THE

TAPROOT

OF YOGA VOL 1

The True Yoga Sutras

A rare, accurate, and authentic translation.
Sanskrit definitions are contemporary with Patanjali.

Beck Anamin

PREFACE

As an introduction to the authorship of this book, I ask you to consider the following quandary. What are you to do if you come to revere a wondrous Swami and he tells you that the moon is blue, though you perceive it as yellow? And if you then move your allegiance and love to another equivalent Master who tells you it is green, and yet another says it is red. What are you to do when the game rules tell you to incontestably accept whatever your great guru tells you? The following quote from the Gautama Buddha (even though we do not know if he really said it this way) tells you what this one yogin did:

> "Do not accept what you hear by report, do not accept tradition, do not accept a statement because it is found in our books, nor because it is in accord with your belief, nor because it is the saying of your teacher. Be lamps unto yourselves. Those who, either now or after I am dead, shall rely upon themselves only and not look for assistance to anyone besides themselves, it is they who shall reach the topmost height."

THE BOOK AND ITS INTENTION

The intent of this book is to fill a vacuum by providing a direct translation of the *Yoga Sutras*. To accomplish that, the author strove to create a carefully researched book, unlike all currently available offerings. No pure direct translation exists, nor is one likely to come into existence in the future. None of the authors of available books wrote and researched as the Buddha advised. All wrote within a preexisting cultural context, already possessing beliefs about what the *Sutras* said. No one wrote as a seeker of the true meaning.

Through decades of effort, the author had one driving motivation, to find the full truth of Patanjali's words. That truth is, of course, imperfect. No one but Patanjali could fully understand his intents and meanings. The author believes, though, that the result is far more accurate, objective, and unbiased than any 'translation' or interpretation available at this time in history. While fully understanding and accepting that the book necessarily has errors, the author believes that it is unlikely that any future work can surpass its accuracy. The natural factors that caused the authors of current books to stray from the path of truth and accuracy would affect future writers as well. The researching and writing of this book took place in solitary occupation of 'No One's Land,' a land where no one owns people or viewpoints. Located in the space between ideological encampments, it is an isolated land where outside influences are absent, a land populated solely by seekers of truth. Becoming an occupant of No One's Land is a yogic step that few take.

The personal translation of the Sanskrit became necessary when it became clear that it was not possible to integrate or resolve the wide and significant differences among the existing 'translations' and interpretations, much of what was labeled as 'translation' when it was not that. Awareness had solidified that the life experiences, mistranslations, influence of religions, personalities, personal orientations, beliefs taught by others, ego, the effects of having 'followers,' desire for profit, and the evolutionary levels of the author had created diverse intellectual products lacking a common base of understanding. Among the most egregious of the translation errors was the tendency of nearly all authors to model their translations of many *Sutras* around the work of some unknown earlier interpreter, portraying sections of the *Yoga Sutras* to be about obtaining 'mystic powers.' Such 'mystic powers' were not a subject of Yoga discussion until long after Patanjali's life, and derived from Hinduism, not from Yoga. Their inclusion in the *Yoga Sutras* required much manipulation of translation.

Although generalities are never accurate for all members of a group, it became clear that certain trends across authors followed obvious 'rules of thumb':

- The translations of authors deeply involved with a 'tradition' or culturally confined group wrote aphorisms in which group beliefs preempted valid translation.
- Those of authors whose traditions or groups were highly religious portrayed many aphorisms in terms of gods and religious beliefs that are not represented in the *Sutras*.
- Academics overrode translation correctness by researching how earlier writers (primarily Indian) had interpreted the aphorisms, often being equivocal about which interpretation was correct.
- Professional writers (those who depended on writing, often accompanied by speaking engagements), produced books that were less oriented to truth and correct content than to style, and marketability.

The intention of this book is to present the teachings of the *Yoga Sutras* as accurately as possible. It is the hope and intention of the author to record the baseline Truths delivered through Patanjali in the *Yoga Sutras*, so that time does not erase them. There is no intention to 'change the world,' obtain followers or 'believers,' or interfere with the valuable teachings by others who do not understand Yoga in these ways. The author refuses to be 'at war' with anyone. The author, though, is constrained and affected by the following beliefs, which he imperfectly adheres to:

- Truth and ego are counterbalancing forces. This is not a competition of wills or intellects.
- Names are carriers of ego. Personal authorship is counterproductive to Truth seeking. This book must be anonymous.
- Desire for profit weakens the zeal for truth.
- Desire for a personal image and acceptance must be avoided.
- The seeker of Truth must be a pure individual, having no one to follow and no followers.
- Guru after guru has lost authenticity and wandered far from their path by yielding to the lures of ego, materialism, or the drive to hold or expand

the size of their following. Their growth as yogins stagnated, or sometimes reversed.

THE YOGA SUTRAS

The *Yoga Sutras* (Union Threads) consists of 196 aphorisms describing the
philosophy and practice of Yoga. An Indian Saint known only as Patanjali
wrote them at about 2250 years ago, at an interesting time in Yoga history. Yoga had existed for more than 1500 years before that writing, as the
ever-evolving philosophy of Union, then expressed as the Samkhya philosophy. Yoga is the philosophy and practice of bringing the mind of the individual self through multiple levels of consciousness experience; ultimately
experience the existence of the primal existence. The primal existence is what
perhaps 500 generations of our uniquely aware species variously identified as
'divinity,' 'godhead,' 'the Absolute,' 'God,' or many other things. The primal
existence is equivalent to what many call God-transcendent, which is beyond
the universe, and is the Source of the universe. In the Sanskrit contemporary
with the *Yoga Sutras*, it is '*brahman*,' the Absolute. Although in modern usage,
the variations of names equivalent to 'God' usually refer to God-immanent
(within the universe), not God-transcendent, terms such as 'God' and 'divinity' are sufficiently non-specific that they could refer to God-transcendent or
God-immanent. God-immanent is not eternal and would disappear if the
universe ended. God-transcendent is eternal: it always was and always will be.
The book will use *brahman* to represent the genderless, nontheistic, formless,
primal existence, which it would be appropriate to envision as godness-tran-
scendent. Like many Sanskrit words, *brahman* translates to many meanings,
depending on the stage of language evolution and context of its use. In this
context, it can equally mean either 'the Absolute' or 'the Eternal.' It is also the
'universal Soul,' but that is only one of its characteristics.

In the details of Yoga philosophy, probably coming from early in its
evolution, a distinction exists that the *Yoga Sutras* does not clarify. The philosophy tells us that *brahman*, the equivalent of God-transcendent, created
an aspect of itself called *isvara (ishwara, ishvara, iswara, izvara)* to oversee
all universes. *Isvara* then created God-immanent figures as the overseers of

universes. In our universe, that overseer could be either *sat*, or *isvara*. The *Yoga Sutras* usually use the word *isvara* to refer to the God-immanent (sat) aspect that is in control of our universe: the *Sutras* do not reference the subject of multiple universes. However, the dividing line is not that clear. *Isvara* often appears in the *Yoga Sutras* as identical to *brahman*. This is appropriate in the sense that *isvara* truly is one aspect of *brahman*, but has all its characteristics. The formless *brahman*-immanent (*isvara or sat*) is, of course, equivalent to the God-immanent to those who envision a god (or goddess) with form.

The primary theme of the *Yoga Sutras* is that the human being is capable of evolving progressively to higher stages of spirituality through experiencing seven stages of consciousness. Those stages of consciousness are the ascending stages of consciousness, in reverse order of the descending stages of consciousness of the universe as it evolved. For the seeking yogin, the final stage of consciousness experience is that of *brahman*, the creator of the universe. This comes about through clearing away all influences on the mortal mind so that it can become as still as the immortal soul of the individual (self, *atman, jiva, or purusa)*, the soul of the universe (*isvara, sat*, atman, *purusa*) and the *brahman* oversoul. Attaining that undisturbed harmony of total and permanent stillness is the goal of personal evolution. When experienced, the individual has no further need for reincarnation to a new mortal life.

By the time Sri Patanjali lived, the basic Union philosophy had evolved in the *Samkhya* philosophy. Seekers of the spirituality that *Samkhya* promised were asking that their teachers show them how to enact the pure philosophy in their daily lives: just knowing the philosophy did not sufficiently ease their longing, reduce their suffering, or help them to travel their path. The first of what would become many 'traditions,' Kriya (Action) Yoga was just then beginning to fill that need. Sri Patanjali wrote the *Yoga Sutras* (Union Threads) as the bridge between *Samkhya* philosophy and the Yoga of action, Kriya Yoga.

THE DIFFICULTY OF LEARNING
THE YOGA SUTRAS

As simple as the lessons of the *Yoga Sutras* are, they describe a world and way of being in that world that is foreign and off-putting to many people. Even when presented in modern language, the deep religiosity of some translators, the esotericism, and vocabulary in the translation/interpretations is daunting. Those who work through the challenges of language and culture may find that some translations available to them are too specifically religious for their world-view, not realizing that Yoga itself is nonreligious, but many religions, most importantly Hinduism, incorporate it in the religious practice. Few realize that like Asian poetry, the *Sutras* have multiple levels of meaning, requiring multiple readings as experience develops and the seeker evolves. During early study, the words may seem esoteric in some places, and overly obvious and simplistic in others, consisting of pieces that do not fit well together. Yet, as linkages and cross-linkages develop, the pieces begin to fit, and beauty and excitement rise in the heart. Perhaps for some that is when the magical realization emerges that there is no turning back, only going forward: the path has become a permanent quest.

At some point in the process, the seeker of the Truths that lie within the philosophy realizes that it is all about personal evolution toward a better, happier, more fulfilling life, in harmony with the purposes of what some call Spirit (*sat* or *brahman*). Somewhere along the path, the seeker realizes that spirit-uality has emerged. As doubts slowly dissolve, the philosophy eases toward Truth. Truth continually builds through study and meditation: from that Truth, wondrous knowledge emerges as the levels of meaning steadily open. The understanding becomes continually easier and more natural.

A DANGER TO YOGA IN TODAY'S WORLD

Since the 1960s when the Indian gurus began to bring their teachings to the West, mostly within self-contained ashrams, Yoga has successfully broadened into the community at large: the many modern variations, though, have not successfully carried their pure Yoga ancestor along. Although valuably serving a large portion of the community and its needs, the spontaneously generated trends have taken on lives of their own, hiding the stable oldness beneath exciting newness. Physical culture, body building, fusion with nonyogic practices, reducing Yoga to the lowest denominator to meet marketplace demand, competition, commercialization, and downplay of its higher qualities and its spirituality have all taken a toll. It is hard for most to recognize Yoga as a way of life, well beyond the posture regimen and bits of Yoga information brought to them by their local teacher. New interpretations and 'translations' of the *Yoga Sutras*, sometimes with beautiful poetic appeal, have recently appeared. With no true understanding of the original teachings, or of Yoga itself, they hide the Truths and reduce the teachings to a single level, adding another barrier to living a Yoga life in which the individual can evolve and experience higher consciousness and its soul.

THE AUTHORS REFERENCED IN THIS BOOK
A NUTSHELL VIEW OF THEIR ORIENTATION

All Compared Authors

When the author began Integral Yoga teacher training in 1972, Swami Satchidananda had his right-hand monk of the time carry a copy of 'How To Know God' to him. It was then the most respected version of the *Yoga Sutras*. The monk dutifully recited the message, 'Swamiji said to tell you, 'This is Yoga. Study it.' Thanking him, the author reached for it and received an additional message from his Swamiji, 'Buy your own.' For a variety of appropriate reasons, the paths of the guru and the aspirant later separated, but the charge had imbedded in his heart as an unbreakable connecting link with the Swami.

The mysteries and difficulties of *How To Know God*, and inconsistencies with what he had come to know Yoga to be, caused him to find other translations and interpretations. The differences among them amazed him, and he began to search out more *Yoga Sutras* texts, looking for the most authentic one. With seventeen versions on his desk and no resolution of the search, he decided to do a detailed and careful comparison, thinking that he could eliminate the 'erroneous' parts from each and save the 'authentic' parts. He narrowed the field to the six apparently 'best' versions, and did write a version of the *Yoga Sutras* in that way. In rereading it, he discovered many things that did not seem right, and began translating the Sanskrit to resolve the issues.

After much translation, he realized that all versions, including his first try, were far from the actual meanings intended in the Sanskrit. The reasons were clear. Some versions strongly reflected belief systems within religions and used religious terminology. Others promoted the beliefs and teachings of a cloistered 'tradition.' A number of them were simply essays on what an individual personally thought the *Sutras* meant, without substantiation. *How to Know God* and others did not provide any translation notes. Even the seeming best did not seem to rigorously pursue direct translation.

During creation of his first version of the book, combining the thoughts of the other authors, it rapidly became clear that five of the seventeen were not worthy of consideration as serious texts. As the comparison of texts proceeded, three others slowly dropped out of the process. Their lack of translation documentation, and strong differences from others and from actual translation impeded comparison and thoughtful consideration. As his own translation from the Sanskrit began, he saw that the eight selected for comparison to his fresh translation had issues that affected their results. They include:

- Lack of rigorous attention to correct translation
- Promoting personal beliefs
- Using the interpretation by a previous writer as a model for a sutra
- Creating their own translations with no dictionary basis
- Using translation definitions not contemporary with Patanjali, derived from later texts
- Promoting religious viewpoints
- Promoting the views of a 'tradition'
- Expanding or restricting meanings by adding words or ideas
- Mistranslating toward grandiose results
- Much copying of wording from one author to another

Among the practices most damaging to truth and accuracy, nearly all authors erroneously translated a significant number of *Sutras* around the concept of 'mystical powers.' Patanjali, though, did not write about the mystical powers: the concept did not exist during his lifetime, and was never part of core Yoga philosophy. It later arose in Hinduism, with the 'powers' being those of the god Siva. As people began to think of high gurus as being gods, they attributed the same powers to them. Emphasizing 'powers' preempted the authors from seeing the core theme of the *Yoga Sutras*, personal evolution through meditation.

There is no attempt or desire to demean the valuable products of the highly accomplished, well-known, respected, authors: the prime attempt here is to find and portray accuracy and Truth, thereby improving the baseline knowledge of true Yoga. The reader should understand that those authors portrayed what they knew from their experience and exposures. They often followed well-established leads from other respected people. They needed to honor the teachings of their teachers or traditions. They did not want to seem to criticize, reject, or disagree with popular trends of interpretation. Teaching, speaking engagements, serving followers, running ashrams or large Yoga organizations, worrying about business and financial necessities, and writing books fully occupied their lives. Due to pressures from publishers, their ego, financial restraints, income needs, a feeling that they owed it to the community, or other reasons, they needed to complete the book and publish it. They did not have time for decades of the solitary fresh-start research necessary to accuracy.

The result of all these factors is that all reviewed books naturally interpret the *Yoga Sutras* in Modern Yoga versions, often far removed from the original *Yoga Sutras* meanings of 2000 years ago. Their interpretations do not portray how Patanjali understood and described Yoga, which is the Truth this author sought.

Eight Authors Reflected In The Comparative Notes Of This Book

Bouanchaud, Bernard, *The Essence of Yoga, Reflections on the Yoga Sutras of Patanjali*

A French student of the greatly respected Krishnamacharya, Bernard Bouanchaud prolifically authored Yoga texts.

Although the book provides lists of multiple possible definitions for most Sanskrit words, with the usual mix of accuracy and inaccuracy, the statement of the aphorisms often uses none of the listed definitions. Many of the words that are used are modern definitions, not meanings contemporary with Patanjali. Added words are often expansive and poetic, and far too often produce a quite different meaning than the aphorism intended. The associated commentary/explanation is hard to follow, often off the mark, and often not based in Yoga philosophy. As a unique feature, the book provides a list of questions for self-exploration, but they would not be helpful to the serious student.

Bryant, Edwin, *The Yoga Sutras of Patanjali, A New Edition, Translation, and Commentary*

Edwin Bryant has taught Indology and Hinduism at such major institutions as Harvard, Columbia, and Rutgers and has authored multiple books. As typically happens when writing from an academic viewpoint, much of the commentary reflects the interpretations of later sages and gurus in place of personal understanding.

As with almost all the books, there is a list of potential translations for each word of an aphorism, but many of them are erroneous. Creative renditions of the aphorism often replaced usage of the listed potential definitions. The distance between actual meaning and the book's purported meaning was often far greater than in the other reviewed books.

Carrera, Reverend Jaganath, *Inside the Yoga Sutras, A Comprehensive Sourcebook*

Reverend Carrera is an obviously brilliant man, who trained in Integral Yoga at Swami Satchidananda's Yogaville. He subsequently founded the Yoga Life Society, a New Jersey teaching group. It is not clear what affiliation the title of 'reverend' relates to, but the book shows the Hindu influence of Integral Yoga. Most likely through permission, the 'translations' and statements of aphorisms are those of Swami Satchidananda, word for word. Even obvious mistranslations by the revered Swami remained uncorrected. The associated commentaries and interpretations of those aphorisms are repeatedly from personal beliefs and musings.

Feuerstein, Georg, *The Yoga Sutras of Patanjali, A New Translation and Commentary*

Georg Feuerstein is a highly respected and broadly known scholar who has written much about Yoga and 'Eastern' philosophies and religions. Although his writings, including this one, are good source for historical perspectives on Eastern teachings including Yoga, his portrayal of the *Sutras* falls far short of what a seeker of Truth should expect. His understanding of Yoga is academic, and that academic approach shows in his writing. The translations are often far from accurate. The statements of the aphorisms often contain added, changed, or deleted words and ignored suffixes that change meanings. The commentary is often equivocal; not taking a position, instead quoting varied opinions of earlier writers and sages, or providing a history of opinions, leaving the reader without clear understanding.

Govindan, Marshall, *Kriya Yoga Sutras of Patanjali and the Siddhas, Translation, Commentary and Practice*

A follower of the modern Kriya Yoga movement, Marshall Govindan's book reflects the understandings and beliefs within that community, often inserting excerpts from its texts. For reasons unknown, but certainly with the permission or collaboration of Swami Satchidananda, the wording of many aphorisms is identical in the Satchidananda and Govindan books. In those cases, the positives and negatives of the Satchidananda book carry over. The book often lists multiple potential translations of a Sanskrit word, without using any of them in the actual statement of the aphorism.

A feature of this book is instructions on how to practice the aphorism. They are interesting personal observations, sometimes helpful, sometimes related to Yoga philosophy, and sometimes not. The reader should be aware that the modern Kriya Yoga promoted in his book is not the Kriya Yoga that Patanjali melded with *Samkhya* philosophy for his book. No records exist for the original Kriya Yoga, and there are no connecting 'traditions' during the

2000 intervening years. Several modern yogins have 'discovered the ancient secrets of Kriya Yoga' and started new 'traditions.'

Iyengar, B.K.S., *Light on the Yoga Sutras of Patanjali*

Mr. Iyengar has a world reputation for being the most advanced, competent, successful, careful, and gifted teacher of postures. Having studied for a time under the revered Krishnamacharya, he left that sanctified environment to follow his mission to study the body in a way that enhanced his ability to teach posture perfection.

Although there are lists of multiple potential meanings for each Sanskrit word, many of the meanings did not exist in dictionaries. The aphorisms often did not use any of them. Instead, they became expansive, non-translation, flow of consciousness statements that often seemed to depict personal beliefs.

The lengthy and broadly knowledgeable associated commentary contained valuable information from Hindu philosophy and religion, or other sources, but the mixture of translation, personal belief, philosophy, religion, ideas from other sources, and extensive detail from the texts of other writers interfered with understanding of the *Sutras*.

Saraswati, Swami Satyananda, *Four Chapters on Freedom, Commentary on the Yoga Sutras of Patanjali*

A revered and well-known Yoga leader, Swami Satyananda Saraswati was a devotee under Swami Sivananda before becoming a traveling monk. He then founded the International Yoga Fellowship, the Bihar School of Yoga, and other organizations. During that time, he wrote 80 books. He later renounced that life and became a solitary monk. As revered as he is and as brilliant as he is, this version of *Yoga Sutras* exhibits many of the errors noted in the above paragraphs. The insights in his knowledgeable commentaries go well beyond the content of the individual *Sutras*, detailing many technicalities of later Yoga philosophy and overshadowing the intended translation. The text drifts far from translation, reflecting the unique perspectives of the Sivananda tradition.

Satchidananda, Sri Swami, *The Yoga Sutras of Patanjali, Translation and Commentary*

Swami Satchidananda was one of the first high gurus to come to America. He is the founder of Integral Yoga and the Integral Yoga Institute, which initially earned a large American following. Now deceased, he earned the great respect of many, including this author, his student. His book is among the better ones, but has many of the flaws listed above. His religious orientation colors what should be a non-religious book. The misconstruing of many aphorisms, failure to provide commentary for some of them, and generally reflecting modern cultural belief in the place of real translation, all decrease the value of the interpretation. Compared to many others, it is an easy to understand westernized book, but that ease of understanding necessarily comes at the expense of authenticity and accuracy. The commentaries are interesting; often containing entertaining stories, and are insightful. They are also sometimes wrong.

Three Potentially Valuable Authors Set Aside During Review For This Book,

Prabhavananda, Swami, and Isherwood, Christopher. *How to Know God*

A book that will always be close to this author's heart, earning gratitude for transportation to a new realm of understanding and living, it eventually generated disappointment over the content and lack of authenticity of the text. Having no translation notes it was impossible to substantiate the statement of aphorisms or to understand why they were stated the way they were, often far different from others and from true translation. Continually trying to sort out the true meanings, this author came to understand the common practice of having a student with writing skills publish a book that interpreted the words of his guru, and how powerfully Ramakrishna and Vedanta teachings influenced the book. As always, the attempt at westernization diminished the truth.

Savitripriya, Swami, *Psychology of Mystical Awakening, Patanjali Yoga Sutras, A New World Translation*

Swami Savitripriya describes herself as a "Siddha Guru and master of Shaktipat-Kundalini Yoga, in the non-dual tradition of Kashmir Shaivite Hinduism." She has written twenty books. A skillful translator, the tone of words in her translation at first seemed close to the proper understanding of aphorisms. However, there was great modification and expansion of the meanings of many *Sutras*. The word lists were helpful by themselves, often providing opportunities for good translations, but when they became part of the statement of the aphorism, the validity evaporated. What the reader would expect to be a direct statement of what the *Sutra* meant was instead a discourse on an aspect of Yoga belief and philosophy as seen through the eyes and mind of a follower of a chosen religious tradition. It was not possible to cross-relate or compare the views to those of the others.

Stiles, Mukunda, *Yoga Sutras of Patanjali*

Mukunda Stiles has world recognition for his unique book *Structural Yoga Therapy* and as a speaker 'on the circuit.' He has many decades of experience in India and the United States, is active on boards of Yoga organizations, and has been the director of Yoga centers. Because of his written promise to provide an accurate translation direct from the Sanskrit, his book originally became part of the set of authors included in this comparison. At first, the list of translations of Sanskrit words appeared valid, although there were multiple potential translations with none flagged as the choice for the aphorism. The aphorism statements had initial appeal, but it quickly became apparent that the poetic form of the writing often changed the meaning. Further, the commentary necessary for understanding was not there. It later became clear that this interpretation was victim to most of the errors of the other authors, such as following predefined models, mistranslation, leaving out words, using modern representations of meanings rather than contemporary translations, orientation toward interpreting in terms of mystical 'powers,' and so on.

Other Acquired Texts

Aranya, Swami Hariharananda (Samkhya-yogacharya), *Yoga Philosophy of Patanjali*

Swami Hariharananda Aranya, a Samkhya-yogacharya, and founder of the Kapila Monastery in India spent most of his life in meditative solitude that enabled writing of many books. His book on the *Yoga Sutras* is a wonderful reference containing inspiration and insights for crosschecking against any translation. However, the text was not useful in this search for truth and accuracy. It did provide the Sanskrit, but in its original pictogram form with no accompanying modern script and no translation notes. The aphorism statements generally conveyed ideas similar to the ideas in this and other texts. However, those ideas were often greatly expanded, sometimes tilted to a religious perspective, sometimes with reversed subject and object, and sometimes too confusing to understand properly. The statement of the aphorism often used a mix of Sanskrit words (in modern form) and English words. The usual expansion of aphorism meaning reflected understanding and insights arrived at through sources beyond translation.

Dvivdedi, Manilal Nabhubhai, *The Yoga-Sutra Of Patanjali*

Professor Dvivdedi produced a version of the *Yoga Sutras* based on the writings and teachings of respected Yogins from earlier times. After discussing the deficiencies and wrong approaches of the other major translations of his time, he promised to provide a literal translation presented in terms that eased understanding. Yet, there is no provision of the Sanskrit to be translated or its translation. In some places the aphorisms carry the same meaning as the translations presented here or other books, but often differ. It seems that the definitions were as they existed in modern times, not contemporary with Patanjali's life. The aphorisms do not seem to be direct word for word translations, but a flow of words representing personal understanding.

Hartranft, Chip, The *Yoga-Sutra of Patanjali*

A local figure of some repute in Massachusetts, a student of Buddhism, Yoga, and what he terms the "Krishnamacharya Traditions,' Chip Hartranft has molded them into a teaching he terms a 'blend of movement and stillness.' His book on the *Yoga Sutras* was not useful to writing this book. There is nothing to help consider the accuracy of the 'new translation,' no Sanskrit for the aphorisms and no translation notes. The statements seem to be opinion, more than translation.

Miller, Barbara Stoler, *Yoga, Discipline of Freedom*

Professor Miller claims to have produced a 'translation' of the *Yoga Sutras*, but provides nothing to support that fact. The Sanskrit to be translated and the translation of its words are both absent. The aphorism statements often pick up the sense of the aphorism, but that sense is generally distorted and it often embellishes or warps the true translation. Some aphorism translations seem to represent personal understanding. Others use terminology that is associated with a 'tradition' or time. Religious terminology and concepts not found in the *Sutras* are prevalent.

Shearer, Alistair, *The Yoga Sutras of Patanjali*

Alistair Shearer studied Transcendental Meditation under Maharishi Mahesh Yogi, did extensive post-graduate work in Sanskrit, and then became a lecturer. The first 85 pages of the book of 132 pages consist of personal ruminations on the nature of Yoga and many things 'Eastern,' including Hinduism and Buddhism. The remainder is a simple presentation of a version of the *Yoga Sutras*. There is no Sanskrit and there are no translation notes. The aphorism statements seem to be personal understanding of what the *Sutras* mean. They are sometimes poetic, sometimes expanded, sometimes contracted, sometimes right, and often wrong.

Vivekananda, Swami, *Raja Yoga*

Swami Vivekananda was among the impressive swamis who evolved under the guidance of the great Ramakrishna. Swami Nikhilananda edited and produced the book post-mortem, from Swami Vivekananda's accumulated notes. It was not used here as a source for this comparison and translation because there were no translation notes to compare. Although a bit freeform, the trend of the aphorisms was in alignment and agreement with those of the reviewed authors, but failed the tests of correctness and authenticity. Further, language and thought structures typical of his Ramakrishna's traditions colored and obfuscated many of the statements.

CONTENTS

CHAPTER ONE

YOGA - PHILOSOPHY AND PRACTICE

PERSPECTIVE

The Aware Species

At the end of the most recent 'Ice Age,' at about 10,000 years ago, or maybe a little earlier, something extraordinary happened. A highly varied set of similar Homo-sapiens-to-be creatures (us) that had evolved from interbred offshoots of earlier Homo species, had occupied all regions of the planet. By comparing them to earlier types and species along the two million year 'human' chain of evolutionary events, we think of them as advanced. Their abilities until then, though, continued to be extremely limited, though creativity was beginning to emerge.

With evolutionary suddenness, a worldwide change came about. Those creatures all settled into a single type. In every corner of the world creativity became rampant. Civilizations suddenly formed, many of them built around the widespread arrival of cultivated crops and herding. The species began to process metal, ending the 'Stone Age.' Travel across water, pottery, weaving, huge structures, and many inventions became everyday things everywhere in

1

the world. No one can tell you how it happened or why, but activation of dormant gene sets, perhaps due to the sudden change in climate, is an acceptable viewpoint for this easy recap.

Although scientists and others point to a variety of differences from past beings as '*the one thing*' that most characterized our Homo sapiens species, the least spoken of is the most obvious. All living beings have consciousness of some level or type. That of a virus differs from that of bacteria. Bacterial consciousness differs from animal consciousness. Plant consciousness differs from that of animal consciousness. The consciousness of Homo sapiens differs greatly from that of all other animals. A vast change in the creature's consciousness and its relationship to mind had come about, causing the awareness of the surrounding world, the creativity, decision making, organization, social structuring, projecting into the future, remembering the past, and many other things.

Insight From 'Beyond'

The scientists do not formally recognize the ability to receive insight beyond normal sensory awareness as perhaps the most important enhancement. However, it did not take long for some people to discover that our new species has a unique ability to discipline our minds so that we can experience higher levels of consciousness. The appearance of mystics, seers, sages, and shamans may well have started early, soon after the genetic arrival of our young species. Those words 'mystics,' 'seers,' 'sages,' and 'shamans' are nearly interchangeable, as people who can enter experience of higher consciousness, but each implies a different locale and a different use of the ability.

Although they may have been present 8,000 or even 10,000 years ago, we are certain that shamans were important in villages of the Indian continent and elsewhere by 6000 years ago. They gained their importance by entering those levels of higher consciousness and returning with intuitive insights that would help their community.

A Philosophy

In addition to helping the villagers live better lives, the insights they provided began to build toward a holistic philosophy. The philosophy dealt with basic concepts of how the world works, examining such things as Truths, the nature of existence, causation, Reality, where the universe came from, how the universe evolved, the nature of humanity and its interplay with godness, and the nature of that underlying eternal creative existence that we name in so many ways.

By 4500 years ago, in the northwestern corner of the Indian continent, that philosophy of the Absolute Source existence and its creation of our universe were in full bloom, associated with a wondrous collection of truths and insights. Seers, rishis, and mystics added more insight from the 'beyond.' The philosophy evolved into the pure *Samkhya* (modern spelling is Sankhya) philosophy, which those who experienced higher consciousness continued to expand. With the fervor enabled by the new consciousness, cultures began to build on the foundation. Known as *brahman* in non-religious Yoga, the formless Absolute took religious form in many places: the hymns, known as the Vedas, to and about a god, came about and expanded. By 4000 years ago, the Vedic religion spread through India and the religious fervor took the same teachings through Persia into Europe in worship of the god Mithras.

The pure, nonreligious philosophy kept growing in India; carrying the message that we humans can experience union (Yoga) with the creator's consciousness by getting our material world orientation out of the way. *Samkhya*, for which no current reliable descriptions or texts exist, contributed much about personal evolution and the relationship of the individual to the presence of the Absolute Source in the universe. At about 2200 years ago, the first of what would become 'traditions' that converted the passive *Samkhya* philosophy to active practice, Kriya Yoga, came into being.

The Philosophy In Action

A high rishi of the time, Sri Patanjali, meticulously, and with great genius, wrote a book documenting the marriage of *Samkhya* philosophy and the action oriented Kriya Yoga. His book focused on personal evolution, setting the philosophical parts about cosmic evolution aside. However, his wonderful presentation of how the human ability to move into experience of progressively higher consciousness levels was in exact reverse order to the stages of cosmic evolution. Each succeeding step into experiencing higher consciousness took the seeker once step backward through the creative process that had evolved materiality from spirituality. Sri Patanjali shows us how to travel from materiality back to spirituality, experiencing the cosmic consciousness levels that existed at each step, eventually to the pure spirituality that started it all.

Please be clear that Yoga is a philosophy, and no one should automatically 'buy' anyone's philosophy. Philosophies are human words put together to describe how things work. The presented philosophy is usually a combination of a person's history, personal beliefs, and discovered truths. You should not make a philosophy yours until you have self-verified it. There are many that will tell you that this philosophy is correct because it was derived from mystics who entered the world of Truth and brought the pieces back with them, not an intellectual process. As true as that may be, it cannot be true to you until your heart tells you it is true, largely resulting from your own study and experience. That is how this book came about.

There Is Only One Story

During the 4000 years or more since the philosophy of union (Yoga) first entered the minds of humans, Great Teachers have sporadically appeared to teach *brahman's* core lessons, the lessons of the Absolute, godness, or God: there have been no more than a half-dozen of the super-Greats, each adapting the teachings to the language and cultural environment of the time and location. It is as if one master teacher, great avatar, or god-on-Earth figure repeatedly appeared where and when humanity needed the lessons. They did not speak on their own: they were receptors through which the words flowed.

The receptor that this book flowed through is a yogin, not a high one, and not a Master, but a simple receptor in search of receiving Truth. Certainty about the oneness of the Great Teachings entered his heart one winter afternoon. Another of his unrelenting questions had caused him to stack books three feet high, to search for something he knew he had seen long before. His effort took him through review of the index of one book after another. As the stack shrank and he removed another book, his copy of the *Dhammapada* appeared beneath it. He had accepted its loss and given up the search two years before that day. Its reappearance filled him with joy and gratitude.

Setting the held book aside with his left hand, his right hand reached for the small paperback. As the fingers and thumb of his right hand closed on it, a shockwave of energy traveled the extended arm, seeming to enter every cell of his body: propelled by the energy, he collapsed backward in his chair. An internal voice spoke. It was simply there, not from a person or a god. 'A book is a sacred book when it becomes sacred to *you*.' After moments of savoring the thought, understanding came that he had been trying to make the *Dhammapada* sacred. With renewed energy, he opened its yellowed pages. His eyes found a target: the words that hit him delivered an even stronger shockwave of energy, again propelling him backward. It ended his quest for an answer. Pierced by the meaning of the words that flashed on the page he slumped into full collapse, becoming resistance-free, an open receiver. He had seen the same word-symbols many times, but in such different forms that the commonality had escaped him. As the Truth they bore seared into permanent residence, his eyelids seemed to become a movie screen, with images of books floating across: each held long enough for recognition before dissolving. The *Quran, Tao Te Ching, Holy Bible, Bhagavad Gita, Dhammapada, the Yoga Sutras*, and others paraded before his awareness. The voice again spoke, 'There is only one story.' He spent much of the next day reading the *Dhammapada* from cover to cover. At the end, a firm and clear realization settled within him; the *Dhammapada* would not serve his interests or fulfill his spiritual needs. It was for others. To him, it was not sacred.

ILLUSION-FREE YOGA

An inevitable result of sincere and consistent aspiration and practice is the removal of all illusions and delusions. If you want to understand Yoga in an illusion-free way, finding what lies behind the cotton candy cloud of Western presentation, start with this. Under the auspices of, and directed by, the one Primal Existence (Spirit-Infinite-Presence-All-Source-Absolute-Being-*brahman*), the god immanent (godhead-God-Allah-Siva-Yahweh-Zeus-Vishnu-Mithras-Brahma-sat ... *isvara*) created you, so that It could experience through you. The meaning of life is as simple as that. The meaning of your personal life is the experience you are having in this lifetime.

You Are Divine

Brahman creates universes through agents that it creates with its own imagination, from its own essence: its essence is the only 'stuff' that is available for making anything. Because of that, you, everyone else, and everything else, are materialized god-essence. That is what yogins mean when they say you are divine or you are God. You are. Everything is. There is only one thing. It is the ever-manifesting primal existence, the transcendent god-being. Because you are, the omniscient consciousness of *brahman* is available to you, but it is human nature to block it. It is accessible only through practice and learning that takes you through progressive experience of multiple consciousness levels within the sphere of the universe, ultimately experiencing the consciousness of the divine-immanent and divine-transcendent, *isvara and brahman.*

Your ego, just as everyone's ego does, places opaque shields between you and that consciousness. That ego stubbornly and obsessively focuses you on your material being. You have the ability and opportunity to bypass the obstructive work of the ego and experience higher consciousness. You are a member of the only Earth species that can do it. Yoga is a process of personal evolution to progressively experience higher forms of consciousness. Its objective is to guide you home, where you will retire.

Your Four Parts

Sutra 2.19 tells us that the gunas (three counterbalancing forces - inherent in everything) established the progression of the universe from the initial *prakrti* (Nature), the primal prana, into three forms. To describe them, this book artificially labels them as 'creative (or causal) prana,' 'subtle prana,' and 'physical prana.' The bodies of the universe and of all physical things in the universe always consist of those three entities. To reflect modern language for them, the book further labels them as the *causal body,* *subtle body,* and *physical body.*

You, the individual living being, have three parts that you cannot see or detect, and one that you can. All four are 'mission critical.' If any were missing, you would not be here. They are of two types, all 'physical' matter and all 'subtle' matter in the universe. 'Physical matter' is sense detectable, measurable, and detectable. 'Subtle matter' is none of those things, invisible and undetectable, but equally present as a part of the creation. The universe and everything in it also has a less-mentioned *causal body,* a realm separate from the *physical body* and *subtle body,* but also subtle. The fourth you, the *soul* (often represented as 'self'), is part of the spiritual realm, as an aspect of the eternal transcendent *brahman* and the immanent *brahman* (*isvara*), not part of the bodies of the universe.

You are a physically mortal body complex that lives an active noticeable life, and then dies. The *physical body* then disintegrates. That *body*-you lives only for decades, before becoming food and soil, never to live again. 'Living' also requires the second you, the invisible and undetectable inner body, the *subtle body.* The *subtle body* provides the raw capabilities for intellect, mind, ego, feeling state, and judgment ability. The *subtle body,* like the *causal body,* is an existence defined in the *Yoga Sutras*: the detailed functions and activities described here and elsewhere come from later philosophy.

The third you, the *causal body,* communicates *soul* initiated developmental intentions to the *subtle body,* concepts that will shape an upcoming new life. Both subtle matter invisible bodies are immortal. They exist for as many Earth years as are required, carrying from lifetime to lifetime, until the individual's evolution completes, and then dissolve. They are not eternal.

The fourth you is the spiritual *soul,* which is eternal and has all the characteristics of the Source, *brahman/isvara.* It is an aspect of *brahman/isvara,* not a separate being, an aspect dedicated to the individual. According to *Sutra* 4.18 and others, it maintains its eternal stillness while observing even every thought of that individual. It never changes, controls, or acts. Its active role is to emit divine guidance that energizes the other bodies. It does not command that an act be taken; it provides choices and alternate paths for selection. It puts signs along our path, places roadblocks in our way, and communicates in many ways, sometimes with 'the voice.' Those that have an active connection will increasingly see, hear, feel, and understand. That spiritual guidance paired with freewill action is an ongoing dance between the material and spiritual. The *soul* also acts as a force that causes creation of the bodily form and communicates karmic intentions for the current life to the *causal body*. Beyond that, individual *souls* do not play an active role in governing a life, but do play a role in starting and ending the phases of the physical lifecycle - death to life and life to death. *Souls* are the connecting links between the *oversoul* of *brahman/isvara* and the individual beings made up of the three body-you identities. You could think of a *soul* as analogous to the port on a computer.

The *soul* is pure divinity, *brahman/isvara* immanent in the individual. The *physical body*-you, *subtle body*-you, and *causal body*-you, and the *soul*-you exist together in mutual encasement, truly as an individual life-packet. For ease, this book will sometimes call the three nonphysical entities the 'soul-packet.'

When the *Sutras* say that *brahman/isvara* and the *soul* are 'eternal,' 'eternal' means that there never has been a beginning and never will be an end. Technically, *isvara* is not eternal, because it will not exist if the universe falls into nonexistence. The *subtle body* and *causal body* seem eternal, but they are not. They will stay in the individual's participation in the game of life for the individually necessary many cycles until reaching the goal of Yoga through evolution, Absolute Unity (*kaivalya*), as written in *Sutra* 4.34. That is what the definition of Yoga as 'union' means. The popular term for that *kaivalya* state of Absolute Unity is 'Emancipation.' Although it is not a translation of *kaivalya*, this book will sometimes use it. The term is descriptive of the teaching that there is then freedom from future material living cycles. *Kaivalya* evolves when the individual mind (citta) becomes so invariably quiet that it can permanently harmonize with the total quietness of the individual *soul* and the *oversoul* of *brahman*. The *subtle body* and *causal body*, along with the individual's *gunas*, disintegrate when that happens, leaving the eternal *soul* as the remaining individuation of you, the eternal you. It was you through all those iterations and it remains you. Your lifetimes are part of the history in *brahman's* omniscient knowledge.

These are the pure baseline 'bodies' that Hinduism, Vedanta, the Upanishads, and Yoga philosophers have expanded and explained in their own ways, whether from mystical revelation, received insight, intellectual processing, or other ways. Although the resulting layers of expansion are sometimes similar, similarity yields to differences with partial overlapping as three bodies (or sometimes 'sheaths') become four or five. The modern creation of Kundalini Yoga, has defined ten.

Some modern writers often refer to the *subtle body* as the *astral body* or *energy body*. Those who use 'astral' also refer to the *subtle body* of the universe as its '*astral body*.' They describe a conscious existence of the *soul-packet* in that astral realm during the time between physical living experiences. The term '*energy body*' refers to the role the *subtle body* plays as controller of pranic energy in the *physical body*. Several levels of philosophical exploration and interpretation exist.

When described, these four seem separate, but they are not so. According to later Yoga philosophers, the *subtle body* exercises much control over the *physical body,* causing its form to generate, and then it maintains interaction with the body. *Citta* (often misspelled as *chitta*), the 'thinking principle,' or mind, is within this *subtle body*, but has an active partnership with the physical brain. Since the word 'citta' sometimes, even in the *Sutras*, refers to different aspects of itself, attention to the context of the moment is necessary to proper understanding. In one context, it may play the role of discriminative intelligence (*buddhi*), or mind (*manas*) in another context. The home of emotions, it is also the location of the feeling state of 'heart,' which is the overall feeling state of the individual when all of the counterbalancing feelings merge. For example, someone carrying a little love and a lot of hatred has an overall feeling state of hatred, a hateful 'heart.'

The *soul* weighs all of the factors of the karmic influences (*Sutras* 2.12 - 2.17 and others) to select new life situations in rebirth after body death. In the expanded Yoga, the *causal* body functions in the light of guidance from the *soul,* which triggers it to inform the *subtle body* in the formation of a new *physical body* and its karmic situation. The *subtle body* then functions in conjunction with those intentions relayed by the *causal body*,

Have you ever read or heard descriptions of something leaving a body at death? In *Sutra* 4.9 Patanjali implies that the *soul* carries karmic memories from life to life, but does not specifically say so. The more developed philosophy portrays that three-member *soul-packet* as departing from the no longer useful *physical body*, readying to build and experience another body in another lifetime, meanwhile residing in the 'subtle realm.' Some say it exits through the third eye, while others describe other paths. There are ample reports of visualizing a ghostlike being drifting out and away.

You will have many cycles of alternating material world and subtle world existences, during which personal evolution will slowly do its job. Throughout both sides of the cycle, the eternal individual *soul* aspect of the *oversoul* of the Absolute (*brahman/isvara*) is completely aware of everything that is happening.

Enlightenment

Many see 'Enlightenment' as the goal of Yoga, but it is only a major benchmark along the way, one not mentioned or delineated in the *Yoga Sutras*. The characteristics defined for blocking future accumulations of *karma* in *Sutra* 1.50 and 'awakening' in *Sutra* 3.9, though, are a major step upward in consciousness experience and are similar to those reported by those who claim the experience. However, that enlightenment is not the same as what graced the Gautama Buddha.

The likelihood that the individual physical you, one of the billions of people currently sharing Earth-lives, will receive enlightenment during this lifetime is statistically low. During your lifetime on this planet of hundreds of billions of people, perhaps a few hundred might reach enlightenment. Few will reach the higher attainment of Absolute Unity. You too will reach both enlightenment and Absolute Unity during some lifetime, because living a material life is all about evolution in that direction. Those results are as unstoppable as the tide, but it will take far more lifetimes than you can imagine to attain the high consciousness experiences necessary to that end.

The human species is continually evolving, one soul-packet after another, so that eventually a higher percentage of its Earth-living members will experience and act out higher, more evolved, lives at the same time, improving life on the planet.

The Buddha, Jesus Christ, Krishna, and many others were born so highly evolved that they were naturally closer to union than others, and drew themselves toward it with every thought and every action. They were born that way because they had already evolved that far, carrying into their next life the love of their 'God,' their deep commitment to becoming absorbed in the Absolute, or whatever drove their Truth seeking. You might be born to experience abuse, alcoholism, starvation, riches, addiction, sickness, femaleness, maleness, a sexuality that does not match your body, scientific curiosity, artistic drive, musical drive, mechanical skill, being unskilled at anything, skilled at something, or into any of millions of other situations. Each of your situations will present a new challenge to your evolution. It is enough that you meet that new challenge and evolve during that lifetime experience. You may accelerate that by how you live, and get more evolution than if you just waited, but you will not prematurely force enlightenment or union to happen. They will happen when you are ready for it.

If you aspire to enlightenment, you should be aware that some movements, traditions, or cults have solved the problem of enlightenment taking long practice across many lifetimes. It is most clear in some forms of modern Buddhism. Their solution is straightforward and simple. They say that it is available to anyone, or even to the masses. To make it so they surreptitiously redefine what enlightenment is. By treating one or more of the early stages of *samadhi* as enlightenment, they make it available to anyone. One Zen teacher, who has declared himself enlightened, when he is clearly not, makes a good living by lecturing on the ease of attaining it. Observing the desperate hope and crushing disappointment in people attending one of his lectures or workshops is saddening.

The Life Experience

Believing in reincarnation, other than by blind faith, is a huge step that requires preparation through deep understanding of many aspects of Yoga. Whether you believe in it or not, practicing Yoga will improve your life experience. If you do or do not believe in a divinity-existence, regardless of whether you might think of it as immanent (God, *isvara*), transcendent (God, *brahman*), with form (God), or without form (the Absolute, *brahman*), practicing Yoga will improve your life experience, and may change your understanding or belief about divinity. That improvement may be as simple as being more happy and contented, or any minor or major stepping along the chain of higher consciousness. When you truly believe in the existence of a divinity, Yoga will naturally improve your life experience in other ways. Your interaction with divinity will increase.

The true meaning of life is the experience you are having. You are learning and evolving through it. All life is about evolution. In fact, all aspects of the universe are about evolution. It is the constant directional thrust. Although no one can safely say what 'intent' *brahman* has, evolution seems to be Its intent, or perhaps Its natural drive. The seeking individual can influence his or her evolution by life choices and actions. Yet, all individuals, even the poor, downtrodden, and criminal evolve without Yoga. It cannot be accidental that by advancing everyone's evolution over time, It advances the evolution of the species.

The directional thrust of personal evolution is toward sanity, steadiness, equanimity, happiness, contentment, peace, harmony, oneness, joy, love, and spirituality. The directional thrust of evolution is away from insanity, chaos, misery, suffering, anxiety, internal and external warring, separateness, hatred, and materiality. Unless you insist on maintaining your status quo, or on reversing your progress while seeking to get material/sensory rewards, you will progress. You will become increasingly happy and joyful (fun, happiness, and joy are three different things) in your current life. That is enough, without ever thinking about carrying that happiness or anything else to a future life.

Not Root Yoga

You can use Sanskrit words in your practice of Yoga, for the spiritual qualities and their great mystical intonations, but root Yoga does not require it. You can reach any level of Yoga benefit while speaking English, Arabic, Chinese, Japanese, Mongolian, French, German, or any language that has become natural to you. You can approach it from the perspective of a Catholic, Muslim, Lutheran, Hindu, Methodist, Buddhist, Jew, Zoroastrian, Pagan, Taoist, Shintoist, atheist, agnostic, or any other religious or nonreligious orientation. *Brahman* understands all the languages that Iτ created through Its immanent Presence, and knows your intent before you do. You can do your grand variety of physical body postures all you want, and receive the huge benefits they can give you. They are a magnificent add-on, but you do not have to. They are not a part of root Yoga and you can achieve even the ultimate union without them. You cannot achieve union through them alone. In root Yoga, the only posture you need is one of comfortable stillness that you can remain in for a while. You can chant to Vedic or Hindu gods, in Sanskrit, Urdu, or Hindi language for the wonderful feelings, spirituality, meditative effect, and calming, but you do not have to: root Yoga has no god names or gods. There is only the One, the eternal absolute singularity that is everything, *brahman*. Iτ is not a god: Iτ is a state of being, the primal existence and the Source of all other existence and states of being. Humans have perceived Iτ as a god, declared Iτ as one, described Iτ in many forms, and named Iτ by many names. No name or description has had longevity or universal acceptance. New names, descriptions, and concepts always replace them. The Absolute primal existence does not care which name you use for either its transcendent or immanent Presence, or if you use one at all. Iτ knows your mind and thought structures. You will learn more of that as your study of the *Sutras* progresses. You will come to understand that any thought, emotion, feeling, or prayer directed toward Iτ is as good as any name.

YOGA IS UNION

A marvelous, astounding, underrated, and misunderstood event happened about 1400 years after Krishna taught the core lessons intended for all humanity in India, in a manner appropriate to the culture that existed. That event happened 400 years after Zarathrusta taught the lessons based on the universal teachings that had passed through Persian portal between Eastern and Western worlds, 300 years after Lao Tsu taught them in China, and 250 years after the great Gautama Buddha taught them in India. It was 250 years *before* Jesus Christ taught them in the western world, and nearly 1000 years before Muhammad taught them in the Arabic world. A revered Indian rishi, a mystic, with genius for concise clarity and organization of thought, known only as Patanjali ('Sri Patanjali' to show respect) wrote a short book. That book documented the underlying philosophy and the techniques for actively living by those teachings. The philosophy he documented was first formulated ages before that by mystics - those who had yoked (the valid translation of Yoga in Patanjali's time) their mind to the primal consciousness that underlies everything - as early as 2000 years before Patanjali lived, even before Krishna and the other Great Teachers lived. The core teachings he documented as the philosophy of Yoga, has become known as the philosophy of 'union,' a somewhat later valid meaning of yoga. It derived from the second of two consecutive *Samkhya* philosophies, that may have existed for two thousand years, and were the root of the first Asian religion, Vedism. The structure of its teachings is evident in the teachings of each of those Great Teachers.

Patanjali could not have had the intuitive understanding necessary to accomplish his writing without a personal evolutionary experience of high consciousness. His expanded consciousness experience was probably more akin to a prophet, such as Muhammad, not nearly as high as that of a Christ, Buddha, Krishna, or perhaps even to the lesser experience of teachers such as Zarathrusta and Lao Tsu. The names used for the highest consciousness experience within the universe, Cosmic Consciousness, often reflects the Great Teachers, naming it as Christ Consciousness, Krishna Consciousness, Buddha Mind, or God Consciousness. Those are names for the root consciousness of the universe and its immanent-Presence on our planet, *isvara*. With equivalents in many languages, that universal common consciousness has broad recognition as a reality.

In one short and succinct book of just 196 crisp aphorisms, Patanjali not only documented a wonderful way of life, but also revealed the mystic's answers to great mysteries that tantalize our minds. Where did our universe come from? What is God? What is the purpose of life? What is consciousness? Do we have an afterlife? He showed us how the consciousness experience of our individual mind evolves toward experiencing the ultimate, beyond the universe, consciousness of *brahman*. Among many other things, he unveiled the secrets of how to gain mental power, become serene, and live by our intuition. In the marvelous Asian way of writing for multiple levels of under-standing, he documented in detail how the processes of cause and effect, informally called the *Law of Karma*, work in our lives.

Because our current culture has sidelined Patanjali's writing, we do not have the foundation we need for understanding the true Yoga and for seeing how it could help our living. In that absence, people do not understand that the practices leading to union provide tools for the everyday experiences of the masses - not just those for the high level seeker of Truth: for the masses, the practices aim at ending 'suffering.' 'Suffering' is the mental chaos we bring on ourselves. Even the initial movement of a life toward the goals of Yoga begins to move us away from that chaos: it moves us toward its opposite, serenity, even though few go to the higher experiences, and very few to the highest.

Many focus their understanding of Yoga on the small elite population who have become the great Masters, become enlightened, or attained supra-normal powers. They think of that as Yoga. Many practice the traditional and continually invented postures in the ever-growing approaches to Hatha Yoga, striving to perfect them, competing with others: they see that as Yoga. Others employ techniques of breathing and management of life energy (*prana* or *chi*) that will take them to some undefined place that is vaguely 'good.' They see that as Yoga, and strive for perfection. Particularly in India, millions become renunciates, forsaking the material world in the hope of attaining the ulti-mate goal of Yoga, or at least happiness: vast numbers of them hybridize it with worship of a god or with a religious practice. Many hope for fast track completion of their trek toward union, which is not yet to be theirs. Few see Patanjali's *Yoga Sutras* as a book about how humans evolve, complete with 'how to' guidance aimed at happier living, while being a guide for the Truth-seeker at the same time, a book about root Yoga.

We rarely think of the obvious truth, that as with baseball, piano playing, soccer, or dancing, *those with natural talent* for the game and *who practice the most diligently* get to the Carnegie Hall, Olympics, or Absolute Unity of their domain. Yet, all participants benefit from whatever amount of practice they put in, according to their needs, nature, talents, *karma*, and drives. Patanjali hits at this point early in the *Sutras* (1.13-1.16), saying that the prime tools of Yoga are practice, and relinquishing attachment to worldly things. Practice is the dedicated practice of all limbs and aspects of Yoga (*Sutra* 2.28) as a full way of life: it is practice of many elements, as an integrated way of living. Its effects vary with the effort given to practice. By practice and relinquishing our need for worldly things, we can move toward the positive effects of living by the philosophy of union, just as we can become an Olympian or renowned artist.

PATANJALI'S YOGA SUTRAS (UNION THREADS)

Pure Yoga - At The Root Of All Practices Of Yoga

Patanjali's unimaginable written description of Yoga appeared 200 years or so before the birth of Jesus Christ. The exact date is unknown, and there is no known history or information about his life. Yet, billions of people know the name, and billions have benefited from his gift to us, the *Yoga Sutras*. Those two words on his Title Page are in Sanskrit, a language in which words have many meanings that depend on their context, usage, and historical date. Here 'Sutras' literally translates to 'Threads.' 'Yoga' translates to 'union,' or some prefer 'yoking,' the meaning contemporary with Patanjali. A *Sutra* is a concise boil-down of a principle idea in as few words as possible, to convey its essence: It is similar to what we call an aphorism. By reading this, you have become a recipient of this gift, because you reached for it, wanting to know more. Perhaps that places you, or will place you, in the special class of people who are looking for a path to something more. Perhaps it will put you in the larger class of people who simply want to improve their life.

The teachings of the *Sutras* and Yoga philosophy are in the heart of teachings within many religions that use god names, but the *Sutras* were and are nonreligious, a philosophy that is neither theistic nor atheistic. Based on *Samkhya*, the philosophy has withstood the tests of time for thousands of years, far longer than any religion has. It has been the base philosophical and/ or spiritual reference point for billions of people. Being universal, the principles within the *Sutras* exist in the sacred texts of virtually every religion of the world, often in the words of the wondrous world teachers, Jesus Christ, Gautama Buddha, Muhammad, Zoroaster, Lao Tse, and others.

Indians revere the sainted Patanjali as a rishi, a highly evolved person experiencing high consciousness and portraying great wisdom, but not as a genius who invented a philosophy. Many view him as higher than prophets, and more spiritually advanced than many mystics, but not as an avatar. Whatever the proper characterization, it would be impossible to have the level of knowledge and insight evident in the *Sutra*s without being highly evolved, without access to high consciousness. The *Yoga Sutras* also shows his genius at organizing and concisely stating wisdom that began in prehistory, thousands of years before his remarkable life occurred. He skillfully unfolds the philosophy and its practice in progressive, easy to understand steps. His sequence and logic of presentation, though not obvious at first, produce awe as you begin to experience them.

Patanjali lived at the optimal time to produce this breath-taking book. The philosophy of *Samkhya* had solidified, spread widely, and attracted deep respect. Yet, it was pure philosophy and its followers were what some writers of today refer to as *jnana* (knowledge) yogins, those who seek wisdom along the path of knowledge. Opportunities to put the philosophy into daily practice through following action (*kriya*) paths were just emerging. Responding to that need, an action path for the nonreligious philosophy, the nonreligious Kriya Yoga (Action Union) was already falling into place alongside the heavily ritualized and complex religions of India. Patanjali documented the way to combine philosophy and action, while maintaining the purity and completeness of each. *Samkhya,* as portrayed through his amazing work, is the root source for and foundation of all Yoga and meditation practice in all forms. Study of the aspects documented in the *Yoga Sutras* provides a firm foundation for the practices leading to union and for living a Yoga life. It is as accessible and as meaningful to today's world as it was to ancient cultures. As with religions, though, today's Yoga is the result of extensive interpretation, reinterpretation, massaging to fit needs, adaptation to audiences and cultures, reinventing, and sometimes abuse and commercialization. A student of Yoga must know his or her own needs and understand that no single source will be enough to help fulfill those needs. It is always necessary to search it out.

The Eight Limbs Of Yoga Practice

Picture a solitary tree on a vast landscape, with eight branches going progressively up the tree in the manner of a spiral staircase. Lets call the tree 'Root Yoga' and envision that it has four equal zones. The zone nearest the ground carries the label '*Mastery of Living*,' and has two branches. The label on the lower of those two branches, says, 'Limb 1 - Self Restraint.' The next one up says, 'Limb 2 - Restraint of Mind.' The second zone from the bottom will say, '*Mastery of the body*,' with branches labeled, 'Limb 3 - Sitting' and 'Limb 4 - Restraint of Breath.' On the third zone, we see the label, '*Mastery of Attention*.' Its branches are 'Limb 5 - Withdrawal,' and 'Limb 6 - Concentration of the Mind.' The highest zone will be '*Mastery of Consciousness*,' with 'Limb 7- Religious Meditation' and 'Limb 8 - Intense absorption.'

Description of those eight limbs required only 30 of the 196 aphorisms in the *Yoga Sutras*, the whole of which provides broad-based, holistic guidance toward living a full life that evolves toward union. Due to the emphasis of teachers on a few of the eight limbs, the rich Yoga practices and philosophy in the remaining 166 of the *Sutras* are less known. Although they represent only a sixth of the *Yoga Sutras*, many consider those eight limbs to be the heart of Yoga practice. Others know them as the only Yoga practice, while others yet hardly know of their existence. The way they exist in the world is fully dependent on who talked or wrote about them, how they modified them, and how the students who received them understood them and passed them on to others. In a strong way, their existence today is like the existence of saplings carried from their original source to many parts of the world, with subsequent generations mutating and adapting to the local situation as needed, depending on the soil and environment. Some environments yielded single or double branch trees, while others thrived fully with all eight limbs and others yet died or dwindled.

The real world and its many Yoga 'traditions' (movements, organizations, sects, cults, or cultures -- choose a word you like) show us the highly variable results of continually transplanting eight-limb Yoga saplings for two thousand years. Although they usually claim otherwise, almost all modern 'traditions' have roots no deeper than two generations. If you found one with deep and continuous roots you could theoretically (but not really) trace the history backward. If you were successful, you would encounter a chain of perhaps 50 to 70 gurus. Your tracing would eventually bring you to an early Master who introduced a first variation from root Yoga. Tracing further backward you would always arrive at Patanjali's *Yoga Sutras,* which describe root Yoga. That would be true for current traditions, as well as earlier traditions that had died out. You would end at the same place. It does not matter whether you were considering a full-blown holistic Yoga tradition that had maintained its purity, or what some call Karma Yoga, Jnana Yoga, or Bhakti Yoga. It is the same if you are starting from Kundalini Yoga, Kriya Yoga, Hatha Yoga, Breathing Yoga, Restraint Yoga, Partner Yoga, aerial Yoga, Sex Yoga, or any other type. Although it is hard to see today, even the recently invented traditions derive from the same teachings. Your tracing would show you that the early traditions, nearest to Patanjali provided the only holistic Yoga.

The tracing of those roots would be difficult to impossible and could well be the subject of an entire book, but this book will take it no further. It is important to know, though, that historians refer to the time between 2800 years ago and 2200 years ago as the Axial Age, the time of the early great teachers. They tell us that it was a time of great philosophic, literary, and scientific giants who suddenly explored new ground. They do not tell us that it was then that the Buddha, Hebrew prophets, Confucius, Lao Tzu, Zoroaster, Socrates and Plato transformed the world's philosophical views, providing the foundations that Christ, Muhammad, Joseph Smith and others later taught from. It was then also, that Patanjali wrote the *Yoga Sutras,* which described the root ideas beneath all those views. Whether it was within Taoism in China, Buddhism or Hinduism in India, or Monotheism in Iran and the Middle East, a worldwide ethic of common ideas was present.

Among other things, all ethical/philosophical systems aimed at providing a method to deal with the pain of life ('suffering') to enable us to live in peace and harmony. All portrayed an absolute Reality that transcended the world, representing It in names such as God, Yahweh, Allah, Siva, Tao, the All, the Infinite, or *brahman*. All tried to integrate the knowledge within those teachings with everyday life, believing that we humans had lost touch with the fundamentals and with the Absolute primal existence (by any name), causing much to go bad. All of today's philosophies and religious practices spawned from these axial thinkers in China, India, and Iran. All those practices in those places spawned from the earlier teachings in India. Yet, the God's or other deities of religious practices tend strongly to be representations of the immanent god-essence not the transcendent one.

Paraphrasing The Limbs

Looking at the limbs less formally can provide insight to their intentions as guidelines for how to reduce our personal suffering, reach serenity, and evolve:

Limb 1. Brings unbreakable root principles as the measuring rod for your life.

Limb 2. Brings you to continuous awareness of the life style you are living.

Limb 3. Bring your body to a state of quiet readiness for performing meditation.

Limb 4. Breathing stills your mind, builds prana, and strengthens focusing.

Limb 5. Withdrawal overcomes the domination by your senses.

Limb 6. Concentration strengthens your single point focusing on anything.

Limb 7. Lets your mind explore reality.

Limb 8. Lets your mind harmonize with the higher consciousness.

To the degree that we attain this yogic life, we yoke many things into a unified force. That force moves our life in a direction, with continually less need for our tugging on the reins, or controlling the situation. Among them are:

Limb 1. Provides distinctive irrevocable personal identity and a sense of autopilot.

Limb 2. Establishes direction and meaning in your life.

Limb 3. Generates a platform of prana, quietness, and single-pointed attention.

Limb 4. Trains us to escape the power sensuality has over our life.

Limb 5. Takes us from sensory awareness to mind awareness.

Limb 6. Gives us the power of concentration.

Limb 7. Transcends the mind to receive insights and higher consciousness.

Limb 8. Leads to even higher consciousness experience, eventually to union.

The Hidden Truth Of The Eight Limbs

The Yoga Sutras are completely about progressive quieting of the mind. Starting with the first two, which enormously decrease inner conflicts and turmoil, each limb adds a powerful new technique of quieting.

A Full Way Of Life

The *Yoga Sutras* describes a full way of life. If we choose that way of living, it moves us in gentle steps toward an increased internal quietness and a serene, centered way of being in the world. Using the unique capability humans have to evolve their personal consciousness experience, it moves us from full focus on our everyday sensory experience to interplay with the pervading, unrecognized, always present, consciousness that is beyond normal experience. In doing so, we move from full focus on sensory existence toward increasing attention to our spiritual existence (*Sutra* 2.45). During that evolution, seven levels of *samadhi* consciousness beyond the mind level come into play before reaching the eighth and final experience. The seven begin with experiencing oneness with physical objects and lead eventually to experiencing divine joy and deep understanding of the egoless experience. The only thing left to experience beyond that is the pure consciousness of *brahman* in *nirbija samadhi*.

However, none of us truly lives in sensory experience alone. We experience gradations and mixes of consciousness levels. From our material/sensory consciousness, we continually go in and out of the mind and other consciousness states, beyond our thoughts. We often unknowingly stay in that other consciousness for an extended time when we become deeply absorbed in something. Perhaps while in that state you have heard someone strongly suggest that you return to your home on earth and recognize his or her existence. When you return you may realize that you have not heard or seen anything through some unknown lapse of time. Perhaps sometime when you have been puzzling through a problem you have entered something like a trance, and when you awake the answer is there. On rare occasions, when we have escaped our sensory experience and moved even beyond that mental consciousness, we realize that some marvelous insight or understanding has come to us.

With meditative practice, we can increase both the frequency and the level of these nonsensory consciousness experiences. We have the capability to control the mix of spirituality and materiality and evolve our capability for higher consciousness. We can also remain contented with things as they are and not reach for higher consciousness. We can even regress from higher consciousness if it frightens us, or if we decline the prices that we must pay to be there. Our way-of-life choices affect that.

We rarely think about the power and beauty of even our everyday consciousness and how it so dramatically differs from that of all other living things, without exception. We rarely appreciate that our many similar predecessor human-like species, up to and through the recent Neanderthal species and the Cro Magnon forerunner varieties of our current Homo sapiens species, probably did not have our capability. It is likely that we have had it for no more than 10,000 years, starting when the forces of Nature unleashed our mental power and creativity. That ability to train our mind to move to progressively higher levels of consciousness experience is just one example of the blessings our still infant species received then. Perhaps you can feel the awe of that. If it were not for that consciousness blessing, meditative yoga could not have come about.

STUDYING YOGA

The Search For Truth

As we progress, our Yoga practices lead us toward Reality and away from fantasy and illusion, toward finding correct meaning and discarding incorrect meaning. The *Yoga Sutras* (1.7, 1.29) and high teachers tell us that study of our selves and of the words of others are important to achieving that. Studying of the words of others, though, does not mean that wen should blindly accept them. It has been traditional in Yoga for the seeker to accept the words of a guru without question and follow whatever instructions the guru provides. We are each, however, responsible for our own journey, acceptance of our *karma*, and evolving during our lifetime. The Gautama Buddha told us that to have inner peace and move toward 'awakening,' the equivalent of Yoga's *kaivalya*, we must discard false thinking, know our true state of being, and continually search for Truth. His teaching emphasized accepting nothing that we see or hear from anyone: we must learn for ourselves and trust our inner understanding.

True knowledge is not intellectual, though we must use the intellect for studying in support of our aspiration to find it. True knowledge is intuitive inner knowledge, beyond the intellect and mind, received from the realms beyond the mind. Our intuitive being understands that the material world intellect and mind, driven by the ego, are the creators of our false views and illusions. Our intellects and minds do not know that they do that, leading us to treat falsity as truth. To obtain True knowledge, we must clear away the noise of the mind, and the stubborn insistences of the intellect and ego, all of which resist intuition. The ego acts as if such awareness is an enemy threatening its power.

Studying Yoga is not different from studying other things. For the moment we will use Buddhism s an example, although the same exploration would apply to Christianity, Sikhism, Islam, Hinduism, Judaism, Vedism, Taoism, Shintoism, and many others. If you were to begin studying Buddhism, you would most likely begin with a modern book written for ease of understanding. If the thirst for pure knowledge began to drive your life, you would begin to read more books. Eventually you would discover that the modern books derive from older Buddhist books, whose teachings have been corrupted (changed). Perhaps you would already see that the modern books were often intellectual overexpansion, far from the original teachings of the Buddha. Maybe you would thirst for the real teachings. If you began reading older books, you would see that they are more difficult to read, but contain hints at Truths that the modern books do not provide. Perhaps you would eventually conclude that the older books do not go back far enough to be helpful in finding the seed teachings. You might even perceive the beginnings of great distortion. As you became more accustomed to the teachings, you would identify certain writings as characteristic of a particular sect, branch, or subset, and come to recognize their signature distortions. Maybe a few undistorted survivor elements would become part of your learning. You would come to understand the process. You would see that revered teachers, having obtained personal reward, success, and followers through a personal Buddhist ideology, guided students in that direction, and momentum toward a sect began. You would soon learn that a base in the teachings of the Buddha was in each sect, but that the alterations would be so great that the original teachings would not be evident. Your search for the truth could finally seriously begin, becoming an obsessive drive to overcome the obstacles, to find your way through the fog with nothing to guide you.

If your thirst became a fire within, you would begin to search for the seeds of ultimate Truth wherever you could find them, using your fire to burn away the onion-like layers of interpretation, personal musings, and intellectualization covering the seed. Perhaps your intuition would eventually lead you to look for the direct source, something close to being the Buddha's own words. You might search through even earlier writings, evaluating and integrating everything new with everything old, rejecting some things and accepting others. If graced with sufficient time, fire, focus, and information, you might peel your way to the seed. The same would happen if your passion caused you to devote your life to Jewish, Christian, Mohammedan, Muslim, Taoist, Zoroastrian, Vedic, Jain, Sikh, Hindu, Shinto, or Yoga teachings. The many levels would deeply hide the seeds.

Available Translations

In all human activities, whether of lawyers, doctors, plumbers, artists, accountants, farmers, yogins, gurus, or anything else, a small number of those that do it are very good at it and a small number are very bad at it. The rest are somewhere on the scale between those extremes. That natural Law applies to people who write books also, including books about the *Yoga Sutras*. A small number of 'translations' (which are not always translations) and interpretations are available in our language. Most are not easy: difficult and unfamiliar language structures are often intermixed with indigestible ancient words and esoteric ideas.

Some *Yoga Sutras* books bear the names of authors with worldwide reputation. The fabulous B. K. S. Iyengar, unarguably the best posture teacher in the world, is one. Integral Yoga's Swami Satchidananda, who popularized Yoga in America in the sixties with his appearance at Woodstock, his intention to westernize Yoga, and his ashrams, left us his version before he passed from our planet. The hugely respected and accomplished Georg Feuerstein produced a frighteningly intellectual and challenging translation and interpretation. His version, though, is too often not true to the Sanskrit. The revered Swami Satyananda Saraswati has contributed an illuminating, exciting, and sometimes breathtaking version, which is often wrong. The widely acclaimed *How to Know God – The Yoga Aphorisms of Patanjali* is also among this collection of translations. Its commentary by Swami Prabhavananda and Christopher Isherwood made it the standard bearer for sixty years, but it is a collection of beliefs, not a translation.

Sanskrit is not an easy language to translate properly: words in dictionaries have many different meanings that depend on context, originating culture, and historical time. In using the dictionaries, it is important to recognize that the varying words reflect the changing of meaning over thousands of years. Translating the *Yoga Sutras* requires finding meanings contemporary with Patanjali or earlier, excluding later meanings. The strongest and most damaging example of non-contemporary meanings is that all authors interpreted many of the *Sutras* to be about the eight or more 'mystical powers.' Writing and discussion of those questionable and highly variable mystical powers, though, did not exist at the time of Patanjali's life, arising much later in a religious context. Before anyone claimed that Yoga Masters could attain them, they were powers attributed only to the god Siva. When some gurus began to claim to be living gods, or followers saw them as that, it was natural to assume they had the same powers.

Though much commonality exists in the most authentic of the modern translations, great differences exist, and each provides unique added content that does not come from the *Yoga Sutras*. Each book reflects the teachings of the tradition, religion, or culture that influenced the author's yogic education, personal evolution, and understanding of things. Each provides the insights and learnings of an individual's lifetime of Yoga. Yet, each book is far from perfect, often greatly wrong in some places, some more so than others.

We must recognize that 2000 years elapsed between Patanjali's writing of the *Sutras* and the translations and interpretations available to us. No translations from the intervening millennia are available. All are modern. Much massaging of Patanjali's words occurred during that long time, just as priests, ministers, monks, intellectuals, kings, and others have massaged and reinterpreted the words of Christ, Buddha, and Krishna. That massaging reflects in the translations and interpretations, just as it does in the writings and teachings of others schooled in a tradition, religion, cult, or cloistered culture. Modern gurus and the most respected authors differ greatly from each other in their understandings and portrayals. There is one huge difference, however. Patanjali's words as he wrote them are available for study, uncorrupted. The words of the Great Teachers did not appear until hundreds of years had passed.

Christ, Buddha, Muhammad, Lao Tsu, Krishna, Zoroaster, and others conveyed many of the same teachings as those presented by Patanjali, but used the words and cultural style of their local civilization. Their styles and cultural conformity inadvertently veiled the common meanings across their teachings. It is no different with Great Swamis from modern times, such as Sri Paramahansa Yogananda, Sri Yukteswar, Sri Ram Dass, Sri Sivananda, and Sri Mahasaya. They, and revered learned beings such as the wondrous Osho and Ramakrishna, also refer to the teachings of the *Sutras* in different ways with different words and interpretations, often very wrong, because the events and conditions of their lives necessarily influenced their words. Yet, they all carry some of the same core lessons. It is as if the lessons wore different clothing.

KARMA AND LIFE PATHS

The source of our human individual uniqueness and variety of needs extends far beyond the genetic inheritance and cultural/environmental influences we normally associate with it. According to Yoga philosophy, every human born to this Earth planet has lived lives before this current one and will live more after it. Each of those lives created accumulations of karmic memories, which carry from current life to every future life. (In *Sutra* 4.9 and eight others Patanjali called the karmic memories 'impressions.')

The karmic history and needs that we each carry across our material world lives create unique individual complexity. That karmic complexity leads the soul-packet to create the next life situation of genes and environment that will provide the needed Earth-bound experience: it may or may not be pleasant or positive, but it will always satisfy the karmic need. No matter who or what we are, we will evolve, or perhaps even devolve, during this lifetime. We will not remain static. What happens to each of us depends primarily on the choices we make. What happens to the aspirant of Yoga depends on the combination of *karma* and personal will applied through attitude, discipline, commitment, as well as life choices.

Both those who know nothing about Yoga and those continually practicing Yoga evolve. The current levels of personal evolution and the current karmic needs of an individual are unique to each of us, and are greatly varied. As yogins, we have the opportunity to choose to affect that *karma* and the flow of our life toward the possibilities available to us, but nothing forces us to take that opportunity. It is a free-will choice. We can reach high, but we cannot all attain the various high levels of consciousness experience.

The purpose of a given lifetime is to have experiences that will affect your next phase of evolution. Those experiences may be good, bad, mundane, or exciting. Nothing guarantees that our next life will be a 'better' experience. The many life experiences will include things from both sides of the 'good/bad' coin. The practice of serious yogins intends to move them through experiencing progressive levels of higher consciousness over time by progressive stilling of the mind. Evolution moves at different rates for different individuals and circumstances. Sometimes evolution slightly regresses, or remains static for a replay, but it always returns to forward movement.

As we progressively enter new birth situations, any situation will provide mixed experiences of chaos, serenity, and everything between. That mix will be unique for each. A small number of evolution-resistant people who do not learn from it repeat horrible lives at the chaos end of the scale, bringing misery. Some highly evolved yogins begin new lives on the established platform of higher consciousness experience. Whether yogin or not, most of us lead average existences with unspectacular, but steady, growth from life to life.

Regardless of the path they chose, those that attain the highest spirituality perceive it in the same way. The trek that enabled them to reach it readies them for it by altering how they perceive: that permanently altered perception eventually ends the differentiation between *brahman* consciousness (pure spirituality) and the material things that manifested from *brahman*. All things become one thing. Those yogins still lower on the progress scale travel through different places and have experiences unique to their paths. Paths may be long, short, high, low, comfortable, difficult, slow, or fast, but still take the long-term seeker to the highest level.

This is all strongly analogous to different mountain paths existing for hikers of varying skills and abilities, some leading directly to the summit for the smaller numbers prepared to go there. Paths up mountains are not always easy to find. Less used paths are not well defined, making them difficult to find and follow. Not all hikers or aspirants want the higher and more challenging paths, and fulfill their personal needs in the foothills. That is as it should be. Those not yet experienced in the ways of the mountain, whether the physical one or a metaphoric Yoga one, will do well to avoid the higher paths until they are ready for the rigors, isolation, and self-dependency. With many paths available to accommodate the varied personal needs, karmic push moves each individual toward a path consistent with a level of involvement that is appropriate to that unique life and path.

ADDITIONAL PERSPECTIVE

Continual Emergence Of Practices

People in most corners of the world know about Yoga, but few understand its true nature, or that it existed for 4000 years leading up to our current forms of practice. Four thousand years is a long time. More than 200 generations of parents, grandparents, great grandparents, and so on passed between its birth and today's practice. It progressively developed formal shape for 2000 years before becoming the philosophy and practices that the *Yoga Sutras* documented.

Then, in the 2000 years after Patanjali's life, multiple formal sets of practice derived from his *Sutras*, some forming 'traditions.' Along the way, Yoga enhanced the lives of billions of people and still does today. The earliest traditions that developed from the *Sutras* maintained the purity and full form of eight-limb practice that Patanjali described, strictly taught and monitored by Masters who had seriously practiced them. As generations accumulated and cultures became further separated from the source of the teachings, new movements gravitated toward a less holistic practice of a few limbs. With the passing of centuries, cults, offshoots, branches, 'traditions,' and philosophical encampments derived from existing practices: much modification, redefinition, exploration, and interpretation changed the teachings.

Current Yoga practice has a strong focus on postures, which became not only a mistranslation, but also a replacement for Limb 3 (*asanas* = sitting). New 'traditions' and their practice models continually emerge, only rarely following the teachings of old-school Masters: some derive from gurus with shallow training and roots, and some from smart, market-oriented lightly trained yogins. A few are pure inventions founded on only a vague personal idea of what Yoga is. At least in the West, few gurus remain. None of these cult-like movements have developed successor Masters as leaders: most exist as fads with little potential for longevity. Some are close to disappearance from the Yoga scene.

The Goals And Purposes Of Yoga

Teachers and books describing Yoga focus on different aspects, often making Yoga seem like different things, confusing anyone seeking to understand its reality or its common base. To further confuse this, many recent books are about what we could fairly call 'applied Yoga,' Yoga used for a purpose such as alignment, acupressure, sex, health, restoration, strengthening, purifying, or sports preparation. The variety of uses is both astounding and overwhelming. Yet, far more astounding than the variations are the commonalties that flow through all true Yoga (not applied, recreational, gymnastic, or athletic Yoga), commonalties that have withstood the tests of time for 2000 years or more. To begin with, all true Yoga is a quest for union of the individual with *brahman* - the eternal essence of godness, the Absolute. Whether perceived as ITs transcendent form or as ITs immanent form of *isvara/sat* does not matter. The absolutely still consciousness is common to both. Even the references to *brahman* have varied greatly over time as people sought a way to identify it. In philosophical representation of that nameless existence, IT has been the Ground of Being, Reality, the Source, the All, Truth, Spirit, the Supreme, and many others.

That naming varies even more when it leaves philosophical ground and enters the ground of religion. Hinduism baffles outsiders with its seemingly unending list of gods, each of which represent some aspect of the *isvara/sat* existence. Buddhism does not name a separate being, focusing on the internal self (soul, but not named as that) as the ultimate entity. Sufism, Taoism, Jainism, Christianity, Islam, Judaism, and many others add their variations. Hundreds of names have existed for gods and goddesses that have either limited or all-inclusive roles. Yet, everywhere we look, behind every name for the eternal existence, we see the human reaching for union, the harmony between the individual and their god-image, the Absolute, the ultimate Reality. Some approach that union through intermediaries, such as Jesus, but the quest for personal connection is always there.

The word for that connection of the individual mind with that presence beyond everything in the material world is also difficult to nail down. 'Yoking' at the time of Patanjali has been union, reunion, merging, remembering, integrating, awakening, and so on at different times in different places. The difficulties in naming arise from a paradox. We are separate, but we are one being, one existence with many aspects. In the philosophy of Yoga, the individual and that which is beyond all materiality are inseparable: more than inseparable, they are the same entity, a unity with no separation other than in the imagination of the divine consciousness. Recognizing that 'imagination' is only an ability of humans, many yogins refer to the conceptualization of things and beings by *brahman* as Its 'dream images,' a god ability, not a human ability. Some say that dream images are one of the ways that the divinity communicates with us. Considering that the individual and the divinity are inseparable, teaching that the word 'union' means that we need to unite them is inappropriate. We can neither unite nor reunite the already united. The other definition of Yoga as 'yoke' provides a better mental image, but what we truly aspire to is experiencing the existing union.

We are certain that we somehow lost something that we need to get back. It seems like a missing connection, but it is truly a missing awareness of the connection. A gap exists where there should be no gap. No word properly describes that unique awareness of unity. No word can adequately show that we have somehow blocked it, hidden it, forgotten how to tap it, buried it under our debris of life, or run from it in fear. It would be wrong to say that the unity is broken, because not even death can break the eternal oneness. The Buddha's term 'awakening' to its presence is perhaps the best we can do. In *Sutra* 3.9, Patanjali uses the word *vyutthana* for 'awakening,' as a specific stage of evolution. Considering the other side of the awakening coin, it would be proper to say that we ignore the oneness, or are asleep to its existence.

When we find it again, we end our ignorance. In the *Sutras* (2.3-2.5 and 2.24), 'ignorance' (*avidya*) is 'lack of spiritual knowledge.'

The Word Yoga

The usual modern translation of Yoga is 'union.' It could also mean 'unite,' 'join,' 'harness,' 'contact,' 'yoke,' 'connect,' 'direct your attention toward,' or 'find communion.' It further carries a strong implication of taking action to achieve a result. The target is to eventually experience the union of the individual material mind with the consciousness of the spiritual soul. Yogins accomplish that by disciplined practices of stilling the mind to gradually experience higher consciousness levels. When the yogin's mind permanently becomes as still as the unchanging consciousness of the soul, *isvara/sat*, and *brahman*: that stillness brings permanent absorption in *brahman*. That is *kaivalya*, or *nirvana*, the 'Absolute Unity' that we loosely call Emancipation.

To accomplish that, Yoga uses the established techniques documented by Patanjali to gradually yoke the mind into harmonic union with the soul of *brahman* and Its Earth presence as *isvara* (*sat*). Barriers that keep us from experiencing the higher consciousness states through a stilled mind slowly erode under the influence of Yoga practice. We progressively move from experiencing one level of consciousness to experiencing the next higher, being unaware of the lower forms while experiencing the higher ones.

Along the way, Yoga practice results in qualities such as poise, sureness, steadiness, clarity, sincerity, and compassion. Those qualities enable us to look at and accept all aspects of life with calmness and serenity. The knowledge, personal adjustments, and physiological changes that come about from this eventually enable us to experience and accept *brahman* as Reality, the ultimate and only Reality of which we are part, which we could not otherwise do. Ultimate arrival on the mountain peak comes from progressive development of mind stillness, eventually becoming absolutely still - no thoughts or activity of any type. We need to remain mindful, though, that Yoga practice slowly evolves through many life-improving changes. Targeting or expecting the ultimate result, which will happen over many lifetimes, would lead to desire, attachment, disappointment, greed for results, and other progress-blocking negative conditions. We can only improve our life in that direction, through our practice, noticing and enjoying the benefits, letting the evolution happen without directing it.

The Interbreeding Of Yoga And Religion

For 4000 years, the core philosophy has fed, and crossbred with, the religions of India. The religious and parallel philosophical teachings have always been so similar that without the god names it is hard to distinguish them from one another. Pure Yoga teaching may portray the same idea that a religion does, but it will assign only an identifying word to an aspect, power, force, or ability of *brahman* or its creations, without assigning qualities of godness. In Yoga teaching, for example, *isvara* is an aspect of the great underlying primal existence, *brahman*. It plays the 'delegated,' or 'on behalf of,' role of overseer, cosmic soul, and Immanent-Presence in our universe. As an aspect of *brahman's* consciousness, *isvara* has all Its powers and characteristics. In a religious context, *Isvara* is the name for the God-immanent that rules this universe. Depending on the religion that owns it, and on the time-point in that religion's history, that same God-immanent might be God, Brahma, Siva, Sat, or any of many others. Some sects of Hinduism claim that Krishna has 1000 names.

To better understand the interrelationship of Yoga and religions, picture an upside-down A-shaped rose-trellis leaning against a wall: its side-rails are joined at the bottom, with a long cross-rail at the top. On the wall near the base, someone has written 'Philosophy.' That common point represents the situation before the first of the Vedas and the earliest Indian god concepts of perhaps 4000 years ago. For some time before that, probably a long time, meditating mystics were delivering Truths received from the unseen 'beyond' to their culture. They described the world beyond the material world and the relationship of humans to it. That was not Yoga, not even close, but the enduring root principles were present and the philosophy was evolving. Without rituals, dogma, organization, hierarchies of leaders, and god names, it had no similarity to religion

Although no religion existed then, the innate human drive toward knowing, naming, and reaching for a god-thing was omnipresent. When humans later began to assign godness and god names to the natural force aspects of Nature and the Absolute, momentum started toward organizing religions and their practices. Now have your mind label the left rail of the ladder as Yoga and the right rail as religion, both energized by philosophy. Let the rungs crossing between represent the flow between the two. In that image, the flow went on for many centuries as mystical revelations that affected both Yoga and religion fed the cross-flow. As the distance between them steadily increased, the recognition of their commonality decreased.

The Indian religions as they have evolved until now and Yoga as it has evolved until now have the same starting point in time and content. Their intricate houses share a foundation, but the philosophy has retained its pure godless Yoga form, while the religions developed rich and complex depictions of gods. Although the philosophy that matured into Yoga also energized a series of religions, Yoga never became one. Nor did it become a god-free, ritualized, quasi-religion in the manner of Buddhism.

No religion or ritual-based practice named Yogism exists. No gods exist within root Yoga. Yet, other than it has no form, human or other, *brahman* has all the standard god qualities. Many westerners, including practicing yogins, believe it is religious, because many Indians combine their Yoga with worship of Vedic or Hindu gods or the practices and beliefs of the Vedanta philosophy/religion. That belief hardens in anyone who attends Yoga classes today where chants pay homage to gods, and the furnishings contain Vedic or Hindu statuary, tapestries, and symbols. The teachers and the students think it is a natural part of Yoga. They rarely differentiate the two.

Evolution Of Yoga

Root Yoga clearly revolves around *brahman*, a formless godness existence that has no beginning or end and has the qualities we ascribe to gods. Yet, the philosophy does not reference it as a named god or provide any religion-like rituals or dogma. As two thousand years passed, though, revered Yoga Masters provided a long string of spin-offs from root Yoga and progressively away from the teachings of their predecessors. Many came to merge them with a religious movement or sect they were part of, establishing Yoga traditions that did worship gods. Their students and students of their students carried the religious influences into the future. Some traditions of today still do take their god(s) seriously. Teachers in other places tell their students that the god names they hear and see are there for the wonderful spiritual flavor, perpetuating the myth that Sanskrit was a spiritual language. Where the god names appear in chants, non-religious teachers may say, 'we just chant for the vibrations.' Most of the time, they say nothing at all. Because students often do not know what the Sanskrit words that they chant mean, and have no background context for understanding, they often do not know that they are chanting god names, making appeals to god-forms, or engaging in a defined religious ritual.

There is nothing right or wrong in any of that. The Masters were all establishing paths for people to follow, paths that worked well for them. The point here is that root Yoga, without any reference to gods, is also a path, but the path is not familiar to students of today. Yoga can be a pure, full, holistic, and fully rewarding practice while maintaining awareness of an unnamed, formless godness reality. Gods and religions are important to and supportive of billions of people, but they solidly stand on their own without Yoga and Yoga can also stand alone.

Yet, truthfully, Yoga is a bit scary. Root Yoga is like taking your coffee black and turning your back on the Starbuck's that was once important to you. Although the Source has no eyeball, metaphorically it means approaching the formless Source of all that there is 'eyeball to eyeball,' without blinking or feeling fear. It means saying with the deepest reverence and respect, 'Yes, I accept that I am made of primal existence stuff, *brahman* stuff. I understand that I deserted my god-essence-ness. I am ready to come home. I am ready to enter the life with deep commitment.' That requires huge changes and giving up much that we think is mandatory to a good life. To use a valuable word that Patanjali does not use, it requires becoming a 'renunciate,' renouncing the material world and its sensuality.

WHAT IS IN THIS BOOK

The Volumes And Chapters

First understand that Patanjali organized the 196 aphorisms into four '*padas*' (parts). A part is equivalent to a chapter.

This book has two volumes containing three chapters and one appendix:

VOLUME 1

- Chapter One is this introduction to the philosophy and practice of Yoga.
- Chapter Two presents the *Sutras* in their pure form, without explanation or translation detail. It includes each of the *Sutras* four parts (padas, chapters):

  Samadhi pada - Intense Absorption

  Sadhana pada - Practice

  Vibhuti pada – Superhuman

  Kaivalya pada – Absolute Unity

  The aphorisms in each pada have standard identifying numbers (e.g. 3.10, 4.26).

- Chapter Three provides translation details and an extended commentary for each *Sutra* in the four parts.

  Samadhi pada - Intense Absorption

  Sadhana pada - Practice

  Vibhuti pada - Superhuman

  Kaivalya pada - Absolute Unity

- Appendix 1 provides a cross reference of words used in the *Sutras*

VOLUME 2

- Volume 2 explains the translation of each word and each of the 196 *Sutras*, while analyzing how the modern books became so different from the original.

Information Added To The Sutras

Documenting the flow of Patanjali's presentation is important to full understanding. Captions within the text of Chapter Two and Chapter Three are there to show that flow. They emphasize the interconnections among the aphorisms, and point to the transitions to new subjects.

No captions existed in the original text. The captions that exist in some of the modern translations vary greatly from author to author, are often misleading, are frequently wrong, and do not catch the flow.

Where parentheses appear within the text, they enclose clarifying notes.

Truth

This book attempts the huge task of conveying Truth, but it is not possible to apprehend Truth fully and completely, unless having personally evolved to close in on the ultimate goal of Yoga, *kaivalya* (Absolute Unity). All Truth short of that is partial. Humans seem to be the only being on Earth that can come progressively closer to it, each in his or her individual way, traveling their unique path. On the other side of the Truth coin, unlike any other species, it is human nature to promote unverified beliefs conveyed to them by others, warp, modify, obfuscate, hide, downplay, and exaggerate. Truth seeking is not a popular pastime, and not sanctioned by religions, cults, adherents to scientific theories, yoga 'traditions,' media, companies, or organizations.

As well as providing the relative Truth of a direct and careful translation, this book provides extensive notes on how even the most respected and accomplished authors arrived at erroneous interpretations and translations. It provides you with an opportunity to confront and examine this attempt at conveying the meaning of the *Sutras*, while accepting your personal responsibility to accept or reject parts or the whole.

To Inform, Not To Convince

This is a book about the taproot of Yoga as described by Patanjali. It exists for you to examine, explore, and consider. It is here for your potential benefit, in the way that it fits the needs of your current life. It is not here to convince you or lead you, only to inform you, to give you choices.

CHAPTER TWO

PURE YOGA
THE 196 SUTRAS

SAMADHI PADA

THE PART ON INTENSE ABSORPTION

(Sutras 1.1 - 1.51)

Patanjali's first part (*pada*) describes higher consciousness experiences, and the nature of the cosmos and of divinity.

THE PRECEPTS OF YOGA

1.1   *Now the precepts of union (Yoga).*

RESTRAINT OF MIND ACTIVITIES

1.2   *Meditation is restraint of mind activities.*
1.3   *At that time, the one who sees comprehends the situation of their own nature.*
1.4   *Or else, devotion to meditation brings assimilation with the deity.*

FIVE STATES OF MIND IN EVERYDAY LIFE

1.5   When not in religious meditation, the mind is restrained to five states. Each state can have pain or be free of pain.

1.6   The five states of mind are:

Means of acquiring certain knowledge

Misapprehension

Imagination

Sleep

Attaining remembrance

1.7   Within means of acquiring certain knowledge there are:

Perception by the senses

Inference

Study

1.8   Misapprehension is incorrect knowledge, not with regard to the natural base (of the thing observed).

1.9   Knowing, following as a consequence of the absent correct expression of the real, is imagination.

1.10   Your state of sleep is the foundation for conception of entities that do not exist.

1.11   Memory follows as a consequence of not letting drop any special worldly object, aim, matter, or business.

ASPIRING TO PURITY OF MIND

1.12   While in continual meditative restraint, the mind exerts effort to remain in the unmodified condition of purity (stillness, spirituality) through indifference to worldly things, life, and pain.

1.13   Under those circumstances, devoted zeal brings the mind effort necessary to remain in its unmodified condition of purity (sattva).

EVOLUTION TO EXPERIENCE HIGHER STATES OF CONSCIOUSNESS

1.14   *A step is to be strong in meditation as long term uninterrupted consideration of a thing, while firm in practicing assiduously.*

1.15   *Having experienced that which is derived from tradition and sensual enjoyments, a yogin free from desire, subjugates notions, and becomes indifferent to worldly objects and life.*

1.16   *Afterward, there will be perception of the Supreme Being and indifference to even the constituents of prakrti (Nature).*

FOUR PROGRESSIVE MODES OF HIGHER CONSCIOUSNESS

1.17   *Thereupon to enter into accurate knowing (samprajnata samadhi): the modes are uncertainty, consideration, joy, and egoism.*

CESSATION OF MIND ACTIVITY AND THOSE HIGHER EXPERIENCES

1.18   *In the effort of the mind to remain in its unmodified condition of purity, cessation of notions is previous to the end of the inexhaustibleness of the impressions.*

1.19   *Thus, arising from that basis, deliverance through release from the body, absorption in the original producer of the material world.*

1.20   *The wisdom from intense absorption is different from that of the earlier faith, valor, and memory.*

1.21   *For the ardent, intensity of onset is indeed near.*

1.22   *Seeking excellence near fading away, you may be mild, moderate, or excessive.*

1.23   *Or, consume profound religious meditation on the Supreme Being.*

THE NATURE OF THE SUPREME BEING

1.24   A superior soul, the Supreme Being is untouched by the afflictions, actions, consequence of actions, or their stock (of impressions).

1.25   Therein, a receptacle of unsurpassed omniscience.

1.26   Going constantly without separation over the course of time, quickly going after the ancients and any venerable or respectable person.

OM

1.27   The mystic (or sacred) symbol (om) signifies it.

1.28   Therefore, raise one's eyes, whisper, and accordingly direct one's thoughts to the meaning.

THE OBSTACLES TO HIGHER CONSCIOUSNESS

1.29   And, extended, one whose thoughts are turned inward or upon himself surely accomplishes absence of obstacles.

1.30   Sickness, apathy, doubt, carelessness, sloth, intemperance, erroneous understanding, not obtaining your next degree, and instability become distractions of the mind, are regarded as obstacles.

1.31   Endure appearing together with the distractions, pain, dejectedness, your causing the body to shake or tremble, panting, and very hard breathing.

ATTAINING PURITY

1.32   Therefore prevent, for the motive of achieving a single true principle, the mind remaining in its unmodified condition of purity (sattva).

1.33   From that time, benevolence, compassion, joyfulness, indifference to pleasure, pain, virtuousness, wickedness, and the organs of the senses, bring gladness of mind.

1.34   Or, retention of exhalation of his breath until it hurts.

1.35   Or, perseverance in bringing the risen mind to a state of bondage to a sensuous cognition.

1.36   Or, without sorrow there is purity.

1.37   Or, a mind that is desireless for objects of the senses.

1.38   Or, sleep dreams are a foundation for higher knowledge.

MEDITATION CAN BE ON ANYTHING

1.39   Or, by consuming profound and abstract religious meditation as desired.

1.40   Whether the meditation targets an infinitesimal particle or infinitely great state of being, its end will be the same.

SAMAPATTI
ONENESS OF THE OBSERVER, THE SENSES, AND THE OBSERVED

1.41   Born in consequence of diminished mind activity, like a crystal, the one who perceives, the organs of sense, and the objects of sensual perception assume the color of a near object, consequently causing becoming the object.

THE STAGES OF HIGHER CONSCIOUSNESS

Stage 1 Of Higher Consciousness
Focusing On A Physical Target
savitarka samapatti samprajnata samadhi

1.42   Then the object of the senses, its name, knowledge of it, and false notions are mixed, falling into a state of uncertain samadhi. (Specifically and technically, savitarka samapatti samprajnata samadhi.)

Stage 2 Of Higher Consciousness
Focusing On A Physical Target
nirvitarka samapatti asamprajnata samadhi

1.43   Inconsiderate (i.e. inconsiderate samadhi) is purified memory nearly void of the own form of the object of the senses and entirely without description. (Specifically and technically it is nirvitarka samapatti asamprajnata samadhi)

Stages 3 and 4 - Focusing On A Subtle (Nonphysical) Target
savicara samprajnata samadhi
nirvicara asamprajnata samadhi

1.44   Moving even nearer, with consideration given (i.e. samadhi with consideration), and without consideration given (i.e. samadhi without consideration), relate to the subtle sphere. (Specifically and technically these are savicara samprajnata samadhi and nirvicara asamprajnata samadhi).

1.45   Your subtle sphere, moreover, has no distinguishing marks or termination.

1.46   Inviolably the same, these are intense absorptions (samadhis) containing seed.

STAGE 4 EXPERIENCE

1.47   Not needing consideration (nirvicara samadhi), there is the infallible tranquility of the Supreme Spirit.

1.48   Therein, there is truth-bearing knowledge.

1.49   Knowledge from teachings or reflection pleases; there is a difference from that of the sphere of inexhaustibleness you go constantly striving to obtain.

1.50   Another impression is produced, preventing new impressions.

HIGHER CONSCIOUSNESS 'WITHOUT SEED'
nirbija samadhi

1.51   That is near to complete control and suppression - seedless intense absorption (nirbija samadhi).

SADHANA PADA

THE PART ON PRACTICE

(Sutras 2.1 - 2.51)

Patanjali's second part (*pada*) describes the holistic practice of Yoga.

THE ACTIONS THAT LEAD TO UNION

2.1   Religious austerity, reciting to one's self, and profound religious meditation on the Supreme Being are Action Yoga (Kriya Yoga).

2.2   The reason is the promoting of intense absorption, as well as the reason of causing the afflictions to attenuate.

THE FIVE AFFLICTIONS THAT DISTURB THE SERENITY

2.3   The afflictions are spiritual ignorance, egoism, vehement desire, repugnance, and affection.

2.4   Attain domination over the place of origin of spiritual ignorance, whether it is inactive, small, interrupted, or great.

2.5   Spiritual ignorance is the perception of the transient, impure, trouble, and corporeal as possessing supremacy over the eternal, the pure, the effort to win future beatitude, and the soul.

2.6   Egoism is perseverance in understanding perception as if the same as the individual soul.

2.7   The effort to win future beatitude is repentant of vehement desires.

2.8   Trouble is the consequence of the act of repugnance.

2.9   In that manner, desire for one's own goods, and causing corruption to flow, spring up from affection.

2.10   When these subtle things are gone, one returns to the original state.

MEDITATION BRINGS STILLNESS

2.11   *And, the tendency toward arrival of activity comes to an end resulting from meditation.*

PREVENTING CONSEQUENCES AND DIFFICULTIES

2.12   *Afflictions are the root of the actions to be felt as the stock (of karmic influences) in present and future lives.*

2.13   *That acquisition is the root of consequences, as the form of existence fixed at birth, a life, and experiences.*

2.14   *Gladness or sorrow result, by reason of your purity or impurity.*

2.15   *Indeed, various of the wise say that change, pain, their troubles from (karmic) impressions, and conflict with activities of the constituents of prakrti (the gunas) bring difficulties.*

2.16   *A future with difficulties is to be avoided.*

2.17   *A condition to be avoided is one who examines the visible through direct material contact.*

THE PURPOSE OF THE VISIBLE (MATERIAL/SENSORY) WORLD

2.18   *The purpose for the visible, composed of manifestation, activity, resistance to motion, a natural way of acting, that which exists, and the faculty of sensing is experience and final beatitude.*

FOUR BASELINE STATES OF THE UNIVERSE

2.19   *The constituents of prakrti (gunas) divide things into essential difference, uniformity, having characteristics, and elementary matter without characteristics within.*

2.20   *And perceiving that basis, one who sees (i.e. the yogin) sees matter unmodified (i.e. by the mind).*

2.21   *And, the only reason it is visible is the principle of life and sensation.*

2.22   *Upon gaining that, objects of the senses disappear; nevertheless, since they are in a constant state of being common to all, they are unimpaired for another person.*

THE EGO

2.23   *The ego is the master of attachment, one's own circumstances, acquisition, and means of contact.*

2.24   *It is the cause of spiritual ignorance.*

CESSATION OF SPIRITUAL IGNORANCE

2.25   *Non-existence of that (ignorance), going constantly in the absence of direct material contact, and relinquishing the power of seeing, absolute unity.*

2.26   *Unconfusing discriminative perception is the means for escaping.*

2.27   *It (cessation of ignorance) is in seven parts: finally it is wisdom.*

THE EIGHT LIMBS OF YOGA

2.28   *Consuming performance of the limbs of Yoga, the impurities wane, and the light of knowledge leads toward discrimination of perception.*

2.29   *The eight limbs within are self-restraint, restraint of mind, sitting, restraint of breath, withdrawal, concentration of the mind, religious meditation, and intense absorption.*

The First Limb - Self-Restraint

2.30   *Self-restraint is not injuring anything, being truthful, not stealing, living in the state of an unmarried religious student, and being destitute of possessions.*

2.31   *That great duty is uninterrupted by the form of existence fixed by birth, place, time, or circumstances, and relates to all conditions of the mind.*

The Second Limb - Restraint Of Mind

2.32   *Restraint of mind is the practice of purity of mind, contentment, religious austerity, reciting to oneself, and profound religious meditation on the Supreme Being.*

2.33   *To remove doubt, direct one's thoughts to the opposite side.*

2.34   *Earlier than doubt, injury, and lack of compassion, whether acquired, brought about (in others), or (considered) acceptable, and whether slight, moderate, or excessive, there is eager desire, anger, darkness of mind, or delusion, bringing the consequences of difficulty and spiritual ignorance of the eternal. Thus, direct one's thoughts to the opposite side.*

Results Of Self-Restraints

2.35   *In this manner, with steadfastness in not injuring anything, those who come near him will abandon enmity.*

2.36   *In this manner, when in the state of steadfast truthfulness, the actions have their effects.*

2.37   *In this manner, being steadfast in not stealing places one near to all gifts.*

2.38   *Steadfastness in being in the state of an unmarried religious student brings attainment of energy.*

2.39   *With perseverance in being destitute of possessions, there is perfect understanding of the state of your life.*

Results Of Mind Restraints

2.40   *Constant purity of mind brings dislike of one's own body and no intercourse with your others.*

2.41   *And mind purification, cheerfulness, one-pointedness, conquering the power of the senses, procure fitness for perception of the soul.*

2.42   *Attain consuming unsurpassed contentment while in the effort to win future beatitude.*

2.43   *Religious austerity contributes to your success in constant waning of impurities in body and faculty of sense.*

2.44   *Recitation (of texts) to one's self brings union with the cherished divinity.*

2.45   *Constantly paying attention to the Supreme Being brings your success in intense absorption.*

The Third Limb - Sitting

2.46   *Sitting is firm and comfortable.*

2.47   *One falls into a comfortable state with relaxation of the endless active effort.*

2.48   *From that place, there will be no damage by the pairs of opposites.*

The Fourth Limb - Control Of The Breath

2.49   *From that gain, breath restraint (pranayama) is procuring drawing breath (inhalation), breath away (exhalation), and interruption of motion (retention).*

2.50   *Your practice of stoppage (retention), being outside (exhalation), and being inside of (inhalation) can be richly experienced by relating to number (count), portions, and being deep or subtle.*

2.51   *Drawing together being inside of (inhalation) and being outside of (exhalation) is the fourth sphere.*

2.52   *When that is extended, it makes an end to the covering over the light.*

2.53   *Moreover, fitness of the mind incites concentration of the mind.*

The Fifth Limb - Withdrawal

2.54   *Withdrawal of the power of the senses from your own objects of the senses disconnects your mind, in some measure resembling your own nature.*

2.55   *Extending that to the highest degree brings fitness for subjection of the power of the senses.*

VIBHUTI PADA

THE PART ON SUPERHUMAN

(Sutras 3.1 – 3.56)

The third of the parts describes the attainment of high consciousness experiences that are not available to the normal human mind.

THE THREE HIGHEST LIMBS

The Sixth Limb - Concentration

3.1   *Concentration of your mind is binding your mind to a place.*

The Seventh Limb - Meditation

3.2   *Thither, when the mind is inviolably fixed on one object only, a notion, is meditation.*

The Eighth Limb - Intense Absorption

3.3   *Intense absorption (samadhi) is in consequence of that way of acting, when there is only the matter itself without brightness, as if void of its own nature.*

INTEGRATION OF THE HIGHEST LIMBS

3.4   *Unified-restraint consists of three kinds in one.*

3.5   *In this manner, being constant in victory over the senses, there is the light of knowledge.*

3.6   *Its use is brought about in stages.*

3.7   *In the aforesaid effort of the mind to remain in its unmodified condition of purity, these threefold limbs are internal.*

3.8   *Assuredly, going forth in this manner, a devoted man goes to his seedless state.*

EVOLUTIONARY PROGRESS TOWARD THE END

3.9   *Awakening through suppression impressions that overpower and destroy manifestations at any instantaneous point in time following mind restraint.*

3.10   *With that, there is tranquility of mind with a constant flow of purification.*

3.11   *Evolution in intense absorption comes forth when all objects inviolably wane in the mind as it becomes one-pointed.*

3.12   *Extended further, evolution comes about with risen tranquility, when notions in your mind in like manner become inviolably one-pointed.*

3.13   *At this time the inaccessible evolution of the world, creation of the faculty of senses, the law, and array of forms are told in full.*

3.14   *Tranquil, following as a result of communication from the not to be defined nature, the yogin knows the law.*

3.15   *Evolution differences interweaving are the cause of succession differences.*

TWO UNIFIED-RESTRAINTS

3.16   *Consumed in threefold unified-restraint on evolution, the yogin will gain knowledge of the past and future.*

3.17   *A thing, its right word, and notions, constantly erroneously transferring from one to the other bring intermixture confusion, therefore constant unified-restraint on the parts brings knowledge of how all the world is divided.*

HIGH KNOWLEDGE

3.18   *Constantly producing the impressions before one's eyes, there is knowledge of prior forms of existence (as man, animal, etc.) produced by birth.*

3.19   *There is knowledge of their past mind notions.*

3.20   *And at that time there is no procuring of the foundation, that constant state of being of the past is out of reach.*

UNIFIED-RESTRAINTS ON THE BODY AND ON FATE

3.21   *Constant unified-restraint on the nature of the body, and suppression of occupation with the objects of sensual perception, brings disappearance through the absence of connection between appearance and the faculty of seeing.*

3.22   *In the manner said, sound and so on will disappear.*

3.23   *Being consumed in unified-restraint on fate with commencement and without commencement, then a natural phenomenon boding approaching death or knowledge of future end of life will come.*

BENEVOLENCE, VIGOR, AND VISIONS

3.24   *Benevolence sets in motion the first fruits of vigor.*
3.25   *Vigor brings forth the noble-minded strength of an elephant.*
3.26   *Manifesting vision may deliver knowledge of minute, concealed, and distant things.*

COMPONENTS OF THE NATURAL WORLD AS TARGETS

3.27   *In constant unified-restraint on the sun, one gains knowledge of living beings.*
3.28   *(Unified-restraint) on the moon brings knowledge of the form of a fixed star.*
3.29   *(Unified-restraint) on the eternal brings knowledge of the meaning of its being.*

PARTS OF THE BODY AS TARGETS

3.30   *(Unified-restraint) on the depression of the body at the navel brings knowledge of the orderly arrangement of the parts of the body.*
3.31   *(Unified-restraint) on the hollow within the throat will bring cessation of hunger and thirst.*
3.32   *(Unified-restraint) on the tortoise tube brings steadiness.*
3.33   *(Unified-restraint) on the head brings perception of light as the unalterable divine principle of life.*
3.34   *Perhaps consuming manifold intuitions.*
3.35   *(Unified-restraint) on the heart, brings thorough knowledge of the mind.*

SEPARATION FROM MATERIALITY

3.36   *Constant practice of unified-restraint on the ideas that existence and the Supreme Being are perpetually unmixed, that there is non-distinction during experience, and that self-interest is dependent on something else, brings knowledge of the Supreme Being.*

3.37   *Expanded intuitive knowledge comes with victory over enjoying perception by the eyes, and perception by the ears.*

3.38   *Consumed by absorption in meditation together with letting go, one unalterably attains awakening.*

3.39   *Attachment to this world is a cause of depression, wandering perception of your mind, and being openly occupied with the body.*

CONTROL OVER THE FLOW OF TWO PRANA FORMS

3.40   *And conquering the udana (upwards vital air), one is liable to begin trying to move without the obstacles of water, mire, and thorns.*

3.41   *Conquering the samana (common vital air) brings fire.*

THE BODY AND THE SURROUNDING ETHER AS A TARGET

3.42   *Consumed in unified-restraint on the organs of hearing and the connection with the ether, the yogin gains divine hearing.*

3.43   *With unified-restraint on the connection between the body and the ether, the yogin can attain falling into a state of being as light as cotton and go to the ether.*

3.44   *Extended, apart from your natural occupation with the intellectual principle and being bodiless, there is destruction of the covering on the light.*

UNIFIED-RESTRAINT ON YOU, THE TANGIBLE, AND THE INTANGIBLE

3.45   *Consumed in unified-restraint, according to your purpose, on the association of the tangible, one's own nature, and the intangible, brings victory over the world.*

3.46   *In that place, consequently knowing the law, beginning with the smallest particle, manifestation of body excellence, they will cause no damage.*

3.47   *In the robust state of body excellence, there is the splendor, loveliness, and strength of a diamond.*

HIGHER EXPERIENCE LEADING TO ABSOLUTE UNITY

3.48   *Consumed in unified-restraint according to your purpose on the association of an organ of sense, one's own nature, and egoism, one gains victory over the power of sense.*

3.49   *And consequently of being deprived of organs of sense and your quick mind, there is victory in being in the state of the original source of the material universe.*

3.50   *And perception comes of the difference between the existence of the soul and its elementary matter in various states, and that the Supreme Ruler state of being knows all states of being.*

3.51   *At that time, with freedom from worldly desires and deficiencies, waning of the remaining seeds, and detachment from all other connections come about.*

3.52   *In the event of pride in worldly attachment to offers from those being in the right place, causing absence of action in the opposite direction will be disadvantageous.*

3.53   *Consumed in unified-restraint on the instant and its course, there is knowledge born from discrimination (i.e. the power of separating reality from mere semblance or illusion).*

3.54   *Extended, there is perception of the differences in those of comparable wel-*
       fare where non-distinctions constantly go on in their forms of existence (as
       man, animal, etc.) fixed by birth, characteristics, and place.

3.55   *Born from that knowledge, the yogin is enabled to pass over all sensuality*
       in the highest degree, and happening at once, any special worldly objects,
       aims, or matters of business, thus gaining the power of separating the invis-
       ible Spirit (brahman, sat, isvara) from the visible world.

3.56   *Thus, having equal purity, the mind and the Supreme Being are in abso-*
       lute unity.

KAIVALYA PADA

THE PART ON ABSOLUTE UNITY

(Sutras 4.1 – 4.34)

The fourth of the four parts (pada) describes closing in on the goal of Yoga,
absolute unity.

FACTORS LEADING TO SUCCESS

4.1   *Attaining success is produced by birth, herbs, prayer or song of praise, reli-*
       gious austerity, and intense absorption.

MAN, ANIMAL, ETC., ARE TRANSFORMATIONS OF THE PRIMAL SUBSTANCE

4.2   *The constantly abundant original passive power of creating the material*
       world (consisting of 3 constituent essences or gunas) transforms into differ-
       ent forms of existence (as man, animal, etc.) fixed by birth.

4.3   *Instrumental causes have no effect on the original producer of the material*
       world (consisting of 3 constituent essences or gunas) in its act of choosing
       changes: it has extended authority, like the owner of a field.

EGOISM AND SEPARATION OF INDIVIDUAL MINDS

4.4   *Forming within mind, egoism is of the material world.*

4.5   *Progressing with that distinction leads to the mind that happened only once being separated.*

SOME ASPECTS OF KARMA

4.6   *There, while in continually consuming meditation there is no stock (i.e. karmic influences).*

4.7   *Actions of those regarded as devotees are not black and not white. Those different from them have three kinds.*

4.8   *After that, consequently with maturing, manifestation is only according to the impressions of anything remaining unconsciously in the mind.*

4.9   *Moreover, since birth, place, and time incline toward separation of immediate sequence, your forms of memory and impressions are identical.*

4.10   *They are in a state of having no beginning, and zealousness to overcome them is a constant innate state of being.*

4.11   *Seeking nullity and consequently non-existence is the foundation on which the state of being collected from cause and effect depends.*

4.12   *Past and future exist in one's own form; the journey changes, holding to the law.*

THE BODY CONSISTS OF THE PHYSICAL, THE SUBTLE, AND GUNAS

4.13   *Regard the whole body (i.e. 'the person or whole body considered as one and opposed to the separate members of the body.') as perceptible by the senses, subtle objects, and the constituents of prakrti.*

TRANSFORMATION TO INDIVIDUAL THINGS FROM PRIMAL ONENESS

4.14   *The tattvas (the 24 true principles of Nature) cause transformation of the oneness (of the primary substance) to the real.*

MORE ABOUT MIND

4.15   *Constant differences in minds on the sameness of the real move variously.*

4.16   *And moreover, therefore, the real is not dependent on a single mind. How could that be, even in the case of small incorrect knowledge.*

4.17   *And, it is required that one's mind be affected for the dawning of that which is known from that which is the unknown.*

THE SUPREME BEING AND INDIVIDUAL MINDS

4.18   *So also, the Supreme Being master, which is a state of being of constant unchangeableness, continually cognizes the mind behavior as it froths up.*

4.19   *It is not so that its (the mind's) own light produces the visibility state of being.*

4.20   *Yet, you cannot newly have both kinds at the same time.*

4.21   *And if a mind were visible to another, an intellect would procure intellects for itself: excessive attachment would yield memory confusion.*

4.22   *Causing perception that has no intermixture, that form enters a state that has its own power to form conceptions from perceptions.*

4.23   *For all objects of the senses, the mind influences the one who sees the visible.*

4.24   *And, the innumerable different impressions of anything remaining unconsciously in the mind, and your acts work together for another.*

CLOSING IN ON ABSOLUTE UNITY

4.25   *Understanding the individual soul, the distinction between reality and not-reality comes to an end.*

4.26   *At that time, in the depth of discrimination, the yogin is not far from meditation into absolute unity of the mind.*

4.27   *At that time, during openings of the practice, notions arise from the impressions.*

4.28   *Seeking getting rid of them, affirm that said about the afflictions.*

ENDING IN CONSCIOUSNESS STATE OF THE LAW CLOUD

4.29   *One uniting to meditation without gain, procuring the highest degree of discriminative knowledge, attains intense absorption in the Law Cloud.*

4.30   *Extended from that, afflictions and effects cease.*

4.31   *At that time you are free from obstruction and impurity, and your higher knowledge drives toward immortality with trifling little to be known.*

4.32   *Extended from that, purpose thus accomplished, indeed the constituents of prakrti complete their succession of evolution.*

4.33   *At this point of extreme end to a yogin's evolution, it is a suitable moment for perceivable succession.*

4.34   *The soul thus void of purpose, indeed the constituents of prakrti return to their original state, with one's own nature standing very still, the layers of attachment end. Absolute unity.*

CHAPTER THREE

COMMENTARY ON
THE SUTRAS

SAMADHI PADA

THE PART ON INTENSE ABSORPTION

(Sutras 1.1 - 1.51)

Comparisons For All Aphorisms

Sanskrit words often contain letters with markings over or under the character. Marked characters are often additional letters in the alphabet. An 'a' with a line across the top is not the same letter as an 'a' without it. Authors and dictionaries, such as on-line dictionaries that do not have access to Sanskrit fonts, use capital letters in the place of such markings. The capitalization, such as the SA in *anuSAsanam* in 1.1, indicates a marking on the letter. The same word, but with or without markings, can have different definitional meanings. Similarly, a marked 'n,' 'm,' or 'h' at the end of a word indicates a manner of pronunciation. Some of these markings indicate pronunciation or breath patterns, such as spoken while exhaling. Dictionaries often drop ending characters.

ON THE TITLE FOR PART ONE OF FOUR

Patanjali presented the *Sutras* with wonderful word economy and orderliness, displaying the essence of Yoga without editorial or explanatory content, carefully unfolding its parts. He displayed the raw seed of Yoga, around which the obfuscating layers of the onion have formed. Each of his words was critical to bringing out his intended meaning. What little 'fluff,' ambiguity, or exaggeration appear to exist, may result from subtle meaning that our modern culture does not relate to, just as jokes or examples from old literature can be meaningless today. His actual book, without the extensive interpretation and explanations that fill the pages of current translations, was probably no longer than a dozen of modern pages.

The title of the first of four parts, *samadhi*, which translates to 'Intense Absorption,' is a wonderful example of his use of words. It captures the essence of Yoga, boldly and without equivocation stating the intent of its practice. Placing what could nicely be the end of the book first, as if he were writing for the already accomplished yogi, has puzzled many. It has generated criticism from second-guessing pundits who believe that the second *pada*, 'Practice,' should have been first. To their eyes, it seems less esoteric, more practical, a more natural order, or 'what people really want to know.' Perhaps that only means that it is the part the pundits prefer to emphasize. No two human minds perceive the world in the same way, nor will they ever.

Whether you recognize and accept Patanjali as a channel for divine communication, or see him as a genius that purposefully constructed it that way, it was truly the right way to start the book. It takes many readings and much insight to feel Patanjali in your heart and thrill to the intent and flow of his writing. It then becomes clear that his first priority was to emphasize where Yoga takes us, its directional momentum, immediately announcing the ultimate intent of the philosophy and practice. He begins with the purpose of the game, without equivocation, before describing how to play it.

In light of that immediate emphasis, it is shocking to realize that the carefully chosen perfect title word 'Intense Absorption,' or even 'absorption,' rarely arises in Yoga books or discussions. Few Yoga students have come across it or have any concept of that being the essence of Yoga. Even those whose fascination, curiosity, obsession, or need for better understanding drives them to extensively read today's books on Yoga will not see it often, if at all. Accidentally tripping over it in writings outside the mainstream will help little, because the culture has long preempted the idea through use of easier words with different meaning.

Layer upon layer of intellectual massaging has clouded the original meanings. Several current translations name that first part only in Sanskrit, 'Samadhi,' without translation. Where those authors provide preamble notes for this first of the parts, their excellent insights only rarely include translation of *samadhi* to the dictionary meaning of 'intense absorption.' A few authors do include the word 'absorption' in their chapter title, but in books by others the reader will find such non-translation titles as 'Yoga and its Aims,' 'Contemplation,' or 'Integration.' The author of one modern interpretation, who does not claim it as a translation, does capture the essence wonderfully with, 'On Being Absorbed in Spirit.' That is exactly the point of Yoga, to ultimately become absorbed in the consciousness of *brahman*, the primal existence, also known as Spirit. Patanjali started his book with that thrilling idea, which so many in today's Yoga miss.

Perhaps the biggest 'absorption annihilator' is the current popular usage of the word 'Meditation.' Through 2000 years, in the way that everything naturally loosens over time, the meaning has shifted from the very specific seventh limb intent in the *Sutras* to a loose nonspecific usage that covers broad ground. The shift to that loose use of 'meditation' erases the distinction between Patanjali's three types of meditative practice, *concentration, religious meditation,* and *intense absorption*. It hides the powerful meaning of being in the absorbed state, and covers the mountaintop with so much fog that we do not know the mountain is there.

THE PRECEPTS OF YOGA

1.1   Now the precepts of union (Yoga).

atha   Yoga   anuSAsanam
now   union   precepts

The opening line of the *Yoga Sutras* often draws chuckles, but does not get the attention it deserves. It simply tells us what the book is about, the underlying precepts for the philosophy and practice of Yoga. That simple statement reveals so much more than is at first seen. It clearly signals a different style of writing and composition, reflecting the culture of the time. It also announces the clarity and simplicity that Patanjali intends. Further, that simple and clear statement announces that this book is Patanjali's current effort, differentiating it from other books he has written, or might write later.

Gifted with intelligence on the high end of the IQ scale, and graced with experience of consciousness near the top of the scale, Patanjali did compose two other books. According to Indian history, he authored the first book of Sanskrit grammar and the original text on Ayurvedic medicine. With little known about his life, Westerners have spread doubt that any one person could have written all three, sometimes claiming that three people with the same name were the authors. Indian people object strongly to such downplaying of their revered saint and 'rishi' (seer or mystic), seeing it as racist diminishment of the achievements of their people.

If the Indian version is as true as it seems, it is easy to visualize Patanjali's life as driven by a passionate desire to organize known information. His *Yoga Sutras* was an effort to create a readable and organized description of Yoga life for those who adhered to the philosophy that had passed forward through history for thousands of years.

The evolved Yoga that existed while he lived had already passed through more than 100 generations and received the contributions of many mystics and gurus. At the time Patanjali wrote, the ancient teachings had become the highly organized and venerated *Samkhya* philosophy. *Samkhya* is pure metaphysical philosophy about godness, evolution of the universe, the nature of life, and evolution of the individual. Although many definitions exist for *Samkhya*, including 'reckoning' and 'counting up,' the definition as 'discrimination,' referring to the discrimination between the material and spiritual (Spirit-ual) natures of the universe, is most appropriate. *Samkhya* describes the goal and purpose of life as being evolution toward perfection so that the individual will ultimately escape the confines of Earth-life. It is a complex and whole philosophy, much of which the *Yoga Sutras* succinctly describe.

The movement to define the daily life *actions* necessary for the seeker to live a yogic life had by then matured as the practices of Kriya Yoga. Developed in parallel with *Samkhya*, long after the philosophy was well established, it helped define a path to personal evolution by enacting what *Samkhya* defined. Breath control, meditation, and many spiritual practices were among its methods. Scientific in its rigor, it guided seekers toward union, starting with development of self-control preliminary to enabling withdrawing the mind from sense objects. With that accomplished, training focused on fully disconnecting the mind and intellect from the senses. With the senses out of the way, the discipline shifted to experiencing higher levels of consciousness.

In beautiful symbolism that easily hides the seeds of its nature, the Bhagavad Gita, which became the prime religious text for Hinduism and other religions, preserves pure and true Yoga as the detailed exposition of *Samkhya* philosophy. The writing date and author are unknown, but it first appeared within the Mahabharata at the time of Jesus Christ. The earlier *Yoga Sutras* also preserve the pure and true enactment of *Samkhya*, but straightforwardly, in simple aphorisms, compared to the complex allegories of the Gita. They subtly portray Yoga as a tension between the material/sensory nature and the spiritual nature, the main allegorical theme of the Bhagavad Gita. Both provide uncorrupted, that is to say essentially unaltered, views of Yoga, as it was early in its history, and how to practice it.

Contrary to the popular belief that Kriya Yoga was lost and held the mystical secrets to everything, it was certainly a simplex set of practices. Masters later enhanced the practices of *pranayama* and meditation. Whereas physical postures are a key part of today's reinvented Kriya, they were not in the practice at that time. The Hatha Yoga postures that we know and practice today gradually evolved many centuries later, as enhancers of Yoga.

The skill at organization displayed in the *Yoga Sutras* would certainly be present in Patanjali's other books. Just as he did not invent or self-create the wondrous complexity of Yoga, Patanjali did not invent or create the great complexity of medical treatment of the time. Understanding it deeply and fully, he organized it in written form. Similarly, it is doubtful that he would have created rules of grammar. More likely, he observed the use of grammar and documented it, perhaps increasing the formality.

atha   Yoga   anuSAsanam

atha	now
yoga	union
anuzasana (for anusasanam)	precept

RESTRAINT OF MIND ACTIVITIES

Meditation Is Restraint Of Mind

1.2   Meditation is restraint of mind activities.

YogaS   citta   vRtti   nirodhaH
meditation   mind   activity   restraint

The first *Sutra* after the identification of the book's purpose focuses on 'Yogas.' It has become customary to translate that as meaning *Yoga*. As a result, a wide portion of the world believes that the first real aphorism says that 'Yoga is about stilling the mind.' As true as that statement is, that is not what this aphorism says. *Yogas* has only two very specific meanings, 'meditation' and 'religious abstraction.' Although the highest form of meditation is in fact 'religious abstraction,' this interpretation uses the word 'meditation' in order to downplay the baggage carried by today's use of any variation of the word 'religion.'

Patanjali was a careful and succinct writer who wasted few words and had a teaching goal for every aphorism. This profound opening statement was neither careless nor accidental. His very first words provide critical information, without which Yoga has no context. The entire book, and all of true Yoga, is about stilling the mind through meditation. Every Yoga practice builds toward increasing our ability and skill for meditation. Thoughts, sensory contacts, memories, emotions, and other things cause mental activity. Stopping them brings stillness. The final words in his book will bring this idea of meditative stillness to its most full meaning. Every aspect and every limb of Yoga intends to move the follower toward greater stillness.

To our disadvantage as students, for whatever valid or invalid reasons brought it about, a significant number of translators consistently translate the second word in the aphorism, *citta*, to 'consciousness,' rather than the correct meaning of 'mind.' That error diminishes the precedent that Patanjali has just firmly established, a foothold that will enable continued discussion of 'mind' and its relationship to consciousness. He has purposefully directed our attention to the mortal mind within our personal material being and implied, 'That is where the game is. We want to bring our individual mind to stillness.' He does not yet tell us the full Truth that achieving that stillness is necessary to experiencing the eternal true self, the soul.

Who cannot recognize how our fast-paced minds race about from one subject to another, never stopping, never resting? How many have ever thought it possible to bring the mind under personal control, to quiet it through will? How could even imagination predict what might happen? If you keep on studying Yoga, you will see the importance of gaining control over the things that control you, whether they are mind and its thoughts, or senses, emotions, body, breathing, ways of being in the world, and the principles we live by.

Most people who practice Yoga will notice the developing stillness in terms of a sense of well-being, increased internal quietness, and stress release. They do not know that they are experiencing the intent of Yoga, to still the thoughts and other mind activities, so that they can experience higher levels of consciousness. The everyday relief is plenty for them; they do not want more. More experienced students may grow into a beginning understanding that their awareness of the world has evolved, bringing new insights and experiences. If they pursue the Yoga life, they may come to experience progressive levels of consciousness, from 'mind consciousness,' through the progressive states of '*samadhi*' (intense absorption in single-pointed awareness).

Those whose dedicated practice brings them further may come to understand that the ultimate stillness they are evolving toward is the absolute stillness that lies within our inner being and the consciousness of the soul, *isvara*, and *brahman*. Nearing evolution to attain awareness of the highest consciousness, where no mental fluctuations exist, the seeker will see that the individual consciousness (that of the soul or inner self) and primal consciousness states of *isvara* and *brahman* are equally still and quiet. They will know that the stillness was always there, and that the active mind was keeping them from it.

For the advanced seeker, Patanjali's ultimate message will become intuitively clear, that the purpose of Yoga and of life is to evolve toward attaining stillness equal to the eternal stillness, and that meditation is the tool for accomplishing that. That may seem unlikely, impossible and even undesirable to many, but it is possible that it is the way the world will gradually evolve to a better world: as soul after soul evolves, over many lifetimes, the infant species will evolve to a more mature species.

YogaS citta vRtti nirodhaH

yogas	meditation
citta	mind
vrtti	activity
nirodha (for nirodhah)	restraint

We Can Comprehend Our Root Nature

1.3   At that time, the one who sees comprehends the situation of their own nature.

tadA   draSTuH   sva   rUpe   avasthAnaM
at that time   one who sees   comprehend   one's own   nature   situation

This aphorism widely opens the game, guiding you to why you would want to meditate. Patanjali has said that humans have a hidden nature that is open to exploration. He has said what we could never imagine, that it is possible to spend time in that reality: through stilling, we can eventually discover and enter that true nature of individual being, the 'soul,' the ultimate situation for our life. The yet undeclared reverse is also true: without that stilling, the true nature of individual being will remain hidden.

The soul exists as the true reality of individual human existence. It is a *brahman*-differentiated portion of the unbeginning, unending, infinite 'oversoul,' or 'common soul,' which is an aspect of *brahman*. Living the yogic life will take us down the path toward that reality hidden behind everything in the material world, but this is just Patanjali's first hint of it. He is constructing the foundation for *Sutras* that follow.

For the everyday person this is a reminder that the inner being or soul exists, and that humans can become aware of that reality. The highly evolved yogin, for which Yoga is a holistic way of life with many interlocking pieces, naturally moves toward the ultimate abiding in that soul experience: along the way he or she falls into complete and full-time dedication to, and absorption in, the guidance and flow of the spiritual force. There are many phases of progressive experience.

tadA draSTuH sva rUpe avasthAnaM

tada	at that time
drastr (for drastuh)	one who sees
sva	one's own
rupa (for rupe)	nature
avasthana (for avastahanam)	situation

Assimilation With The Deity

1.4   Or else, devotion to meditation brings assimilation with the deity.

vRtti sArUpyam itaratra
devotion to   assimilation with the deity   else

This closes the subject of stilling for the moment, by describing what happens if the mind remains quiet through devotion to meditative practice. As Patanjali will continue to show, the higher levels of consciousness experience progressively move toward deep experience of divinity. Divinity can take any of many forms, or can be formless. It can, and does, appear in a religious or non-religious context.

This all depends on progressively quieting the mind. If the mind remains unquiet, you fall into the trap of following the mind's lead to wherever it takes you, allowing it to control your life. If you do not dominate it and take control, you never gain the opportunity to experience the vital parts of your being that the mind activity hides, those other levels of consciousness. When you experience only the mind, you have no way of knowing that the other part of your being is available to you. It is natural and normal for humans to believe that their true nature is in the body and mind. It is not possible to understand the existence and nature of the other levels of consciousness, and of the soul, other than by experiencing them.

The meaning of this *Sutra* will change for anyone whose Yoga life continues to grow, expand, and evolve. It does not take long for a Yoga student to recognize how busy, hectic, wild and uncontrolled the mind is, leading to later acceptance that stillness is positive, something to be encouraged and sought. As students work on stilling, they realize how little open mind-space they have. As they begin to open up mind-space with Yoga practices, particularly with meditation, they invite serenity, calmness, and other effects. They begin to intuitively sense the existence of a deeper reality and want to come closer to it, understanding how the mind-noise limits and prevents their becoming receivers for it. After years of practice, with awareness that the real self (the soul) truly exists, they may begin to comprehend that minds are time-limited, since they are native to mortal existence, a part of what 'dies' at the end of a given life experience. They can then begin to sense the eternal immortality of the inner being, or soul, which does not experience time or death, except when observing mortal life through an individual experience.

As they develop further, the yogins minds become increasingly still. Stillness and spirituality - the opposites of activity and materiality - advance together, and they reach understanding that their true nature is in the soul. This is not intellectual understanding. It is a different form of knowledge, separate from mind. As stillness advances, they come ever closer to the soul, experiencing its nature sporadically. Near the highest levels of stillness and spirituality, they experience the stillness of the soul and the god-existence (*brahman*, *isvara*, the Absolute) for longer periods. As experiencing for longer periods brings about additional evolution, they eventually reach total stillness, and their individual stillness will meld with the stillness of the god-existence.

Patanjali reveals none of this yet. Here, he simply describes the bottom line for Yoga aspiration, leaving the seekers to find new meaning in his aphorism with each stage of their evolutionary progression.

vRtti sArUpyam itaratra

vrtti	devotion to
sarupya (for sarupyam)	assimilation to or conformity with the deity
itaratra	else

FIVE STATES OF MIND IN EVERYDAY LIFE

Five States Exist

1.5   When not in religious meditation, the mind is restrained to five states. Each state can have pain or be free of pain.

vRttayaH paNcatayaH kliSTa akliSTaH
religious meditation gone restraining five-fold state painful not painful

Patanjali now describes the everyday states of the mind, as they exist when a religious practice of meditation is not occurring. Although he uses the term 'religious' here, he clearly did not write his book to be a religious or sacred text. For at least this writer, it means practicing religiously (in a constant and ongoing manner) while keeping a focus on the underlying source of all things. It does not mean practicing a religion.

The mind is the vehicle through which we perceive the world that exists: it is the baseline state of consciousness for everyday material/sensory life. To experience the higher consciousness states that meditation delivers we need to move beyond the mind, progressively moving farther away from it.

This aphorism tells us that there are five states of mind: the next *Sutra* will identify them. It further tells us that the mind can experience pain (sorrow) or be free of pain. This pain is the pain that the Buddha, The Christ, and others called 'suffering.' We can experience that pain or be free of it while in any of the five states. The message is clear that the pain is an option. The practices of Yoga lead to that freedom from pain or suffering, again a goal shared with Buddhism, Christianity and other religions and philosophies.

It is an inherent human condition that while in any of the five mind states we cannot experience the others, just as when we are experiencing one consciousness state, we have no awareness of any other. At some level of personal development, we will see this *Sutra* as pointing to the mind as being the nonspiritual (material) side of a two-sided coin. Mind-free higher consciousness states are the spiritual side of the coin.

vRttayaH paNcatayaH kliSTa akliSTaH

vrttayah
vrtta	gone
ya (for yah)	religious meditation

pancatayah
pancata	five-fold state
ya (for yah)	restraining

klista	painful
aklista (for akliSTaH)	not painful

The Five States

1.6   *The five states of mind are:*
  Means of acquiring certain knowledge
  Misapprehension
  Imagination
  Sleep
  Attaining remembrance

pramANa viparyaya vikalpa nidrA smRtayah
means of acquiring certain knowledge   misapprehension   imagination

sleep   attaining remembrance.

Again laying groundwork, this *Sutra* unambiguously defines the five mind states of ordinary living. The aphorism provides the foundation to differentiate the active states of the human mind that we continually experience from the higher consciousness states that are available outside of ordinary experience. This discussion does not include the consciousness states of other types of living beings - squirrels or plants, for example - or those of rocks or planets. Everything in the universe has consciousness at some level, but Patanjali focuses on the human condition.

The statement is so simple, clear, and easy that it may cause you to question it, to attempt coming up with other states that humans can experience. It would be a good exercise for you to question if the list is complete and accurate, or even use it as a meditative target, exploring types on your own. Perhaps when you first read this *Sutra*, you found yourself arguing its merits, looking for those other options, because the five categories just did not seem right. You might play with creating your own, modify these to see what happens, or do mind experiments to test the correctness. You might temporarily accept them as 'interesting' or 'useful' and go on, translating the words into the most meaningful understanding you can make from your previous experience and use of language.

Although the words are self-defining, we can use terms closer to everyday usage for better understanding. 'Certain knowledge' means perceiving something as it truly is and knowing that you do. Be clear, though, that the mind state is that of being in the process of acquiring the knowledge, not the certain knowledge. It is easy to see 'misapprehension' as 'getting it wrong' or failure to grasp the right meaning. More formally, it means misunderstanding that which you have become aware of only through your senses. 'Imagination' simply refers to those things that are a creation of the mind without anything else as a source. Although some authors refer to 'sleep' as deep sleep or some other form, it clearly refers to all forms of sleep, the time when all voluntary functions are suspended. Patanjali carefully used 'attaining remembrance' to point to the active process of retrieval, not the memories themselves.

As intuition develops through yogic practice, these words will take on new meaning, their intent becoming clearer. At some higher level of consciousness, joy will follow the reading of these words, as they harmonize with new understanding of the universe, and you may then clearly see that there really are no other options. At a much higher level of consciousness, you may understand why the universe built things that way and what the purpose of each is in the scheme of this complex human creation that experiences living in ways that no other creation does. You might see that sleep, for example, crosses the boundaries between the spiritual and the material worlds. Highly spiritual people often need less sleep, because their complex of body, mind, and energy has evolved along with their consciousness, and the needs fulfilled by sleep are satisfied in other ways.

pramANa viparyaya vikalpa nidrA smRtayah

pramana	means of acquiring certain knowledge
viparyaya	misapprehension
vikalpa	imagination
nidra	sleep
smrtayah	
smrta	remembrance
ya (for yah)	attaining

The Mind State Of Certain Knowledge

1.7   Within means of acquiring certain knowledge there are:
Perception by the senses
Inference
Study

pratyakSa anumAna AgamAH pramANani
*perception by the senses   inference   study   within
means of attaining certain knowledge*

Means of acquiring certain knowledge is the first of the five states; it requires aspiring to that condition and working to achieve it. The world is there to provide individual experience: you will not perceive correctly without experiencing it and studying your experience. You can directly perceive through your senses and use your intelligence, independently of the intelligence of others, to understand what your senses have perceived, bringing you closer to understanding reality. You can also infer things from that experience. If you live near a pond and never see ducks on it as you do on nearby ponds, you can infer that there are no fish for them to eat. Yet, if you are to grow and gain correct perception, you will need to question your experience and verify your interpretations. Perhaps ducks avoid certain algae blooms.

No one can remain independent and isolated from the interconnected world of other minds: evolution also requires learning what others perceive and how they have processed their experiences. The beliefs, conclusions, and observations they provide may be right or wrong. Those that want to know Truth need to study what the others pass on to them, using their independent intelligence to assess the information. Yet, they cannot forget that the Buddha and many Masters have stressed the importance of self-learning; the importance of not assuming that things that any of the senses detect is correct, and that parroting and faithfully accepting the words of others does not yield knowledge.

When you read the *Sutras* for the first time, as an average person living in the everyday world, you are likely to be excited by the idea of certain knowledge: you will probably feel that it is a good thing. As you accumulate results of Yoga practice, you may begin to feel that it is a desirable goal, something worth some effort. Along the way, you will see that what you perceive directly through your senses is not always correct, because your experiences and beliefs color it. At some intermediate stage of development, you will understand that intuition is vitally important to having correct direct perception and correct inference. You will have begun to understand by then how important it is to study the experiences and views of others. Yet, all that studying may just sit there until some intuitive higher consciousness effect becomes a catalyst to synthesize it with other perceptions and insights, producing a flash of understanding. That flash will wean you from some of the incorrect perceptions and solidify the correct ones.

At a higher level of consciousness yet, you may perceive the words 'certain knowledge' to be connected to reaching union. In the state of union, all knowledge is certain.

pratyakSa anumAna AgamAH pramANAni

pratyaksa	perception by the senses
anumana	inference
agama (for agamah)	studying
pramanani	
pramana	means of acquiring certain knowledge
ni	within

The Mind State Of Misapprehension

1.8   Misapprehension is incorrect knowledge, not with regard to the natural base (of the thing observed).

viparyayo mithyA jNAnam atad rUpa pratiSTham
misapprehension incorrectly knowledge not with regard to natural base

Our lives overflow with <u>misapprehension</u>, the second type of active consciousness. There are too many paths to erroneous perception to fully explore them, but your senses and your experiences are the sources. What you take in through them helps form the base for your beliefs, value systems, ideas, and perception of reality. It is easy and normal to accept them without subjecting them to continuing scrutiny and challenge. They imbed as programs that guide your life. Humans, by both nature and cultural conditioning, easily accept untruths as truths, incorrect as correct, and wrong as right. Yogins in training do not perceive for a long time how vital to Yoga the elimination of false perception is, or how difficult that is. When they have been deeply involved with Yoga and that message has come to them in many ways, they learn it by seeing how it affects their lives.

viparyayo mithyA jNAnam atad rUpa pratiSTham

viparyaya	misapprehension
mithya	incorrectly
jjana (for jnanam)	-knowledge

atad

  a   not
  tad   with regard to that
rupa   nature
pratistham   base

The Mind State Of Imagination

*1.9   Knowing, following as a consequence of the absent correct expression of the
real, is imagination.*

Sabda   jnana   anupAtI   vastu   SUnyo   vikalpaH
*correct expression   knowing   following as a conse-
quence   the real   absent   imagination*

The English dictionary says that 'imagination is the ability to form images and ideas in the mind, especially of things never seen or experienced directly.' Patanjali clearly understood that in describing it as a state in which the perception of the real existence is absent. Aside from precisely defining imagination, the *Sutra* tells us that it is a specific state of mind: when we are experiencing imagination, the mind locks out all other states of mind or consciousness.

Some say that this aphorism is about 'delusion,' or more narrowly about 'verbal delusion.' Not only is 'delusion' not a translation of *vikalpah*, it is usually used to describe a symptom of mental illness. Patanjali does not explore such states, only the everyday 'normal' states of being human.

Further along your path, as you recognize that the individual self's drive for individualism and self-discovery will cause you to question and impeach all words received by sight or sound. You will come to accept as Truth only what your deep intuition tells you to accept. You will often be judgmental and emotionally reactive to everyday information and its suppliers, but that will disappear as you grow. At a high level of consciousness, you will see imagination as part of the process of evolution, and understand the role it plays, coming to know that it is neither 'bad' nor wrong-minded.

Sabda   jnana   anupAtI   vastu   SUnyo   vikalpaH

zabda (for sabda)	correct impression
jjana (for jnana)	knowing
anupatin (for anupati)	following as a consequence
vastu	the real
zunya (for sunyo)	absent
vikalpa (vikalpah)	imagination

Mind State Of Sleep

1.10   Your state of sleep is the foundation for conception of entities that do not exist.

abhAva   pratyaya   AlambanA   vRttir   nidrA
non-entity   conception   foundation   state your   sleep

The aphorism tells us that no 'entities' (things) are present in the mind during the sleep mode of mentality. In Yoga terms, thoughts, abstract ideas, and other nonphysical entities are just as surely things, as rocks, books, and tables are things. While in the sleep state, those subtle material things are not available to the mind. Although it is not pure Yoga philosophy, it seems true that mental experience during sleep is through symbols: symbols are similar to the dream-ideas, or imagination, of *isvara*, *brahman*, and the soul. Symbols seem to be the language of that zone. Again, it is not Yoga philosophy, but the experience of this yogin is that they are more spiritual than either subtle-material or physical-material.

Humans spend a third of their lives in the fourth state of mind, the state of sleep. Individually, collectively, and even scientifically, we know little about what happens during sleep. It is clear that we use a different language while in a state of sleep, which we can think of as a universal language of symbolism, which is more useful to our intuition than to our intellect. Otherwise, that conceptualization through intuition is accessible only at higher levels of consciousness, not in the active mind states of everyday consciousness. A greatly different experience, sleep performs a largely unknown and unexplored, but vitally important, role. The need to shut down all other states for hours to experience sleep is a signal of its importance.

abhAva   pratyaya   AlambanA   vRttir   nidrA

abhava	non-entity
pratyaya	conception
alambana	foundation
vrttir	
vrtti	state
ir	(indicator of second or third person) your
nidra	sleep

Mind State Of Memory

1.11 Memory follows as a consequence of not letting drop any special worldly object, aim, matter, or business.

anubhUta   viSaya   asaMpramoSaH   smRtiH
following as a consequence of   any special worldly object, aim,
matter, or business   not letting drop   memory.

Memory state, the fifth of Patanjali's active states, is simply mentally holding onto a past event. Other consciousness states are not available while we are remembering. Memory can be of incorrect perception, correct perception, sleep consciousness, or delusion, but it is a distinctly different state of consciousness, experiencing the past in the present time. Whether as a result of the actual event or of its memory, the past affects and defines the future. The *Sutras* will later teach how to reduce the effect that memory has on future events.

This *Sutra* is seemingly perfectly clear on first reading, with no further explanation needed. We all know we have mind and brain, and that memories are somehow stored there. Yet, as the developing yogin reaches distinct points of higher understanding, new knowledge of what 'mind' and memory are will change the meaning of this *Sutra*. At some point, it will become clear that mind is separate from the physical brain - a processing engine for it and sensory inputs, with which they harmoniously interact. At another point, the yogin will automatically recognize that 'memory' refers to both mind memory and the karmic memory of the subtle body, sometimes called 'soul memory.'

Patanjali introduced this critical subject early, so that it could weave through the *Sutras* that teach such things. Deeper insight will be necessary to understanding the seeming paradox of having memory that we must ultimately abandon to achieve the goals of Yoga.

anubhUta viSaya asaMpramoSaH smRtiH

anubhuta	followed as a consequence
visaya	any special worldly object, aim, matter, or business
asampramosa (for asampramomah)	not letting drop (as from memory)
smrti (for smrtih)	memory

ASPIRING TO PURITY OF MIND

The Mind Exerts Effort Toward Purity

1.12 While in continual meditative restraint, the mind exerts effort to remain in the unmodified condition of purity (stillness, spirituality) through indifference to worldly things, life, and pain.

abhyAsa vairAgyAbhyAM tan nirodhaH
the effort of the mind to remain in its unmodified condition of purity (sattva)
indifference to worldly objects and to life pain continually restraint

The *Sutras* have shifted from the five active everyday states of mind, now discussing the stillness of the passive higher consciousness states attained through meditation. The term 'meditative restraint' is a specific high-level type of meditation that Patanjali will later emphasize. This *Sutra* tells us that once we have attained a high degree of mind stillness we can maintain it only by being indifferent to all worldly things, including our life and worldly pain. For whatever reason, perhaps convention, most authors replace the wording of 'indifference' and 'meditative restraint' with 'relinquishment of attachment' and 'practice.' Those ideas are valid and roughly reflect the theme of the aphorism, but far more narrowly. They are not translations, and do not provide the scope and accuracy of the actual translation.

Indifference to worldly things and meditative restraint are vital to stilling mind activity that masks the higher levels of consciousness: without both, progress will wane. The task of achieving higher consciousness experience, to any degree, is no different from that of becoming an opera singer, drummer, or athlete. Continual dedicated effort is a necessity to an aspiration to reach high in any field. Yogins progress in proportion to degree of dedication. Yet, becoming indifferent to the presence of worldly things (having no interest) is as difficult as continual meditative restraint. Both come about through hard and continuous awareness of the intent and practice. Meditative restraint comes about only after years of progression through several forms of meditation, and the range of worldly things that require indifference is huge. Many factors are invisible to us: searching them out requires personal volition, will, devotion, and motivated drive. The recognizable things, such as possessions and people are easy to recognize, but hard to let go of. Indifference to ideas, beliefs, patterns, habits, self-image, the way others see you and treat you, pain, pleasure, foods, alcohol, coffee, and things like anger and pride are hard to achieve.

As yogins progress, the nature of indifference will change. At first, they may be able to move away from some gross material world things, addictions, or habits. Later some cherished thoughts and beliefs will no longer be important to them. Materialism and physical things will dramatically diminish in importance over time. As consciousness progresses further, they see that progress requires making large, sometimes earthquake-like, changes: they gravitate away from ways of being and personal relationships that are harmful or poisonous, long held understandings of what 'divinity' means, greed, and many other things. As they approach the highest levels, their emotional loads, embedded perceptions, ego-needs, and self-identification become unimportant. They can then begin to give up interest in the material world itself, moving toward spirituality. They would never see the need for those things in their early understanding of Yoga. They must let experience and personal evolution take them there.

abhyAsa vairAgyAbhyAM tan nirodhaH

abhyasa	the effort of the mind to remain in its unmodified condition of purity (*sattva*)
vairagyabhyam	
vairagya	indifference to worldly objects and to life
abhyam	pain
tan	continually
nirodha (for nirodhah)	restraint

Devoted Zeal Brings Purity

1.13   Under those circumstances, devoted zeal brings the mind effort necessary to remain in its unmodified condition of purity (sattva).

tatra   sthitau   yatno 'bhyAsa
under those circumstances   devoted zeal   the effort of the mind to remain in its unmodified condition of purity (sattva).

Patanjali nails the idea down in this *Sutra*, emphasizing that devoted zeal is vital to the goal of stilling the activity of the mind. The goal of stilling the mind to enable experiencing higher consciousness often becomes lost as you progress through the many aspects of practicing Yoga. Continual practice ensures that it stays in view.

When we first begin Yoga, most will go to Yoga classes once a week. Many pay the same weekly attention to Yoga that most people pay to their religion. Many of their teachers train them to call that weekly or occasional practice their *sadhana* (practice), not telling them that *sadhana* is the life commitment to zealous practice that Patanjali intends here. Some escalate to two or three classes a week, or more, while others become teachers who practice and teach many times during the week. Continuing the analogy with practicing religion, Yoga often does not exist for them between their class sessions, other than perhaps acknowledging the need for honesty, not harming, or some other Yoga principle. They are not carrying that aspiring zeal for higher consciousness.

tatra sthitau yatno 'bhyAsa

tatra	under those circumstances

sthita (for sthitau)	devoted
yatna (for yatno)	zeal
abhyasa (for 'bhyasa)	the effort of the mind to remain in its unmodified condition of purity (*sattva*).

EVOLUTION TO EXPERIENCE HIGHER STATES OF CONSCIOUSNESS

Practice Meditation Assiduously

1.14   A step is to be strong in meditation as long term uninterrupted consideration of a thing, while firm in practicing assiduously.

sa   tu   dIrgha   kAla   nairantarya   satkAra   Asevito   dRDha   bhUmiH
meditation   be strong   long time   uninterruptedly   consideration of a thing   practiced assiduously   firm   step

Continuing the teaching about meditation, the aphorism tells us that a step toward the goal is to be strong in meditation as long term uninterrupted consideration of the target chosen, while being firm in assiduous practice. It is necessary to moving in the direction of experiencing the higher consciousness levels of *samadhi*.

The *Sutra* prepares us for the dedication necessary to building a meditative Yoga life style. Many benefits are available to you; in proportion to the amount that you invest. The eventual union is the experience of a *consciousness state*, not an event. To reach that state, practice of meditation must be long, consistent over many years, and it must be uninterrupted during your sessions. Benefits accumulate with repetition and practice. You gradually move toward a stilled mind through reorienting your being, purging incorrect views, stilling and calming all aspects of yourself, cleansing your impurities, and building a new foundation. The degree of progress depends on the priority that you assign and the investment you make.

The results, in all cases, slowly accumulate. Once they are there, like having trained the muscles and reflexes to ride a bicycle, they remain there. If life calls you away, when you come back with rededication you build from where you were. Although the rate of growth varies among people, the process will not be instant. The intense absorption of *samadhi* is not a game of immediate gratification.

   sa tu dIrgha kAla nairantarya satkAra Asevito dRDha bhUmiH

sa	meditation
tu	be strong
dirgha	long
kala	time
nairantarya	uninterruptedly
satkara	consideration of or regard for a thing
asevita (for asevito)	practiced assiduously
drdha	firm
bhumi (for bhumih)	step

Freedom From Desires, Notions, And Worldly Life

1.15   Having experienced that which is derived from tradition and sensual enjoyments, a yogin free from desire, subjugates notions, and becomes indifferent to worldly objects and life.

dRSTa AnuSravika viSaya vitRSNasya vaSIkAra saMjNA vairAgyam
   experienced   derived from tradition   sensual enjoyments   one free from desire   subjugating   notions   indifference to worldly objects and to life

A vital part of Yoga philosophy lies with subtlety within this wording, which will develop further as the *Sutras* unfold: we are here to experience material-world life, in order to enable our movement beyond that experience. We cannot escape from the sensuous allure, our minds, and our emotions until we have appropriately experienced the material world. Practicing Yoga leads to freedom from responding to the 'siren call,' through equanimity, inner quietness, and priority shifts.

While absorbed in that material world, most humans relinquish recognition that there is a nonmaterial aspect of life that is just as life-critical as the physical body and its functions. The material world is so clearly present, intrusive, and familiar that we focus all our attention on its things: those things become prime objects of attachment. Attachments to cars, comfort accessories (such as machines and electronic equipment), homes, image items (jewelry, cosmetics, clothing), and other physical goods are often obvious, to those who care to look for them. With Yoga progressively diminishing the desires for more, our attachments to worldly things, and the tyranny of our mind and its notions, we eventually become indifferent to each. Separating from them, we can experience our spirituality.

It is not as easy to see the attachments to notions, such as thoughts or beliefs created by material world active consciousness. 'God is good.' 'I am a good parent.' 'Humans are built in the image of God.' 'Christianity (or Buddhism, Islam, Judaism, Zoroastrianism, Taoism) is the right teaching; the others are wrong.' 'My kid does not use drugs.' 'I cannot get a better job.' 'Krauts, Chinks, Charlies, Arabs, Gringos, Goyim, Japs, North Koreans (but not south Koreans), Gays, Lesbians, Conservatives, Liberals, Republicans, or Democrats are evil.' 'I must succeed financially.' 'I must be perfect.' 'I will fail. I know it. I have always failed.' 'I must get all A's.' 'A grade of C at this school is as good as an A at another.' The list is endless. We either blindly accept ideas and concepts instilled by others or personally develop them with our own mentality. Once we have them, we do not want to give them up. Such attachments drive lives and lay the groundwork for choices and decisions. It is extremely hard to question them. The answers as to whether they are good, bad, or benign influences on life, and on living it, are always fuzzy. Gut instinct (intuition) is the only valid choice-maker, but that game is too risky for many. Yoga develops intuition.

The recognition of the need to relinquish specific attachments comes about slowly and progressively. After first reading of the *Sutras* and during early practice, you will recognize the need to give up only the most obvious physical things, because your orientation is so heavily to material/sensory existence and awareness. As your first offering to your future life, you will probably give up things that do not matter and are easy to let go of. As you evolve, you will perceive the need to relinquish habits, addictions, engrained ways of being, thoughts, emotions, ideas, perceptions, beliefs, and rituals. As you move into higher consciousness, you gain insight leading toward relinquishment of hard to give up things that block your spirituality, perhaps sensory delights, or false views of *isvara* and the cosmos. You slowly, but surely, move away from the material world to experience the spiritual world of higher consciousness.

dRSTa AnuSravika viSaya vitRSNasya vaSIkAra saMjNA vairAgyam

drsta	experienced
anuzrava (for anusravika)	derived from tradition
visaya	sensual enjoyments
vitrsnasya	
vitrsna	free from desire
sya	(3rd person indicator) one
vazikara (for vasikara)	subjugating
samjja (for samjna)	notion
vairagya (for vairagyam)	indifference to worldly objects and to life

Indifference To Even Basic Elements Of Nature

1.16   Afterward, there will be perception of the Supreme Being and indifference to even the constituents of prakrti (Nature).

tat   paraM   puruSa   khyAter   guNa   vaitRSNyam
afterwards   Supreme Being   perception   constituents of prakrti   indifference

The yogin who reaches that nearly full separation from the world will perceive the Supreme Being and lose interest in the workings, even the roots of Nature. There will be indifference even to the inception of the constituents of *prakrti* (the *gunas*), the very knowledge that he or she has diligently attained. It does not matter. It just exists. This is the achievement of the state called *paravairagya* in Sanskrit, where desire in all its forms is absent. It is the higher of two states of *vairagya*.

When you can perceive and then believe in your nonmaterial existence - the state of existence of your soul, and in the Supreme Being, the soul of the universe, which is not obvious but always present, it becomes natural to completely relinquish the material world. Experiencing the spiritual aspect of existence gives rewards of pleasure, happiness, and joy that are more enticing than the sensory pleasures and the comforts of material things. The experience of that spirituality defeats the power that sensual materiality wields. In full acceptance and trust, you allow a nonmaterial, spiritual, life to control how you are in the world, displacing your infatuation with your material/sensory life.

The true meaning of this will only be clear to those who have advanced to high levels of consciousness where intuitive learning prevails. The *Sutra* provides little direct meaning or guidance to those in early stages of their evolution: it speaks of the endgame of Yoga. Eventually they will come to understand the gunas, the basic elements of *prakrti* (Nature in its rawest primal form); they will acquire some enabling insight, only to give it up when your understanding evolves further. Yet, only those experiencing very high consciousness will feel the full impact of the function and activity of the gunas, their relationship to the universe and to individual life. Only a consciousness nearing Absolute Unity (Emancipation) will perceive what it truly means to relinquish attachment to even that knowledge, to be indifferent to having it or not having it.

tat paraM puruSa khyAter guNa vaitRSNyam

tato param (for tat param)	afterwards
purusa	Supreme Being
khyati (for khyater)	perception
guna	constituent of *prakrti*
vaitrsnya (for vaitrsnyam)	indifference

FOUR PROGRESSIVE MODES OF HIGHER CONSCIOUSNESS

Within these four modes there are six 'seeded' stages of samadhi.

1st and 2nd experience samapatti - falling into a state of oneness

1st and 3rd experience samprajnata - mind still distorts things

2nd, 4[th,] 5[th,] and 6th experience asamprajnata - no mind distortion

'Seeded' means to be still affected by karmic memories.

To be discussed later, the 7th and final stage,
nirbija samadhi, is 'without seed.'

*1.17   Thereupon to enter into accurate knowing (samprajnata samadhi): the
modes are uncertainty, consideration, joy, and egoism.*

vitarka   vicAra   Ananda   asmita   rupa   anugamAt   saMprajNAtaH
*uncertainty   consideration   joy   egoism   modes   to enter into
thereupon   known accurately*

Even beginner yogins recognize that consciousness exists beyond the
senses, but they do not usually understand that it has multiple levels; they do
not know its import to Yoga, its relationship to evolution, or its relationship
to material world living. Most accept intuition, the 'sixth sense,' as being
nonspecifically 'real.' Intuition as experienced in meditation will become
meaningful only after having the experience and the sure knowing that the
experience happened. It will be different from any prior expectation.

The word *samadhi* has a ring of beauty and wonder to the spiritual seeker,
but those who have not yet evolved to begin experiencing the *samadhi* levels of consciousness will be unable to perceive what that could be like. The
highest *samadhi* is a state without senses, mind, or concurrent awareness of
the world and its material/sensory mode of consciousness. It is an experience
of the root reality beyond the material world, in which nothing differentiates
from anything else: there is nothing but pure primal existence-consciousness.
The descriptions of those who have briefly reached that consciousness can
only give clues of what it is truly like. True knowledge of it can only come
through experience.

In this aphorism, Patanjali is introducing the first six of seven stages of
samadhi, progressive levels of higher consciousness experience. The full story
of these stages of higher consciousness will slowly unfold throughout the
book: it begins here by introducing four progressive 'modes.' *Sutras 1.42 -
1.44* will say that two of these four modes each have two steps, bringing the
total among those four to six. For ease of proper understanding, this book
calls them 'stages.' A meditator will only enter the first of these by beginning
separation from the five states of everyday active material/sensory mentality.
Successful long-term practice gradually leads through the sequence this aphorism portrays, continually exposing deeper levels of Nature. Each deeper level

of Nature exists at a higher (closer to divine) level of consciousness than the one before.

In introducing these progressive levels here, Patanjali used the term *samprajnata*. The *Yoga Sutras* specific translation used here is 'accurate knowing,' but it does not convey the intended meaning. Using the prefix 'sam' creates the intention 'accurate knowing to be disturbed.' Patanjali later clarifies that in those cases the active mind disrupts the pure understanding. As the stages progress, the degrees of mind involvement and mind understanding decrease as intuitive knowing increases.

Patanjali does not use the term *samadhi* in this aphorism, but each of the stages is a form of *samadhi*. In the first and third of the six sequential stages, the mind is involved (*samprajnata*) while meditating, while in the second and fourth there is no mind involvement. That lack of mind involvement characterizes *asamprajnata samadhi,* as discussed in other *Sutras*. The end of the fourth stage is a dramatic turning point: an evolutionary development will occur in which all stages after that will be without mind involvement.

Stage 1

Vitarka - Uncertainty

Savitarka - with uncertainty

Samprajnata - mind involvement

Samapatti – falling into a state of oneness

(*savitarka samapatti samprajnata samadhi*)

The first of the six stages is the portal between active material/sensory consciousness and meditation, experiencing the consciousness of the mind itself. Thoughts may arise, but the meditator leaves logic and analysis (reasoning) behind. The thoughts will often conflict with the observations and give rise to doubt and uncertainty. The mind is active with its load of uprising thoughts and previous knowledge of the object.

This is the practice within the sixth limb of Yoga, 'concentration,' which uses a physical object as the object (target) of meditation. 'Physical (tangible) objects' are anything detectable by the senses, and may include not just rocks, flowers, art forms, and created items, but also breathing, body functions, body parts, a candle flame, scents, tastes, sounds, tactile feeling, or vision. The meditator focuses all of his or her sensory awareness on observing the object, using all senses with no deliberate thinking or intellectual activity. However, existing mind activity and previous knowledge about the object distort the insights, the *samprajnata* effect.

<u>Stage 2</u>
Vitarka - uncertainty
Nirvitarka – without uncertainty
Asamprajnata – without mind involvement
Samapatti – falling into a state of oneness
(*nirvitarka samapatti asamprajnata samadhi*)

The <u>second of the stages</u> comes about when the meditation becomes free of mind effects, bringing 'certainty' of the perception. With highly accomplished sensory focus, the meditator merges into 'oneness 'with the rock, flower, or other object and non-deliberately exists for a brief time in the experience of being a rock or flower. Insights may arrive concerning its deepest nature, its individual beingness.

<u>Stage 3</u>
Vicara - consideration
Savicara - with consideration
Samprajnata - mind involved
(*savicara samprajnata samadhi*)

In <u>the third stage</u>, having evolved past the ability to see the gross physical existence in its depths, the meditative focus shifts to leaving the senses behind and allowing the mind to observe subtle objects: this is the meditative skill of the seventh limb, 'meditation.' The target of focus may include such things as the relationship of the *cakras* (modern spelling is *chakra*) to prana flow, prana, divine *mantra*s, mudras, symbols, complex yantras (symbolic patterns), the divine sound, or the divine light. Anything abstract might be a target, including concepts such as love, compassion, god, evolution, or the meaning of life. A deeper knowledge of the raw truths of Nature and existence emerge. The

insights received are far more subtle, esoteric, and related to more foundational aspects of existence than those of the previous stage.

Here the mind automatically considers the subtle object, independent
of personal will and intellectual processing, without thinking or analysis.
Eventually, this level of consciousness is sufficiently clear and the mind sufficiently quieted that it is open to the insights that flow in from 'beyond.' As
those insights accumulate, opportunities arise to synthesize them into increasingly significant portions of knowledge and Truth. However, the mind is still
warping those insights through its previous knowledge and understanding of
the meditative target.

Stage 4

Vicara – consideration

Nirvicara – without consideration

Asamprajnata – mind not involved

(*nirvicara asamprajnata samadhi*)

In stage 4, the perception of meditation's subtle target is no longer
warped by the mind. Similar to the previous physical target, this time with
a non-sensory, non-physical, subtle realm target, the meditator merges into
a sense of oneness with the target, derived from deep understanding. This
is not, though, *samapatti*, which occurs only with meditation on physical
objects. Insights may arrive concerning its deepest nature, its true symbolism,
or the meaning apart from normal human impression. As discussed in regard
to other *Sutras*, this is a point of accelerated progress in the seeker's evolution,
and may be the experience that many refer to as enlightenment.

Stage 5

Ananda - joy

Asamprajnata – mind not involved

(*ananda asamprajnata samadhi*)

The stage 5 state of 'joy' comes about when the meditator automatically
experiences the tranquil (*sattvic*) nature of the soul, while focusing meditative attention on spiritual targets. Identifying with and meditatively focusing

on Spirit brings experience of the bliss and love that Yoga philosophy says underlies and supports everything, the eternal characteristics of the soul, and of *isvara* and *brahman*. However, it is not truly clear whether this characterization of godness as 'love' is from Yoga or Hinduism. The *Sutras* do not define it as such.

The stage occurs at the transition from the skills needed for the seventh limb religious meditation (*dhyana*), and those skills needed for the eighth limb abstract meditation (*samadhi*): it is free of thoughts for longer periods, and absent of the perception of physical and subtle bodies experienced in the first four stages of *samadhi*. There is deeper intuition and greater understanding of the nature of everything.

We cannot truly relate to this level of higher consciousness, 'joy' (bliss), except through experience. Words cannot properly describe its nature, but you will know without any doubt when you have experienced it. When it happens, you have clearly entered another level of existing in which words, symbols, and intellectual reasoning have no meaning. It is definitely a state of feeling, but different in quality from the feeling of an emotion, such as happiness. In whatever way someone experiences it, it will contain the common ground of a sense of great clarity and joy that is not comparable to any sensory or mental experience, and will often generate enormous gratitude.

<u>Stage 6</u>
Asmita - egoism
Asamprajnata – mind not involved
(*asmita asamprajnata samadhi*)

The word *asmita* directly translates to 'egoism,' but conventional ways of speaking of it at this level include 'I-am-ness,' 'I-sense,' and 'ego-sense.' The egoism <u>sixth stage</u> of consciousness experience requires the developed skills and experience of eighth limb *intense absorption*. The meditator becomes absorbed in the 'sense of I-am-ness,' the foundation for the sense of individual separate existence, a primal characteristic of universe evolution, as later defined in the expanded philosophy based on *Sutra* 2.19.

In that, during early evolution of the universe, the all-pervasive sense of ego enabled individuation of souls from the common soul and minds from the common mind. This sense preceded the formation of material being. When the seeker experiences that consciousness, great knowledge and insight are available, and fear and doubt dissolve. In this state, there is awareness of individuality and one's root existence. The sense of 'I am' abides, but the meditator is not yet at the point of, 'I am the One,' or 'I am the god-essence.'

vitarka vicAra Ananda asmita rupa anugamAt saMprajNAtaH

vitarka	uncertainty
vicara	consideration
ananda	joy
asmita	egoism
rupa	mode
anugamat	
anugam	to enter into
at	thereupon
samprajjata (for samprajnatah)	known accurately

CESSATION OF MIND ACTIVITY AND THOSE HIGHER EXPERIENCES

Cessation Of Mind Activity Must Occur

1.18   In the effort of the mind to remain in its unmodified condition of purity, cessation of notions is previous to the end of the inexhaustibleness of the impressions.

virAma pratyaya abhyAsa pUrvaH saMskAra SeSo'nyah
cessation   notion   the effort of the mind to remain in its unmodified condition of purity   previous to   impression   end inexhaustibleness

Having identified the first six stages in 1.17, this *Sutra* previews experiences to come later. Those experiences move toward the seventh stage, *nirbija samadhi,* and final resolution at the spiritual endpoint, *kaivalya.* This and following *Sutras* set the stage for a stream of aphorisms that speak of that forward movement. The *Sutra* begins by saying that the mind is naturally on a continuing quest to remain in purity (stillness). It tells us that the ultimate stillness will derive from ending (deactivating) the seemingly inexhaustible stock of active impressions (karmic memories). Karmic memories (impressions) do not just affect the future flow of life experiences: as long as they are active they generate vibrations in the mind, and those vibrations disrupt the sought after total stillness. That is why even the high consciousness experience that comes from going beyond senses and mind activity is not yet perfect stillness. Deactivation of remaining impressions, though, will not proceed without full cessation of disquiet to the mind from thoughts, notions, sensual stimulus, and other activities. Even that is not the end game, since there are still steps to take after the activity stops, but it is a necessary late stage step on the way to *nirbija samadhi*, and on to the end game.

This conquering of mental activity is part of the evolutionary pattern that the *Sutras* continually lay before us. We live in a zone of everyday mentality and consciousness, experiencing the five aspects of material world mind. The aspiring yogin begins the journey toward the highest consciousness beyond the material world and ultimate Absolute Unity by entering the first stage of *samprajnata* (mind involved) meditation, in which mind effects disrupt the necessary stillness. Through those evolutionary steps, the mind becomes progressively less active and involved. As shown above, all stages after the first four have that withheld mind characteristic. No objects remain in the mind during the high consciousness experience, and no thoughts, sensory signals, or other material world distractions exist to ripple the mind. This is a rare state, which few reach. Only the karmic memories, which Patanjali terms as 'seeds,' interrupt the mind stillness as the spiritual end approaches.

The core of this aphorism describes a transitional step toward having no remaining karmic memory (seed) activity, *nirbija* (without seed) *samadhi*, which is at the threshold to Absolute Unity (*kaivalya*).

virAma pratyaya abhyAsa pUrvaH saMskAra SeSo'nyah

virama	cessation
pratyaya	notion
abhyasa	the effort of the mind to remain in its unmodified condition of purity

purva (for purvah)	previous to
samskara	impression (impression on the mind of acts done in a former state of existence)
seso'nyah	
zesa	end
anya	inexhaustibleness

Absorption In The Primary Substance

1.19   *Thus, arising from that basis, deliverance through release from the body, absorption in the original producer of the material world.*

bhava pratyaya videha prakRti layAnAm
arising from   basis   deliverance through release from the body
the original producer of the material world   absorption in   thus

This continues the meditative evolutionary progression that characterizes Yoga philosophy, personal consciousness experience evolving backward to the original state of spiritual consciousness that created the universe. In what some modern describers call devolution (evolution of consciousness experience as the reverse sequence of evolution of the universe) the developing yogin experiences a state that preceded the development of the ego sense of I-am-ness referred to earlier. Nearing this final step in his or her evolution the experience is of the original substance of the universe, the early form of *prakrti* and its *gunas*, from which all physical and subtle material things derived. This is very near to the final evolutionary step of reaching *kaivalya*, freedom from living another material life, but not quite there.

The aphorism goes further, to state that the seeker is now experiencing as Spirit experiences, without the body, experiencing the consciousness of the *prakrti* that *Samkhya* philosophy tells us was the passive creative power that produced the material world, or Maya. Maya is another word for all of Nature, a word meant to indicate 'illusion.' In Yoga philosophy, the world of Nature is illusion created by Spirit (*brahman*) while the world of Spirit is reality. Nature is one side of the cosmic coin, with Spirit being the other.

bhava pratyaya videha prakRti layAnAm

bhava	arising from
pratyaya	basis
videha	deliverance through release from the body
prakrti	the original producer of the material world
layana (for layanam)	
laya	absorption in
ana (for anam)	thus

Different From Previous Experiences

1.20 The wisdom from intense absorption is different from that of the earlier faith, valor, and memory.

> SraddhA vIrya smRti samadhi prajNA pUrvaka itareSAm
> *faith valor memory intense absorption wisdom earlier different from*

The *Yoga Sutras* make it clear here that the practice of Yoga is different from the seeker's earlier practices of religion. It specifically tells us that before the practice of *samadhi* (intense absorption), faith, valor, and memory were instrumental in attaining wisdom (spirituality), but the results were different. Since the listed factors may not all be obvious, it is worthwhile to reflect on them.

Faith has many aspects, some of which are common to both Yoga and religion. Particularly for Yoga, the seeker must have faith in the rightness of the goal and in the underlying philosophy. Faith in your interpretation that it is the right life for you, perhaps that it is indeed your *karma*, is paramount, because doubts will continually spring up. Faith in the practice and process is necessary to continuing them. Although many gurus would say otherwise, true yogins must have faith in their ability to search out the truth of Yoga on their own. At the highest level of faith, the yogin has faith in the leadership and guidance of the divine, a personal relationship. For those taking a religion seriously, it is mandatory to have faith in their teachers and leaders: individual searching is discouraged. Those seekers of God must have full faith in truth of the written and handed down scriptures and documents.

Faith without the valor to maintain it is weak faith. While on your path, religious or yogic, many will challenge you, seeing you as aberrant from their view, separated from the rules and guidance of their culture. There will be intense peer pressure to be more like others. You will need the courage to sacrifice things once important to you, and to choose new things that may be risky. You must have the courage to persevere, direct your energy, and take the steps into the unknown. Unlike religious seekers, perhaps the most important valor of the yogin is in the questioning of everything seen and heard, and discarding things that previously seemed true.

You cannot easily understand what Patanjali meant by memory in this case, without combining it with the adjacent definition, "the whole body of sacred tradition or what is remembered by human teachers." The meaning of the word 'memory' in this context is as a much bigger word than you would immediately anticipate. The *Sutra* is specifically referring to memory of all that the seeker has ever learned. A huge body of teaching has engulfed the devotee over the years, whether originating in sacred texts, books, hymns, teachers, insights, practice, observation, or anything else.

The state produced by intense absorption in the experience of consciousness, has already received much attention, and does not require further explanation here. The *Sutra* includes *samadhi* as a specific practice and experience differentiating Yoga from religion. It is the key factor, the ultimate practice, without which union does not come about. The whole of Yoga practice evolves toward and supports meditative practice. The whole of meditative practice evolves toward and supports progressive stages of intense absorption.

Although some correctly translate *prajja* as 'knowledge,' the very high level effect of 'wisdom' is the meaning here. In Yoga terms, wisdom is spirituality.

SraddhA vIrya   smRti samadhi prajNA pUrvaka itareSAm

zraddha (for sraddha)	faith
virya	valor
smrti	memory (the whole body of sacred tradition or what is remembered by human teachers)
samadhi	intense absorption

prajja (for prajna)   wisdom
purvaka   earlier
itaresam
    itara   different from
    sam   (indicates grouping)

Ardent Desire Brings The Result

1.21   For the ardent, intensity of onset is indeed near.

tIvra   saMvegAnAm   AsannaH
ardent   intensity onset indeed   near

The preceding series of *Sutras* has described how the yogin advances to the highest levels of intense absorption. The described progression has moved on from the evolutionary development to experience *samprajnata samadhi*, which the mind affects with its previous knowledge, to *asamprajnata samadhi*, which is free of mind activity. In that state, however, the yogin still carries active impressions (karmic memories) that must deactivate to achieve the ultimate state and enter the doorway to Absolute Unity, *nirbija samadhi*, the *samadhi* that is 'seedless.' At this point in the progression, Absolute Unity is imminent for ardent yogins: they are indeed on the threshold.

We must realize, though, that this is a rare event: it is not easy and only comes about after years and lifetimes of evolving toward it. Many come to believe, and are often encouraged to believe, that they can become enlightened overnight, and even reach Absolute Unity during this current lifetime, that it is within reach. That is an incorrect perception. Reaching enlightenment and going on to Absolute Unity requires many more lifetimes than you would imagine. Everyone's path and potential is different, because the needs and capabilities of people are different, and because each one has a different karmic starting point for their current lifetime. Few will be born into their current lifetime carrying the potential for Absolute Unity. The ways of modern writing and teaching make it difficult to extract the idea that benefits accumulate, taking you through intermediate states and benefits that evolve in a direction. The rates and heights of progression will be different for each person.

tIvra saMvegAnAm AsannaH

tivra	ardent
samveganam	
sam	intensity
vega	onset
ana (for anam)	indeed
asanna (for asannah)	near

Effort Varies Nearing The End Game

1.22 Seeking excellence near fading away, you may be mild, moderate, or excessive.

mRdu   madhya   adhimAtratvAt   tato'pi   viSeSaH
mild   moderate   excessive you   fade away near   seeking for   excellence

The continuation of the series that relates to being near the endpoint of personal evolution becomes clear with the inclusion of the term 'near fading away.' There is a tendency in all translations to say that the degree of your effort, from mild to excessive, determines the speed of your last steps of evolution or whether they happen at all. However, there is no wording to make that connection. The *Sutra* simply says that when that seemingly non-willful and spontaneous effort arises it may be mild, moderate, or excessive.

mRdu madhya adhimAtratvAt tato'pi viSeSaH

mrdu	mild
madhya	moderate
adhimatratvat	
adhimatra	excessive
tvat	(2nd person indicator) you
tato'pi	
tas (for tato)	fade away
api (for 'pi)	(expresses nearness) near
vizesa (for visesah)	seeking for excellence

Meditation On The Supreme Being
Also Brings The Result

1.23   Or, consume profound religious meditation on the Supreme Being.

Isvara   praNidhAnAd   vA
Supreme Being   consume   profound religious meditation   or

The multiple appearances of this meditation in the *Sutras* emphasize its importance. The reader will see it in varying contexts in 2.1, 2.32, 2.45, and 3.36. The simple wording tells us to practice 'profound religious meditation,' where 'religious' synonyms of 'spiritual,' 'sacred,' 'devout,' or 'religiously' carry the proper intention, more than 'religion' does. Religion did not exist in Patanjali's framework.

It is important to recognize that the Sanskrit purposefully refers to the divine as *isvara* (the Immanent-Presence), not to *brahman* (the Transcendent-Presence). No dictionary representation over time takes *isvara* beyond the universe. Some yogins naturally assume that meditation and prayer focused on the root cause of everything in all universes, *brahman*, is better than a focus within the universe. For the *Yoga Sutras*, this *Sutra* clearly keeps the focus within the universe. Remembering that the entire progression of the meditation experience Patanjali describes moves us through the consciousness experiences in the reverse order of the *Sutras* universe evolution (devolution to some) puts that in perspective. *Isvara,* which equates to *sat* (the Immanent-Presence) in the *sat-om-tat* of the creative trinity of Vedism and Hinduism, is their deepest cosmic evolutionary point. Before *isvara*, the universe did not exist.

Throughout the *Sutras*, it becomes clear that there are many paths to the experiences of higher consciousness. This dedicated meditation on the root divinity of the universe is high on the list, without ever changing to a god name. This book will not judge whether personal *karma* and choice identifies divinity as *isvara, sat*, godhead, Lord, God, Allah, Brahma, Siva, Zeus, primal existence-immanent, or whatever symbol or framework the local culture established. It assumes that all religions were seeded and stimulated by the godhead and recognizes that most claim similar high experiences.

Whether considering a god with form or the formless Absolute, the dedication that leads to profound absorption in meditation is not easy. The degree to which a seeker externally vocalizes, or internally pictures, commitment and belief does not matter: it often does not express the yogin's true reality. In the context supplied by Patanjali, *isvara/soul/purusa* observes all aspects of the truth of your existence, knowing your thoughts, actions, and the status of how you are in the world. Dedication of a life requires full acceptance of the Yoga life in all its forms, and of your personal path, with your actions reflecting your ability to follow the guiding spiritual lead. It means giving up all attachments. It means committed discipline. It means rejecting all illusions, fantasies, delusions, desires, wishes, hopes, expectations, and fears, the Judas Goats that lead many from the path.

Complete devotion to the life and path comes naturally and easily to some, as if they were born to it, and some may well have been. Most humans, though, remain absorbed in everyday consciousness of life, and do not have the necessary yogic tools to move beyond it. What view they have of the primal existence, or being-ness that they are committed to accepting as Supreme, is hazy and colored by layer upon layer of teachings from others. Unschooled and unpracticed in Yoga, they do not understand the role of dedication, the need for tremendous focus of their attention, the nature of the target of their devotion and meditation, the results that may come, the need to individuate for learning, or the purposes.

Isvara praNidhAnAd vA

izvara (for isvara)	Supreme Being
pranidhanad	
pranidhana	profound religious meditation
ad	consume
va	or

THE NATURE OF THE SUPREME BEING

The Supreme Being Is Not Touched By Anything

1.24   A superior soul, the Supreme Being is untouched by the afflictions, actions, consequence of actions, or their stock (of impressions).

kleSa   karma   vipAka   Asayair   aparAmRStaH   puruSa   viSeSa   iSvaraH
*afflictions   actions   consequence of actions   stock   their
untouched   soul   superior   Supreme Being*

The Supreme Being (*isvara, sat, purusa*) is a singular oversoul encompassing all other souls in the universe. Although it simultaneously experiences what material beings experience, the experiences do not affect it. It does not experience the effects of the five afflictions that the *Sutras* will discuss in *Sutra* 2.3, or of emotions, thoughts, desires, or karmic memories, and is not subject to the laws of cause and effect. Conflicts - the mental stresses all humans endure - do not ripple within that immanent primal existence, *isvara/sat/ purusa*, the transcendent primal existence, *brahman*, or the individual soul (*purusa*): the primal consciousness that is common to all three exists in undisturbed absolute stillness. No actions by anyone or anything can affect that consciousness: it is impervious. No underlying motivators, in the way that humans understand motivation, influence it.

The Supreme Being is a unique state of being, a unique existence, and the root from which all other states of being in the universe emerged. Yoga philosophy differentiates between our normal way of being, which focuses on materiality ('ignorance' in Yoga terms) and the opposite way of being that is full spirituality ('wisdom'). Being fully spiritual, the Immanent-Presence (*isvara, sat, purusa*) shows not even a hint of being a material manifestation until It creates the material universe: the material world of *isvara/sat/ purusa,* though, is really the Transcendent-Presence, Great Spirit or *brahman*, self-manifested in materiality.

Being subject to the Laws of Karma, human actions, motivations, thoughts, emotions, desires, and many other things affect the future of the individual being and its corporate being in oneness with others, but they never affect the great and original transcendent Source, the immanent god-presence (the oversoul of the universe), or the individual soul. Yet, the consciousness that is common to all beings continually experiences them through us and through all the other things It creates.

It may require much study and much received intuitive insight before a yogin can picture an invisible beingness, a primal existence superseding all

other existence, that has no beginning, end, or form; a pure spiritual beingness which is totally still, that manifests itself as a material universe. The
yogin may comprehend and believe those words early on, but will not then
feel them or see the implications or full meaning. Understanding what it
means that an eternal primal Law binds and constrains *brahman*, while at the
same time *brahman is* that Law that constrains It will await a yet higher level
of experience.

At some point in the evolution into attaining higher consciousness experiences, the intuitive awareness will arrive that shows that the root beingness *is* also a primal creative drive that exhibits indecipherable intention and
direction. The consciousness will be quite high when the yogin sees how
the drive of the primal existence (*brahman*) causes universes and individual
beings under Its Law and that the Law controls all evolution within the universe. It may require higher consciousness yet to truly understand that the
primal being knows nothing of time or sequence; that everything happens
simultaneously, that in Its reality there is no past, present or future, and that
Its Immanent-Presence created time within our universe, and that time is
material and not spiritual. Nearly all humans are far from comprehending
or experiencing the infinite omniscient knowledge of the Absolute original
being, in the way that the yogins of highest consciousness can.

kleSa karma vipAka Asayair aparAmRStaH puruSa viSeSa iSvaraH

kleza (for klesa)	affliction
karman (for karma)	action
vipaka	consequence of actions
asayair	
azaya (for asaya)	stock (of impressions)
ir	(denotes second or third person plu-
	ral) their
aparamrsta (for paramrstah)	untouched
purusa	soul
vizesa (for visesa)	superior
izvara (for isvarah)	Supreme Being

The Supreme Being Is A Receptacle Of Omniscience

1.25 Therein, a receptacle of unsurpassed omniscience.

tatra   niratiSayaM   sarvajNa   bIjam
therein   unsurpassed   omniscience   a receptacle

The ancient philosophy tells us that the *Supreme Being*, on behalf of *brahman*, is like a bucket. Every awareness of the ultimate consciousness, from the finest detail and tiniest occurrence, pours into that bucket: none is to be forgotten even in the most infinite future, although past present and future are concepts of the universe, not of infinity. All physical things are there as well as all subtle things, including every thought you ever had.

Without the force and eternal presence of the Absolute in every *thing* from the tiniest particle and subtle object, there would be no consciousness and knowledge. Without the original timeless consciousness that has no beginning or end, nothing could exist. It is the Source of everything, including all knowledge. The eternal beingness, godness, amid all its other characteristics, has the characteristic of ultimate, infinite, omniscient knowledge. It has that knowledge because it is the owner of everything, the creator of everything, the observer of everything, and the voyeuristic experiencer of everything.

At first exposure to the idea of all knowledge and all things, your mind might settle on world events and the daily activities in your life, seeing *isvara* as the observer/recipient of it all, aware of everything that is happening. Seeing It as the 'source' of all knowledge and everything else is a bigger step. At some level of yogic evolution, understanding will come that every bit of knowledge and experience that anyone has ever had came from that single receptacle of everything. It may take longer to focus on the word 'unsurpassed.' If the word becomes a puzzle that your mind plays with and reaches for insight, you might see that it means the 'highest quality of knowledge,' untainted Truth, and that all other knowledge is lower quality, devoid in many ways of Truth. The yogin will not have that perfectly pure and unsurpassed knowledge.

At some point in your higher consciousness journey, insight can burn into you that the source of everything must be a vast warehouse that holds within Its awareness everything that ever happened. Insight arrived at in an even higher consciousness could be a life-altering trigger, as you sense that acquiring that Truth requires passionate devotion to the life, more practice, and relinquishing more things. At nearly the highest level of consciousness experience, while in the state of experiencing oneness of all physical and subtle things, you will see that the One does not behold the things that happened in the universe as sequences. You will see that It miraculously holds all moments of universe time that ever existed simultaneously in its awareness, and that time and sequences do not exist at that level of consciousness.

tatra niratiSayaM sarvajNa bIjam

tatra	therein
niratisaya (for niratisayam)	unsurpassed
sarvajja (for sarvajna)	omniscience
bija (for bijam)	a receptacle

The Supreme Being Is Not Separated, Urges Us On

1.26   Going constantly without separation over the course of time, quickly going after the ancients and any venerable or respectable person.

pUrveSAm api guruH kAlena anavacchedAt
ancient going after quickly and any venerable or respectable person
the course of time not separation to go constantly

In the true translation, Patanjali tells us that *isvara* is constantly with us, not separated, and always has been over the course of time. Few teachings of Yoga are more important to understand. From varying perspectives, several other *Sutras* tell us that the eternal presence of the god-essence is always with us, observing us, correcting us, and using us for Its purposes, not ours. It never goes away and is there in all of us.

Contrary to the idea that it teaches only the great teachers such as Buddhas, Christ, and Krishna, and prophets like Muhammad, the wording tells us that It 'goes after' the earliest people, focusing on 'venerable or respectable persons.' It does not say, but we can properly assume, that the purpose is to pass on the teachings. The wording is powerful. By omission, it is bringing our attention to the idea that the disrespected and those without wisdom are

not worthy of It urging them toward the goals of Yoga. From the very beginning of our species in the most ancient of our men and women, *isvara* has
quickly approached them to begin the teachings.

Isvara teaches in many ways. It guides parents, those who have earned
wisdom, and respected leaders toward educating the upcoming generations.
It teaches Great Teachers how to teach the mass of humanity, to provide the
horde with guidelines for living. While focusing the higher spiritual teaching
for the appropriate people, it is always teaching all of us all the time. It uses
every person as an actor on the great stage of life, to show others the results
of their way of living. All results of acts are lessons, whether good, bad, or
indifferent. It builds situations from which the earthbound material beings,
housing their invisible spiritual souls, learn from experience and evolve. It
places symbols before us in endless diversity. It leads us to understand the
results of our actions. It empowers us to observe the workings and agonize
over the mysteries of the universe and of existence itself.

It can be easy to absorb this *Sutra* and say, 'Of course that's true.' Anyone
who knows of the teachings of Krishna, Jesus, Muhammad, the Buddha, Lao
Tsu, or any other Great Teacher, can easily accept the words of each as coming
from the Source. Yet, ask yourself the impossible to answer question of what
other insight about this might be available if you had evolved to experience
consciousness at a higher level. With that higher insight might you easily see
that they all said the same things, taught the same lessons, but dressed them
in the languages and thought structures of widely separated cultures?

Would it be possible for you to see and accept that the earliest seeker or
teacher was not the Christ, the Buddha, or even Krishna who walked on Earth
2000 years before those two great ones? Without high insight and study, do
you think you could intuitively understand that the pre-Harappan people of
5000 years ago, who began passing on the Samkhya philosophies that led to
Yoga - which said the same things as those later teachers did - were not the
earliest teachers? What would it do to your mind structure and beliefs if you
saw that even the shamans who taught people the same lessons through their
connection with the Spirit more than 8000 years ago were not the earliest
teachers? At a higher level of consciousness yet, insight could grace you with

knowledge of just when our species became sufficiently sentient that *isvara* could begin teaching a species on this planet.

A wonderful passage in the Bhagavad Gita has Lord Krishna telling Arjuna that from time to time, when good and evil get out of balance, he sends an avatar to earth to teach, so that it can find balance again. In Yoga terms, 'good' and 'evil' are not what you think they are in your modern mind. Good is simply 'right living.' Evil is 'erroneous living,' making choices that effect your life and your evolution negatively.

Would you thrill to it, or have some other reaction, if your insight showed you that all The Great Teachers are one soul that sporadically appeared in a body when and where needed, to teach through the local language and culture? Would you see that you are a teacher with an equivalent soul, one who has a different role to play during this lifetime journey, one who has a special place on the stage?

pUrveSAm api guruH kAlena anavacchedAt

purvesam		
	purva	ancient
	esa (for esam)	going after
	am	quickly
api		and
guru (for guruh)		any venerable or respectable person
kalena		the course of time
anavacchedat		
	an	(negation) not
	avaccheda	separation
	at	to go constantly

OM

The Sacred Symbol For The Supreme Being

1.27 The mystic (or sacred) symbol (om) signifies it.

tasya   vAcakaH   praNavaH
it signifying   the mystic (or sacred) syllable (om)

The *Sutras* say that *om* is a mystical syllable representing the Supreme Being. Over thousands of years, many intellectual and mystical explanations and descriptions have come forward for *om*. Some say that it is the name of the primal existence, which it is not. The primal existence has no name, but has the nongod designation as *brahman*. *Brahman* is a genderless, formless 'It,' not a 'he,' or 'she.' You may have seen many other designations that are not names, which point to it, things like Source, Absolute, Spirit, Presence, All, or Supreme. This aphorism tells us that *om* is specifically the symbol for the imminent presence of *brahman* in the universe, *isvara* (*sat*, *Supreme Being*), not the transcendent *brahman*.

Some teachers point to *om* as being the original and continuing vibration or 'sound' of our universe, and there is Truth in that, but even when passing through an atmosphere the continuous vibration is not an audible sound. Reflecting a later view, they also tell us that it is one member of the indivisible creative trinity of *sat/tat/om*, and there may be Truth in that. However, this *Sutra* tells us that the word (often referred to as 'the syllable *om*') is a human symbol to represent *isvara (brahman-immanent. sat)*. Discussion of whether *brahman/isvara* taught us that ancient symbol by revealing it to a mystic, or whether it is a human creation will never yield a firm result.

The symbol provides an opportunity to focus attention on the godness existence by focusing on the symbol. If you come to automatically call forth the symbol when reflecting on the All, your awareness will move toward the All whenever you think of the symbol or see it, supporting the idea of devoted deep meditation. That is not different from a Christian's awareness moving toward the Christ or God when seeing a cross.

tasya vAcakaH praNavaH

tasya	
ta	it
sya	(3rd person indicator)
vacaka (for vacakah)	signifying
pranavah	the mystical or sacred syllable (om)

Finding The Meaning Of The Symbol

1.28 Therefore, raise one's eyes, whisper, and accordingly direct one's thoughts to the meaning.

taj japas tad artha bhAvanam
*therefore raise one's eyes whisper accordingly meaning
direct one's thoughts to*

The heart of the aphorism is the focusing of one's thoughts on the meaning of *om*. 'Whisper' depicts a verbal context, not just mental. 'Raise one's eyes' recommends a reverential attitude toward that which is beyond materiality, whether it is religious, prayerful, devotional, or otherwise. It is important to note that Patanjali has not used any word that he normally uses for meditation, instead using *bhavana*, 'direct one's thoughts.' The practice engages the mind, not stilling it in the way meditation intends. However, if the yogin becomes deeply engrossed and continues the practice it will have meditative effects and will yield valuable insight to the nature of *om* and to Nature (the material world).

Om, the great symbol for *isvara*, the universe creation god-drive, exists in pictograph, and alphabetic characters, not just in sound forms, and it is more than a symbol. Over thousands of years, Masters, mystics, the wise, and many who are less masterful, mystical, and wise have interpreted, reinterpreted, and described the many aspects of *om*. One is the creative trinity of *sat-om-tat*, discussed above, in which *om* is the initial vibration of the universe; passing through the primal essence of *sat*, causing material forms (tat) to arise. More recently, and perhaps more fanciful, some say that when all the sounds of the universe combine, they make that sound. Another intellectual portrayal treats the three sounds as primary sounds, just as the colors of the universe have three primary colors. Other characterizations range from the simple, such as each of the three letters having symbolic meaning, to complex.

Particularly at the start of focusing the mind on this, the seeker could plant some understanding of *om* in the mind and work from there, or just letting an empty mind explore. *Om* as the initial vibration of the universe, or *om* as a member of the trinity, would be wonderful for the mind to explore.

However, the characterizations above and many others do not derive from authentic Yoga philosophy. Unknowingly picking a popular, but incorrect, characterization of *om*, or a religious explanation from a religion you do not share, could lead to reinforcing wrong as right and lead down erroneous paths.

Beyond the 'direct one's thoughts' of this aphorism, varied meditative techniques that employ *om* do exist. Close to the guidance of this aphorism, but absent of intent to use the intellect to find meaning, many yogins use *om* as a chant or verbal *mantra*. This can be loud, whispered, or anything in the range between them. The sound symbolizes the creative godness in exactly the same way pictorial or alphabetic symbols do. By focusing on the sound, thereby stilling the mind, awareness can continually move toward *isvara/brahma*. Keeping awareness directed toward that immanent god-essence by repeated utterance increases harmony with It, brings stillness, and can yield insight. This will not happen without truly understanding and accepting that the symbol represents the creative, all-pervading *isvara*, and having a heart that strives for spiritually moving toward it. In effect, the chanter is stating an aspiration to come closer, to know the Spirit better. Over time, as the aspirer becomes more receptive, the true meaning of the symbol and what it represents will reveal itself.

Silent repetition can also be valuable. For silent practice, one needs to do little more than plant the word in the mind and mentally repeat it, while generating an aspiration to known its meaning. The repetition can be in harmony with the rhythm of some detected body activity, whether it be breathing, heart beat or perhaps internal energy flow, or it can be independent and at whatever pace works well for the individual. Over time, the yogin will move toward the personally most appropriate and useful technique. With proper practice and experience, the mind explores independently and may deliver intuitive answers.

The non-meditative and meditative approaches to gaining insight to *om* are apparent easy formulas, practices that even the beginner can comprehend, but they are not as easy as they appears in words. Although they are potentially potent, a direct route to understanding divinity, even the novice can practice them and derive some benefits. The novice, though, does not yet understand the forms and variations of practice, and has not developed the skill platform, discipline, stillness, or the evolution of body and mind to attain full success. Over time, with purification of the body through Yoga practices, concentration of the mind, and other skills, the committed seeker will become more adept.

taj japas tad artha bhAvanam

taj (= tad)	therefore
japas	
jap	whisper
as	raise one's eyes
tad	accordingly
artha	meaning
bhavana (for bhavanam)	direct one's thoughts to

THE OBSTACLES TO HIGHER CONSCIOUSNESS

Inward Thoughts And Self-Study Remove Obstacles

1.29   And, extended, one whose thoughts are turned inward or upon himself surely accomplishes absence of obstacles.

tataH pratyakcetanA adhigamo 'py antarAya abhAvaS ca
extended   one whose thoughts are turned inward or upon himself
to accomplish   surely   obstacle   absence   and

Patanjali has completed the discussion of *om* by telling us that it is a symbol to reflect on and seek its true meaning, a deep exploration of the spiritual realm. He now extends his guidance to take in the other side of the coin, pairing the spiritual with an exploration of the personal material self. Exploring the spiritual nature and the material nature will each be important to progress on the path up the Yoga mountain. In this regard, he introduces two new things. The first is that yogins can study their self by turning their thoughts inward. Some interpret 'self' as used in this *Sutra* to mean the true self or soul, but he does not use any of the words he usually uses that specifically refer to that. He clearly means that we should study our persona and how we are being. Studying the self introduces the second new subject, the obstacles the personal self will encounter while seeking union.

In his next aphorism, he will specifically detail those obstacles, but for now, he is telling us that inward study will remove them. He clearly indicates that this is not casual study, but extensive and extended over a long time. Such self-study is just a step in the Yoga process, not a miraculous end in its own right. It helps with progressively moving toward higher consciousness experiences and on to eventual Absolute Unity.

As you practice this inward discipline, you may begin to perceive the core pattern within your life, through seeing repeated scenarios: you may become aware that it relates to the cumulative state of your being and to why you are in the current karmic life situation. Those insights will help generate the faith, commitment, and discipline necessary to the removal of obstacles: they will bring the new understanding that will counter false understandings that preserve the obstacles.

tataH pratyakcetanA adhigamo 'py antarAya abhAvaS ca

tata (for tatah)	extended
pratyakcetana	one whose thoughts are turned inwards or upon himself
adhigama (for adhigamo)	to accomplish
api (for 'py)	surely
antaraya	obstacle
abhava (for abhavas)	absence
ca	and

There Are Nine Distractions, Regarded As Obstacles

1.30 Sickness, apathy, doubt, carelessness, sloth, intemperance, erroneous understanding, not obtaining your next degree, and instability become distractions of the mind, are regarded as obstacles.

vyAdhi styAna samSaya pramAda Alasya avirati bhrAnti
darSana alabdha bhUmikatva anavasthitatvAni
citta vikSepAs te'ntarAyAh
*sickness apathy doubt carelessness sloth intemperance
error understanding unobtained degree your instability   the mind*

distractions become   obstacles regard as

Nine typically human things block access to the higher consciousness experiences of Yoga. To the degree that we do not recognize the presence of nonmaterial being, these things are so normal to our daily material/sensory life that we do not see them as obstacles to experiencing the consciousness.

Sickness is the first and easiest to see. If we do not proactively protect and enhance our bodily health, we are more likely to fall into physical or mental ill health. When we are in bad health of any type, we become more disquieted. Our attention to our health draws us away from other things. Our personal strength and clarity diminish. Our energies become absorbed in healing. The discomforts and ripple-effect problems captivate us.

Few among us have not known the feeling of falling into apathy at some time and for some period, short or long. For some, it is a regular part of life, while for others it is a rare experience. There are many reasons why it comes about, but all produce a similar effect. We simply cannot charge our battery. Nothing works and we even lose interest in trying to activate ourselves. Often we sit and wait for something to happen. We may feel dull. We may experience life as slow motion activity. The worst of it is that we cannot help ourselves escape it. Even the prospect of escape cannot capture our interest. Often the state seems so natural that we do not even see it as something we need to correct. Yet, if we are to thrive and evolve, we need to work proactively to cure it. We cannot continue our practice or examine our life or state of being while in such a state, because we simply do not care. If it becomes a chronic condition, interfering with our life and growth, strong and willful action is necessary. We must find strategies to shake loose from what has arrested us.

All seekers experience doubt, some more than others do. While on the spiritual path, there are no benchmark points left by surveyors, maps, trail markers, or reinforcements from the world around us. God-voices are not whispering instructions in our ears, and no Master or teacher is nearby to give guidance. We are on our own. We have made a risky decision to invest in a different life. We naturally want to mitigate the risk, make the commitment partial. We fear it will take us over, capture our life. Wanting to keep it from becoming obvious to others, we flow unobtrusively through the surrounding culture, without stating who we are or sharing our struggle. Our minds play endless games with us, as if our new direction were an enemy to be defeated. In a true way this new direction is an enemy, but one that we do not recognize. We have set out to break the patterns that hold us in position, to break through our internal fortresses and walls separating us from reality. Everything that our minds and ways of being have become accustomed to is under threat. We are riding on pure faith in the rightness of what we are doing. Keeping that faith and rightness in mind, and remembering our intention, may be our only defense.

Buddhist and Yoga teachings often include reminders to maintain mindfulness, as the best defense against falling into carelessness and lack of attention to our lives. It is so easy to stop caring, to become careless. Caring requires work and continual attention. Caring requires a foundation of values, priorities, and philosophy. Those foundation pieces require continual reinforcement, or they will decay, dissolve, and crumble. We need to measure our lives with them, or they have no value. This requires the hard work of continual awareness of our actions, thoughts, motives, emotions, interactions, and effects on everything and everyone outside of our personal being. It also requires awareness of the effects of everything outside our selves on our selves. This is mindfulness. This is caring about our lives.

Sloth, the fifth of the obstacles, is similar to apathy and closely linked to uncaring. This obstacle, however, does not stem from the physical, metabolic, dietary, chemical or other agents of lethargy, as apathy sometimes does. It is purely attitudinal. We simply do not want to take on the work. The tradeoff between effort and benefit does not come out the right way for us. Perhaps we just want to have fun, go to the beach, or find some other escape from self-work. To the degree that we let an attitude of noninvolvement enter our lives we will step off the path we have been traveling. We will lose the reasons, forget the intention, and discount the rationale or intuition that brought us to the path.

Yoga students, and often their teachers, when presented with the idea of intemperance often do a mental jump to sexuality. The *Sutras* do not contain any 'thou shall not' prohibitions. They, instead, warn seekers of dangers to their being and to their path, so that they can weigh the risks. Intemperance refers to lack of self-control, which excessive desires of many types bring about, often for sensual gratification. We humans are sensual creatures. We want to hear the best sounds, see wonderful things, feel great sensations, taste fantastic foods, and smell exotic things. Dangers exist in each of the senses. Sounds have enormous effects on the psyche and mentality. Different kinds of music, for example, produce different effects, both long-term and immediate. Music can spur us to romance, violence, peace, and many other things. It can damage or heal the aspects of our being.

You have probably noticed how visual images, whether moving as they do in films, as static drawings, or of real scenes and events can generate deep emotional effects and convince us of realities that may or may not be true. The after-effects are sometimes long lasting. Governments, marketers, politicians, and public relations experts constantly barrage us with visual images, using the power they contain. As with all other things that we use our senses for, those images can be harmful, benign, or helpful to us. Like all other senses, the visual sense can become addictive or obsessively close to it. Consider pornography as an example. Anything addictive, that is to say anything we attach to obsessively, interferes with our freedom of choice and ability to progress on our path, and our ability to exercise self-control to define the path for our life. Excessive and obsessive interest in Internet pornography is an excellent modern example.

Our sense of taste gets us into continual trouble. We love the taste of fatty food, sweets, alcohol, and other things that are not good for us. Just as we can become obsessive about music or visual imagery, we can become obsessive about what we taste. We can move it to a high priority in our lives. Eating tasty food and constant visits to restaurants can cause us to ingest many things that we do not realize are there, as well as to eat and drink far more than is good for us. Similarly, aromas of food, sex, intoxicants, or marijuana can lead us to into situations that are not good for us. It all requires awareness, decision-making, and maintaining freedom to choose. It requires anticipating the effects that the actions will cause.

Picture yourself walking through the Golden Arches, yearning for a hamburger and fries. Imagine the delicious taste. Picture the millions of people that go there for that taste. Then understand this. Food manufacturers have a deliberate strategy of using the best tasting fats, which are the least healthy ones, and huge quantities of salt in their products. They do it because they know that those tastes naturally draw humans, and their customers are not going to think about their health, only about the taste, the fun, and riding the popular cultural wave. The same is true of sugar and caffeine. Did you ever watch a Dunkin Donuts, Starbucks, or Krispy Kreme employee shovel sugar into their 'Smoothies,' 'Lattes,' or whatever the currently hyped product is? The only problem with all of this is that you have not decided to master your senses, to exercise your self-control over them. You are not making deliberate choices. That enables others to manipulate you.

All the senses can be very alluring. As alluring things, they can easily bring attachment and intense desire for more. They can easily put us in opposition to attaining our freedom, by choosing through attachment to the things we have come to value and to the fanciful images about them that our minds create. We often choose only the food, music, movies, art, body sensations, and obsessive activities that our surrounding culture sanctions, those that peer pressure selects for us. Those attachments and desires are lures from the path. Intemperance, the lack of self-control, is among the strongest obstacles on the path.

Sense gratification and erroneous understanding are the most emphasized obstacles, because they are among the most prevalent and seductive of our behaviors. Each of them causes a feeling of possessiveness: in the cases of the senses, we not only want to keep the good things coming, but we also want more of them, which then brings greed into the picture. In the case of perceptions and understanding of things, we struggle to form the ways we see the world, building up a huge investment in them. Once we become convinced of something like 'the weather changed on Earth after those men landed on the moon,' our resistance to changing the idea increases with time and opposition from others. We protect our perceptions, defending them against potential threats. Each of us carries a load of those delusions, illusions, wrong ideas, false understandings, prejudices, bigotry, dogma injected by others, values, and attitudes that we never question. The Truth-bearing seed of what we truly are, and the higher consciousness that takes us to it, lie beneath those layers, so far down that we do not even guess that they are there. Every false belief is a block to finding and understanding that reality. By peeling the false layers away, we can find Truth and Reality. It is also important to understand that every false belief, illusion, delusion, and misperception sets up a tension that will prevent calming the mind.

Yoga is cumulative work with progressive effects. We keep laying foundation pieces and building on them. Patanjali is pointing that out to us by saying that an obstacle lies in our failure to obtain the next degree of evolution to a new state of consciousness experience, by not persevering toward it. Anyone who has traveled the path toward union will verify the seditious nature of that failure to persevere. It is natural to become comfortable in staying at the level we have reached, and to perhaps fear the effort necessary to moving on. It is so easy to become discouraged through watching our progress toward the goals: watching involves expectation, and expectation yields false perceptions of our progress. If we focus on how well we have done with part of it, such as living by principles, we may lose motivation to work on another part, such as breathing or meditation.

Using varying contexts and symbolisms, teachers often tell their students that the mind and the ego are fearful of our getting control over them: they act as if they are seditious beings, putting all sorts of negative thoughts and perspectives in our way, trying to break our progress and keep things as they are. We become accustomed to how we are, how we think, our habits, movements, values, style, priorities, beliefs and everything else about us. Changing anything is a major threat. We cannot do it without holding to faith in the value of doing it. Without that faith, we cannot progress to the next stage.

Once progress occurs, instability is the last of the nine obstacles. Most of us can relate to it, having experienced it in some part of our lives. 'Two steps forward and one back' is a way of life for many of us (which is far better than the reverse ratio, resulting in continually sliding backward). The *Sutras* are warning us to be wary of this obstacle, because people who have engaged in these practices of Yoga have fallen into exactly that trap so often. Having formed a solid base in some aspect of the work does not mean that it is a stable base. It can crumble at any time: we need wariness and recognition of the possibility of reversal. Foundations need continual maintenance. It may become easy to think it is time for a vacation, or to put the next step on hold for a while. 'I will back off for a couple of days,' becomes a week then a month and so on. If we do not make the practices 'automatic pilot' parts of our lives, we may forget and drift away. Perhaps a long-held principle will seem unimportant on one day. Just a small light-hearted foray into putting a drug into our system will be alright for just a Saturday night, perhaps because we need a 'kicker,' we are feeling boring, or we think people see all our practice and dedication as something unattractive. If mindfulness about what we are saying or doing is not automatic, if we are still reminding ourselves to do it, the comfort of leaving it behind can easily become permanent withdrawal from it.

vyAdhi styAna samSaya pramAda Alasya avirati bhrAnti darSana alabdha bhUmikatva anavasthitatvAni citta vikSepAs te'ntarAyAh

vyadhi	sickness
styana	apathy
samzaya (for samsaya)	doubt
pramada	carelessness
alasya	sloth
avirati	intemperance
bhranti	error
darzana (for darsana)	understanding
alabdha	un-obtained
bhumikatva	
bhumika	degree
tva	(2nd person personal pronoun) your
anavasthitatvani	
anavasthitatva	instability
ni	(untranslated)
citta	the mind
viksepas	
viksepa	distraction
as	become
te'ntarayah	
te	(untranslated)
antaraya	obstacle

ah   regard as

1.31   *Endure appearing together with the distractions, pain, dejectedness, your*
       causing the body to shake or tremble, panting, and very hard breathing.

   duHkha   daurmanasya   aNgam   ejayatva   SvAsa   praSvAsA
                  vikSepa   sahabhuvah
   pain   dejectedness   causing to shake or tremble your   body   panting
   very hard breathing   distraction   appearing together with   endure

Although the interpretations and translations of this list vary somewhat
from author to author, Patanjali is giving us an inventory list of negative
results that derive from the 'obstacles' that distract us from our path. He certainly did not mean it to be a complete and invariably biblical list, but to be
representative of the things that happen.

The *Sutra* tells us that if we allow such things to divert our mind, we will
experience mental pain and chaos, a dejected or depressed psychological state,
physical effects on the body, and breathing disruption: these are all recognizable as things we have experienced, not esoteric events. The underlying message is that we need a solid base for living a yogic life. Without the disciplined
life that will keep us from illness, give us a feeling of proactive excitement for
our living, and provide the faith to keep it all going, those negative results will
overtake us. They can become despair if doubts bring us to lack of decisive-
ness, commitment, or clarity. Doubt often produces ambiguity, which causes
depression if we come to a state in which we do not know which way to turn.

Visualizing a spiritual monk or nun strolling though a garden may help
you understand: he or she is perfectly centered, calm, relaxed, inwardly drawn
and displaying a slight smile. It is hard to imagine the happening of those
negative conditions that Patanjali describes while in that equanimity. Change
the picture to a different person, one who lives a chaotic life at or near the
illusion/delusion end of the sanity scale, perhaps self-dissipating with drugs,
alcohol, tobacco, and too little sleep. Such things as depression, tremors,
and breathing irregularities are easy to picture in that person, because that
often happens in such situations. Expand that negative vision to include the

presence of non-lethal poisons in the body and the effects will be even easier to see.

Calm living without stress, and with equanimity, confidence, and the natural purging of adrenaline, poisons, and impurities from the body bring steadiness and normal functioning. Such practices as meditation and *pranayama* condition the nervous system, the complex of *prana nadis* (energy channels), and the physical tissues, preventing the symptoms pointed to in this *Sutra*.

If we adopt these practices, care about our lives, resolve our doubts, develop positive enthusiasm, work to maintain our health, and avoid the disappointments and traps that come with sense gratification, we will become calm, steady, and centered. Since the mind affects the body, the body will follow along. We will not be as subject to the wildness of breathing that follows emotions and adrenaline pumping activity, because we will not be experiencing those emotions.

This is not a one-time 'clean up your act' practice. Even the highest yogins need to continually practice and be mindful of all of these things to keep from regressing, or to recover from regression.

duHkha daurmanasya aNgam ejayatva SvAsa praSvAsA vikSepa sahabhuvah

duhkha	pain
daurmanasya	dejectedness
angam	
anga (printed dictionary)	body
agga (on-line dictionary)	body
ejayatva	
ejaya	causing to shake or tremble
tva	(indicator of second person pronoun) your
zvasa (for svasa)	panting
prasvasa	
pra	very
zvasa	hard breathing
viksepa	distraction
sahabhuvah	
sahabhu	appearing together with
vah	endure

ATTAINING PURITY

Patanjali begins a series here that will carry through *Sutra* 1.39. It emphasizes that the intent of Yoga is purification. Purification is the progressive stilling of the mind. The series covers a broad range of ways to achieve it. He does not say that the seeker must practice them all. Indeed, by continually using 'or,' he implies that any approach will work. Yet, most are illustrations of activity related to the practice of one of the eight individual limbs of Yoga. None of the aphorisms in the series directly illustrates Limb three, sitting (called 'postures' today), but its practice is necessary to *pranayama* and meditation. *Sutra* 2.28 counters that implication by emphasizing the consummate practice of all the limbs as a path to success.

Prevent The Distractions

1.32   Therefore prevent, for the motive of achieving a single true principle, the mind remaining in its unmodified condition of purity (sattva).

tat pratiSedha artham eka tattva abhyAsaH
therefore   prevention   motive   single   a   true principle
the effort of the mind to remain in its unmodified condition of purity (sattva)

In telling us of the effects of preventing the distractions, Patanjali is revealing the trajectory of all Yoga practices. By preventing all the distractions, our minds will be still and we can exist in the calm purity of our inner nature, the state of spiritual existence (sattva). That pure stillness is the 'single true principle.' At its ultimate expression, it is the pure quietness of *brahman*, *isvara*, and soul. There are two ways to interpret the phrase 'single true principle.' First, aspiring to that stillness is the first principle of Yoga practice. Second, that stillness is the first principle of everything, from which everything descends. As the *Sutra*s move forward, that theme will continue to play out.

tat pratiSedha artham eka tattva abhyAsaH

tad (for tat)	therefore
pratisedha	prevention
artha (for artham)	motive

eka	single
tattva	a true principle
abhyasa (for abhyasah)	the effort of the mind to remain in its unmodified condition of purity (*sattva*)

Gladness Of Mind From Yogic Qualities

*1.33   From that time, benevolence, compassion, joyfulness, indifference to plea-
sure, pain, virtuousness, wickedness, and the organs of the senses, bring
gladness of mind.*

maitrI karuNA muditA upekSANAM sukha duHkha
puNya apuNya viSayANAM bhAvanAtaS citta prasAdanam
*benevolence compassion joyful indifference pleasure pain
virtuous wicked the organs of the senses subdue producing from that time gladness of mind.*

The *Sutra* describes a result from continuing Yoga practices that overcome
the obstacles and lead to that purity of mind. 'Gladness of mind,' is a continuing state of inner happiness that comes with lessening of mind activity. It
is a state that cumulatively results from the yogic life style. Through continued dedicated practice, that gladness will be the base for later joy and bliss.

Imagine what it would be like to continually feel and act benevolent
toward others, always feeling kindness and goodwill, and never being critical,
judgmental, or wishing them harm. Perhaps you can see that it would bring
you toward happier internal feelings and a quieter mind. Compassion comes
from truly understanding the suffering of another being, and acting in a way
that honors that knowledge. This does not mean imposing a load on yourself
to solve the problem of the other, but to feel the love that comes with that
understanding and do what your heart (the summation of all your count-
er-balancing internal feelings) causes to happen. This again requires growing
past the opposites of being judgmental, critical, blaming, and condemning.
The result is the same as with benevolence, a happier inner feeling, and a
quieter mind. A feeling of joyfulness that you convey outward will affect others and increase your own happiness. These are not platitudes: they are real

advantages we can gain for our lives: they are true drivers of our momentum along our path toward spirituality.

Developing indifference, or equanimity, in all things under all circumstances, increases the purity, which is the stillness. Polar opposites continually come about as occurring events, but they no longer bring disquiet to the mind. Pleasure, pain, virtuousness, and wickedness are just a few of the world factors that cause us to attach to and become involved with our subconscious meanings and cause our mind to become positively or negatively judgmental, critical, or involved in plotting or planning. When we reach the point at which we observe without emotion, obsessive thinking, or other mind work, we can let our intuition guide our actions and we can have a quieter and more peaceful mind, a mind that feels 'gladness,' the first happy step toward feeling true spiritual joy and bliss.

Indicative of the time and practice required, the result comes when the seeker has also gained control over the sense organs, becoming indifferent to their temptations, a factor discussed in other aphorisms. Such internal 'gladness' (intuitive happiness and peacefulness), clear of the mind-caused disruptions, is necessary to higher forms of meditative practice and living, and to the purposes of Yoga. Methods to overcome the distractions and achieve this peacefulness are within our reach.

Picture again the monk or nun visualized earlier, and now see him or her walking the earth as a radiant benevolent being, emitting waves of compassion and joy, being a generator of that compassion and joy. Visualize the calm centeredness again, able to maintain equanimity in all situations. The waves from others and the world, which continually bounce against that person, are not changing the attitude: he or she is indifferent to them. The wave-generating person is making joy and compassion available. He or she has no obligation or need to ensure that people accept it, and expends no energy in trying to achieve a result. The seeker is on the path, doing the work of the path. Faith is present. Evolving to that attitude and projecting it to others as your visualized monk or nun did, comes to the yogin of devoted practice. When we evolve to a position of continual friendliness, compassion, joy, and indifference in the face of happiness, unhappiness, virtue, vice, and the lures of the material sensory life we attain the higher consciousness.

maitrI karuNA muditA upekSANAM sukha duHkha puNya
apuNya viSayANAM bhAvanAtaS citta prasAdanam

maitri	benevolence
karuna	compassion
mudita	joyful
upeksana (for upeksanam)	indifference
sukha	pleasure
duhkha	pain
punya	virtuous
apunya	wicked
visayanam	
visaya	organs of sense
anam	(untranslated)
bhavanatas	
bhavana	producing
atas	from that time
citta + prasadanam	
cittaprasadana	gladness of mind

Breath-Control As A Step Toward Purity

1.34   Or, retention of exhalation of his/her breath until it hurts.

pracchardana   vidhAraNAbhyAM   vA   prANasya
exhaling   retention hurt   or   his/her breath

There is an astounding insight here that is difficult to comprehend correctly, and often misinterpreted and misrepresented. Although retention of inhalation or exhalation is a widely recognized part of *pranayama* practice, this *Sutra* specifically focuses on having the highly evolved yogin hold an exhalation until it 'hurts,' excluding all reference to inhalation. It would be wrong to take the word 'hurt' too literally, since pain will distract the mind by bringing attention to its presence. The guidance is to hold the exhalation for the maximum endurable period. That condition can be deeply uncomfortable, but does not hurt in the normal sense of the word. The result is increased purity (stilling) of the mind.

Yoga and Buddhist teachings often point to a connection between the breath and the mind, suggesting collaboration. Neither the *Yoga Sutras* nor the core Yoga philosophy provides explanation of why this would be true: the knowledge of the result comes from the experience of early yogins. It seems reasonable to guess that extended exhalation provides more time for the physical purification of the blood by removing the carbon dioxide, impurities, and modified prana, as well as fully emptying the lungs.

Even low-level practice by inexperienced Yogins, extending the exhalation by chanting, sighing, or deliberate *pranayama* techniques would have the same effect. That effect, though, will also be low-level.

pracchardana vidhAraNAbhyAM vA prANasya

pracccchardana (for pracchardana)	exhaling
vidharanabhyam	
vidharana	retention
abhyam	hurt
va	or
pranasya	
prana	breath
sya	(3rd person indicator) - his

Using Sense Objects As A Step Toward Purity

1.35 Or, perseverance in bringing the risen mind to a state of bondage to a sensuous cognition.

viSaya vatI vA pravRttir utpannA manasaH sthiti nibandhanI
*sensuous cognition or risen mind perseverance
to bring into a state bondage*

The use of the terminology 'sensual cognition' is powerful and certainly not accidental. It describes the first level of meditative practice, perception of something through the senses alone. It comes about when we fix our attention on something physical without thinking about it, just letting the senses explore it. This first of the progressive steps toward higher consciousness and union employs the skills of concentration of the mind (dharana), which is the practice of the first of the three meditative limbs (limb 6 of 6, 7, and 8).

Having acquainted us with the idea of higher consciousness and how we can reach it by focusing the mind, the *Sutra* tells us that the yogin can advance toward increased purity by perseverance in binding the mind to some sense detectable target.

We can use any or all of our five senses for single-pointed attention, focusing our sense of hearing, sight, feel, taste, or smell on a target. The target can be any physical object, although natural objects are preferable. At earlier levels of yogic practice, the meditator should avoid objects that have religious or symbolic significance, but such targets may be natural to more experienced meditators. Multiple senses may come into play for many such objects, or the meditator might choose objects that engage only a single sense. Spoken *mantra*s and chants are targets for deep concentration using the sense of hearing. Candle flames, visual symbols, and yantras are examples of visual sense targets, grouped under the term 'trataka.' Focusing fully on tasting something, such as a piece of fruit or spice, is a practice of focusing the mind on the sense of taste. Similar practices exist, or you can easily create them, for the senses of smell and feel. Later *Sutras* detail some special effects that come about through focusing specific senses on specific targets. As with Limb 4 breath control (*pranayama*), Patanjali's book provides no guidance as to details of practice or technique. Just as they have with breathing practices, Masters have developed techniques for sensory meditative work over many hundreds of years.

viSaya vatI vA pravRttir utpannA manasaH sthiti nibandhanI

visaya-vati-pravrtti	a sensuous cognition
va	or
utpanna	risen
manasa (for manasah)	mind
sthiti	perseverance
nibandhani	
nibandha	bondage
ni	to bring into a state

In The Absence Of Pain There Is Purity

1.36 Or, without sorrow there is purity.

viSokA   vA   jyotiSmatI
cessation of sorrow   or   pure

The meaning of this aphorism is simple and clear. *Sutra* 1.5 tells us that all five states of the mind can have pain or be free of pain. Pain creates mental activity. Sorrow is a specific type of pain, that of the mind. When our Yoga practices have brought us to a point where mind experience has no sorrow, we will achieve a higher state of mind purity, a fuller state of stillness. That is part of the progressive evolutionary game of experiencing higher states of consciousness. It is, though, just one factor in the movement toward perfect purity, not a single magic event. The *Sutras* will show that other factors also affect our moving toward the total stillness that brings Absolute Unity. The stages of meditation and their resultant levels of intense absorption enter the equation as prime factors in attaining that stillness. Toward the end, the 'impressions' (karmic memories, soul memories) that have not yet deactivated are the final obstacle.

viSokA vA jyotiSmatI

visoka	cessation of sorrow
va	or
jyotismat (for jyotismati)	pure

Being Desireless For The Material World Brings Purity

1.37   Or, a mind that is desireless for objects of the senses.

vIta   rAga   viSayaM   vA   cittam
desireless   object of sense   or   mind

In case you have not yet caught the drift, bring your awareness to this. The people who developed the philosophy, and Patanjali who documented it, understood that we are all so different that we need a variety of tools for reaching higher consciousness. The *Sutras* have already presented attitude, breathing, mind fixation on sensual objects, and cessation of sorrow. They now provide an illustration of fifth limb withdrawal from the senses as a means of moving toward greater purity. As our connection to the outer world, the senses bring us to desire repeats of all good things we have experienced and to fantasize those we have not experienced. Those desires and sensual fulfillment trap us in material world living.

vIta rAga viSayaM vA cittam

vitaraga	desireless
visaya (for visayam)	object, especially of sense
va	or
citta (for cittam)	mind

Sleep Dreams

1.38   Or, sleep dreams are a foundation for higher knowledge.

svapna nidrA jNAna AlambanaM vA
dream sleep   higher knowledge   foundation   or

Dreams appear as symbols to give us direct intuitive insights while we are in sleep consciousness. That is their function, their way of communicating to us from higher consciousness. We all have dreams, and we all experience times when the dream makes no sense to us in our everyday consciousness. On those occasions, we do not have waking understanding of the meaning of the dream, but the intuitive communication has affected us at a deeper level. At other times, we are conscious of beautiful insights to the meaning of the dream. Care is required though, because we sometimes self-create what we think is an intuitive insight.

Although it is not the intent or thrust of this aphorism, at least one author validly tells us that we can use the dream as our meditative focus, by simply putting the dream in our awareness and focusing our attention on it. The amount of dream content that returns for a rerun during such meditation, even when it has not come forth to normal awareness, may surprise you. This is particularly potent if we have already received an insight and use that insight as our meditative focus.

svapna nidrA jNAna AlambanaM vA

svapna	dream
nidra	sleep

jjana (for jnana)   higher knowledge
alambana (for alambanam)   foundation
va   or

MEDITATION CAN BE ON ANYTHING

You Can Choose Any Meditative Target

1.39   Or, by consuming profound and abstract religious meditation as desired.

yathA   abhimata   dhyAnAd   vA
as desired   consume profound and abstract religious meditation   or

This is perhaps one of the most astounding things revealed in the *Sutras*. The scope of meditation is not limited to those specific targets that the *Sutras* define. The aphorism tells us that it does not matter what you focus on as a consuming meditative target. You can choose others that suit your individual nature and use them to fully absorb your mind.

Patanjali has purposefully used the word for *religious meditation* (*dhyana* - limb 7), not the one for *concentration of the mind* (*dharana* - limb 6), the one for *intense absorption* (*samadhi*), or the one for the integration of those three skills, *unified-restraint* (*samyama*). He intended to restrict the subject of this aphorism to that, signaling that meditation has a different character than the other meditative practices, allowing that broad range of target selection. However, he did not use the pure word dhyana: he used a suffix to emphasize consuming practice of meditation.

yathA abhimata dhyAnAd vA

yathabhimata   as desired
dhyanad
        dhyana   profound and abstract reli-
                                     gious meditation
        ad   consume
va   or

Meditation Can Be On the Smallest Or Largest Thing

1.40   Whether the meditation targets an infinitesimal particle or infinitely great state of being, its end will be the same.

paramANu   paramamahattva   anto'sya   vasIkAra
an infinitesimal particle   infinitely great state of being   its end   the same

This expands the message of the previous aphorism, telling us that we cannot only meditate on anything we desire, but it can be on the smallest possible scale or the largest one, both of which would be meditation on aspects of Nature itself. In bringing this out, Patanjali may have recognized that the normal mind would not have recognized those possibilities, and that it takes much meditative experience for those possibilities to open for us.

When we begin our practice, our range will be naturally limited. Many potential targets just will not occur to us, not be comfortable, or be beyond our range. Our range broadens as we progress. When we have reached a high level, we can choose a meditative target such as the nature of the root particles for our universe, the creation, the entire cosmos, the nature of the god essence, or the meaning of love or compassion, whatever we need to move us along our path. As we progress in our personal evolution, we will have full freedom to choose targets, including things we would not have the insight to choose at lower experiences of consciousness. The most abstract targets are characteristic of the eighth limb, intense absorption.

paramANu paramamahattva anto'sya vasIkAra

paramanu	an infinitesimal particle
paramamahattva	
paramamahat	infinitely great
tva	the state of being
anto'sya	
anta	end
sya	(3rd person indicator) its
vasikara	the same *(This is a linguistic idem' - it indicates 'the same as that previously referred to' - in this case that would be the state of purity)*

DISCUSSION
THE FORMS OF SAMADHI

Patanjali deliberately began his book with this part (*pada*) about *samadhi* (intense absorption), the revered states of high consciousness. At the highest and iconic development of *samadhi*, a total stilling of the mind enables experiencing that intense absorption in the pure state of *primal consciousness*. Few attain that state, though, and the word *samadhi* (intense absorption) covers seven consciousness states, seven types of *samadhi* that evolve stepwise. This progression is one of the more confusing and daunting sections of the *Sutras*, in part due to the variability in translations, interpretations, and 2000 years of reinterpretation and adaptation contributed by ever-changing gurus, sects, 'traditions,' and religions. To help overcome that, these paragraphs provide a background for the following ten difficult aphorisms.

As outlined above, much of the difficulty with understanding those ten aphorisms stems from three Sanskrit words, *samapatti*, *samprajnata*, and *asamprajnata*: their descriptions in the modern books on the *Yoga Sutras* are often unclear and they significantly vary from one author to another. Adding to the difficulty of comprehension, after careful exposure of progressive steps, Patanjali has now suddenly introduced the full range of states of beyond-the-mind consciousness experience. They are a huge step into a zone of existence that yogins only experience after serious long-term practice of a Yoga lifestyle. The serious business of *samadhi* is suddenly before our eyes here, with no preparation, softening, or simplification. He does not tell us that the meditator and the meditative practice would necessarily each go through sometimes great transformation to reach advancing stages of *samadhi*, including the *samapatti* introduced in *Sutra* 1.41, the next Thread. He leaves it to us to recognize where beginner's meditation evolves into something more.

It is easy to become confused and intimidated by the, sometimes esoteric, interpretations. It becomes easier when you understand and accept that *samapatti* is not a separate type of *samadhi*, but simply a state of oneness that can characterize *samadhi* states resulting from meditation on physical objects (and only when meditating on physical objects). Literally, *samapatti* translates to

'coming together,' or 'falling into a state, or condition.' *Sutra* 1.41, for example, tells us a factual truth: when a highly experienced meditator has attained
great skill at prolonged single-pointed focus on a physical meditative target,
a flower for example, the meditator's mind will be free of all other activity.
In that state, the perceived object (the flower), the perceiver (i.e. the meditator), and the sense organs detecting the object 'come together.' When that
happens, they become one thing, with no distinction between them. That
is *samapatti* oneness, and it applies to the meditative state that results from
meditatively focusing the senses (not the mind) on elements of the physical
world. The *Sutras* will tell us that *samadhi* states with names containing the
element *vitarka* (i.e. *savitarka* and *nirvitarka*) potentially have that *samapatti*
characteristic of oneness with a physical object.

Although meditation on subtle objects and higher-level spiritual meditation also generate oneness, the word *samapatti* does not apply, because the
senses and sense organs are not involved. Samapatti refers to oneness with
physical objects only. To be clear, the states that are higher than *savitarka* and
nirvitarka (*savicara, nirvicara, ananda, asmita*, and nirbija, are not *samapatti
samadhi*, even though they bring an experience of forms of oneness: those
oneness experiences are progressively more global and less object-centered.

In 1.17 Patanjali lists four progressive consciousness states within two
categories, the first (*savitarka*), which is in both the *samapatti* category and
the *samprajnata* category, because the mind is involved and because a physical object with its potential for oneness is involved. In *samprajnata* experiences, the meditator's previous perspectives of the target of meditation,
gained through experience in the material/sensory realm, will taint the newly
gained intuitive knowledge of the target. The second, *nirvitarka*, is even more
subject to *samapatti* physical oneness, because it is *asamprajnata* (not *samprajnata*), with no min involvement. The third (*savicara*) is *samprajnata* (mind
involvement), but is not *samapatti* because the object of meditation is in the
subtle realm, not the physical realm. No other *samprajnata* experience exists.
Experience of *samadhi* levels 4-6 (*nirvicara, ananda*, and *asmita*) is always
asamprajnata: the mind is not involved.

To be clear: the physical objects of *nirvitarka* and *savitarka* meditation are anything that is made of particles and takes up space. From a meditative target standpoint, it is anything that we can detect with our senses. The *savicara*, *nirvicara*, *ananda*, and *asmita* meditations involve targets from the subtle realm. A subtle realm target might be a symbol, thought, idea, abstract concept, or any of such philosophical ideas as the subtle elements of the universe, the five bases for the senses, the five organs of activity, the five 'earth' elements, or many other things. The highest form before Absolute Unity, *nirbija samadhi*, is void of mind content of any type and has a greater form of oneness: it is the oneness of everything, the experience of the pure unblemished consciousness of the divine

The *nirbija* state employs no objects as targets and carries no material world knowledge and no impressions. It is neither *samprajnata* nor *asamprajnata*. It has the characteristic of oneness, but there is no physical object to know. The oneness is with the entirety of the cosmic creation.

The chart below shows the progression of the six consciousness states that lead to the seventh state of *nirbija*.

Vitarka (uncertainty) (two types of *samapatti* - achievement of physical oneness)

1. *Savitarka samapatti samprajnata samadhi*
   Physical object meditative state with uncertainty and consideration (mind)
2. *Nirvitarka samapatti asamprajnata samadhi*
   Physical object meditative state with certainty, non-consideration (no mind)

Vicara (consideration)

3. *Savicara samprajnata samadhi*
   Subtle object meditative state with uncertainty and consideration (mind)
4. *Nirvicara asamprajnata samadhi*
   Subtle object meditative state with certainty, without consideration (no mind)

5. *Ananda asamprajnata samadhi*
   Meditative state without consideration (no mind) experiencing Divine Joy
6. *Asmita asamprajnata samadhi*
   Meditative state without consideration (no mind) experiencing I-am-ness
7. *Nirbija samadhi*
   Seedless meditative state experiencing the (Primal Consciousness of *brahman*)

Patanjali's definition of the evolution of the universe in *Sutra* 2.19 has been the basis for much added philosophical definition over time, with little information about the sources. The trend of those advancements shows the progress of personal evolution through experiences of ever-higher consciousness states is exactly the opposite flow of the evolution states of the universe; since universe evolution moved progressively toward ever-lower consciousness states, some have dubbed it as 'devolution' (de-evolution). In keeping with the philosophy that the creator does not experience past, present, and future; all of the universe's progressive consciousness states still exist for the seeker to experience.

Summary Of Universe Evolution And Personal Evolution

The progressive universe evolution, as outlined below, comes from sources other than the *Sutras*:   the inclusion here is to provide insight to the relationship between evolution and devolution, and does not claim to be an authoritative or completely accurate view of those details.

PRE-UNIVERSE EVOLUTION

Source of universe evolution - *brahman*

The primal soul/source, transcendent of the yet-to-come universe

PERSONAL EVOLUTION

Kaivalya, the end of mortality

FIRST PHASE OF UNIVERSE EVOLUTION

Foundation of the universe - *isvara, sat*

The Absolute, immanent in the universe

Carries twenty-four principles for universe creation, the Laws, and the *gunas*

The creative trinity of sat-om-tat is in place

SEVENTH STAGE OF PERSONAL EVOLUTION

Experience of soul, *brahman*

Seedless *nirbija* - complete unity

SECOND PHASE OF UNIVERSE EVOLUTION

Mula prakrti (*Prana*)

Carries the twenty-four principles for universe creation, the Laws, and the *gunas*

Primal conscious energy/force of the universe

Unity of the I-sense, presence of the ego

SIXTH STAGE OF PERSONAL EVOLUTION - experience of root ego, *Asmita* - I-am-ness

THIRD PHASE OF UNIVERSE EVOLUTION
 Maha Prakrti (Creative *prana*)
 Establishes the seven powers of universe creation
 Christ/Krishna/Cosmic consciousness is active as the seventh power

FIFTH STAGE OF PERSONAL EVOLUTION
 Experience of cosmic consciousness
 Ananda - joy

FOURTH PHASE OF UNIVERSE EVOLUTION
 Para Prakrti (Subtle *prana*)
 Establishes causal and subtle bodies of the universe
 Creates 5 Great Elements in subtle form (tanmatras)
  (Earth, fire, water, air, and aether)
 Creates 5 instruments of perception in their subtle form
  (jnanendriyas)
  (Hearing, seeing, feeling, tasting, and smelling)

THIRD AND FOURTH STAGES OF PERSONAL EVOLUTION
 Experience of subtle universe
 Savicara and nirvicara - subtle object meditative states

FIFTH PHASE OF UNIVERSE EVOLUTION

Apara prakrti (Physical *prana*)

Creates 5 Great Elements in physical form (mahabhuttas)
(Earth, fire, water, air, and aether)

Creates 5 instruments of perception in their physical form
(jnanendriyas)
(Hearing, seeing, feeling, tasting, and smelling)

Creates 5 principles for performing actions (karmendriyas)
(Procreate, excrete, talk, walk, and manual skill)

Creates 5 types of physical *prana*
(Crystallizing, assimilating, eliminating, metabolizing,
and circulating)

Creates sensory mind - (*manas*)

Creates feeling state of mind - (*citta*)

FIRST AND SECOND STAGES OF PERSONAL EVOLUTION

Experience of physical universe

Savitarka and nirvitarka - physical object meditative states

SIXTH PHASE OF UNIVERSE EVOLUTION

Fully created Physical/Subtle/Causal Universe

PRE-EVOLUTION OF PERSONAL CONSCIOUSNESS

Human consciousness condition - Everyday active consciousness

SAMAPATTI
ONENESS OF THE OBSERVER, THE
SENSES, AND THE OBSERVED

1.41 *Born in consequence of diminished mind activity, like a crystal, the one*
who perceives, the organs of sense, and the objects of sensual perception
assume the color of a near object, consequently causing becoming the object.

kSINa vRtter abhijAtasya iva maNer grahItR grahaNa grAhyeSu

tat   stha   tad   aNjanatA   samApattiH
diminished   activity   born in consequence of it   like   crystal   one who
perceives   an organ of sense   the objects of sensual perception
assuming the color of any near object   consequently   causing   becoming

Compared to his slow, small-step exposure of the elements of a Yoga life, Patanjali has now taken a large step toward announcing and describing the higher results of purification through stilling the mind: what he tells us here sounds esoteric and unreachable at first reading, but multiple readings and experience will lead to more accurate comprehension. Many *Sutras* presented before this one have attempted to bring us to understand that the point and purpose of Yoga is to purify the mind through stilling of its activity. That stilling through our meditative practices can produce a state of 'oneness' with a physically sensed object, the state of *samapatti*. This *Sutra* intends to improve our understanding of 'oneness.'

Three things must always come into play while meditating on a physical object: the meditator (the one who perceives), the sense organs that enable the perception, and the object of perception. The result comes about after dedicated practice, when those three factors enter a state of mutuality in which no awareness of their separateness occurs. From a consciousness viewpoint, which obviously differs from a physical world viewpoint, we 'become' the object of our meditative focus. The *Sutra* defines it as coloration of all three factors in the way a clear crystal absorbs the colors that are nearby.

Characterizing this from another angle, when the mind is strong in its single-pointed focus on an object, the vibrations of that single focus can cause the effects of outside vibrations to dwindle so significantly that there is little more than the single set of mental vibrations caused by the object. In that purified situation, the target object that emits the vibrations, the sensory apparatus that perceives them, and the mind of the observer resonate, becoming indistinguishable from each other in the 'oneness' of *samapatti*.

From another compatible perspective, when we succeed in harmonizing the mind, sense organs, and object through our meditative practice, we no longer evaluate the object, describe it, or make relative judgments. Our awareness hones in on its root nature, becoming one with that for the duration of the experience.

Patanjali does not yet reveal the truth that this is just a preamble: when the yogin experiences higher levels of consciousness and begins to understand the root nature of the universe, everything truly is just one thing, a unity, or 'oneness,' with no separations and distinctions. Individuation is an illusion that came to exist at a specific phase of universe evolution. The type of *samapatti samadhi* described here is an introductory experience of that ultimate state of unity, a beckoning to continue.

kSINa vRtter abhijAtasya iva maNer grahItR grahaNa grAhyeSu tat stha tad aNjanatA samApattiH

ksina	diminished
vrtti (for vrtter)	activity
abhijatasya	
abhijata	born in consequence of
sya	(3rd person indicator) it
iva	like
mani (for maner)	crystal
grahitr	one who perceives
grahana	an organ of sense
grahya (for grahyesu)	the objects of sensual perception
tatstha	assuming the color of any near object
tad	consequently
anjanata	cause
samapatti	becoming

THE STAGES OF HIGHER CONSCIOUSNESS

Many think of *samadhi*, 'intense absorption,' as a single thing, but it is not: *samadhi* is a category for multiple named levels (steps or stages), of evolutionary progression. This next section, which includes 1.42 through 1.44, describes the first four progressions within that state. These are all 'with seed' (*sabija*). 'Seed' means that karmic memories also affect the perception. Only the highest level, *nirbija*, is 'seedless,' pure experience of high consciousness with no karmic memories. Patanjali will wait until the end of his final *pada*, at *Sutra* 4.29, to describe that state.

You should be aware that, for all types of *samadhi*, the experience dissipates before returning to the everyday world. It holds only during the meditative episode. Yet, resultant permanent and progressive change takes place in the physical body and the mind: these changes leave noticeable cumulative effects and bring changes to the life of the meditator. As they accumulate, it becomes easier to enter *samadhi* states and to stay in them for longer periods.

Please be aware that Vedism, Vedanta, Buddhism, Hinduism, later interpretations of the *Sutras*, and other sources have introduced alternate *samadhi* naming schemes and classifications. Some of them propose additional stages of *samadhi*, and redefine Patanjali's stages. Since all those variations add confusion and do not meaningfully cross-relate, this book stays strictly to the language used in the *Yoga Sutras*. It is also helpful to maintain awareness that the meanings of Sanskrit words have evolved during its long history: dialects have developed, and authors sometimes mix Sanskrit with Pali, Tamil, Hindi, and other languages. Because of that, the spellings of words can vary from one book to another.

When Patanjali later introduces us to the eight limbs of Yoga, we will see that three stages of evolution of consciousness experience follow progressively from mastery of sense withdrawal, the fifth limb. The first progression comes about through *concentration of the mind* (*dharana*), the sixth limb practice, with physical objects as the target. Seventh limb *meditation* (*dhyana*), with subtle realm of mind as the media, and eighth limb *intense absorption* (*samadhi*), where the meditator becomes absorbed in experiencing even higher levels of consciousness follow that. The discussion here precedes that explanation, and of the integration of those three practices, which Patanjali introduces as *samyama*, 'three kinds in one,' in *Sutra* 3.4. It is informally called '*unified-restraint*' in this book.

Stage 1 Of Higher Consciousness
Focusing On A Physical Target
savitarka samapatti samprajnata samadhi

*1.42 Then the object of the senses, its name, knowledge of it, and false notions
are mixed, falling into a state of uncertain samadhi. (Specifically and technically, savitarka samapatti samprajnata samadhi.)*

tatra   Sabda   artha   jNAna   vikalpaiH   saM-
kIrNA   savitarkA   samApattiH
*then   name   object of the senses   knowledge   false notions   mixed
uncertain   falling into a state*

This *Sutra* builds on the preceding one, which describes the baseline condition of *samapatti*, the state in which the meditator, sense organ, and targeted
object merge into oneness. The formal Yoga terminology tells us that this first
of four samadhi states that are about to unfold is *savitarka samapatti*, a meditative condition with doubts and uncertainty, which is the 'uncertainty' level
of consciousness introduced in 1.17. (Note: to be clear, this is *savitarka samapatti samprajnata samadhi*). The 'objects' of meditation in this case and the
next one (1.43) are sense detectable, from the physical realm of the universe.
Sutra 1.44 discusses objects that are not sense detectable, being in the 'subtle' realm of the universe. The *Sutras* will later show that physical objects are
targets for the skill of 'concentration,' the practice of the sixth limb of Yoga.
In that limb, observation of physical objects uses the senses, and only the
senses, to examine an object. Focused concentration using the senses can only
target physical material objects. The senses cannot experience subtle objects.
When focusing the attention on a stone, flower, or other physical object we
can reach the first two stages of higher consciousness, shown in this aphorism
and the next, 1.43, but only those two. To experience higher levels than that
we will need to shift the focus to the subtle realm, as described in *Sutra* 1.44.

Focusing the attention so fully that nothing other than the object enters
it, enabling the oneness, is the full realization of this practice. Insight about
the root nature of the object then arises. This is not a mind event, a thing of
reason. It is an experiencing of the object from the point of view of a different
consciousness, as if we were the objects.

The 'uncertainty,' or lack of certainty in the accuracy, arises because the
insight provided by this first stage is not pure. The effects of our everyday
knowledge of the object, including its characteristics and uses, are present

during the meditative experience. We may experience its name, the emotions it generates, memories that are associated with it, its physical characteristics, history, and much more. We also have false ideas about the object that we do not readily set aside. The intuitive, insightful experience we gain, arguments, or doubts from the mind (manas), combined with all these things affect the experience. The result is an unclear, imperfect, and uncertain understanding of the object.

tatra Sabda artha jNAna vikalpaiH saMkIrNA savitarkA samApattiH

tatra	then
zabda (for sabda)	name
artha	object of the senses
jjana (for jnana)	knowledge
vikalpa (for vikalpaih)	false notion
samkirna	mixed
savitarka	uncertain
samapatti (for samapattih)	falling into any state

Stage Two Of Higher Consciousness
Focusing On A Physical Target
nirvitarka samapatti asamprajnata samadhi

1.43   Inconsiderate (i.e. inconsiderate samadhi) is purified memory nearly void of the own form of the object of the senses and entirely without description. (Specifically and technically, it is nirvitarka samapatti asampraj-nata samadhi)

smRti   pariSuddhau   sva   rUpa   SUnya   iva   artha
mAtra   nirbhAsA   nirvitarkA
*memory   purified   its own   form   void of   nearly   object of the senses
entirely   without description   inconsiderate*

If the sensory concentration on a physical object has sufficient focus and prolongation, a feat achieved through accumulated practice, native ability, or both, the meditator can reach the second stage of higher consciousness, the *nirvitarka-samapatti* stage of *samadhi (nirvitarka samapatti asamprajnata samadhi).* In this second stage, the targeted object of the senses is just barely in the mind, which is not thinking about it, and has no awareness of descriptions, definitions, or other previous knowledge. He or she comes to know the object perfectly and intimately, as an experience, not as an intellectual examination. All knowledge is intuitive, coming directly from the zone of consciousness the yogin has entered. The insights that arise about the nature of the object are pure, untarnished by our past experience or learning, or by the mind in any way. Due to the non-involvement of the mind, which could color things, it is free of doubt and uncertainty.

smRti pariSuddhau sva rUpa SUnya iva artha mAtra nirbhAsA nirvitarkA

smrti	memory
parizuddha (for parisuddhau)	purified
sva	its own
rupa	form
zunya (for sunya)	void of
iva	nearly
artha	object of the senses
matra	entirely
nirbhasa	
nir	without
bhasa	description
nirvitarka	inconsiderate

Stages 3 And 4 - Focusing On A Subtle (Nonphysical) Target

savicara samprajnata samadhi
nirvicara asamprajnata samadhi

1.44 *Moving even nearer, with consideration given (i.e. samadhi with consideration), and without consideration given (i.e. samadhi without consideration), relate to the subtle sphere. (Specifically and technically these are savicara samprajnata samadhi and nirvicara asamprajnata samadhi).*

etayA eva savicArA nirvicArA ca sUkSma viSayA vyAkhyAtA

> *moving come near   even   that to which consideration is given   not*
> *needing any consideration   and   subtle   sphere   to relate*

The advancement of personal evolution into experiencing a new level of *samadhi* continues. Since the senses are not involved, the word *samapatti* does not apply to the stages described in this *Sutra* or to any stages higher than this one. One *Sutra* covers two stages in the evolutionary process, both of which come about when using subtle realm (nonphysical) objects as targets. All invisible, undetectable, conceptual, or abstract things are nonphysical objects, as well as all the underlying forces, nonphysical elements, energies, and such. Those not having familiarity with those deeper constituents of the universe could target love, compassion, hatred, time, space, infinity, consciousness, mathematics, life, symbols, ideas, memories, insights, or many other things as abstract meditative targets. With no physical object to detect through the senses, the target object exists within the mind. When focusing on that subtle target has become sufficiently single-pointed and prolonged, so that the meditator reaches full understanding of it (a different oneness): intuition will provide new insight about the nature of the target.

The first of these two, the third stage in the evolution of consciousness experience, is the *savicara* stage of *samadhi* (*savicara samprajnata samadhi*), in which the mind independently considers the subtle object during meditation. As with *savitarka*, previous learning and experience will taint the insights gained. The knowledge of the object (subtle this time) will be great and the interruption by thoughts less than in any stage up to this point.

The fourth stage is a continuing evolution, an extension of the *savicara* state of consciousness experience: this is the *nirvicara* stage of *samadhi* (*nirvicara asamprajnata samadhi*), a stage 'without consideration,' that is to say 'without mind involvement.' The intuitive realizations at this stage will be pure identification with the subtle target, experiencing its natural reality without any distortion by the mind's involvement with previous knowledge, names, words, thoughts, or anything else. The meditator will experience the pure evolutionary consciousness level of the subtle realm of the universe.

Patanjali will make clear that this fourth stage is a deeper, different, and more fulfilling experience, bringing great advancement and permanent changes to the mind and physical body.

etayA eva savicArA nirvicArA ca sUkSma viSayA vyAkhyAtA

etaya		
	eta	come near
	ya	moving
eva		even
savicara		that to which consideration is given
nirvicara		not needing any consideration
ca		and
suksma		subtle
visaya		sphere (of influence or activity)
vyakhya (for vyakhyata)		relate to

1.45   Your subtle sphere, moreover, has no distinguishing marks or termination.

sUkSma viSayatvaM ca aliNga paryavasAnam
subtle   sphere your   moreover   no distinguishing marks   termination

Having introduced us to *samadhi* states of *savicara* and *nirvicara* resulting from meditation on subtle targets, the *Sutras* now tell us that things of the subtle world are not like things in the physical world. The subtle things have no distinguishing 'marks' or characteristics, no dimensions, and no atoms or other physical entities. They just 'are.' More importantly to us, the aphorism points to our own individual subtle 'body,' one of the three 'bodies' of our being. It tells us that our personal subtle sphere of influence, as much as we like to describe it as being the same shape as the physical body, has no dimensions or identifying characteristics.

sUkSma viSayatvaM ca aliNga paryavasAnam

suksma		subtle
visayatvam		
	visaya	sphere
	tvam	(2nd person pronoun) your
ca		moreover

alinga   no distinguishing mark (see
                                          notes above)
paryavasana (for paryavasanam)   termination

All These Types of Consciousness Are 'with seed'

1.46   Inviolably the same, these are intense absorptions (i.e. samadhis) contain-
ing seed.

tA eva sabIjaH samadhiH
inviolability   same   containing   seed   intense absorption

All types of consciousness experience discussed so far are 'with seed.' A popular misconstruing of this *Sutra* interprets the 'seed' to be the target, the object that is the starting point for a meditative session, but it is not that. Seeds are the deep eternal 'impressions,' residues of actions and events that accumulate under the process of *karma*. Informally and inaccurately, but often used, authors call them 'subliminal impressions,' 'subliminal activators,' 'karmic memories,' 'soul memories,' 'deep memories,' or 'subconscious memories.' Seeds always produce mental vibrations that interfere with stillness: the most evolved yogins can eventually reach a pure vibration-free meditative state, a state of full stillness. Only the very highest form of *samadhi, nirbija samadhi*, is 'seedless.' In that seedless state no *active* seeds (impressions) remain.

Patanjali will clarify the concept of a seed (*bija*) later, as he shows how karmic memories accumulate and how Yoga practice deactivates them. In all consciousness states explored so far, even through the very high *asmita samadhi*, seeds remain active after the consciousness experience passes. Although many Yoga practices enter into the deactivation of seeds, the reaching of such high level stages of consciousness experience does not directly affect them. Yet, neutralizing the seeds is one of the ultimate goals of Yoga, necessary to the ultimate freeing the yogin from the effects of *karma*.

This *Sutra* is a stage-setting statement, preparing us for later discussion of what happens to seeds when a yet higher level of consciousness occurs.

tA eva sabIjaH samadhiH

ta	inviolability
eva	same
sabija (for sabijah)	containing seed
samadhi (for samadhih)	intense absorption

STAGE 4 EXPERIENCE

Stage 4 Experiences Root Tranquility

1.47 Not needing consideration (nirvicara samadhi), there is the infallible tranquility of the Supreme Spirit.

nirvicAra vaiSAradye' adhyAtma prasAdaH
not needing any consideration infallibility Supreme Spirit tranquility

Reaching *nirvicara asamprajnata samadhi* is a transitional event of large magnitude. For the first time, free of contamination by the mind, the yogin experiences the consciousness level of the Supreme Spirit oversoul, the root nature of all. The yogin, at least briefly, experiences that ultimate peace. Insight comes as to the relationship of the immanent and transcendental soul to the Absolute. At first, the periods of absorption in soul consciousness are intermittent and brief, but the connection stays active even during the return to normal consciousness. This makes reentry easy and automatic when the yogin is ready for it. The yogin at the high end of this experience, when nearly ready to move on to the next level, becomes absorbed in peace for longer periods, free of the suffering that is the human condition. When that suffering-free absorption becomes continuous, the next phase will begin.

nirvicAra vaiSAradye' adhyAtma prasAdaH

nirvicara	not needing any consideration
vaizaradya (for vaisaradye')	infallibility
adhyatma	Supreme Spirit
prasada (for prasadah)	tranquility

Truth-bearing Knowledge

1.48 Therein, there is truth-bearing knowledge.

RtaMbharA   tatra   prajNA
truth bearing   therein   knowledge

In entering the new zone of knowledge, we have entered the zone of ultimate Truth, the Truth that underlies our transient false views of things. At the peak of this experience, we receive knowledge that exists in the hidden Reality - truth-bearing knowledge, but not all of it. The rest will unfold at higher levels of experience. It comes to us unbidden, as a surprise, while we experience the deep consciousness. Neither the intellect nor the sensory apparatus provide it. It is intuitive insight.

RtaMbharA tatra prajNA

rtambhara
    rta (for rtam)   truth
    bhara   bearing
tatra   therein
prajja (for prajna)   knowledge

Higher Knowledge Is Different Knowledge

1.49   Knowledge from that taught or reflection pleases, there is a difference from that of the sphere of inexhaustibleness you go constantly striving to obtain.

Sruta   anumAna   prajNAbhyAm   anya   viSayA   viSeSa   arthtvAt
taught   reflection   knowledge please   inexhaustibleness   sphere difference   to strive to obtain to go constantly you

This knowledge is unlike any that we have known before. No matter how much it pleases us, or convinces us, no teaching by anyone, sacred tradition, or study of scriptures, philosophy, learned books or personal reflection could provide it. We cannot attain it with consciousness held in the material/sensory domain or with activity of the mind: we must enter the sphere of higher consciousness. It is not possible to project into that zone and anticipate what it would be like. It is different in both content and quality of knowledge. It is a revelation from the subtlest and deepest consciousness, where knowledge of the root nature of everything resides. Yet, although it is knowledge of Truths, it is not yet omniscient knowledge, knowledge of everything.

Sruta anumAna prajNAbhyAm anya viSayA viSeSa arthtvAt

zruta (for sruta)	taught
anumana	reflection
prajnabhyam	
prajja (for prajna)	knowledge
bhyam	please
anya	inexhaustibleness
visaya	sphere
vizesa (for visesa)	difference
arthtvat	
arth	to strive to obtain
tva	(indicates 2nd person) you
at	to go constantly

New Impressions (Karmic Memories) Are Prevented

1.50   Another impression is produced, preventing new impressions.

tajjah saMskAro'nya saMskAra pratibandhI
produced impression another impression being prevented

Patanjali tells us here that the greatly increased purification produced by the *nirvicara* experience not only brings truth-bearing knowledge, but also generates a special karmic memory that will block accumulation of future karmic memories. The *Sutras* will later tell us that the key to full purity leading to Absolute Unity is the deactivation of the last active karmic memory. If we were to continue adding active impressions, we might never deactivate all of them.

The arrival at this new state means the yogin can begin to reduce the remaining count of such impressions. It is perhaps the most dramatic turning point in a yogins life, a point of no return. Though it is a life-altering event, it does not end the game. Life will never be the same again, but the altered person will return to the world and live an externally normal life. Life will go on and personal evolution will continue. The seeker will still seek, but with a different viewpoint and an altered way of being in the world.

A Speculation About Enlightenment

Some who have achieved a state that they call 'enlightenment' tell us that while experiencing that consciousness, nothing else exists. The flash of awareness stills all memories, surroundings, sensations, thoughts, equivocations, emotions, and everything else. The seeker is temporarily within pure still consciousness, the state of oneness with everything. According to some, intuitive implants such as 'I am He who has become I and all things,' 'I am God,' 'God is the only reality,' everything is one thing,' or 'the Absolute is all that exists' might arise. On return to normal consciousness, the ego will no longer function, but is still present. The I-sense that generated the individuality of consciousness remains active. The yogin will now walk earth without ego, having no remaining attachments, having immunity from accumulating additional karmic memories, and be in a state of equanimity. It is a lasting experience: it does not go away on return to normal consciousness. Later experience in higher consciousness states will enhance it and build upon it. Many future actions will be actions that follow the will of the divine, not personal will.

These descriptions are the descriptions we hear from those who have experienced that extremely high state of consciousness along the evolutionary path toward Absolute Unity. Although Patanjali never uses the term 'enlightenment,' this may be the earliest of the stages at which something akin to it occurs, or even the one stage at which it occurs. Support for this is in *Sutra* 3.9 where Patanjali refers to this stage as a stage of 'awakening,' the term used by the Gautama Buddha, long before Patanjali was born. We only recently began to use 'enlightenment' in its place, which has no specific spiritual meaning.

An unresolvable puzzle exists that this speculation cannot attempt to resolve. Many mystics and gurus have been 'enlightened,' but the experience has not affected their later behavior and teaching in the same ways or in the way that enlightenment affected the Gautama Buddha. Perhaps its after-effects are stronger or different in some seekers than in others. Perhaps it is simply because the individual *karmas* called for different roles to play, cultural influences enhanced how they acted, or there are different levels of whatever enlightenment is, if it is a real and specific thing. Even harder to resolve, there can be little doubt that Jesus Christ and Krishna taught from the same level of consciousness, without any talk of an enlightenment-like experience. Prophets, such as Muhammad, could not have brought their extensive teachings to the world without a divine connection.

Perhaps the best perspective is that 'enlightenment' has become an impressive modern catchall term covering a range of high experiences. Sects of modern Buddhism, for example have lowered the bar significantly. Telling followers 'enlightenment' is within everyone's reach, without saying that they are not referring to 'awakening,' or defining what 'enlightenment' means.

tajjah saMskAro'nya saMskAra pratibandhI

tajja (for tajjah)	produced
samskaro'nya	
samskara	impression
anya (for 'nya)	another
samskara	impression
pratibandhin (for pratibandhi)	being prevented

HIGHER CONSCIOUSNESS 'WITHOUT SEED'
(nirbija samadhi)

In *Sutra* 1.51, Patanjali begins to show the evolutionary step that brings the yogin to experience the level of *samadhi* that is the doorway to Absolute Unity, the 'without seed' (*nirbija*) state, which occurs when no active impressions (seeds, karmic memories) remain. In 4.29 of the *Sutras*, he will describe the Dharma Cloud state that results from it. Experience at the just-discussed *savicara* level began the momentum toward the deactivation of seeds. Later in the book, Patanjali will show many factors entering into the seed deactivation during the two stages between *savicara samadhi* and *nirbija samadhi*. Although it may seem quick and easy as you read the *Sutras*, it is a slow evolutionary process. It will vary from individual to individual and, depending on personal *karma* situations, may span additional physical lifetimes.

Unlike earlier states, *nirbija* is not a temporary stage; the acquired stilling is permanent, allowing the meditator to continually experience Spirit (*brahman*) and its creative energy. Understanding the process of creation, the yogin may now intuitively (not intellectually) understand what it means to say that each created thing, including the self, is a wave or vibration within godness, in which the individual four-part being (soul, causal body, subtle body, physical body), and all bodies and things within the universe are a single existence. During the experience, no awareness of materiality exists. The universe does not exist. Everything is spirituality, godness. The seeker will see that the material universe and all its things are illusions formed within the godness; all differentiations between them dissolve.

In this highest and final stage of *samadhi*, on the threshold of the ultimate Yoga experience of liberation from materiality (Absolute Unity) there is a supraconsciousness experience of pure soul intuition, direct unimpeded perception of the soul. No mental processes remain, and full transcendence of the individualized ego needs has occurred. There is nothing but immersion in the omnipresence of *brahman/isvara*.

There is not immediate death as some assume, but a return to finish the final living experience. On returning to the living world, the state of ecstasy continues and the seeker perceives the world differently. There is now permanent and irrevocable unity of the *brahman/isvara*, with the aspirant in the suffering-free state. In this state, the yogin now experiences unity of the individual soul, the local god-force (*sat, isvara*), and the underlying Absolute primal existence (*brahman*), as well as all intermediate levels of existence. Freedom from all past and present karmic influences has come about and the meditator experiences the 'peace that passes all understanding.' The yogin exists in the realm of material/sensory consciousness, but is without an ego and free of all attachments.

1.51   That is near to complete control and suppression - seedless intense absorption (nirbija samadhi).

> tasya   api   nirodhe   sarva   nirodhAn   nirbijaH   samadhiH
> *that   near   control   completely   suppression   seedless   intense absorption*

Over many lifetimes it is possible to evolve to experience yet another level of consciousness, approaching the ultimate goal of Yoga (yoking or union), the state of Absolute Unity. Few reach it during any generation, but the Gautama Buddha is a prime example. His followers tell us that in reaching *nirvana* he was 'extinguished,' or 'liberated.' from having another material life. This 'seedless' state of consciousness, *nirbija samadhi*, transcends all ego, motivation, mind, and impressions. All *samskara* impressions (karmic memories) are inactive. In this state, the meditator fully experiences primal consciousness, not just harmonizing with it or tasting it, but perceiving the universe in all its detail, with even past, present, and future merged into oneness without distinction. The seeker, soul, and god-essence are all one timeless thing.

The yogin returning from this experience will be an obviously different person in the eyes of others. All ego experience will permanently cease. No karmic memories will ever reactivate and new ones will never form: the state of being is pure, still, and unmotivated. The person knows his or her identity and remembers his or her life history, but those things no longer affect the life as they previously did. Little separates the being from Absolute Unity, except to complete the current lifetime.

tasya api nirodhe sarva nirodhAn nirbijaH samadhiH

tasya	
ta	(pronoun indicator) that
sya	(3rd person indicator)
api	near
nirodha (for nirodhe)	confinement
sarva	completely
nirodhana (for nirodhan)	
nirodha	suppression
an	(untranslated)
nirbija (for nirbijah)	seedless
samadhi (for samadhih)	intense absorption

SADHANA PADA

THE PART ON PRACTICE

(Sutras 2.1 - 2.55)

Buddhism, Christianity, Hinduism, and Islam, among others, share Yoga's intent to provide tools that enable us humans, to self-reduce the suffering (mental chaos and pain) that is a companion to human awareness. Each has performed superbly in fulfilling that intention. However, the teachers of each share an illusion that they have the singular answer to solving humanities woes. "If they only knew" drives them toward the goal of bringing their wonderful teachings to all humanity. It has never happened and will never happen, and many wars that increase suffering have resulted from it. Vast numbers among the masses live in horrible conditions that could never respond to these offerings, because starving, homeless people strive for survival alone. Within the reachable populations, relief is not universal, even among the religious communities; many never receive the relief and even worsen. Great numbers of people do receive some relief, often significant. A large number are able to conquer a great measure of their suffering. Small numbers reach the apex where no suffering remains.

It is all individual, not a thing of the masses. The masses improve only as the summary count of improved individuals rises. These wonderful efforts and teachings offer tools that individuals can choose to use. Much of the differentiation between individuals is just the natural order of the universe. Given any activity, small numbers of people will be at the positive and negative extremes and a large number will be at points between the extremes, most being average. Genetics, circumstances, and *karma* all have roles in determining where an individual falls on that curve, and they are all beyond the immediate direct control of the individual. If you are interested in spreading the word of Yoga broadly, try the following practical exercise. In a city, sit at an outdoor coffee shop table observing the stream of people in a special way. As each comes into full view ask yourself, "Could I bring Yoga to this person." You will understand many reasons why you could not. Then guess at the number of people who live in the city where you are sitting and the number who are doing Yoga.

Among those who do accept Yoga as a life style, which is a small percent of those who do Yoga, there are many obstacles to moving toward serenity and away from chaos. They are often self-created and are self-controllable through awareness and practice. One obstacle is in the human nature to want to reach for the ultimate, to get the best there is as fast as possible. The discipline, life commitment, sacrifices, and process required for the high attainment that many come to expect or desire, together with lack of visible progress, cause many to drop out. Only those who come to understand the goal, how the game is played, and the tradeoffs of what you get for what you give up will hold to an aspiration for union. It is a long-term game of slow and steady cumulative personal evolution, which encompasses many lifetimes. Others may buy into the popularized negative image of austerity and sacrifice, become frightened by it, and never begin a committed practice. The media attention that misrepresents, belittles, makes fun of, and generally degrades gurus, yogins, and spiritual people will cause people who fear being 'different' to back away.

Similarly, the flow of the *Sutras* naturally carries the attention toward Absolute Unity as the goal of Yoga. By reaching for that, rather than letting it happen when you are ready, you can easily discount the strong accumulating benefits that are quickly available even to people who will invest less energy in that practice. Every bit of practice yields some benefit. That benefit builds over time. The initial benefits of clarity, calmness, and stress reduction are plenty for most people. Since the *Sutras* do not deeply explore this benefit-along-the-way, people tend to overlook it.

The presentation of the *Sutras* will progress to the subject of *karma*: some call that 'destiny,' but destiny is a weak substitute. Although the most commonly used translation of *karma* is 'action,' our language does not provide a word that matches the meaning of *karma* in the context of Yoga philosophy. When the *Sutras* begin the *karma* discussion, it will become clear that we each have our own lessons to learn, activities, priorities, and ways to live. These are important to the differing roles we each play. It is a highly varied world, with everyone both giving lessons and receiving lessons. The pieces of different lives fit together to form a world community. It would not work if everyone became a Buddha or an enlightened mystic. It would not work if we were all The Christ, Muhammad, Mahatma Ghandi, or any other great being. What would a world with only Albert Einsteins, florists, dentists, truck drivers, or loggers be like? Since we all have different destinies and purposes for being here, we certainly cannot all go the same distance or enter awareness of the same level of consciousness through the practice of Yoga. We will each go to the level that is appropriate to our life and get the appropriate benefit. The benefits along the path toward union are wonderful. We should not lose awareness of them. Only those who practice receive them. Benefit is world-cumulative. The more we individually receive benefits; the more benefit the world receives.

THE ACTIONS THAT LEAD TO UNION

Action Yoga

2.1   Religious austerity, reciting to one's self, and profound religious meditation on the Supreme Being are Action Yoga (Kriya Yoga).

tapaH   svAdhyAya   Isvara   praNidhAnAni   kriyA   yogaH
religious austerity   reciting to one's self   Supreme Being   profound religious meditation   Action Yoga

Human expectations or wishes for free rides always lead to disappointment. Everything has a price. The currency of payment is as varied as human experience and not always obvious. The price of attaining the higher consciousness experiences of Yoga is devotion to taking the positive actions that will meet the intent. Maintaining that devotion to action requires having faith in the rightness of the path. Without them, we cannot endure the many difficulties on the path. Those hard times will severely test our faith, and devotion will weaken and strengthen in proportion to the faith. Perhaps that is exactly why hard times exist. Patanjali reminds us of the work by opening his second pada, *Practice*, with three lifetime actions necessary to arriving at union, austerity, study, and meditation on the Supreme Being. This is the first mention of the Yoga of Action (Kriya Yoga): it is the *Yoga Sutras'* partner as forerunner of the many 'traditions' (types of practice) that developed during the past two thousand years.

The introduction of Kriya Yoga, Action Yoga, at this point in the *Sutras* puzzles many. Yet, the reason for its presence is clear, simple, and awe inspiring. *Samkhya* philosophy, the philosophy of union with the divine, had existed for nearly 2000 years without clear guidance for how to live by and act within the philosophy. At the time of Patanjali's life, the pressure for guidance toward that living practice had yielded the practices of Kriya Yoga. Patanjali documented both the philosophy, as it existed at that time, and the Kriya Yoga action steps to live by it. The student of Yoga should keep awareness, though, that many 'traditions' of today are no more than one or two generations deep, and that today's 'tradition' of Kriya Yoga is a modern invention, not the original practice, no matter how strongly the adherents claim that it is a 'rediscovery of ancient teaching.' There are no records of its practice, leaving the door open for false claims of rediscovery.

'Religious austerity' (*tapa*) is positive, but the loaded cultural view of austerity makes it easy for us to misunderstand its true meaning. For some, there is a natural tension and unresolved mental conflict between religion and spirituality, and they may not approach a spiritual practice if they see it as 'religious.' For others, the view of the popular culture supported by some translators, that austerity means self-harm, nearly starving, extreme ascetic behavior, or living in a cave, makes it difficult to accept. The reality of religious austerity is far easier than that. It is the type of austerity practiced in many religious and spiritual environments by monks and nuns. They live quiet, studious, reflective, plain, simple lives, without luxury, or self-indulgence. That is the life of a yogin. As the Buddha pointed out after going to ascetic extremes and nearly dying, the "middle-way" is the best way.

Reciting to one's self (*svadhyaya*) means to continuously study and recite your spiritual truths and findings to yourself until they firmly embed in the mind. It is also possible to translate *svadhyaya* as 'reciting the Vedas,' but that would interpret Kriya Yoga as a religious practice that aligns with Vedism. With no other evidence to support that orientation, it would be a mistake to use a religious translation. In either case, constant repetition of anything is very meditative in that it subdues thoughts and other mind activity.

The *Yoga Sutras* represent a merger of *Samkhya* philosophy and Kriya Yoga, but neither is Vedic or oriented to any religion. However, over many hundreds of years Yoga evolved into many divergent traditions, many of which merged with religions. For those who practice Yoga in a religious context, the intent of the aphorism would have them study the scriptures, writings, and teachings available to them, reciting them endlessly so that they will be permanently absorbed. For those who practice Yoga in a nonreligious context, the intent would have them study and recite everything about Yoga that they can find. Depending on individual needs and orientation, the nonreligious seeker might include religious texts in their studies. Both the broader idea of study in general, and the idea of studying scriptural or spiritual writing are Jnana Yoga, the path of knowledge. To the jnana yogin, the accumulated wisdom of the world is the fuel that drives them toward deeper knowledge and realization of Truth. Some claim that knowledge by itself can bring attainment of the higher goals of Yoga, but Patanjali does not promote that view.

Wise people whose words you study have been through the process of study of wisdom from others, to learn the Truths as they see them and pass them on. Since all of us are imperfect, and we can never be sure if a Truth from someone is a correct Truth or a false Truth, the wise seeker compares the purported truths from many until personally satisfied with the knowledge. The Gautama Buddha taught that we should accept no Truth from anyone and should rely on our own searching to find it. Particularly in this time, when the few great and accomplished gurus are no longer among us, and false or unevolved gurus abound, it is not a good idea to turn our life over to someone's control and accept their knowledge as Truth. It is, though, always wise to observe and reflect on what others have to say. You can learn many lessons from them about Truth, reality, and how to approach the study. You can learn much about their amazing discoveries that you might never discover on your own. Even learning what they were wrong about can be greatly valuable.

Profound religious meditation means everything it implies. It is meditation well beyond the norm: it is profound, and continually practiced with the attitude of the religious aspirant, though no religion is involved. 'Profound' means that it strives to meet difficult and strict standards, taking it to the extreme of practice, separated from ego needs, not showy for others. As the *Sutras* go on, the power of meditation and its results will be increasingly clear. Meditation *is* Yoga, and Yoga *is* meditation. The advancement of degrees of purification of the mind through stillness is dependent on the increasing rigor of and devotion to meditation. *Sutra* 2.43 specifically addresses that point and tells us that it sanctifies the body and the faculty of sensing.

However, we should be clear that the highly motivated yogin applies that rigorous effort to every aspect of Yoga, not just meditation, while avoiding buildup of possessions and needs. Developing consistent disciplined practice is a problem for many, but it is mandatory for traveling on the path toward higher consciousness. The committed seeker will train to do it and stick with it for the entire trip. None of the obstacles will yield without it. Virtually everything attained is at least partially dependent on that disciplined energetic practice and forsaking all other things. It requires continual awareness of actions, thoughts, emotions, and being, of all aspects of living. The result will always be proportional to the energy expended. Yet, it does not have to be work. It is both acceptable and desirable to make it fun and joyful. The joy will increase as you progress.

Meditating on the Supreme Being (*isvara*) helps you understand its nature, its constant presence and interplay with beings, and the way of life of a yogin who intends union with that beingness. Faith in its presence and interplay allow you to reduce much of the work, agony of decision-making, fear, risk, uncertainty, doubt, and other energy consumers, by putting yourself on automatic pilot. You 'ride the wave,' 'catch the flow,' and give up your resistance. Automatic pilot status slowly phases into your life as you yield to your inner-awareness, intuition, and the guidance of the divinity. As your faith in its presence and the rightness of what you are doing increases, trust in that underlying consciousness becomes easier. You become more confident and more able to maintain equanimity while 'rolling with the punches' of life. Since the existence of such guidance is not provable, following it requires extreme and consistent faith that it is there waiting for the seeker to recognize and accept it. A yogin capable of that degree of faith figuratively 'jumps from a cliff-edge into the waiting lap of the divinity.'

tapaH svAdhyAya Isvara praNidhAnAni kriyA yogaH

tapa (for tapah)	religious austerity
svadhyaya	recitation to one's self
izvara (for isvara)	Supreme Being
pranidhanani	
pranidhana	profound religious meditation
ani	(untranslated)

kriya   action
yoga (for yogah)   the name of the philosophical system

The Reason For The Actions

*2.2   The reason is the promoting of intense absorption, as well as the reason of
causing the afflictions to attenuate.*

samAdhi   bhAvana   arthah   kleSa   tanU   karaNa   arthaS   ca
*intense absorption   promoting   reason   afflictions   attenuated   causing
reason   as well as*

In his wonderful way of weaving patterns, Patanjali now emphasizes the
importance of the three actions of Kriya Yoga that he has just summarized.
He tells us that they are tools to help us achieve deep meditative absorption
and be antidotes to the five afflictions that he will begin describing in the next
aphorism. Reducing the incidence of the afflictions that interfere with the
goal of union by making absorption difficult, these tools are vital to attaining
union. The tools he gave us earlier, practice and developing indifference to
worldly things, a two-edged sword, now have a new value: they not only lead
us down the path to higher consciousness, they also help move those interfer-
ences out of our way.

samAdhi   bhAvana   arthah   kleSa   tanU   karaNa   arthaS   ca

samadhi   intense absorption
bhavana   promoting
artha (for arthah)   reason
kleza (for klesa)   affliction
tanu   attenuated
karana   causing
arthas   reason
ca   as well as

THE FIVE AFFLICTIONS THAT DISTURB THE SERENITY

The Five Afflictions

2.3   *The afflictions are spiritual ignorance, egoism, vehement desire, repugnance, and affection.*

avidyA asmitA rAga dveSa abhiniveSAh paNca kleSAh
spiritual ignorance   egoism   vehement desire   repugnance   affection
afflictions

Five types of afflictions stand in the way of stilling the mind and experiencing levels of higher consciousness. The character of these five aspects is different from the character of the 'obstacles' of sickness, apathy, doubt, carelessness, sloth, intemperance, erroneous understanding, not obtaining your next degree, and instability. The obstacles are ways of being in the material world, how we behave and exist, and things that block our practice. These afflictions are all 'subtle world' mental/attitudinal factors that counter our spirituality. They are more under control of our direct decision-making than the obstacles are. The following *Sutras* independently explain each affliction.

avidyA asmitA rAga dveSa abhiniveSAh paNca kleSAh

avidya	spiritual ignorance
asmita	egoism
raga	vehement desire
dvesa	repugnance
abhiniveza (for 'bhinivesah)	affection
panca	(left untranslated)
kleza (for klesah)	affliction

Attain Dominance Over The Source
Of Spiritual Ignorance

2.4   *Attain domination over the place of origin of spiritual ignorance, whether it is inactive, small, interrupted, or great.*

avidyA kSetram uttareSAM prasupta tanu vicchinna udArANAm
spiritual   ignorance   place of origin   attain dominant

latent   small   interrupted   great

Though not fully obvious, this current set of *Sutras* is about overcoming spiritual ignorance, commonly shown as 'ignorance.' This *Sutra* emphasizes that. Spiritual ignorance is lack of spiritual knowledge: its opposite is wisdom, having spiritual knowledge. Its origin is in the mind. Yoga is largely about disciplining the mind, to invert the balance of power by gaining dominance over it.

Ignorance, and the other elements of the tenacious hold to materiality as well, are not like on/off switches: they exist in varying degrees. They can be currently inactive, active, interrupted and awaiting a trigger, and of any strength or size. Until we reach full wisdom, ignorance and its potential activity are always there. Evolutionary progress toward union depends on attaining victory over it. In the everyday world, the mind has great power over us. When we attain power over it, we can still it. When we still it, we can move from the field of ignorance (lack of spiritual knowledge) to the field of wisdom (having spiritual knowledge).

avidyA kSetram uttareSAM prasupta tanu vicchinna udArANAm

avidya	spiritual ignorance
ksetra (for ksetram)	place of origin
uttaresam	
uttara	dominant
es	attain
am	(left untranslated)
prasupta	latent
tanu	small
vicchinna	interrupted
udaranam	
udara	great
anam	(untranslated)

Ignorance Is

2.5   *Spiritual ignorance is the perception of the transient, impure, trouble, and corporeal as possessing supremacy over the eternal, the pure, the effort to win future beatitude, and the soul.*

anitya aSuci duHkha anAtmasu nitya Suci
sukha Atma khyAtir avidyA
transient impure trouble corporeal to possess supremacy eternal pure
the effort to win future beatitude the soul perception spiritual ignorance

Everything in the material universe and the universe itself, without any
exception, is perishable. Some things last for very long times, but all things
die or decompose. Its opposite, the spiritual eternal, had no beginning and
will never end. We humans tend to believe that our everyday experience of the
material/sensual world is the ultimate reality. What thoughts we give to the
existence and nature of spirituality tend to be secondary and less important.
Our belief in, and focus on, the transient, impure, troubles, and non-spiritual
things keeps us in spiritual ignorance, which is simply the lack of acquired
spiritual knowledge. Without spiritual knowledge, we will fall into difficulties
created by the ego, afflictions, repugnance, and desires. Spiritual knowledge
provides the insight and understanding that enable us to avoid or reduce
those affects. Our effort to win future beatitude (bliss), and our perception
of the eternal and infinite reality behind the apparent material reality, along
with mind purity, bring us to direct spiritual knowledge. Ignorance, then,
comes from perceiving poorly, from developing incorrect knowledge of the
nature of things.

Although purity of the body and environment are important to Yoga,
Yoga philosophy is concerned with purity of the mind. In material existence,
the mind is very active with thoughts and other things. The goal of Yoga is to
eliminate the mind 'vibrations' (the activity) to bring it to stillness. Stillness is
purity if mind. The active mind of the material life brings about much pain
and sorrow. A highly purified still mind brings the experience of spirituality
and the soul.

anitya aSuci duHkha anAtmasu nitya Suci sukha Atma khyAtir avidyA

anitya	transient
azuci (for asuci)	impure
duhkha	trouble
anatmasu	
anatman	corporeal

su	to possess supremacy
nitya	eternal
zuci (for suci)	pure
sukha	the effort to win future beatitude
atman (for atma)	the soul
khyati (for khyatir)	perception
avidya	spiritual ignorance

Egoism Is

2.6   *Egoism is perseverance in understanding perception as if the same as the individual soul.*

dRg darSana Saktyor eka AtmatA iva asmitA
*to understand perception perseverance in
the same individual soul as if egoism*

Patanjali is simply telling us of the most normal of human traits, that we perceive through our perceptive senses; without recognizing that there is a nonmaterial, non-sensuous, spiritual way of perceiving, we treat the sensual perception as if it were the whole thing. In Yoga philosophy terms, this is egoism, relating everything to the personal and individual material being, as if that is all that exists. It drives the false identification of the self with the material world that our senses reveal to us. Because of that, we come to believe that our power to sense and experience is our identity. Yoga terms this the 'false self.' We do not understand that our permanent root identity is beyond the material world, our 'true self' or soul. He will return to this subject, showing us the other power of seeing.

At the everyday practical level, the ego causes us to create a self-definition, a personal mind view of who we are and how things are. It knows nothing except what our senses and mind bring to its attention. An inherent part of our material nature, it has no base in or connection to spiritual intuitive consciousness. It naturally leads us to believe that everything revolves around who we are and what we sense, to believe that what we see, feel, smell, hear, and taste is reality.

Students often say that a teacher told them that they must get rid of their ego. That is not possible. The ego is not removable. It is part of living, as surely as the brain, liver, and skeleton are critical parts of living. What the teachers probably meant, and perhaps did say, is that we cannot let the ego's search for rewards and its unrelenting clinging to false images drive our lives. If we are to attain the higher goals of Yoga, we must purge the ego-created self-image.

Under the ego's guidance, we humans begin our identity creation upon birth. Early in our lives, we form a belief of who we *should* be and establish momentum to create ourselves in that image. Whether we actually succeed in creating that person or not, we come to believe that we have. We look at that creation with pride and admiration. We defend our right to be that person and reinforce it at every opportunity. We believe in its 'goodness' and 'rightness,' no matter what it is. We create false images of world reality to justify and enhance that image. The ego prompts this, as well as most of our cravings, desires, and wants. Our attachments are ego-satisfactions. The ego is in firm control of our lives and defends against any threats to its dominance.

All of this exists within our material world self, our body-mind-emotion complex. Most of us ignore the existence of the soul, which is not within material world existence. The soul, or inner nature, is the true and prime self-identity, because it is eternal individuality, not a temporary mind and body bound to a universe that is also time-limited. The soul is an aspect of the eternal primal existence, equally beginningless, endless, and timeless. The ego does not search for that pure unarguable soul identity: it defends against searches for it. Searches threaten its power and hold.

A fully evolved individual, such as a Buddha becomes egoless in the sense that he or she no longer needs the satisfactions that the ego searches for, nor the attachments that hold to a self-image. If you become free of ego dominance, you will have recognized the existence of your true root nature, the soul (or inner being), as being more real than the images that the mind generates and carries. You will no longer have self-interest.

dRg darSana Saktyor eka AtmatA iva asmitA

drz (for drg)	to understand
darzana (for darsana)	perception

sakti (for saktyor)	perseverance in
eka	the same
atman (for atmata)	individual soul
iva	as if
asmita	egoism

Repent Desire

2.7   The effort to win future beatitude is repentant of vehement desires.

sukha anuSayI rAgaH
the effort to win future beatitude   repentant   vehement desire

Beatitude, receiving the blessing of perfect joy, is a high level attainment of yogis. Elimination of strong desires is a vertebra in the backbone of Yoga teachings. Eventual repenting of that longing is necessary to yogic attainment. Desire strongly binds us to material existence and the things that we acquire responding to that desire are the foundation for attachment. Together they tempt us to break all Limb 1 restraints of not injuring, truthfulness, not stealing, living in the state of an unmarried religious student, and being destitute of possessions. Those outgrowths from desire generate intense mind activity that counters Yoga's movement toward stillness: that unsettling affect on the mind is contrary to the practice and goals of Yoga.

Where other translations have translated *sukha* to 'happiness' or 'joy,' this one uses the philosophical translation of 'the effort to win future beatitude.' Although 'beatitude' is a term for joy, the concept of future is far more appropriate to this aphorism. No yogin can immediately stamp out desire. Its elimination is a gradual process, building over time. That gradual practice establishes the potential for future beatitude.

sukha anuSayI rAgaH

sukha	the effort to win future beatitude
anuzaya/anuzayin (for anusayi)	repentant
raga (for ragah)	vehement desire

Repugnance Earns Trouble

2.8   *Trouble is the consequence of the act of repugnance.*

duhkha   anuSayI   dveSah
trouble   consequence of the act   repugnance

The teaching tells us that there will be karmic difficulties in the future for carrying any kind of repugnance forward. Dislikes, hatreds, and fears can lead to the repugnance, and though they are all on the opposite side of the coin from affections, they have as much power over our lives as affections have. Like affections, they can be good for our material world life or bad, and they too take many forms. Like affections, we may strongly attach to them, not wanting to give them up. A repugnance may be derived through experience and be self-protective, but it may also separate us from the reality of the world. A repugnance of the opposite sex or a racial group may be genetic, psychotic, based on bad experience that brought anger or sorrow, or a mentally generated neurotic fear. If we are so afflicted, we will always view the group in a false light. Repugnance of any group may be healthy in some ways, but will cause us to isolate from parts of society, denying us some understanding of the truly existing material world, and will earn karmic consequences. We may lose the opportunities for learning, self-change, or growth that come from active participation or passive observation of the world. However, it is a two-sided coin: When such feelings separate us from the true world, they deny us the opportunity to observe, while providing us the opportunity to introspect and discover our spiritual side. We need to know that such strong feelings are there, where they came from, and what their effects are, while understanding that they will always bring difficulties and disquiet to our future lives if we do not come to understand and resolve them.

duhkha anuSayI dveSah

duhkha	trouble
anuzaya or anuzayin (for anusayi)	the consequence or result of an act
dvesa	repugnance

The Effects Of Having Affection

*2.9   In that manner, desire for one's own goods, and causing corruption to flow,
spring up from affection.*

sva   rasa   vAhI   viduSo   'pi   tathA   rUDho   'bhiniveSaH
*one's own goods   desire   causing to flow   corrupt   and
in that manner   spring up from   affection*

Affection for people and things also brings karmic results, in this life
and subsequent ones. Affection triggers a strong human drive to hold on to
the things we acquire, and to continually build an inventory of things we
like, without making a move toward spiritual living. That materiality produces unending desire to have more things, more sensuality, more people,
more power, more recognition, and ever more ego satisfaction. All corrupt the
understanding of the world around us, causing us to live in illusion, not in
reality, reducing our chances of finding a more spiritual way of being.

sva rasa vAhI viduSo 'pi tathA rUDho 'bhiniveSaH

sva	one's own goods
rasa	desire
vahin (for vahi)	causing to flow
vidus (for viduso)	corrupt
api (for 'pi)	and
tatha	in that manner
rudha (for rudho)	spring up
abhiniveza (for 'bhinivesah)	affection

Eliminating Subtle World Things

2.10   When these subtle things are gone, one returns to the original state.

te   pratiprasava   heyAH   sUkSmah
these   return to the original state   come to an end   subtle

An important message lies hidden in these words. Beginning at *Sutra*
1.10, Patanjali amply described that the entire material universe consists
of physical world things and subtle world things. Physical world things are
sense detectable and measurable. Subtle world things, such as thoughts,

perspectives, beliefs, emotions, and other mental objects are not. The afflictions are within the subtle world. Since they are not physical objects, but products of mind, they are curable by changing or bypassing the mind.

After introducing Kriya Yoga in 2.1 and saying in 2.2 that its purpose is to promote intense absorption, the seven *Sutras* following them discussed subtle world entities that interfere with that purpose. Seeing this *Sutra* in that light, it is easy and straightforward. If a yogin diligently and energetically practices the aspects of Yoga with an objective of fulfilling its purposes, ignorance, egoism, desire, repugnance, affection, enmity and subtle world afflictions of all sorts will progressively lose their influence and go away. When attachment to them is gone, the yogin is on the verge of Absolute Unity, returning to the original state of *brahman*. Removing the affection for and attachment to products of the mind is among the last steps, occurring after freedom from the affection for and attachments to physical entities.

te pratiprasava heyAH sUkSmah

te	these
pratiprasava	return to original state
heya (for heyah)	come to an end
suksma (for suksmah)	subtle

MEDITATION BRINGS STILLNESS

Meditation Overcomes Activities Of The Mind

2.11 And, the tendency toward arrival of activity comes to an end resulting from meditation.

dhyAna heyAs tad vRttayaH
meditation   come to an end   tend toward any result   and   activity arrival

In a book whose essence and trajectory is meditation, this *Sutra* provides one of the most important lessons: meditation is the process of getting around the mind, stilling the thoughts, reflections, reveries, and other activities. We can only experience higher levels of consciousness by going beyond our mental activity, whether arising from physical or subtle stimulation. To advance to higher consciousness we must get rid of the mind activity, no matter what causes it.

From here on the *Sutras* will keep adding to the teaching about meditation and unfold a larger picture of it. It is important to know here that the many forms of meditatively focusing our attention have one common effect. They all quell the activity of the mind, the source of subtle objects such as those related to the afflictions, leaving increasingly large gaps of stillness. They put our overactive mind on hold so that we can achieve increasingly greater stillness.

dhyAna heyAs tad vRttayaH

dhyana	meditation
heyas	
heya	come to an end
as	tend towards any result
tad	also
vrttayah	
vrtti	activity
aya	arrival

PREVENTING CONSEQUENCES AND DIFFICULTIES

Afflictions Are The Root Of Karmic Future

2.12 Afflictions are the root of the actions to be felt as the stock (of karmic influences) in present and future lives.

kleSa mUlaH karma Asayo dRSTa aDRSTa janma vedanIyaH
afflictions root action stock (of karmic influences) present and future life to be felt as

This *Sutra* begins to unfold how *karma* (action), works under the eternal natural Law that governs everything, even *brahman*. The situations of living and our mental framing of those situations, particularly those generated by the afflictions, cause us to take actions. Actions have results. Among the results are memories. Memories accumulate at the level of the individual mind, but the mind is impermanent and dies when the body dies. To preserve memories over many lives, impressions (karmic memories) record in the soul, which is not mortal, allowing them to carry from life to life. Accumulated impressions condition our future, in this life and subsequent ones. They affect the direction and starting point for your future life, and provide new events as the stimulus for path choices in the current life. We define our future life and lives with every action, no matter how small: we are sometimes aware of the effect, but often are not.

kleSa mUlaH karma ASayo dRSTa aDRSTa janma vedanIyaH

kleza (for klesa)	affliction
mula (for mulah)	root
karman (for karma)	action
azaya (for asayo)	stock (of karmic influences)
drstadrsta + janma	present and future lives
vedaniya (for vedaniyah)	to be felt as

How The Stock Of Memories Is Used

2.13   *That acquisition is the root of consequences, as the form of existence fixed at birth, a life, and experiences.*

sati   mUle   tad   vipAko   jAty   Ayur   bhogAH
acquisition   root   that   consequence   the form of existence fixed by birth
life   experiencing

There are two strong teachings here. The first is obvious: the stock of karmic influences is the root from which experiences grow, including the events that occur during the future of our current life, the very form of our next life, and all of its conditions, circumstances, and experiences. That is all preconditioned by the life we have finished in which the choices and actions we took in response to situations brought on experiences that generated that stock of karmic memories to condition the next life.

A dramatic and deeply meaningful second teaching exists, but is recognizable only by using the *Yoga Sutras* specific translation of the Sanskrit word *jati*, 'the form of existence (as man, animal, etc.) fixed by birth.' Using valid alternate translations such as 'birth,' 're-birth,' or even 'species' conceal the true meaning. This second teaching strongly and clearly addresses a subject that has caused many to wonder why the *Sutras* did not cover it. It tells us that the law of cause and effect with its karmic memories applies to all living things, not just humans. It is how evolution has occurred since the very first life form emerged on our planet, or perhaps anywhere in the universe. The accumulated 'stock' of impressions dictates not only the experience that the being will have in its next life, but the form of existence it will be born into, which authors hint at by translating *jati* to 'species.' The startling insight is that all life forms carry such a karmic stock. It is difficult to comprehend, because other life forms do not have the mentality that would produce such afflictions, and we do not normally think of them as having experiences. Yet, all species evolve by adapting their behaviors to situations.

Examining the five afflictions in a different light, though, is helpful. Since 'ignorance' is the lack of spiritual knowledge, plants, lower animals, fungi and other life forms are ignorant: they certainly lack spiritual knowledge. Since 'egoism' is seeing the self as if it were the entire world, we must agree that other beings are egoistic, because everything revolves around their individual sensing of the world. They cannot relate to other entities. Although the type of 'desire' may vary from one type of being to another, all living beings desire those things that will improve their situation, and with lower beings, those things usually relate to survival and propagation. Those desires bind all living things to material existence. Experience brings all types of living beings into episodes of 'repugnance.' Even the lowliest bacteria rapidly move away from water that has contaminants that are harmful to them, and develops both 'desire' and 'affection' for those things that are beneficial.

The underlying insight is that life, from its very instant of inception on the planet, established a trajectory toward evolution of spiritual creatures that could escape the materiality. We think we are 'it,' the ultimate result of evolution, and cannot possibly predict what we will evolve into when the survival of our species comes under threat.

sati mUle tad vipAko jAty Ayur bhogAH

sati	acquisition
mula (for mule)	root
tad	that

vipaka (for vipako)	consequences
jati (for jaty)	the form of existence (as man, animal, etc.) fixed by birth
ayus (for ayur)	life
bhoga (for bhogah)	experiencing

Gladness, Sorrow, And Purity

2.14   Gladness or sorrow result, by reason of your purity or impurity.

> te hlAda paritApa phalah puNya apuNya hetutvAt
> *gladness   sorrow   result   pure   impure   by reason you*

The *Sutra* continues to tell us of the importance of purity, that is to say 'stillness of mind,' to the goals of Yoga. Those that have not developed that inner stillness will be far more prone to sorrow in all of its manifestations. Those who have spiritually grown to become more pure of mind will experience a greater degree of gladness in their lives. The degree of sorrow or gladness will vary with the degree of purity.

Patanjali will later show that the spiritual life of those experiencing higher consciousness slowly clears the karmic record as the mind develops higher degrees of stillness: At the ultimate level of supreme consciousness, no karmic memories remain active. The entire being then becomes without blemish, pure, equal to the purity of the Absolute.

te hlAda paritApa phalah puNya apuNya hetutvAt

te	(untranslated)
hlada	gladness
paritapa	sorrow
phalah	result
punya	pure
apunya	impure
hetutvat	
hetu	by reason
tvat (= tva)	(2nd person pronoun) you

Even The Wise Are Aware Of The Difficulties

2.15   *Indeed, various of the wise say that change, pain, their troubles from (kar-*
mic) impressions, and conflict with activities of the constituents of prakrti
(the gunas) bring difficulties.

pariNAma tApa saMskAra duHkhair guNa vRtii virodhAc ca
duHkham eva sarvaM vivekinaH
change pain impression trouble their constituent of prakrti activity
conflict with and with difficult y indeed various wise to say

Traveling the path of a yogin requires and brings about continual changes
from an existing state of being to a new one. Although the ultimate results
are serene, the changes bring much pain: attachments are broken, memories
arise, insights develop, perspectives change, habits dissolve, the body adapts,
the mind yields to discipline, and much else. Much of that is response to
pressures from the impressions (karmic memories) that continually lead
to new tests, decisions, path choices, and challenges through presentation
of situations.

We all suffer anxieties, experience difficult learnings and setbacks, wrestle
with internal conflicts, resist change, lose our path, and suffer through material choices and their results throughout the range of human experiences.
We agonize over lost loves or things, yearn for renewal of pleasures we have
experienced, and anxiously protect what we have. This all brings sorrow and
pain into our lives, often called 'suffering.' The Buddha tells us that 'suffering'
is 'innate and continuing dissatisfaction.' That dissatisfaction is the 'constant
mind fluctuation' from our mental turmoil over wants, losses, missed opportunities, decision-making, and many other things. The difficult parts of living
come from even good or positive things, not just negative ones. We cannot
predict all of the long-term and immediate outcomes or ripple effects of our
actions and experiences. Things change. What seemed good sometimes turns
bad. We can predict that pain will be there in some form, and we can know
that the potential for peace is there, awaiting our making of choices.

Patanjali introduces another subject here that he will later expand,
an unseen conflict that places continual pressure on us as we evaluate and
adjust our lives: it is a natural source of great inner disharmony. Three basic

constituents, which act like forces, create and maintain all subtle and physical creations in the cosmos. They are the forces of change, and they war with each other for dominance, but the war diminishes as we move toward greater stillness. They are the three *gunas*: their Sanskrit names are *sattva*, *rajas*, and *tamas*. As core constituent qualities of the universe, they are present in everything. Their descriptions and exact translations vary from text to text, but the core character and function of each is consistent across all translations. You may see *sattva* described as beingness, purity, luminosity, calmness, balancing, or neutralizing. *Rajas* may have a description of activity, vibrancy, passion, or restlessness. *Tamas* may have descriptions of inertness, darkness, dullness, or resistance. *Rajas* and *tamas* oppose each other, while *sattva*, is neutral. *Rajas* is the principle of action. *Tamas* opposes action with its resistant inertia. *Sattva*, the neutral one, is the principle of pure being or existence. Any one of us can be active, resistant, or neutral. To oversimplify it, someone might claim that 'type A' behavior comes about when the *rajas* force within us predominates, that we become couch potatoes when the *tamas* force overpowers the others, and that we are still and spiritual when *sattva* is the controlling one.

To become a serene person, the opposing forces of action and the inertia that resists action must be in perfect balance. It is their nature to be in conflict with each other. Humans have the challenge of resolving those conflicts, harmonizing the forces. Yoga practice moves us toward that harmony. That harmony allows us to reduce inner conflict and quiets the mind.

The true point of the aphorism is that even the 'wise,' those who are spiritually advanced, experience the pain and difficulties to some degree. There is no magic formula to gain instant serenity. All of the pain-producing facts of life gradually diminish over time.

pariNAma tApa saMskAra duHkhair guNa vRtii
virodhAc ca duHkham eva sarvaM vivekinaH

parinama	change
tapa	pain
samskara	impression
duhkhair	
duhkha	trouble
ir	their

guna	constituent of *prakrti* (primal Nature)
vrtti	activity
virodha (for virodhac)	conflict with
ca	and
duhkham	with difficulty
eva	indeed
sarvam	various
vivekinah	
vivekin	wise
ah	to say

Avoid Future Difficulties

2.16   A future with difficulties is to be avoided.

heyam   duHkham   anAgatam
to be avoided with difficulty future

The potential for future pain of transformation, troubles brought on by *karma*, and conflicts with the constituents of *prakrti* (the *gunas*) will always be there and be difficult to avoid. During our lifetimes, we have accumulated an inventory of karmic seeds. Some will cause effects during future lives, while others cause effects during this life. We have no control over them, but we can control how we respond to their effects. We can also reduce the accumulation of new seeds that will bring future difficulties, by how we currently conduct life. As we progress with a Yoga life, our way of living and our choices can actually reduce the load of active *karma*.

Patanjali does not yet tell us the reason for avoiding future difficulty, but the thrust of the *Sutras* implies it: all of our difficulties, including our sadness, pain, sorrow, and chaos derive from the things that disrupt the yogic goal of stillness. As we reduce the disruptions to our stillness, we have a happier more comfortable life in harmony with the directional thrust of the *gunas* toward a more *sattvic* nature. As our evolutionary transformation continues, we move further along the path toward equanimity and the goals of Yoga.

heyam duHkham anAgatam

heya (for heyam)	to be avoided

duhkham   with difficulty
anagatam   the future

Material Contact Brings The Difficulties

2.17   A condition to be avoided is one who examines the visible through direct material contact.

draSTR dRSyayoH saMyogo heya hetuH
one who examines visible   direct material contact   to be avoided condition

According to the Monier-Williams dictionary, "in philosophy, relation or connection is said to be of three kinds, *samyoga*, *samavaya*, and *svarupa*." *Samyoga*, the type in this aphorism, indicates temporary physical encounter, as in a person touching a rock. The second, *samavaya*, indicates inseparability or union, in the sense of a sperm and an egg, or the spiritual union that is the subject of Yoga, two entities becoming one. The third, *svarupa*, indicates full individuality, separating the personal self. In the physical contact relationship pointed to here, whether it is by any or all of the senses, we cause our own unease, sorrow, pain, disquiet, karmic troubles, disharmony with the *gunas*, and other difficulties by having contact only with the physical world. Looking at it from the opposite side, not having a relationship with the spiritual world we miss the opportunity to avoid those difficulties.

In bringing this out as the root condition leading to difficulty, Patanjali again brings us to the importance of discovering and contacting our root nature. If we continue to believe that the root nature is in the material world, we will never be free of the difficulties. If we aspire to Truth and solace, the material world is the wrong place to look. In that world, we will never acquire the quietness, serenity, and peace necessary to our spirituality.

The gradual and incremental recognition and acceptance of our root nature as we continue our practice is one of the most marvelous things about the Yoga effect. The slow pace is a protective mechanism, to avoid transitional shock, while providing an opportunity to fully learn and experience our two natures, material and spiritual. As the next *Sutra* will tell us, we are here to experience our material nature so that we can become spiritual. Just as with the other ever-present dualities, such as love-hate, peace-war, action-inertia (*rajas-tamas*), and existence-nonexistence, spirituality would not be meaningful without materiality to oppose it.

draSTR dRSyayoH saMyogo heya hetuH

drastr	one who examines
drsyayoh	
drzya (for drsya)	visible
yoh	(left untranslated)
samyoga (for samyogo)	contact (in philosophy 'direct material contact')
heya	to be avoided
hetu (for hetuh)	condition

THE PURPOSE OF THE VISIBLE (MATERIAL/SENSORY) WORLD

Purpose Is Worldly Experience Leading To Eventual Beatitude

2.18   The purpose for the visible, composed of manifestation, activity, resistance to motion, a natural way of acting, that which exists, and the faculty of sensing is experience and final beatitude.

prakASa kriyA sthiti sIlaM bhUta indriya AtmakaM
bhoga apavarga arthaM dRSyam
*manifestation   activity   resistance to motion   natural way of acting
that which exists   faculty of senses   composed of   experiencing
final beatitude   purpose   visible*

This is an amazing teaching, because of the things it says, what it does not directly say, and the underlying principle it reflects. The aphorism begins simply enough by saying that *everything* that exists in the visible (physical) world is manifest, has a way of being and acting, is in active motion, and resistant to being placed in motion, and has an ability to sense its environment.

The main point arises in the last few words, an astounding statement that the book expands upon later. In his continuing light and easy way Patanjali has ended the aphorism with nothing less than a statement of the purpose of life and goal of personal evolution, but many will have difficulty seeing it as that, or accepting it as desirable once they do see it. In using the term 'beatitude,' a state of superior blessing, bliss, and joy, the *Sutra* points to arriving on the threshold of the endgame of Yoga, Absolute Unity. In accomplishing ultimate union, the freedom from future earthly experience, to never be reborn, comes to the seeker. We cannot find that freedom except by having earthly experience that enables learning and evolution. Only experiencing the world in ways that generate continually deeper intuitive understanding and awareness of higher consciousness, until primal consciousness becomes the one thing that remains in our awareness, will free us. It alone will liberate us from the earth-bound cycle of temporary entry to the material realm for a life experience, alternating with temporary dying from physical existence to reside in the subtle realm before returning to a new physical experience. While we pursue our evolution through steps of increasing spirituality, we cannot reject the material/sensory world. It is what it is, the only place available to us for living a life; it is the only realm for gaining experience. Evolution and *karma* changes cannot occur in the subtle realm during the between life experience, only during a lifetime in the material realm.

The *Yoga Sutras* that began by telling us that stilling the mind is what Yoga is about will slowly and methodically lead us toward the final explanation of that. At the end of the fourth *pada*, it will speak of what Absolute Unity is, and that it happens at the point of achieving permanent total stillness. Reading about it, though, will not convey the reality, other than through some measure of intellectual understanding. That reality is not easy to accept, and it startles many. Even many in the mid-ground of their evolution do not yet accept the endgame of Yoga, with some still seeing it as undesirable, confusing, senseless, or theoretical philosophy. Along the way, the seeker may find help with this by attaining the intuitive clarity that it is not just about evolving us as individuals, but about evolving the species and life on the planet. Happy anticipation of the ultimate endgame may not come about until we have experienced wonderful tastes of the higher consciousness states, tastes that bring enough insight to no longer fear death.

Only deep insights to the nature of the universe, cosmic divinity, life, and the karmic cycle, which come forth while in higher consciousness, can provide the joyful anticipation of the endgame. Related to that understanding, Patanjali has also provided, through implication, a foundation that he will build on while answering the underlying question of, 'Why does *brahman* create?' Simply said, *brahman* experiences through its creations: it has no way to experience anything in the eternal permanent state of stillness, so it uses its dream-imagination to create *isvara*, then causes *isvara* to create other things so It can have experiences. What use would it be to have omniscient knowledge and the power to observe everything everywhere if nothing existed to have knowledge of or observe.

prakASa kriyA sthiti sIlaM bhUta indriya AtmakaM
bhoga apavarga arthaM dRSyam

prakaza (for prakasa)	manifestation
kriya	activity
sthiti	resistance to motion
zila (for silam)	natural way of acting
bhuta	that which exists
indriya	faculty of sense
atmaka (for atmakam)	composed of
bhoga	experiencing
apavarga	final beatitude
artha (for artham)	purpose
drzya (for drsyam)	visible

FOUR BASELINE STATES OF THE UNIVERSE

The Cosmos Passed Through Four Evolutionary Levels

2.19   *The constituents of prakrti (gunas) divide things into essential difference, uniformity, having characteristics, and elementary matter without characteristics within.*

viSeSa aviSeSa liNga mAtra aliNgAni guNa parvANi

essential difference   uniformity   characteristics   elementary matter   without characteristics within   constituents of prakrti   division into.

Try a mind experiment that it is best not to try in the actual world. Picture approaching a neighbor, spouse, boss, lover, or stranger and say, 'How many evolutionary states of Nature do you know of?' What reaction from that person comes to your mind? Can anyone even relate to the question? Would anyone accept it as a real question worth discussion? Most of us accept the sensory world as existence without questioning it. We do not ponder such things, particularly not strange sounding states such as those in this aphorism. Yet, Patanjali so easily and naturally tells us that the 'stuff' of our universe, that is to say of *prakrti* (primal Nature), passed through four initial evolutionary processes to establish a cosmic foundation. He has already described the primary constituents (*gunas*) that will control this evolution. They are *being, action,* and *resistance to action (inertia)* whose names and characteristics are in 2.15 above.

He now makes an unequivocal declaration that makes our familiar understanding of our material/sensory state of being just one current situation derived from the four early evolutionary developments. The primary conditions that the three constituents orchestrated - are 'uniform,' 'essential difference,' 'with characteristics,' and 'elementary matter without characteristics.'

The *Sutra* does not give any information about sequence of universe evolution, but rich insight about that exists within Yoga philosophy. In simple terms, the universe evolves from the uniform oneness of a primal essence. Formally, this is *mula prakrti*, a form of *prana* dubbed here (and only here) as *primal prana*. That first type of cosmic existence has no form, lacks identifying characteristics, and contains no separation into individuals.

The next evolutionary condition was the 'essential difference' development, *mahat prakrti*. Derived from the initial *mula prakrti*, it provided the foundation of a newer form of *prana* that this interpretation refers to as 'creative *prana*,' and for the Causal Body of the universe.

The 'without characteristics' evolution followed that, creating the subtle matter, *para prakrti*, and the 'subtle *prana*.' Being without identifiable characteristics, it is not detectable by senses in the way physical matter is. Although it is there, we cannot distinguish it from anything else.

As evolution continued the *gunas* created *apara prakrti*, the physical or 'elemental matter with characteristics' portion of the universe made of 'physical *prana*' and physical matter that the senses can detect.

viSeSa aviSeSa liNga mAtra aliNgAni guNa parvANi

vizesa (for visesa)	essential difference
avizesa (for avisesa)	uniformity
linga	characteristic
matra	elementary matter
alingani	
alinga	without characteristic
ni	within
guna	constituents of *prakrti*
parvani	
parvan	division
ni	into

DISCUSSION OF THE FOUR TYPES

Uniform
(The Stage Of The Primal Essence)

Through its universe creation agent *isvara,* the eternal *brahman*, which is equivalent to what some call god-transcendent, brought about the primal *prana*, or primal essence, of our non-eternal Universe. A temporal universe must have an overseer, equivalent to a god-imminent: Yoga represents it as *isvara* and religious others as *sat*. Aside from that, in everyday modern god-speak, it has many names, such as Lord, God, Allah, Yahweh, Brahma, and hundreds of others.

Although using either *sat* or *isvara* is correct, *they are not truly equal. Isvara* is the exact image of *brahman* in all its aspects, extending to all universes. *Sat* is a Vedism and Hinduism representation adapted by later Yoga philosophy for the presence of *brahman* within the universe. Beyond the *Sutras*, it does

not stand alone: it is a coequal partner within an inseparable trinity of powers, *om, tat,* and *sat (om-tat-sat)*, which jointly created our universe.

Our universe first appeared as a unified field of energy that had no internal distinctions, the uniform 'primal essence,' *avisesa*: it is Nature, or *prakrti*,
in its most primitive form of *mula prakrti*. It is also *prana*, the power/energy
effect of *brahman* in this universe. Everything, both physical and subtle, will
evolve from this essence, under the influence of the three constituents (or root
properties) of Nature already present, *sattva, rajas,* and *tamas* - the *gunas*. The
sattva guna provides equilibrium to the triumvirate. The *rajas guna* provides
action, and the *tamas guna* provides resistance to action. The three *gunas* are
in perfect balance while in the primitive situation, with no conflict or struggle against each other's forces. Later disruptions in this balance result in the
differentiations that produce the physical and subtle universe. Because everything in our universe contains the primal constituents (the *gunas*), including
this primal essence and everything that will follow it, those characteristics
are in everything. They always exist together in varying balance: they are
not separable.

Essential Difference Stage
(The Stage of the First True Entity)

Generically, the first stage of differentiation from the undefined pure essence
of *mula prakrti* (Root Nature) is *mahat prakrti*, sometimes dubbed as the
Great Cause: this is Yoga's macro scale 'causal body' of the universe. It is no
longer *avisesa*, uniform, but now *visesa*, which means 'essential difference.'
The previous *primal prana* for the universe, mula *prakrti*, has now manifested
as the Causal Body for the universe with perception capability (*buddhi*), and
its power to create. The evolved substance is a modified form of *prana*, informally labeled here as 'creative *prana*.'

Elementary Matter Without Characteristics Stage
(The Subtle Matter And Mind Stage)

This stage is the foundation for the 'subtle body' of the universe: it carries
the designation of 'without characteristics' (*alinga*) to distinguish it from the

distinct physical body, which has sense-detectable characteristics. It provides pranic energy, forces, influences, abstracts, and mentality.

Although often used interchangeably with the term 'astral body,' the two terms have different origins and carry different implications. The term Subtle Body is early Yoga representation, while Astral Body has a later more modern source. Both terms represent the third portion of our being that exists between the Physical Body (Food Body to some) and the Causal Body. Both terms refer to the vehicle that transmigrates at physical body death to the subtle world realm during periods between births, along with the Causal Body, under the influence of the soul.

We have been correctly viewing these bodies as those belonging to the universe. However, as individuation later occurs in the universe, separate minds, souls, causal, and subtle bodies generate and play a role in forming individual physical bodies. We should have at least working assumptions about the difference between mind and intelligence. Taking a straight and easy line that does not disagree with either our modern dictionary or Yoga philosophy, 'Mind' (mentality) is where thoughts, emotions, ideas and perceptions come from and where memories are stored. Intelligence is the ability to learn and to process from observations. Being mortal, both mind and intelligence are different from consciousness. We always say that *brahman* has consciousness. We never say that It has mind or intelligence. It does not think and process. It exists, observes, and causes. Yet, It has the power to create forms that can think and process on its behalf. When we directly experience consciousness, we experience an aspect of the eternal and spiritual, whereas mind and intelligence are temporal as part of the material world.

With Characteristics
(The Physical Matter Stage)

The universe's soul established the primal essence, and the *gunas*. The *gunas* influenced the formation of the Causal Body containing the *prana* from which the universe manifested. They then stimulated the creation of the Subtle Body, both of which are necessary to the creation of a Physical Body. In the *linga* (with characteristics) phase, matter that the senses can detect manifested, forming the Physical Body of the universe. All the physical objects we know so well manifested over time from the initial physical matter.

Related Consciousness Levels

Although Patanjali has introduced no ideas about the correlation of these four evolutionary developments to levels of consciousness, most authors introduce their personal view of such a relationship, while some openly refute that there is one. Some of the authors' correlations are similar to each other, and some are broadly dissimilar. A perspective follows here, to provide insights gained from a variety of sources, without claiming it as an unquestionable authoritative view and without attributing it to Patanjali. It is there for you to compare to the ideas of varied sources and to provide a benchmark for your continued study.

In our everyday living, we think of evolution in purely physical terms: we do not think of evolution of subtle matter and invisible underlying structures; we also fail to see the far more important evolution of the consciousness of the universe. Yoga philosophy addresses those evolutions. At each step in evolution of the universe, a new subtle or physical form arises and consciousness evolves to a new level, one that is lower (farther from the invariable consciousness of *brahman*) than the last evolved consciousness. The first stage of evolution is that of *mula prakrti* and '*primal prana*,' which this aphorism labels as 'uniform.' It is the level of soul consciousness and I-sense, or the ego of the universe, which yogins experience in the high state of *asmita samadhi*. The second stage, labeled as 'essential difference,' is at the consciousness level of *mahat prakrti* and '*creative prana*.' It is the consciousness state of the Causal Body and is experienced during *ananda samadhi*. 'Elementary matter without characteristics' is the evolution of subtle matter, *para prakrti*, and its consciousness form, experienced by the yogin as *vicara samadhi*, the consciousness of the Subtle Body. This interpretation also characterizes it as '*subtle prana*.' The fourth evolution, *apara prakrti* is the consciousness of 'elementary matter with characteristics,' which is physical matter, experienced in *vitarka samadhi*. The term '*physical prana*' also denotes that development here.

The following chart of these cross-relationships may be helpful to continued study. The names come from the words, *alinga, linga, avisesa,* and *visesa*: because there are many alternate meanings for those four words, there is much inconsistency in the single-word meanings selected by translators.

Uniform (avisesa)
mula prakrti - unmanifested primal essence - 'primal *prana* '
The consciousness level we access during *asmita samadhi*

Essential Difference (visesa)
Mahat prakrti - 'creative *prana*'
The consciousness level we access during *ananda samadhi*
This is the consciousness of the Causal Body

Elementary Matter Without Characteristics (alinga)
para prakrti - 'subtle *prana*' produces subtle matter
The consciousness level we access during *vicara samadhi*
This is the consciousness of the Subtle Body

With Characteristics (linga)
apara prakrti - 'physical *prana*' produces physical matter
The consciousness level we access during *vitarka samadhi*
This is the consciousness of the Physical Body
At That Consciousness Level The Yogin Sees Matter in Pure Form

2.20   *And perceiving that basis, one who sees (i.e. the yogin), sees matter unmodified (i.e. by the mind).*

draSTA dRSi mAtraH Suddho 'pi pratyaya anupaSyaH
*one who sees   seeing   matter   unmodified and
basis   perceiving*

In a simple and straightforward way, the *Sutra* tells us that advancing to experience a consciousness state that brings us to perception of the four states of evolution brings us to a new state of understanding of the material world. During that experience, the yogin has accurate perception of matter with no modification by the mind, as well as full intuitive understanding of the nature of the universe and its states of matter.

This is a very high level experience achieved by a highly evolved yogin. The student of Yoga should understand, though, that any successful meditation experience conditions us to understand the material world to an improved degree of accuracy. This is a further development of the continuing evolution.

This translation and interpretation varies greatly from the 'standard model' found in other books. The translation notes tell you more about that.

draSTA dRSi mAtraH Suddho 'pi pratyaya anupaSyaH

drastri (for drasta)	one who sees
drzi (for drsi)	perceiving
matra (for matrah)	matter
zuddha (for suddho)	unmodified
api (for 'pi)	and
pratyaya	basis
anupazya (for anupasyah)	perceiving

The Reason The Universe Exists Is To Support Life And Sensation

2.21   And, the only reason it is visible is the principle of life and sensation.

tad   artha   eva   dRSyasya   AtmA
and   reason   only   visible   it   principle of life and sensation

This simple statement is profound, answering one of the great questions of existence. It reinforces a private perspective that occurs to many, but never appears in print. A universe has no reason to exist except to provide a workbench for developing sentient life forms that can experience the world though sensation. That has been its purpose from the start. From the moment of the first primal energy, the sensuous life intention has been there, and that life intention has the goal of creating continually more complex and advanced beings.

As with the preceding aphorism, the common translation is far different from this one. The translation notes tell you how and suggest how that came about.

tad artha eva dRSyasya AtmA

tad	and
artha	reason
eva	only
drsyasya	
drzya (for drsya)	visible
sya	it
atman (for atma)	principle of life and sensation

Disappearance Of Physical Objects

2.22   *Upon gaining that, objects of the senses disappear; nevertheless, since they are in a constant state of being common to all, they are unimpaired for another person.*

kRta   arthaM   prati   naSTam   apy   anaS-
Tam   tad   anya   sAdhAraNatvAt
*object of the senses   gained   upon   disappeared   nevertheless
unimpaired   they   another person   common to all
state of being to go constantly*

Beginning with *Sutra* 2.18, the *Yoga Sutras* have presented a series of aphorisms about the material world. The first tells us that it exists to provide for experience and final beatitude. The second tells us about the universe's stages of evolution, which are the reverse of the stages of evolution of material beings. The third tells us that the being that enters the consciousness level of understanding how cosmic evolution works sees matter as it really is. The fourth ties to the first, telling us the purpose of materiality is to support life and sensual experience. This last *Sutra* in the series tells us that when the yogin has gained the experience of truly perceiving matter, the physical objects disappear from the yogin's awareness. Further, it affirms the separateness of the being and the perceived object, clarifying that objects are physically real and not products of the yogin's imagination. When the individual temporarily becomes free of sensual materiality with its separation of things into individual objects, it does not affect others. All others still see the objects in their everyday material nature.

When *Sutra* 2.18 pointed to beatitude, it referred to the high spirituality approaching the edge of Absolute Unity, the freedom from having to live another material life. At the point of readiness for Absolute Unity, the individual experiences the highest possible level of consciousness, in which the individual's consciousness becomes the same as primal consciousness. While in that state, the meditator no longer perceives differences between objects of any type: everything spiritual and material is a unity, oneness, without separation or sequences: the material world (Nature or *prakrti*) does not exist for that person. Patanjali wanted to ensure our understanding that any material world object continues to exist for others. Common to all, beings with their perception focused in material/sensory consciousness continue to perceive them as ordinary objects.

kRta arthaM prati naSTam apy anaSTam tad anya sAdhAraNatvAt

krta	gained
artha (for artham)	object of the senses
prati	upon
nasta (for nastam)	disappeared
api (for apy)	nevertheless
anasta (for anastam)	unimpaired
tad	they
anya	another person
sadharanatvat	
sadharana	common to all
tva	state of being
at	to go constantly

THE EGO

The Master Of Our Material Living

2.23   *The ego is the master of attachment, one's own circumstances, acquisition, and means of contact.*

sva svAmi sAktyoH sva rUpa upalabdhi hetuH saMyogaH
ego　master　attachment　one's own　circumstances　acquisition
means contact

The preceding *Sutras* laid out the nature of the material world and our need to escape from it if we seek the highest goals of Yoga. This *Sutra* now identifies the powerful force that keeps us so deeply involved with it. It is the ego, an inherent drive at the root of existence in all beings. It drives the emotional mechanisms that keep us attached to things. It generates the desires that drive us to acquire things. Minute by minute it works with our mind to select paths and actions that accumulate to form the circumstances of our life. It provides a continuous pressure that drives the way we physically interact with material things, including people. In a strong sense, it is the enemy of spirituality, binding us to sensual material world things, and constantly keeping us away from spiritual-mindedness as if a jealous and competing force. To achieve our goals we must overcome the drive of the ego.

sva svAmi sAktyoH sva rUpa upalabdhi hetuH saMyogaH

sva	ego
svamin (for svami)	master
sakti (for saktyoh)	attachment
sva	ones own
rupa	circumstances
upalabdhi	acquisition
hetu (for hetuh)	means
samyoga (for samyogah)	contact (esp. in phil. ` "direct material contact ")

It Causes Spiritual Ignorance

2.24　It is the cause of spiritual ignorance.

tasya　hetur　avidyA
it　cause　spiritual ignorance

The message of the aphorism is clear. Our potent ego maintains our state of ignorance. Recognizing that the ego is the ultimate 'I,' we could interpret the aphorism to say *'I am the cause of the lack of spiritual knowledge (ignorance).* It is not new ground to suggest that *avidya* (ignorance - that is to say, lack of spiritual knowledge) derives from our wrong-minded belief that our actual individual identity is material. That misconception leads to many issues already addressed. Reintroducing it here, in a unique and subtle way, however, reaffirms its importance and leads us toward correcting it.

The Yoga philosophy says that to achieve the harmonious union of the divine and the material we must recognize and understand the spiritual realm beyond materiality and overcome the normal human focus on that material world. When we know only of the material world, we attach to it. When we know of the oneness of the spiritual world and the material world, our awareness can lead us to spirituality. The ego does not want us to know that. In the marvelous two-sidedness of everything, it is a competitive force against it.

This powerful aphorism indirectly points to the entire process and intent of Yoga. It is the game that the Great Presence established when It created us. It was not an accident. It intended to create a being that would focus its attention on the material world while having the capability and drive to transcend that in order to experience the realm that extends beyond the universe. The pleasures and rewards of materiality, excite us, energize us, satisfy us, nurture us, and motivate us. They continually draw us in. Giving that up is unthinkable. However, once we enter awareness of the spiritual realm, we begin to become enamored of the experience and thrilled that we material beings can accomplish it. That new lure continually grows in the strength of its affect on us. The endpoint of Yoga, the full spirituality of Absolute Unity, is the opposite extreme from full materiality. There the seeker becomes fully spiritual, completely losing awareness of the material world, as well as all ego and traits such as 'enamored.'

tasya hetur avidyA

tasya	
ta	(pronoun indicator) it
sya	(3rd person indicator)
hetu (for hetur)	cause
avidya	spiritual ignorance

CESSATION OF SPIRITUAL IGNORANCE

Result Of Gaining Spiritual Knowledge

*2.25   Non-existence of that (ignorance), going constantly in the absence of direct
material contact, and relinquishing the power of seeing, absolute unity.*

tad   abhAvAt   saMyoga   abhAvo   hAnaM   tad   dRSeH   kaivalyam
   *that   non-existence   to go constantly   direct material contact
absence   relinquishing   and   power of seeing   absolute unity*

The true momentum of the yogin is to eliminate 'spiritual ignorance'
through the various practices of Yoga, to move from a life bound to the material existence to a life bound to the spiritual existence. At one end of the
spectrum of life styles, there is only material world knowledge: in Yoga terms,
that is a state of full ignorance. At the other end of the spectrum, there is
full spiritual knowledge: in Yoga terms, that is a state of wisdom. Yet just
achieving a high level of spiritual knowledge is not enough to cause the ultimate step of entering the Absolute Unity with *brahman*. The seeker gradually
evolves toward it. This eventually leads to a point of full separation from the
bondage to material contact, and seeing through the inner intuitive sight, not
through the material power of eyesight. Patanjali does not discuss stillness in
this aphorism, but those who evolve to total spirituality (wisdom) would be
in total stillness. At the other end of the spectrum, those in total materiality
(ignorance) would be in a state of high mental activity, often chaotic.

Yoga teaching describes the material world as a *maya*-produced illusion
that keeps us in a state of ignorance (lack of spiritual knowledge). The progressive stilling that is the backbone of Yoga philosophy and is the seeker's reward,
goes hand in hand with the progressive reduction of ignorance: both lead to
the eventual separation from material experience, and entering the absolute
experience of Spirit in a state of unity. When our way of living finally elimi-
nates our false view that our identity is in that material/sensory world, and we
detach from need for contact with material things, we will arrive at that state
of wisdom and true stilling. Perhaps Patanjali could have told us at the start
that if we gain spiritual knowledge, eliminate our material bonds, and get rid

of that false view, we will gain the spirituality and stilled mind necessary to unity, but he needed to first tell us how to gain spiritual knowledge.

The few words of this aphorism provide the base for understanding the requirements for reaching Absolute Unity, which some call Emancipation or Freedom, although they are not definitions or synonyms. To intellectually understand this we must give up our material/sensory ideas about the word 'freedom.' This freedom is not the political/cultural freedoms we enjoy in our daily lives; it is freedom from the material/sensory world itself, freedom from the need to ever experience another material lifetime. This simple statement does not yet have the impact, though, that Patanjali will provide at the end of the final part, when he defines it for the third time.

Perhaps it makes it sound all too simple, and even circular - a chicken and egg phenomenon - but the simple antidote to having the anti-spiritual perception of ourselves as material and being addicted to material contact is to gain spiritual knowledge. If we do, the misunderstanding will just go away. Although replacement of the false idea with a new one is necessary, we cannot force it: we must let it evolve from our practices and actions. The correct and powerful idea will displace the old one with time and practice. No intellectual maneuver will accomplish it. The deeply embedded programs that have convinced us that our carried untruths are true are complex, and interwoven. Only the new experiences and meditations that expose us to insight can correct that through deep intuitive learning. We can only get that insight through spiritual practice. Through spiritual practice, we develop spiritual knowledge that gradually displaces false perceptions with true perceptions.

tad abhAvAt saMyoga abhAvo hAnaM tad dRSeH kaivalyam

tad	that
abhavat	
abhava	non-existence
at	to go constantly
samyoga	direct material contact
abhava (for abhavo)	absence
hana (for hanam)	relinquishing
tad	and
drzi (for drseh)	power of seeing

kaivalya (for kaivalyam)   leading to emancipation

Discriminative Perception

2.26   Unconfusing discriminative perception is the means for escaping.

viveka khyAtir aviplavA hAna upAyah
discrimination   perception   un confusion   escaping   means

The *Sutras* have seemingly just introduced different things that will elim-inate the lack of spiritual knowledge (ignorance). That is partially true, but what we have truly seen are ingredients of the final state and the progression that takes us there. The *Sutras* will carefully explore this at the end of *Pada 4* as Patanjali takes the discussion ever closer to *kaivalya*, the Absolute Unity. The discriminative perception he speaks of here is a result that comes about very close to attaining that ultimate experience of high consciousness. It seems like a cumbersome and broad term, but it specifically refers to the power of unequivocally, and without any error, separating the invisible Spirit from the visible world, (or Spirit from matter, truth from untruth, and reality from illusion).

This is far easier to understand than it sounds, but not so easy to do. We overcome the problem of attachment to the *maya*-produced grand illusion (that material world) by becoming able to intuitively separate the nature of the spiritual realm from the nature of the material realm. As part of that discrimination, we develop the ability to know when our current experience is in the lower consciousness level of the material realm or the high spiritual consciousness. We then surely know the difference between illusion and real-ity. The false-world illusion, though, does not disappear until we are able to do so in a continuous and unbroken way.

This subject is not separate from the underlying theme of stillness: the longer you can continuously hold that clear discrimination between the two, the longer you will hold to stillness, seeing through the intuitive 'eyes' of the one Reality. This is not willful action: it is what happens as progress continues.

The progression is becoming clear. Practice and giving up the sensuous world bring you to enter the first levels of higher consciousness. Continued practice takes you higher. You can advance into experiencing higher consciousness through meditative techniques. These practices lead to removing obstacles, the distractions from the path. You become aware of the primal nature of things and receive Truth-bearing knowledge after you have advanced to the fourth stage of higher consciousness. That brings you to a state of pure consciousness. You are then ready to deal with the factors of materiality, overcoming them with meditation and continued practice. As you become more capable of holding your experiences of primal consciousness, the distinctions between the two, as well as their unity, become apparent. This too is progressive, not a sudden event.

Patanjali has brought the subject of higher consciousness to its ultimate form. He is telling us that as this displacement continues away from attachment to materiality and toward full knowledge and acceptance of the reality of the nonmaterial identity, we become more fully able to discriminate between experiencing the material consciousness and spiritual consciousness. Stilling occurs proportionally with the degree of discrimination. Since all aspects of materiality are illusions that cause mental fluctuations, at the ultimate point of discrimination, we fully realize primal consciousness alone and stilling is total. When total stillness holds, the Absolute Unity occurs and we become free from further need to experience the material/sensory world.

viveka khyAtir aviplavA hAna upAyah

viveka	discrimination
khyati (for khyatir)	perception
aviplava	
a	un (negation)
viplava	confusion
hana	escaping
upaya (for upayah)	means

There Are Seven Stages Of Progressive Stilling

2.27   It (cessation of ignorance) is in seven parts: finally it is wisdom.

tasya saptadhA prAnta bhUmih prajNA
it   in seven   parts   finally   wisdom

There are seven stages of consciousness to experience from pure material sensory consciousness to Absolute Unity in *kaivalya*, pure spirituality. Within the seventh experience is wisdom (opposite of spiritual ignorance) attained through the continuous discrimination between material consciousness and spiritual consciousness.

Throughout the *Sutras*, Patanjali has slowly and with subtlety, placed progressive levels of consciousness experience and their associated levels of spirituality/wisdom before us. He now says that this continuous differentiation is the occurrence that resolves things to finality. Although the *Sutras* do not include a handy list of the stages, integration of what they have taught piece-by-piece show the seven stages beyond active material consciousness to be:

1. *Savitarka samadhi*
2. *Nirvitarka samadhi*
3. *Savicara samadhi*
4. *Nirvicara samadhi*
5. *Ananda samadhi*
6. *Asmita samadhi*
7. *Nirbija samadhi*

With this, the *Sutras* have again progressively brought us to the brink of the highest Yoga, Absolute Unity. Experiencing continuous discrimination within *nirbija samadhi*, the path has completed. The ultimate full stilling in the state of union is immanent. Patanjali tells us that the key to opening that door is the differentiation described in *Sutra* 2.26. It should now be clear that Absolute Unity occurs when the discrimination is a permanent situation, but it is not the last time the *Sutras* will make this point. Showing it through several perspectives helps us understand it with increasing clarity. In the final aphorisms, he will return to the subject of differentiation and in *Sutra* 4.29 will ascribe the name *Dharmamegha samadhi* (Law Cloud *samadhi*) to the state immediately preceding the Absolute Unity.

We must retain awareness, though, of what Patanjali does not tell us, that this progression may take thousands of lifetimes to complete. Masters have inconsistently proposed various counts of needed lifetimes, but Yoga philosophy provides no similar perspective. The important piece of information is that, for almost everyone, it is not achievable within his or her current lifetime. The end-result must occur within *some* given lifetime, but we do not know at birth, or any other time, what our karmic needs are, or what level of evolution we have carried forward from a previous life. Those who we know as beings of high consciousness, such as Christ, the Buddha, Krishna, and some high yogins, were certainly born with an evolved level of being that enabled their teaching and the activities that the Laws make available only to the few who attain the mountaintop.

With the seven stages not being easily clear or listed, translators and inter-preters sometimes point to a seven level scheme of Yoga effects invented and proposed by the iconic Vyasa some 400 years after Patanjali died, representing it as a valid interpretation of the seven levels. However, the reporting of his naming and classification varies greatly from one author to another, and there is little correlation with the wording or meaning within Patanjali's *Sutras*. Over the centuries, many others have attempted to describe the intention, and saints and scholars have often described levels of meditation growth that parallel the pattern in the *Sutras*. However, those descriptions do not depict seven levels, with some being as low as four.

tasya saptadhA prAnta bhUmih prajNA

tasya	
ta	(pronoun indicator) it
sya	(3rd person indicator)
saptadha	in seven parts
prantabhumi	finally
prajja (for prajna)	wisdom

THE EIGHT LIMBS OF YOGA

Patanjali now does a surprising thing: having told us how to reach higher con-sciousness through spiritual knowledge, as if preparing us for the end of the book, he seems to hit the restart button, giving us a different way to do it, with no reference to what he has just developed. As the presentation of the *Sutras* seemingly approaches conclusion of this part (*pada*) on practice, he does not even tell us that the perpetual stilling leading to the discrimination he has just led us to is the vaunted goal of Absolute Unity. He, instead, begins to discuss the classical eight-limb practice of Yoga that leads to that Absolute Unity. Through the next 32 aphorisms, he will use declarative statements in the simplest of terms, describing a lifetime practice involving total commitment and great faith. He does not say so, but everything discussed in the other 164 aphorisms is harmonious with this structure. Without altering, diminishing, or redefining the underlying philosophy in any way, these eight limbs provide new clarity, more practicality, precision of technique, additional techniques and disciplines, and context for things he has so far unfolded.

The Result Of Practicing All Limbs

2.28   Consuming performance of the limbs of Yoga, the impurities wane, and the light of knowledge leads toward discrimination of perception.

yoga   anga   anuSThAnAd   aSuddhi   kSaye

jNAna   dIptir   A   viveka   khyAteh

yoga   limb   performance consume   impurity   wane   knowledge   light

towards   discrimination   perception

The *Sutras* have carefully described the highest attainment of Yoga, Absolute Unity, and the stages that lead to it. They have informed the reader about the obstacles to achievement. They now foreshadow the individual descriptions of the eight limbs of Yoga by saying that practice in all those realms will enable that Absolute Unity. The dedicated practice will gradually reduce the impurities of mind and active karmic memories, producing continually greater stillness. The use of different wording here reinforces what the *Sutras* have previously said, that at the highest levels of consciousness experience everything dissolves, including the karmic memories that control the flow of destiny, bringing the seeker into the highest spiritual state. This *Sutra* describes an integrated set of practices that evolve us toward that high spirituality. In effect, Patanjali says here, 'If you want to get there, practice the eight limbs.' Each limb has purposes that contribute to the attainment. What is not said, nor immediately obvious, is that the highest three limbs are the meditative practices related to the already defined states of consciousness. The first five limbs are preparatory to meditation.

Some call these eight limbs and their practice 'Kriya Yoga' (literally, Action Yoga): That is correct, but not fully correct. The eight limbs combine features of Kriya Yoga and *Samkhya* philosophy. In modern Yoga culture, many believe that the word 'ashtanga' is Sanskrit for 'eight limbs,' and that modern Yoga practice of 'Ashtanga Yoga' is the practice of the eight limbs. That also has a degree of correctness, but the term Ashtanga Yoga is a modern term with roots only eighty years deep. Ashtanga is not a Sanskrit, Hindi or Urdu word, but a purposeful combination of the Sanskrit word *astan*, which means 'eight,' and *anga*, which means 'limb' or 'part.' It is likely that when founded, the modern 'tradition' of Ashtanga Yoga reduced Yoga practice to focus on those eight limbs. In actual broad-based practice, though, it has become mostly physical practice of postures and breathing. Iyengar Yoga, which emerged at the same time as Ashtanga Yoga, further reduced Yoga practice to a subset of the eight limbs, with a primary emphasis on posture development. Those two founders of Yoga-narrowing and redefinition, as well as the beloved Indra Devi, each of which gained a great reputation for physical (hatha) Yoga during the 1960s, were dedicated disciples of Krishnamacharya, a Master who was apparently deeply religious (Vaishnavism) and fully broad in his practice of Yoga. Because his students replaced 'sitting' with 'postures' and transformed spiritual Yoga to the greatly narrowed physical Yoga emphasized today, his followers and admirers refer to him as the 'father of modern Yoga.' All things, of course, have two sides.

yoga anga anuSThAnAd aSuddhi kSaye jNAna dIptir A viveka khyAteh

yoga	Yoga (as the name of the philosophy)
anga	limb
anusthanad	
anusthana	performance
ad	consume
azuddhi (for asuddhi)	impurity
ksaya (for ksaye)	wane
jjana (for jnana)	knowledge
dIpti (for diptir)	light
a	towards
viveka	discrimination
khyati (for khyateh)	perception

The Eight Limbs Are

2.29   The eight limbs within are self-restraint, restraint of mind, sitting, restraint of breath, withdrawal, concentration of the mind, religious meditation, and intense absorption.

yama   niyama   asana   prAnAyAma   pratyAhAra   dhAraNA   dhyAna
samAdhayo 'STAv aNgAni

*self-restraint   restraint of mind   sitting   restraint of breath   withdrawal
concentration of the mind   religious meditation   intense absorption   eight
limbs   within*

The eight limbs of Yoga life that lead to union are:

Self-Restraint	(*Yama*)
Restraint of mind	(*Niyama*)
Sitting	(*Asana*)
Restraint of breath	(*Pranayama*)
Withdrawal	(*Pratyahara*)
Concentration of the mind	(*Dharana*)
Religious Meditation	(*Dhyana*)
Intense absorption	(*Samadhi*)

Earlier Masters taught that the *Sutras* intended sequential practice of the eight limbs of Yoga; guiding students to master the first before taking on the second and so on. Typically, that was in a cloistered ashram environment where teachers had full control over the students living. That is not the case in modern cultures. There is some reference to this sequence in the text, particularly with the meditative limbs, but Patanjali does not hit heavily with it. It is, however, a solid idea. We need the foundation of the principles before going higher in practice. Yet, to be too insistent on that would often counter the practice. It would be better to follow your instinct for exploration and remember that all are important. The need for holistic integration of all practices outweighs the need for sequence: it would be better to practice the limbs in parallel or out of sequence than to not do them at all.

yama niyama asana prAnAyAma pratyAhAra dhA-
raNA dhyAna samAdhayo 'STAv aNgAni

yama	self-restraint
niyama	restraint of mind

asana	sitting
pranayama	restraint of breath
pratyahara	withdrawal
dharana	concentration of the mind
dhyana	religious meditation
samadhayo'	intense absorption
asta (for 'stav)	eight
angani	
anga	limb
ni	within

The First Limb - Self-Restraint

2.30   *Self-restraint is not injuring anything, being truthful, not stealing, living in the state of an unmarried religious student, and being destitute
of possessions.*

> ahiMsA   satya   asteya   brahmacarya   aparigrahA   yamAH
> *not injuring anything   truthful   not-stealing*
> *the state of an unmarried religious student   destitute of possessions*
> *self-restraint*

The five self-restraints are:

    not injuring anything

    truthful

    not stealing

    living in the state of an unmarried religious student

    being destitute of possessions

The restraints of this first limb of Yoga sound much like the Ten
Commandments, the Five Precepts of Buddhism, and the similar moral
codes within a variety of religions and philosophies. These are not, however,
'thou shalt not' commands, but self-restraints that will improve your life. No
restrictive rule exists in these restraints, within the 'restraints of the mind' of
the next limb, or any other part of the Yoga philosophy. This is simply wise
advice that if we restrain ourselves in these ways, it will improve our life. The
restraints are important to the seeker as a foundation for evolution. As with
every other aspect of Yoga, practicing each of the self-restraints brings calmness and quietness of mind.

The first of the self-restraints on behavior is 'not injuring anything.' You will see that most translators translate this as 'harmlessness' or 'non-harming.' A few translate it as non-violence, which is not a correct translation. Without the precise translation that includes the word 'anything,' it has become customary to interpret this as not harming others. The intention is broader than that. If you take the warning seriously, you will continually be aware of the many ways in which you can injure or bring harm to anyone or anything. You will continually attempt to reduce the injury you cause. If you try to imagine, or even write a list, of all the possible ways of injuring others, the inventory could become very long. Spend a little more time trying to think of all the ways that you can injure living beings that are not people and imagine how much that could lengthen the list. Having done that, include harm to nonliving things, perhaps to a pond, stream, or hillside where you might dump used motor oil. Now pick a few of those ways of injuring and try the difficult mind work of understanding how each would diminish you if you did it. Perhaps you can see how harming someone brings the mental disquiet of guilt, or other emotions. Perhaps you can see the agony and tension of planning to do the harm, or notice the fear of retribution. Maybe you can see how the ripple effects flow from the harmed person into others in the community.

Obviously, it would be impossible to build a checklist that you either memorize or refer to continually. The wise person who wants to move along the path toward quietness and healthier and more harmonic living will learn to self-monitor, looking for the daily opportunities to prevent events and reduce injury. The practice will eventually become automatic, not requiring conscious evaluation.

The second of the restraints is to being 'truthful.' Many minds will immediately accept that need and may perhaps spring to warnings from parents, clergy, and teachers. Some will expect god-retaliation for untruthfulness. Most of us have been down this road of instruction. It is, of course not always learned or accepted, and sometimes has caused rebellion. Yet, it has been such a powerful message that we at least do not want anyone to catch us at lying. Lying may even yield punishment, rejection, or failure to get what we want.

Most of us can easily see the self-damage of lying. We look over our shoulder a lot. We expect that others are lying to us. We build webs of misinformation that we lose control of. It generates bad feelings about us. It makes us anxious and nervous. It makes us smaller, weaker people. Yet, we do not go the step further and look at the effect in the way a spiritual seeker would look at it. We do not anticipate a destiny effect, a retribution, or payback in kind. We do not think of how strongly it keeps the mind agitated and busy, preventing our spiritual growth.

Yet, truthfulness is far more than not lying. A truthfulness context we do not think of, for which there is no punishment from others, is failure to be authentic. If you fail to become a person consistent with your nature, try to masquerade as something other than your nature, you are going to suffer. Your life will not activate. It will be an unrewarding life of wasted potential. You will not be able to harmonize with the greater consciousness that knows the difference between truth and falsity, or to move along the path toward union.

Then of course, there is the huge untruthfulness of living in fantasy, ignoring reality. We live in a culture that continually misrepresents truth and reality, sometimes extending to gross institutional untruths. We become used to it through television: the weather, news, commercials, and entertainment are so often perversions of reality that we have come to not know the difference. In total, it does great harm to our society. Lack of care about truth, with many seeing it as an obstacle to their success, is warping the view of an entire civilization. Individually, accepting the untruths as if they were truths takes us ever further from reality.

Patanjali has already warned us of several effects on our lives that come from such misperception. If we want to find higher consciousness, we need to focus on discriminating reality from falsity. That discrimination is necessary on all planes of consciousness. When our consciousness is in the material/sensory realm, we must be able to know what is real and false in the world around us. When experiencing other levels of consciousness, we must always be able to discriminate between that level and material consciousness. When we come to understand the Reality underlying and supporting the material world we come to accept new truths that our everyday mind could never imagine.

Not stealing, the third of the restraints, takes on several forms in the Ten Commandments. We know that stealing, much like untruthfulness, is a punishment generator. We know what will happen if we slip ten dollars from our father's wallet, rob banks, 'borrow' from the petty cash fund, or climb up to the cookie jar. Far more laws exist prohibiting stealing than for prohibiting lying. Yet, there are many ways of stealing, some even hard to imagine.

How many ways can you imagine to steal? What are all the injuries that result from stealing, thereby violating the not injuring restraint also? What ways do they affect our lives? If you are a speaker on a panel and two other speakers follow you, is it stealing to use more time than your allocation of the total time? If you deliberately attract the affection of someone away from someone else, is that stealing? If you sneakily plant a row of trees or place a fence ten feet past your lot line, is that stealing? Is it not stealing, whether we like the idea or not, to put up a satellite dish and intercept signals we have not paid to access. Is it not stealing not to pay taxes owed, when we know we can get away with it? Again, we must look not just at the harm caused, but also at the effect on ourselves. We must be aware of how it diminishes us, blocks us, disquiets us, and harms our spiritual growth.

Then we come to the difficult subject of *brahmacarya*, 'living in the state of an unmarried religious student.' This means that those in ardent and sincere pursuit of a yogic life should employ great devotion to continuously study, meditate, and avoid the powerful distractive forces of materialism, sensuality, and sexuality.

Study is extremely important to success in Yoga. The seeker must correctly understand the philosophy, teachings, and practices. Without study, we cannot learn truths that others have learned, and the seeker would not have the stimulus of inspiration derived from others. In Patanjali's time, all study was local. Typically, the student studied specific available texts under the guidance of a guru and came to understand it in the way the local guru came to understand it, through the guidance of that single person. In later times, many gurus told their students to study nothing other than what they provided, and to follow their guidance without variance. It is a practice not sanctioned by, nor originated in, Yoga philosophy or the *Yoga Sutras*.

Today, spiritual study has a far broader base, with an unending supply of information and texts available from around the world. Gurus of varying degrees of knowledge, experience, insight, evolution, and authenticity exist everywhere. Today few of those who call themselves gurus, and even some who carry the respected designation of Swami, have reached the advanced evolutionary status of many gurus of that day. 'Traditions,' religions, personal opinions, commercial interests, and continual alteration over time have affected large amounts of the material available for study. For the spiritual seeker, the need for study to truly understand Yoga still exists. It is a more difficult task today, in which the student must carefully choose sources and reject much inauthentic information to find the seeds of Truth. Study must be continuous and dedicated.

Nearly all translators and interpreters only bring attention to part of the intention of living a student's life, by translating *brahmacarya* to 'chastity,' 'continence,' 'celibacy' or 'sexual abstinence.' Giving up sexuality is such a fearful image to most people of today, and so impossible to hold to, that it can become a major block to pursuing Yoga. Many of us have observed Yoga teachers, speakers, and even swamis dance around that loaded subject with great care. Few of them are willing to lose students or followers over it. Many useful lessons come from those delicate dances. A swami wisely advises that we should not waste our energies; that we need to preserve them for our spiritual practice. Another sage advises not to worry about it at this point; it is a subject for higher-level practice. Some appropriately tie the subject to other restraints, such as truthfulness and nonharming. More than one esoteric entanglement has passed from lip to ear. Stories abound, both parable and real, of those, high and low, who have fallen from the path through their sexuality. There is so much interest in the sexuality aspect that it is hard to get past it to examine the real message of the aphorism. Yet, few tell the students what they really need to know. Self-imposed celibacy does not work. It simply pushes the drive down into pressure cooker status, only to erupt at some future time. Celibacy naturally evolves over time in proportion to the degree of evolution of spirituality.

To make it easier, remember that the whole thing is about what we do to ourselves, to our growth, and to our evolution. With sexuality or anything else, we must ask what it is doing to our life and us. It is always our decision to make. There is no rule to follow. Is our response to whatever situation exists in the moment keeping us on our chosen path, or taking us away from it? Remember that it is a big tradeoff game. Is what you are getting out of it worth the price you pay for it? Do you know what all of the prices are, not just financial?

This issue can raise questions in many aspects of living. The most important of all is our intention. If we have formed a spiritual intention, and defined a path, we need to keep a pure view of that path. That is to say that we cannot allow our trick-able mind to corrupt our intention so that life will be more comfortable. The restraint advises to keep purely to our principles, values, drives, practices, and faithfulness in the philosophy. Losing our pure intention places us in positions of complexity, anxiety, worry, doubt, and conflicting ideas that sap us. Yes, gurus do advise not to waste energy on the alluring things in the material world, but that advice is far broader than sexuality. A huge number of traps, sensual and otherwise, are along the path.

The fifth and last of the restraints is 'being destitute of possessions.' Over the millennia, translators have somehow universally converted this to 'greed-lessness.' That is a valuable attribute in a yogi, but it is a reversal of the idea of not having possessions, perhaps created to make it seem less extreme. In effect, it sanctions having possessions, but cautions against wanting too many of them. However, it is not reasonable or workable to walk the streets with a beggar's bowl in this modern world. We cannot expect a rich person to give us support and housing while we pursue our spirituality as has historically happened in India. We need a place to live, food, sanitation, protection, and other necessities. Those require possessions. The question then becomes one of how to balance living in the world with seeking our spirituality. What minimal possessions do we need to support that, and what is the appropriate way of acquiring them? Yes, the most spiritual people will have fewer possessions than those of lesser spirituality, or perhaps even none, but we are not all destined to be the most spiritual. It is spiritually desirable to reduce the number of possessions we have as we evolve. It is also true that as we evolve we will naturally want fewer possessions.

Perhaps the best way to understand the benefits of all the self-restraints is to play a mind game. Understand first, like it or not, that you are irrevocably and unavoidably a teacher of others. Everything you do teaches someone something. To play the game, with that as a background thought, pick any of the five self-restraints you want to play with: pick just one and come back for another round if you like. Now search your mind for someone who has gone to the extreme opposite of that restraint, so far out that it epitomizes his or her life. If you do not know any person like that, imagine such a life of nearly pathological lying, sex, rejecting study, eating, or whatever. See the effect that it has on their life. Do it without moral judgment. Just see what it does to them personally.

ahiMsA satya asteya brahmacarya aparigrahA yamAH

ahimsa	not injuring anything
satya	truthful
asteya	not stealing
brahmacarya	the state of an unmarried religious student
aparigraha	destitute of possession
yama (for yamah)	self-restraint

Uninterrupted Great Duty

2.31   That great duty is uninterrupted by the form of existence fixed by birth, place, time, or circumstances, and relates to all conditions of the mind.

jAti deSa kAla samaya anavacchinnAH sarvabhaumA mahAvratam
form of existence fixed by birth place time circumstances uninterrupted relating to all conditions of the mind   a great duty

The *Sutra* tells us this self-restraint is not something that one takes lightly, emphasizing its importance. Having accepted the duty to adhere to these principles in our life, it does not matter what the conditions of the karmic birth were, where we are, what the time is, or whatever of a myriad of potential circumstances are surrounding us. The duty is unbreakable. Our mood, excitement state, fear, emotions, or any other condition of the mind cannot become an excuse justifying parting from that duty. These baseline principles are extremely important to fulfilling the purposes of Yoga.

jAti deSa kAla samaya anavacchinnAH sarvabhaumA mahAvratam

jati	the form of existence fixed by birth
deza (for desa)	place
kala	time
samaya	circumstances
anavacchinna (for anavacchinnah)	uninterrupted
sarvabhauma	relating to all conditions of the mind
mahavrata (for mahavratam)	a great duty

The Second Limb - Restraint Of Mind

2.32 *Restraint of mind is the practice of purity of mind, contentment, religious austerity, reciting to oneself, and profound religious meditation on the Supreme Being.*

Sauca saMtosA tapaH svAdhyAya Isvara praNidhAnAni niyamAH
purity of mind   contented   religious austerity   reciting to oneself   Supreme Being   profound religious meditation   restraint of mind

The second limb of Yoga establishes self-discipline over our style of living, our way of being in the world. It recommends five attitudinal commitments that will strengthen the foundation the self-restraints provide. If we can characterize the first limb as being in the realm of commitment to principles, we can characterize this second limb as being in the realm of commitment to a way of being. These are not new subjects. Patanjali has introduced them before, within different contexts.

The first of the mental restraints is purity of mind. In considering this meaning, it is helpful to remember that the emphasis on stillness as purity is a theme that runs through the entire set of *Sutras*. It is among the most important aspects of fulfilling the aspirations of a yogin. This restraint relates directly to that, and is instrumental in achieving that by caringly and mindfully restraining the content of the mind. Mind contents such as thoughts of hatred, jealousy, competition, fear, untruths, greed, judgments, and many others add to the disquiet of the mind. Mind contents of peace, love, caring, sharing, helping, and others are more quieting to the mind. Keeping a pure mental view of our intentions and what the path is that we are traveling is necessary to receiving the blessings of progress. Above all bringing the mind to stillness through meditation is the greatest purification.

Contentment is the second life practice that deserves our continual mindfulness. Few of us are ever content. We want more. We want to do better. We want a different life. We want recognition. We want money. We want spirituality. We want peace. We want control. Wants drive us. Wants lead to attachments. Attachments lead to protection of what we have. Both lead to internal conflicts. Conflicts unsettle our lives and our minds. Again, the problem stems from that image we have of our self as a material being. That image makes us feel in control. We try to control the world, to shape it to our specifications.

If you recognize the Reality behind the material world, understand the presence and nature of your internal being, and accept the existence of *brahman/isvara* you can become content. You will understand that all situations create outside of you, that you have no control over them. You will begin to flow in harmony with Nature. Contentment is another of those things that you cannot directly make happen. You cannot order yourself to be content, but you can firmly establish it as an aspired for result of your practice. Understanding that it is a derivative of living the life and practicing the disciplines helps to bring it about. Like anger or other negatives, you cannot suppress discontent. You can only replace it with content over time, through how you live.

Some translate the Sanskrit word for the third mental restraint simply to 'austerity,' rather than 'religious austerity.' The word 'austerity' carries a heavy load. From the viewpoint of some historical forms of Yoga, austerity would point to self-harm, deprivation, and degradation. Currently, it is a government word for asking us to give things up, while raising our taxes and imposing restrictions. To our minds, an austere person is cold, unapproachable, and usually not attractive. Thinking of austerity in our own lives raises images of poverty, self-denial, wearing hair shirts, and even self-damage. These are negative images. The word 'religious' can have similar effects on people. Yet, in the meaning of this aphorism neither of those words carries those loads. The *Sutra* 2.1 discussion of Kriya Yoga provides the positive perspective of the term, in which the yogin leads a simple, studious, non-sensuous, and quiet life in the way monks or nuns do.

As shown in the 2.1 introduction of Kriya Yoga the translation of *svadhyaya* is 'reciting to one's self.' Not at first obvious, the intent is to have the seeker always recite learning acquired along the path until it firmly embeds in the mind. This learning may be from the many texts on Yoga, or in the case of those participating in some 'traditions,' from religious texts. It may come from listening to or observing others, from insights gained during meditation, or many other sources. However, the seeker has an unceasing duty and huge challenge to purge incorrect knowledge, eliminate fantasy thinking, and test beliefs until they become truths. This translation differs from those of typical translators or interpreters who simply say that the aphorism is about 'study or 'self-study.' The translation notes in Volume 2 describe that difference and tell you why it is an erroneous translation.

The continual emphasis on meditation as the theme of the book appears again in this fifth mental restraint, profound religious meditation, a backbone of the Kriya Yoga introduced in 2.1, where the Supreme Being was the meditative target. Among the many approaches to and uses for meditation in the *Sutras*, Patanjali shows the importance of meditation on the Supreme Being (*isvara/brahma/god/sat*) and meditation on *om*, which is its symbol, by bringing them forward in separate *Sutras*.

Sauca saMtosA tapaH svAdhyAya Isvara praNidhAnAni niyamAH

zauca (for sauca)	purity of mind
samtosa	contented
tapa (for tapah)	religious austerity
svadhyaya	reciting to one's self
izvara (for isvara)	Supreme Being
pranidhanani	
pranidhana	profound religious meditation
ani	(untranslated)
niyama (for niyamah)	restraint of mind

DOUBT

To Remove Doubt

2.33   To remove doubt, direct one's thoughts to the opposite side.

vitarka bAdhane pratipakSa bhAvanam
doubt   removal   the opposite side   direct one's thoughts

Doubt can occur in many ways, including lack of faith, uncertainty, disbelief, and distrust. The key to the aphorism is in the word *pratipaksa*, which means 'the opposite side.' It tells the seeker to move beyond doubt by thinking of the opposite side, but it is not immediately obvious what 'opposite side' means. We could say that it means to reflect on the opposite side of the issue, but doubt can have many facets with no single opposite side. It clearly does not mean that we should meditate on 'non-doubt' as the opposite side of 'doubt.' To understand that opposite side, it is necessary to recognize that the doubt comes about during the mind's interplay with the material world, either subtle or physical. We naturally mind-wrestle the many factors that exist in any situation. The material world that we live in and the spiritual world we aspire to experience through meditation are opposite sides of the coin of existence. Doubt does not exist within the spiritual world. The guidance is to direct your thoughts to the spiritual side of things, when the material side has you doubting. Do it in that quiet, confident, undisturbed way, as exemplified in the monks and nuns in *Sutra* 2.32 above. Entering repetition of a mantra is one good way of doing that. Just six *Sutras* before this, in *Sutra* 2.27, Patanjali said that there are seven stages of samadhi experience resulting from meditation. In the first and third of those stages (*savitarka samadhi* and *savicara samadhi*) uncertainty can tinge the received insights. Doubts do not exist in the other five stages.

vitarka bAdhane pratipakSa bhAvanam

vitarka	doubt
badhana (for badhane)	removing
pratipaksa	the opposite side
bhavana (for bhavanam)	direct one's thoughts to

Cause Of Doubt, Injuring, And Lack Of Compassion

2.34   *Earlier than doubt, injury, and lack of compassion, whether acquired,*
brought about (in others), or (considered) acceptable, and whether slight,
moderate, or excessive, there is eager desire, anger, darkness of mind, or
delusion, bringing the consequences of difficulty and spiritual ignorance of
the eternal. Thus, direct one's thoughts to the opposite side.

vitarkA hiMsA AdayaH kRta kArita anumoditA lobha
krodha moha pUrvakA mRdu madhya adhimAtrA duHkha
ajNAna ananta phalA iti pratipakSa bhAvanam
doubt   injury   no compassion   acquired   brought about   acceptable
eager desire for   anger   darkness or delusion of mind   earlier
slight   middle   excessive   difficulty   spiritual ignorance   eternal
consequence   thus   the opposite side   direct one's thoughts

Doubt, injury of any kind, and having no compassionate feelings for others, do not arise by themselves. They result from personal characteristics such
as overwhelming desires, anger, darkness of mind and delusion. The earned
difficulties and spiritual ignorance are not just from our personal acquisition of those traits, but also from our actions causing those things to come
about in others, and to our deeming them acceptable in others or ourselves.
It makes no difference whether are participation is slight, moderate, or excessive. Unless we are free of them, they will bring some degree of impurity to
the mind, affect our Yoga practice, and impede our personal evolution.

As with the doubt in the preceding aphorism, the seeker should move the
focus to of the spiritual side for relief from the obstacles. Mantras, dropping
into a meditative release, or remembering a spiritual experience could help.
Contemplating how all the factors specified here affect or block spirituality
could reduce future need.

vitarkA hiMsA AdayaH kRta kArita anumoditA lobha krodha moha pUrvakA mRdu madhya adhimAtrA duH-
kha ajNAna ananta phalA iti pratipakSa bhAvanam

vitarka	doubt
himsa	injury

adayah
   a   (negating) no
     daya   compassion

adayah	
a	(negating) no
daya	compassion
krta	acquired
karita	brought about
anumodita	acceptable
lobha	eager desire for
krodha	anger
moha	darkness or delusion of mind
purvaka	earlier
mrdu	slight
madhya	middle
adhimatra	excessive
duhkha	difficulty
ajnana	
a	(negation) no
jjana (for jnana)	spiritual ignorance
ananta	eternal
phala	consequence
iti	thus
pratipaksa	the opposite side
bhavana (for bhavanam)	direct one's thoughts to

RESULTS OF THE SELF-RESTRAINTS

Result Of Not Injuring

Patanjali has just finished presenting the self-restraints and mind restraints, the first two limbs of Yoga, all ten of which require a deliberate approach to living. He now explores the positive results of living by these standards and negative results that come from not living by them.

2.35 In this manner, with steadfastness in not injuring anything, those who come near him will abandon enmity.

    ahiMsA pratiSThAyAM tat saMnidhau vaira tyAgaH
      not injuring anything steadfastness in this manner
        him to bring near enmity abandoned

What a surprising and wonderful idea. Imagine everyone giving up enmity toward us. Perhaps it is hard to find role models who have acted that out in your life experience, or to imagine no one feeling that you are their enemy. Yet, it is easy to comprehend the lesser degree effect of at least some people not seeing you as their enemy, and that the numbers of such people could build as your purity becomes more established. Turn that around and visualize people that you recognize as never causing injury. Can you see that you will not feel threatened by them and will put up fewer defenses? Can you also see that you and others will make fewer preemptive attacks, since there is no need to treat that person as an enemy?

It takes a long time to understand the multitudinous ways that we injure or harm and the messages of potential threat that we send out without knowing we are sending them. Others will always react to potential injury or safety, and the degree of reaction will vary with the degree of threat or its opposite. Toward the extreme, for a few highly evolved yogins, enmity *will* fully dissolve in their presence. All Yoga effects build slowly, being the result of long practice and relinquishing involvement with the world. Can you see how you would be better off if the number of people who thought of you as an enemy slowly dwindled? Would you become slowly happier and more serene? That happens in the life of a dedicated yogin.

This marvelous aphorism, worthy of hanging on anyone's wall, is directly meaningful in its most obvious sense, but it has an underlying message that is a carrier wave for all of the *Sutras*. Patanjali has such faith in the clarity of the teachings that he rarely elucidates. He seems to assume that you have taken his second *Sutra* to heart, understood them, and so fully accept them that they have engrained in your being. The cryptographic key to the carrier wave of the *Sutras* is right here, hiding in plain sight. To find the key on your own, you need to do little more than pose the self-inquiry, 'Why is this important?' Reject your string of false intellectual answers until insight lands within you. Observe that he has not emphasized right or wrong. He has not moralized about the affect you have on the world or others, as useful as that teaching might be. He has not used words like 'good or bad.' He has simply pointed to the effect on you. 'Enmity *toward you* will be abandoned in *your* presence.' What would happen if you never had to worry or fret about enemies? The answer is that you would be more still and serene, with far fewer mind ripples. That is why it is important.

Yet, as true as all that is, and as meaningful as Patanjali wanted to make it for our everyday living, you will be a rare being if you have seen the Truth that he laid before you. The opened yogin of higher consciousness would see it immediately, without puzzlement or surprise. Such a yogin would see the literal Truth of perfect restraint from injuring that causes enmity to 'be abandoned in your presence.' As much as your load of enemies will reduce with your growth in Yoga, be clear that the *Sutra* does not say, and does not mean, that the result will be that you will have no enemies. It is about how people act when 'in your presence.' It is factually true, and often observed and documented that people of certain high consciousness cause a meltdown effect on people who are in their presence. It is impossible to maintain feelings of enmity while in the proximity of such people, whether the effect comes from their radiance, psychic emanations, love, respect, or a combination of many things. Jesus, Buddha, and perhaps every highly evolved person had enemies. Yet, that enmity could often not be active within their local sphere. The power of their evolved nature kept it away. The reactions of the soldiers who came to arrest Jesus and could not do it until he invited it are a wonderful example of this. There are many stories of hostile people approaching Masters, only to wilt in their presence.

ahiMsA pratiSThAyAM tat saMnidhau vaira tyAgaH

ahimsa	not injuring anything
pratisthayam	
pratistha	steadfastness
aya	in this manner
tad (for tat)	him
samnidha (for samnidhau)	to bring near
vaira	enmity
tyaga (for tyagah)	abandoning

Result Of Truthfulness

2.36   *In this manner, when in the state of steadfast truthfulness, the actions have their effects.*

satya   pratiSThAyAm   kriyA   phala   ASrayatvam
truthful   steadfastness   in this manner   action   effect   the state of

If we establish a life of full truthfulness, the *Sutras* say, our words will yield the result they depict. At a simple everyday level, if people do not trust our words, they will be less likely to take them seriously and follow through on what we ask of them or convey to them. They may suspect bad intention or motivation. They will be more likely to resist or rebel against anything we say. Depending on the degree of mistrust or threat they feel, they may even actively work against us. To the degree that people know from experience, or can intuitively sense, our honesty, truthfulness, and good intention they will be more likely to follow our lead.

If we develop such a trusting and non-resisting relationship with people, we will also be at greater peace, in a state of higher equanimity. Again, that is what the Yoga game is about; we evolve toward ever-greater equanimity and peace until we merge into the stillness and peace of the Absolute primal existence, *brahman.* That is the full and final 'effect' that our acts bring. It is not possible to attain it without full truthfulness.

The aphorism points to the benefit that we all can get as well as the effect of truthfulness while in the higher levels of evolution that fewer yogins attain. It directly describes what happens when a highly evolved seeker has attained perfect truthfulness. When such a yogin says something will be true, it will be true. It will be true because that seeker can accurately assess the future, and because the images formed in high consciousness will cause the effect. The yogin is so 'tuned-in' and harmonized that untruth cannot exist. Every thought, word, and action at that level is spiritual, joined with *isvara/brahman.*

One must sufficiently absorb and settle in a high consciousness state before truly understanding the supra-human power of truthfulness and integrating the teaching of this *Sutra* with those of others. A later important one, for example, speaks of mastering the elements of Nature. The physical Laws of the universe allow people at high levels of evolution to cause Nature to respond in ways that seem miraculous to us, but which the Laws truly allow.

satya pratiSThAyAm kriyA phala ASrayatvam

satya   truthful

pratisthayam
    pratistha   steadfastness
    aya   in this manner
kriya   action
phala   effect
azrayatva (for asrayatvam)   the state of

Result Of Nonstealing

2.37   In this manner, being steadfast in not stealing places one near to all gifts.

asteya pratiSThAyAM sarva ratna upasthAnam
*not stealing steadfastness in this manner   all   a gift   the act of placing one's
self near to*

At the everyday level, many experience the gifts that come from living by the principle of not stealing. Both material and spiritual blessings come as we fall into harmony with these principles, always consistent with our needs and our karmic situation. At the highest level, where not stealing is a firm element of the yogin's continuous life style, the relationship between the Supreme Being and the individual is in such harmony that life becomes a wave of gifts that carry the seeker closer to union.

The common message of all Yoga teaching also lies unstated beneath the surface of this *Sutra*. Everything in the *Sutras* relates to the purpose of Yoga to move continually toward equanimity and internal quietness. Stealing will involve plotting, covering up, evading capture, and causing harm: that will place great chaos and turmoil in our minds. If we even consider accepting the opportunities to steal without acting on them, that chaotic mind state will come about from deliberating the possibilities. On the other side of that coin, if non-stealing were to automatically engrain in our life, protecting us from our natural inclination toward the hundreds of ways we can steal, we will be more open to receiving whatever gifts the source sends our way. As others interpret this aphorism, even gems can be near us without causing a ripple of temptation or ambivalence to our principles. We will not strive to attain that wealth that will oppose our equanimity. Yet, as true as that is, it is not what Patanjali teaches in this *Sutra*. Although it is true that each practice increases our equanimity and inner quietness, this *Sutra* focuses on the gift of blessings that derive from a life dedicated to not stealing.

asteya pratiSThAyAM sarva ratna upasthAnam

asteya	not stealing
pratisthayam	
pratistha	steadfastness
aya	in this manner
sarva	all
ratna	gift
upasthana (for upasthanam)	the act of placing one's self near to

Result Of Being In The State Of A Religious Student

2.38 Steadfastness in being in the state of an unmarried religious student brings attainment of energy.

brahmacarya pratiSThAyAm vIrya lAbhaH
*the state of an unmarried religious student steadfastness
in this manner energy attaining*

This aphorism speaks clearly of the yogin's need to 'live the life of an unmarried religious student.' That includes all the things that such a student would do, including religious (or spiritual) study, devotion, having a chaste personal life, praying, meditation, seeking the counsel of those who have gained knowledge, and many other things. It tells us that the orientation will give us energy for the yogic life. That energy comes about in several ways. The very idea energizes us toward the goal. The seeker might redirect the sexual activity or the energy consumed by seeking sensual/material experiences of many types to other activities. If the yogin's practice includes Yoga techniques of breathing and meditation, they further build a supply of pranic energy.

Although that is the true meaning of the term *brahmacarya*, none of the authors of the books referenced by this one, and virtually no modern interpreter, conveys that message. They all restrict their view to a subset of the unmarried student's life with terms such as 'continence,' 'sexual abstinence,' 'celibacy,' 'moderation,' and 'chastity.' That observance causes much discussion and continual reframing to attain greater acceptability. Many teachers of all levels struggle with it, often light-footedly step by it, and sometimes do amazing word dances to provide a 'sellable' perspective, fearing that a reputation for interfering with the powerful sexual drive will keep people away from Yoga.

That modern trend of *brahmacarya* interpretation would have us believe that Yoga has a strict prohibition against sexuality, and that sexual chastity is a necessary discipline imposed on, or voluntarily taken on, by serious yogins. Some modern teaching also dictates that withdrawal from sex should be willfully instant. Pure Yoga does not teach prohibition or instant willful withdrawal: both of those ideas developed within recent Yoga history. The *Sutras* say nothing about prohibition or speed of withdrawal. Gradual personal evolution is far better at achieving that steady state than willful suppression of the sex drive.

The yogin that follows the common misperceptions of today that guide students to willful suppression of the sexual drive faces many short-term and long-term problems. Not only is it nearly impossible to suppress, suppression of anything only strengthens it and buries it deeply, poised to surface again. The efforts at suppression create anxieties, doubts, stress, neurosis, and internal chaos. They take away our peace. Sexual drive only abates as spiritual drive replaces it. Over time, sometimes deliberately, but more often not so deliberately, the yogin slowly evolves toward less interest in sensuality of all types and greater interest in spirituality.

brahmacarya pratiSThAyAm vIrya lAbhaH

brahmacarya	the state of an unmarried religious student
pratisthayam	
pratistha	steadfastness
aya	in this manner
virya	energy
labha (for labhah)	attaining

Result Of Having No Possessions

2.39   With steadfastness in being destitute of possessions, there is perfect under-
standing of the state of your life.

aparigraha sthairye janma kathaMtA saMbodhaH
destitute of possessions perseverance life the what state
perfect understanding

Although gaining access to deep understanding of your state of being for
the current lifetime sounds like a desirable result, the true meaning of that
does not immediately gel, nor does the connection to having possessions. The
restraint and benefit do not appear to relate to each other. If you ask yourself
how having possessions keeps us from access to understanding of our current
life situation, the question may appear difficult.

Abstaining from possessions is a different character of restraint. It more
directly interacts with the physical materiality of the world, attaching us more
firmly to its nature. In that light, they are a perfect pairing, because if you
let possessing things drive your life, you will fix much of your attention on
acquiring and holding them. Having acquired them, attachment to them will
then form, and they will become aspects of your self-created false self-image,
reinforcing that image. If some factor in your life, such as a desire for more
spirituality were to cause you to self-examine that self-image or the drive
for acquisition, the ensuing doubts might cause equivocation about keeping them and about acquiring more. In such a situation, many of us would
choose to hold to the status quo, unwilling to trade in something that gives us
a lot of material or sensual reward for something whose rewards are unclear.
Dealing with possessions and self-examination leading toward spiritual evolution as a yogin are incompatible, creating great internal conflict.

We remove the desire and need for possessions from our life as we naturally
examine our motivations, drives, psychology, fantasies, and history. Realizing
all the new benefits that reducing possessions can provide and knowing the
full range of personal costs for obtaining and holding those possessions might
lead a dedicated yogin to a decision to change. Among those personal costs
would be the degree of our attention and energy that the possessions cause,

and the internal stresses, disquiet, tensions, and conflicts that the protection and continuation generate. However, devoted practice and continual awareness of it require a spiritually oriented, evolutionary perspective with analysis by the intuition, not just by the intellect.

The two are a bound pair of opposites. If we reduce one, the other increases. If the drive for possessions goes up, self-examination and spirituality go down. If self-examination and spirituality go up, interest in possessions goes down. Because we cannot look at ourselves and see the potentials for another kind of life while pursuing goals to have possessions, renouncing possessions yields deep knowledge of the self-situation. The more we move away from possession orientation, the quieter our mind becomes. The quieter our mind becomes the more we move toward the goals of Yoga. As we move toward the goals of Yoga, material needs and desires diminish, and contentment and insights to who we are and how we are being increase.

aparigraha sthairye janma kathaMtA saMbodhaH

aparigraha	destitute of possession
sthairya (for sthairye)	steadfastness
janman (for janma)	life
kathamta	the what state
sambodha (for sambodhah)	perfect knowledge or understanding

RESULTS OF THE MIND RESTRAINTS

Result Of Purity

2.40 *Constant purity of mind brings dislike of one's own body and no intercourse with your others.*

SaucAt sva aNga jugupsA parair asaMsargah
*purity of mind to go constantly one's own body dislike
others your   no intercourse with*

The *Sutra* points to three largely unrecognized and necessary aspects of a yogin's evolution, individualism, moving away from fascination with the body, and separation from others. As purity of mind increases, the path narrows, higher consciousness experiences come about, and many things gradually change. The yogin's viewpoint, insights, confidence, and desire to continue the evolution bring wariness against alteration of thoughts, values, priorities, and many other things by outsiders, in order to maintain and protect the purity of the yogic beingness. The term 'no intercourse with' refers to all interactions with others, including sexual intercourse, which is among the many definitions of the word that Patanjali chose for this aphorism, *asamsargah*. Interactions with others could include talking, playing, arguing, receiving teaching, dining, sharing events, sexual intercourse, fighting, loving, judging, and many other aspects of living. Since they have the potential for altering the yogin in many different ways, becoming obstacles on the path, and diminishing the purity of mind, the experienced seeker intuitively avoids them.

It is good to keep in mind that from their start to their finish the *Sutras* show us a pattern of progressive development. As the true purposes of Yoga clarify through our practice and study, that progressive flow becomes ever clearer. At the start, Patanjali established that stillness of mind is the way to union, and holds to that perspective as the *Sutras* unfold. All practices leading to union are practices that move us from turbulent mental fluctuations at one end of the scale to mental stillness at the other end. That progress simultaneously moves us from focus in the material world to focus in the spiritual world. From another perspective, Yoga practices move us from interest in the physical being, whether narcissistic, sensuous, or other, to interest in our spiritual life. As consciousness evolves, such yogins become wary that the different thoughts and behaviors of others will contaminate their understandings and insights. They become increasingly discriminative about information received from others, recognizing the delusions and wrong perceptions. They may intermix with others, but their mentality will not blend with the mentality presented by others. 'Not blending' is actually another valid definition of *asamsargah*.

SaucAt sva aNga jugupsA parair asaMsargah

saucat
zauca (for sauca)   purity of mind
at   to go constantly

sva	one's own
anga	body
jugupsa	dislike
parair	
para	others
ir	(indicates second or third person plural) your
asamsargah	
a	(indicates negation)
samsarga	intercourse with

Purification Evolves Us

2.41 And mind purification, cheerfulness, one-pointedness, conquering the power of the senses, procure fitness for perception of the soul.

sattva Suddhi saumanasya eka agrya indriya jaya
Atma darSana yogyatvAni ca
mind purification cheerfulness one-pointedness power of the sense conquering soul perception fitness procure and

Continuing the discussion of purification, that is to say stillness of the mind, the *Sutra* tells us that the purification works with other elements of a Yoga life to gradually bring us toward the highest experiences. It is important to recognize the *Sutra* does not say that the purification or other factors instantly give us the result: they 'procure fitness' for it, thereby stimulating the process. Without significant contribution from each, it would be a slower process.

As our Yoga practice progresses, we live less and less with the negative ideas, illusions, delusions, inner turmoil, and struggles that produce anger and depression, all of which keep the mind agitated and unsettled. The resulting cheerfulness is an early step in the movement toward later happiness and joy. Cultivating it helps with the mind stilling.

At first, our practice of the meditative limbs of Yoga faces the difficulties of quelling the thoughts and quieting the mind. As the stilling progresses, we develop our ability to be 'one-pointed' on the target. With continued practice and increased stilling, that intense focus will lead first to oneness with the

target and then progressively on to the higher levels of meditation characterized by even greater focus and stilling.

The five senses constantly provide disquieting stimuli and lure the yogin
toward the pleasures and satisfactions of the material world, often becoming
the source of desires, stress, and a foundation for fantasies, delusions, and
illusions. A continuous internal warlike conflict occurs with the quietness of
spirituality on one side and the sensory stimulation on the other. Conquering
the power those senses have over us is vital to stillness and moving to higher
levels of spirituality.

The final words of the aphorism indicate that the purifying (stilling) is
preparation for the ultimate result of Yoga, experiencing the consciousness of
the soul.

sattva Suddhi saumanasya eka agrya indriya

jaya Atma darSana yogyatvAni ca

sattva	mind
zuddhi (for suddhi)	purification
saumanasya	cheerfulness
ekagra (for eka + agrya)	one-pointedness
indriya	power of the senses
jaya	conquering
atman (for atma)	soul
darzana (for darsana)	perception
yogyatvani	
yogyata	fitness
vani	procuring
ca	and

Contentment On The Path

*2.42   Attain consuming unsurpassed contentment while in the effort to win
future beatitude.*

saMtosAd anuttamaH sukha lAbhaH
contented consume unsurpassed the effort to win future beatitude attaining

For those who aspire to the path of winning future beatitude through
practice of Yoga, it is necessary to attain a personal attitude of keeping to

contentment while following that path, consuming it as if it were a nutrient. That requires great faith in the rightness of the life in the face of doubts and temptations.

Purification of the mind prepares us for attaining that through natural evolution. Just as *Sutra* 2.7 told us that relinquishing desire prepared us for future beatitude, this one tells us that living a life consumed in contentment also does. It does not point to the obvious situation of opposite sides of a scale. As desire diminishes, contentment increases. If contentment should decrease, desire would increase. Desire is a materiality characteristic and contentment is a characteristic of spirituality. Where *Sutra* 2.7 did not qualify the degree of desire, this one points to a situation in which the scale has tipped, resulting in a high degree of contentment and low degree of desire.

The sought after beatitude is a blessed state of serenity, bliss, and joy that comes about in a state of stillness of the mind. Simple contentment, unqualified by degree or dedication to its continuous presence, is an earlier state of lesser stillness when factors common to human life have begun to lessen their disquieting of the mind. A discontented person will always be searching for more, something different, more agreeable, less upsetting, or in line with personal perception of how things should be, never finding satisfaction even with things found in the search. A discontented person can be riding waves of resentment, embarrassment, anxiety, anger, desire, wanting, or greed. All are negative: they will lead to pessimism, doubt, loss of faith, and straying from the path. All require great energy investment. A discontented life requires continual focus on finding what will bring contentment, along with the individual's search that does not end.

Contentment exists in varying degrees, progressively growing as the yogic practice matures. A contented person moves away from waves of distraction. A contented person has available energy and vitality. He or she will be living life as it is right now, not focused on past or future, not looking for more. Such people move toward dealing with whatever comes along with equanimity, not making judgments, characterizing as good or bad, emoting, or wishing for something 'other.' Just as they are not riding negative waves that drain their energy, they are not riding positive waves that sap them through exuberant bursts of energy, captivate their attention, respond to needs of ego, and tempt them toward obsession or addiction. They are steady observers of the moment and receivers for what comes. As is true with so many things in a Yoga life, contentment cannot come about through force of will. It arrives because of Yoga practice.

saMtosAd anuttamaH sukha lAbhaH

samtosad
    samtosa   contented
    ad   consume
anuttama (for anuttamah)   unsurpassed
sukha   the effort to win future beatitude
labha (for labhah)   attaining

Waning Of Body Impurities

2.43   Religious austerity contributes to your success in constant waning of impurities in body and faculty of sense.

kAya indriya siddhir asuddhi kSayAt tapasaH
*body   faculty of sense   your success   impurity
wane to go constantly   religious austerity*

Here the *Sutra* speaks of physical impurity, not mind stillness, expressing the need to purify the body and its sense organs. This is the first time that the *Yoga Sutras* have spoken of cleansing the sense organs. Imagine for the moment that you touch the body of the gender you are attracted to: then imagine that you touch the skin of a peach. Imagine that your sense of smell detects a skunk, and then imagine that it detects pure mountain air. If you continue that experiment with all of the senses, you can see that they can have different effects on the mind, sometimes quieting it, sometimes not.

Our everyday experience can show us that many things ingested in the body have effects on our senses, nervous system, mind, and organs of the body. Experience also shows us that carefulness in selecting foods, fasting, and purification diets cleanse the body and its organs. An impure body brings disquiet to the mind, which is contrary to the goals of Yoga. By purification of the body, its organs, the stimuli of the senses, and its tissues, we support purification (i.e. stillness) of the mind. With greater control over what the body takes in, the body and the senses lessen their linkage to the material world. The religious austerity, first discussed in *Sutra* 2.1, leads to that bodily purification.

kAya indriya siddhir asuddhi kSayAt tapasaH

kaya	body
indriya	faculty of sense
siddhir	
siddhi	success
ir	(suffix denoting second person plural) your
azuddhi (for asuddhi)	impurity
ksayat	
ksaya	wane
at	to go constantly
tapasah	
tapas	religious austerity
ah	(untranslated)

Result Of Recitation To One's Self

2.44   Recitation (of texts) to one's self brings union with the cherished divinity.

svAdhyAyad ista devatA saMprayogaH
recitation to one's self   cherished   divinity   union

Nearly every word adds power and precision to the meaning. Fully understanding the intent of 'recitation to one's self' only comes from seeing it in the context of the single other valid definition contemporary with Patanjali. The two exist as a pair, one religious, and one not religious. The full definition of this non-religious definition is 'reciting or repeating or rehearsing to one's self.' That of the religious definition is 'repetition or recitation of the Veda in a low voice to one's self.' The guidance to the serious yogin is to study spiritual texts and verbally self-recite them until they become ingrained.

The last three words are critically important and largely unrecognized for what they mean. The first of the three, 'cherished' makes it clear that this effect will not come about unless the yogin has formed a deep connection with the divinity, whether it is divinity with form or without it. Second, the use of the generic word 'divinity,' opens the door of Yoga applicability to a broad range of beliefs. Many words and concepts are available to represent divinities. Third, Patanjali has used a word that means 'union,' *samprayogah*, that is a lesser degree of union than 'Yoga' itself, signaling that it is a progressive step, not the end game. The lesson puts us on the path to union through deep belief in an unspecified divinity, while continually becoming absorbed in yogic study and reciting our learning. In today's world, the availability of non-religious texts opens the door to more than just those that some person or group sees as sacred.

The full discussion of the Yoga concepts of divinity and study that is in *Sutra* 2.1 applies here. Patanjali brings two important points to our awareness. The first is the importance of studying independently, by reading and observing everything available about Yoga. In an indirect way he says what the Buddha says directly, that you must learn by yourself, not accepting anything you see or hear as valid. You must sort it out through study. The second point is that it makes no difference what form or formlessness we chose as our personal concept of divinity. As we study, we continually reject more falsity and accept more reality. As that balance shifts to a greater abundance of reality we become more spiritual, in harmonious union with divinity.

Study peels away the illusions, reveals truths about the world and ourselves, and allows us to become deeply aware of every aspect of being. Our whole being begins to narrow to experience of its true state of existence. Removing so much that blocks us, study leads us to an understanding of our root inner nature, our soul. We continually move to experiences of greater harmony and higher consciousness as our nature and the divine nature become clearer.

The *Sutras* do not name gods, pointing only to the divine source of everything (*brahman, the Absolute*). The root philosophy as represented in the *Sutras* is compatible with the gods of all religions and all times, but proposes no god name: many sects and traditions have combined Yoga and religion. In the Yoga view, all named gods represent either the transcendental god-essence or its immanent representation of that god-essence in the universe. All religion-based names of gods are names for that essence in one of these two forms, or in some cases (as in Hinduism) for certain *aspects* of the godness. Profound contemplation of any god by any name, reaching for union with the Absolute, or full dedication to the Yoga life are all equal actions, because all such intentions point to acceptance of the existence of a divine

svAdhyAyad ista devatA saMprayogaH

svadhyaya (for svadhyayad)	reciting to one's self
ista	cherished
devata	divinity
samprayoga (for samprayogah)	union

Result Of Contemplating The Primal Existence

2.45   Constantly paying attention to the Supreme Being brings your success in intense absorption.

samAdhi   siddhir   Isvara   praNidhAnAt
*intense absorption   your   success   Supreme Being
to go constantly   attention paid to*

In each of his four *padas* (parts), Patanjali steadily advances the discussion of progressive stilling through meditation as he presents ever-higher levels of results. Here the *Sutra* tells us that constant focus of our attention on the presence of the Supreme Being (*brahman/isvara/sat*) brings success to our meditative practice. The yogin will not proceed to the highest levels without seeing and accepting Its guidance. Awareness will become automatic as we progress, but we can enhance the process through self-will, which we need to wean from.

There is nothing equivocal about this *Sutra*, and there can be no doubt that the instruction aims directly at evolved yogins, not newcomers. We may work toward complete dedication to reaching out to divinity, release our will to follow its guidance, and enter profound contemplation early in the game, and get great benefits from that work. Higher *samadhi*, though, is not something most of us can gain early in our Yoga life. Nor is it necessarily the highest experience, since multiple levels of *samadhi* experience exist. Entry to those levels begins when we have left the mind behind. Yet, we do not get there until we have learned and developed total devoted involvement with divinity, without necessarily tagging it as that or anything else, a task that is not as easy as it sounds. It must be nonnegotiable and complete. Pretending that we have yielded our life to it, without actually doing it, does not work. Until we have readied through reaching a more pure state, removing illusions and attachments, and have gained a level of equanimity the door remains closed.

This is not a magic pill. Even with the full commitment of a prepared being, the highest consciousness levels are not accessible without the full and dedicated practice of other yogic disciplines. We cannot enter into the more profound levels of meditation without having developed a consistent and dedicated Yoga life.

samAdhi siddhir Isvara praNidhAnAt

samadhi	intense absorption
siddhir	
siddhi	success
ir	(suffix denoting second person plural) your
isvara	Supreme Being
pranidhanat	
pranidhana	attention paid to
at	to go constantly

The Third Limb - Sitting

At the time of the *Sutras*, it is likely that no more than five formal 'postures' may have existed, possibly *padmasana* (lotus), *bhadrasana* (splendid), *vajrasana* (thunderbolt, diamond), *virasana* (hero), and *svastikasana* (auspicious). All five were postures for seated meditation, only varying in the leg arrangement. Yoga was not a posture-oriented practice, other than for meditative sitting positions. The variations in leg arrangement accommodated people of different body builds and flexibility, and have symbolic and energy flow significance. However, Patanjali does not point to specific seated postures or nuances such as changed energy flow, or effects on the body. The objective was simply comfortable stability that would avoid distraction.

According to some, more than a thousand defined postures exist today. All but the original meditative postures are innovations created within the many sects, cults, movements, and traditions that have spawned and evolved since then. Some postures of today are the carefully balanced and purposeful product of Masters, resulting from personal discoveries during their deep practice and meditation, all having long history and formal names accepted across traditions. Some modern 'traditions,' though, have seen value in renaming them, making it difficult to find the commonality. A greater number of today's 'postures' and 'movements' are recent inventive add-ons, casual innovations provided by teachers of all levels of skill and insight. All have value and purposes, but those purposes are not always reflective of the purposes of root Yoga.

Teachers conduct posture classes in many different ways, for many different purposes. If moving toward spirituality, and root Yoga is important to you, you will need to use your discrimination ability to separate practices that support that from others.

Sitting In Firm Comfort

2.46   Sitting is firm and comfortable.

sthira   sukham   Asanam
firm   comfortably   sitting

You may find it strange or heretical, but the truth is that *asana* does not translate to 'posture.' It translates to 'sitting.' The only time any dictionary uses the word posture is in the phrase 'sitting in a peculiar posture according to the custom of devotees.' *Asana* refers specifically to sitting for meditation. The small amount of information in this *Sutra* applies strictly to that. It simply tells us that sitting for meditation should be firm and comfortable. Unsteady sitting and discomforts will interfere with meditation.

When Patanjali recorded the *Sutras*, 2500 years ago, and for 2000 or more years before that, such sitting had a single purpose, to enhance the process of finding higher consciousness through meditation. The postures we revere today are modern innovations and inventions that have no intention in that direction.

The first of what we call 'postures' came into existence hundreds of years after the writing of the *Sutras*. Masters designed them to bring rich benefits to enhance Yoga practice with the intention of doing far more than toning muscles and joints. They cleaned impurities from organs, muscles, and the nervous system, removed blockages in *nadis*, balanced *prana* flow, and were an excellent from of discipline and concentration. When practiced properly they were a form of meditation. In the early 1600s CE, the Hatha Yoga Pradipika documented 16 of these new 'asanas.' At a later point someone documented 84 of them. Today, people claim there are 1000. Every new 'tradition,' movement, and self-empowered local Yoga teacher that claims the right to invent their own or modify others has increased the variety to an uncountable number. Even the poorest postures are good for us, but the serious yogin must always question if they serve the meditative, stilling, and personal evolution purposes of Yoga. In today's culture of entertainment, athleticism, 'pop' fads, and invention of new 'traditions,' postures are offered for many purposes, not all of which recognize or serve the goals of Yoga.

sthira sukham Asanam

sthira	firm
sukha (for sukham)	comfortable
asana (for asanam)	sitting

Effortless

2.47   One falls into a comfortable state with relaxation of the endless active effort.

prayatna Saithilya ananta samApattibhyAm
active effort   relaxation   endless   falling into a state comfort

Having told us that sitting should be firm and comfortable; this following *Sutra* simply says that the comfort derives from giving up all effort and relaxing. Sitting in a state of inactive meditation is not an easy task: in our yogic life style, including our time in meditation, we are forever striving to reach the goal, to make things happen. Striving for meditative results is a mistake made by many. It is counterproductive.

Striving while sitting in meditation will lead the meditator to awareness of the body, produce tension, cause the yogin to monitor for results, and perhaps bring the experience of discomfort and pain: since discomfort, pain, stress, attitude, and wanting something generate thoughts and emotions, meditating with the properly relaxed body and mind eases the job of quieting the mind. The meditator should eliminate all effort, just being present.

prayatna Saithilya ananta samApattibhyAm

prayatna	active efforts
zaithilya (for saithilya)	relaxation
ananta	endless
samapattibhyam	
samapatti	falling into any state
bhyam	comfort

Prevent Awareness Of Conflicting Opposites

2.48   From that place, there will be no damage by the pairs of opposites.

tato   dvandva   anabhighAtaH
from that place   a pair of opposites   no damage

All of Nature is dual; its paired opposites fill our lives. Those dualities can be obvious, hidden, physical, mental, abstract, or in either the physical or subtle realm. Pain and pleasure, and hot and cold are examples of paired physical opposites. More abstractly, long would be meaningless without short: so also would high without low, love without hate, peace without war, faith without doubt, and so on. Everything in our universe exhibits the dualities.

At the everyday level, a comfortable posture facilitates drawing the attention away from the senses, which continually draw us to pleasure and pain. The absence of sensory arousal relieves the mind of dealing with those sensations and the chains of thoughts and emotions they generate. Comfort also establishes an environment in which we can draw the mind away from the conflicts created by nonphysical dualities. The absence of mental conflict is mandatory for successful meditation.

The pairs of opposites are a great source of distraction and disruption of the mind. Setting them aside brings greater stillness. As evolution through meditation progresses, the yogin experiences ever less internal warring, doubt, ambivalence, and involvement with conflicting opposites.

tato dvandva anabhighAtaH

tatas (for tato)	from that place
dvamdva (for devandva)	a pair of opposites
anabhighatah	
an	(signifies negation) no
abhighAta	damaged

The Fourth Limb - Control Of The Breath

As with postures, teachers today teach breath control in many ways, for varying purposes. Not all target the purposes defined in the *Sutras*, mind stilling and improving concentration for meditation. Some do it for energy arousal, getting a high, or movement of *prana* through the *cakras*. When we accept a practice discipline, we need to know the reasons and benefits and orient our practice to our needs. If the root goals of Yoga are important to us, we need to discriminate those practices that lead to stilling from those that do not.

2.49   *From that gain, breath restraint (pranayama) is procuring drawing breath (inhalation), breath away (exhalation), and interruption of motion (retention).*

tasmin sati SvAsa praSvAsayor gati vicchedaH prANAyAmaH
*from that gaining   drawing breath procuring   breath away
motion   interruption   pranayama*

The *Sutras* suggest sequence of practice here. The gain of a relaxed and steady seated posture provides a platform for this practice. The sitting in a meditative practice is a necessary preparation practice for *pranayama* techniques. Having mastered the relaxation in *asana* practice, *pranayama* easily takes place in the same effortless meditative way. The discipline, faith, dedication, and blocking of thought bring about stilling of the mind - the objective of Yoga and its meditation practices - preparing the seeker for higher meditation practices. The intent of the aphorism is to point to the three separate activities of breathing (i.e. inhalation, exhalation, and retention), each of which can be under the yogin's control. The yogin practices the breathing techniques while meditating.

tasmin sati SvAsa praSvAsayor gati vicchedaH prANAyAmaH

tasmin	from that
sati	gaining
zvasa (for svasa)	
zvas	drawing breath
sa	procuring
prasvasayor	
pra	away
zvasa (for svasa)	breath
yor	(untranslated)
gati	motion
viccheda (for vicchdedah)	interruption
pranayama (for pranayamah)	pranayama (name of the three `breath-exercises' performed during Samdhya meditation
prana	breath
ayama	restraining

Types Of Breath Control

2.50   *Your practice of stoppage (retention), being outside (exhalation), and being inside of (inhalation) can be richly experienced by relating to number (count), portions, and being deep or subtle.*

bAhya abhyantara stambha vRttir deSa kAla saMkhyAbhiH
paridRSTo dIrgha suKSmaH
*being outside being inside of stoppage practice your portion
relating to number richly experienced deep subtle*

This *Sutra* directly introduces stoppage (retention, *kumbhaka*) of both inhalation and exhalation, a subject not covered elsewhere. It provides guidance for how to practice it. Using slightly different language than the previous aphorism, the *Sutra* reiterates that *pranayama* has three parts, inhalation ('being inside of'), exhalation ('being outside'), and retention ('stoppage'). Understanding comes easily when looking at the individual words:

- 'Being outside' simply means that exhalation of the breath has happened before stoppage.
- 'Being inside of' means that the breath is inside of the body, following inhalation, before stoppage.
- Stoppage simply means to stop the motion of the breath. The modern terminology is 'retention.' Brief stoppage always occurs in the turn-around between inhalations and exhalations.
- 'Relating to number' is Patanjali's terminology for what modern authors translate as 'counting.' It refers to counting the repetitions of any pattern of practice during a *pranayama* session. Various authors present patterns of counting of exhalations, inhalations, and retentions as if a divinity had etched them in stone. They are different from each other and have no meaning other than being the practice defined by one guru as compared to another. There is no uniformity and no basis in root Yoga philosophy.
- 'Portion' simply refers to the volume of air inhaled or exhaled. Some techniques, such as the *viloma* breath, control the amount. Many authors use the correct word 'place,' where this interpretation uses the word 'portion.' Their descriptions of what 'place' means are inconsistent and not reliable.
- Some techniques use 'deep' breathing while others use nearly unnoticeable 'subtle' breaths.
- 'Time' points to our ability to choose the duration of inhalation, exhalation, and retention. We need to do this with care and guidance, not just experimentation, because *pranayama* practices have psychic and physical effects: the harmful or beneficial effects might be dramatically obvious, unnoticeable, or anywhere between those extremes.

Again, Patanjali gives no direct and detailed guidance, but he delivers a powerful message that a new yogin could easily miss. Just as you can control and dominate your mind and your senses, you can control and dominate your breathing, so that it becomes your servant and you are not its servant. In the *Sutras*, *pranayama* is a practice intended to support and prepare for meditation.

Most Yoga students of today learn to practice '*pranayama*' in varying combinations of inhalation, exhalation, and retention. The dozen or so specific breathing techniques taught and practiced today were originally products of Masters, reflecting their received experience and meditative insights. Masters have even developed ratios for the relative length of the three breath parts, with each ratio producing a different effect. (Note: Many less masterful people have also done this, and you do not know which is which. There is much counterfeit material available, even from well-known gurus.)

These *pranayamas* are highly valuable to Yoga and some are quite old, but none are from the roots of Yoga. The truth is invisible that many current variations on those themes and impressive 'newly discovered' techniques are modernizations far removed from the original practice is invisible. Some carry the name of a technique introduced long ago, but are entirely different from the practice that the Master established. As an example, the popular *Ujjayi* Breath (Ocean Breath or Courageous Breath) has no similarity to the original single nostril technique, or to the more complex Ujjayi breath that came about in the 1600s.

bAhya abhyantara stambha vRttir deSa kAla saM-
khyAbhiH paridRSTo dIrgha suKSmaH

bahya	being outside
abhyantara	being inside of
stambha	stoppage
vrtti (for vrttir)	practice
vrtti	practice
ir	(2nd person indicator) your
deza (for desa)	portion
kala	time
samkhyabhih	
samkhya	relating to number
abhi	by
paridrsta (for paridrsto)	
pari	richly
drsta	experienced
dIrgha	deep

suksma (for suksmah)   subtle

A Fourth Mode Of Breathing

2.51   *Drawing together being inside of (inhalation) and being outside of (exhalation) is the fourth sphere.*

bAhya abhyantara viSayA Aksepi caturthaH
being inside of being outside sphere drawing together the fourth

Patanjali continues this fascinating, surprise-laden sequence of aphorisms about *pranayama* by expanding it further. Before he completes this sequence in the next two *Sutras*, he will show how important it is to the progression of a Yoga life: some may also recognize that little of this special perspective has survived in modern teaching.

Here the *Sutras* point to a fourth mode of *pranayama*, which is different from inhalation, exhalation, and retention. Perhaps because it is beyond the range of shared experience, the simple wording is amazingly hard for people to grasp in a common way. Since Patanjali does not use additional aphorisms to clarify what the fourth mode is, he has left the door open for wide-ranging interpretation and for quoting the guesses and interpretations made by authors, such as Vyasa, who lived 500 to 1000 years after Patanjali.

Regardless of where individual translators take it from there, there is common representation that the fourth mode comes about spontaneously, without willful or purposeful action, unlike the three previous modes. Further, this mode clearly happens only with the accomplished yogin after much practice of *pranayama*. Yet, it may not necessarily happen during a period of purposeful *pranayama* practice: It sometimes happens during meditation. Under the right conditions, an automatic breath comes about easily and naturally. In this different and spontaneous pattern, the breath reduces to such subtlety that it seems to disappear, with no distinction between inhalation and exhalation. Hard to describe and accept until it is experienced, inhalation and exhalation occur simultaneously, with no sequence from one to the next. One author describes that as 'folding into each other.' It is as if the breathing stops while the nurturing it provides continues. Yet, the breathing continues in that mysterious folded way, leaving a distinct sweetness of feeling.

The stillness of the breath matches the stillness of the mind activity. During higher levels of consciousness experience, with greater and longer stillness of the mind, spontaneous fourth mode *pranayama* experience could last longer. At lower and intermediate levels, the stillness will be incomplete and short-lived.

It is important to understand also that many have experienced varying types of involuntary spontaneous breathing that have unusual character. Those who do their postures in a meditative way often experience the spontaneity of an automatic, delicious, subtle type of breathing. During *pranayama* or meditation practice, breathing patterns beyond our control will sometimes occur. They may be fast, slow, subtle, or dramatic, depending on the result that the internal wisdom is after. The farther you advance the more you will notice these events. However, since they all involve separated inhalation and exhalation, they are not the breathing referenced by this *Sutra*.

bAhya abhyantara viSayA Aksepi caturthaH

bahya	being outside
abhyantara	being inside of
visaya	sphere
aksepi (for aksepi)	drawing together
caturtha (for caturthah)	the fourth

Access To Spiritual Illumination

2.52   When that is extended, it makes an end to the covering over the light.

tataH   kSIyate   prakASa   AvaraNam
extended   make an end of   light   a covering

The word 'extended' refers back to the fourth mode of breathing presented in the previous aphorism, saying that when its occurrence has significantly lengthened it will work mutually with meditation and other practices to uncover the light. It is important to recognize that this aphorism does not describe an event that is chronologically the same as the baseline practice of *pranayama* described in previous *Sutras*. It represents a state that comes about in later stages of personal evolution through practice.

To properly understand this *Sutra* it is important to be clear about what 'light' means. You will find many conflicting and confusing representations, some highly esoteric, but it is simply the light of intuitive understanding associated with high spirituality. It is the light epitomized in the following wonderful prayer/chant/mantra that epitomizes a yogin's aspirations, with darkness as the down side of living fully in materiality and light as the up side of living fully in spirituality:

'Lead me from the unreal to the real.'

'Lead me from darkness to light.'

'Lead me from death to immortality.'

It is easy, and even customary, to give this *Sutra* dramatic meaning as a sudden life changing situation. However, the situation is more gradual, similar to the experience of opening the door to a house we have never entered and learning that there are endless opportunities for exploring what is inside. Here, the door has opened, we see that the light is there, and we continue in our exploration of the illumination through *samadhi* experiences. It is not, as some suggest, an experience of ultimate illumination.

To have the ending of the 'covering ' lead to high consciousness experiences, many of the things that block our ability to see the inner being, such as our illusions, delusions, thoughts, karmic influences, sensuality, ego, and attachments to material things have to wither. At the transition from *pranayama* to sense withdrawal, those things would not have withered. The degree of yogic experience does not yet warrant it, but with accumulated experiences and increasingly effective meditation, the fourth mode of breathing can come into play for spiritual illumination.

tataH kSIyate prakASa AvaraNam

tata (for tatah)	extended
ksiyate (= ksi, ksiyati)	make an end of
prakaza (for prakasa)	light
avarana (for avaranam)	a covering

Fitness For Concentration

2.53   Moreover, fitness of the mind incites concentration of the mind.

dhAraNAsu ca yogyatA manasah
concentration of the mind   incites   moreover   fitness   mind

Patanjali again brings the student's awareness to the 'one thing leads to another' nature of Yoga practice. The teaching that breath restraint brings mind fitness as preparation for meditation reinforces the original intention that yogins practice the limbs in sequence. The needed focusing and quieting of the mind through *pranayama* develop the power of concentration for the meditative work that will begin with the upcoming sixth of the eight limbs. Although, Patanjali does not directly state it or define the method, the definitions for *dharana* (concentration) from his time, include 'concentration of the mind (joined with the retention of breath)' indicate that breath retention is part of the sixth limb practice.

The gradual removal of materiality further facilitates concentration. The discipline and practice of breathing intensely focuses the mind and the movement toward *sattva* dominance over *tamas* and *rajas*, bringing greater clarity, peacefulness, and quietness.

dhAraNAsu ca yogyatA manasah

dharanasu		
	dharana	concentration of the mind
	su	incite
ca		moreover
yogyata		fitness
manasa (for manasah)		mind

The Fifth Limb - Withdrawal

2.54   Withdrawal of the power of the senses from your own objects of the senses disconnects your mind, in some measure resembling your own nature.

sva   viSaya   asaMprayoge   cittasya   sva rUpa   anukAra
iva   indriyANAM   pratyAhAraH
your own   object of the senses   disconnection   your mind   own

nature   resemblance   in some measure   power of the senses   withdrawal

A surprising aspect of the *Sutras* appears in this inclusion of 'sense withdrawal' as one of the eight limbs of Yoga, emphasizing its importance to attaining the stillness leading to union. The surprise arises because today's teachers rarely discuss sense withdrawal: when they do, they do not convey the powerful reality the aphorism describes. This possibly happens because sense withdrawal is such a natural and integral part of many practices that a separate practice, replete with techniques, does not seem necessary. Yet, sense withdrawal is critically important to attaining the goals of Yoga. Higher meditative attainment will not occur without withdrawing from the senses and from the external world to which the senses bind us. Withdrawing the senses is exactly what it says, taking them away from sense detectable objects, the targets of the senses, so that the entire field of attention is within the mind. When that happens, the quietness deepens and lengthens and we begin to experience levels of consciousness beyond the mind, eventually that of our true nature, the soul. That experience develops in degrees over time, at first resembling that soul experience and gradually growing into being absorbed in it.

The message is easy and strong. The senses and the mind work together to accomplish external perception. We would know nothing of the outside world without the five senses. The senses endlessly and with little interruption, send signals to the body and mind. That has a huge effect on the mind, keeping it in a state of disquiet as it processes those sensory experiences and develops responses. If we are able to reduce our awareness of sensory input, we greatly reduce the activity of the mind. One way to do that is to be in places where there is less sensory input. If we are sitting in the midst of a rock concert with music blaring, constant movement around us, flashing lights, smoke in our nostrils, and bodies interacting, we experience sensual overload. If the mind processes it into sexual stimulation, excitement, awe, judgment, or whatever else, the overload increases. Toward the opposite extreme, being alone in a dark soundproofed room that has a constant temperature and filtered air will have minimal sensory input.

The other, and far more difficult way to accomplish that is to learn to bypass our senses, locking out their signals. Advanced yogins can be in sensory active places, even have exposure to sudden and dramatic loud noises, such as a gunshot, and never experience any of it. It is not clear whether the nervous system still experiences the sensory input, but it is clear that at least the linkage between the senses and mind is inactive during those times.

However, the key to sense withdrawal is mysterious, no one can teach you to do it. Because it requires going inward and bypassing the mind, there is a close relationship between it and meditation. Patanjali says no more about this, and provides no guidance about how to practice *pratyahara* withdrawal and make it happen. It is interesting though that the first limb of meditation, limb 6 'Concentration,' requires focusing the senses exclusively on an object of the senses, while putting the mind on hold. That process of focusing the senses is surely a step toward greater control over them. The two limbs following that increasingly depend on moving away from senses and the mind.

sva viSaya asaMprayoge cittasya sva rUpa anukAra iva indriyANAM pratyAhAraH

sva	your own
visaya	an object of sense
asamprayoge	disconnection
a	(negation flag)
samprayoga (for	connection
samprayoge)	
cittasya	
citta	mind
sya	(third party voice) your
sva	own
rupa	nature
anukara	resemblance
iva	in some measure
indriyanam	
indriya	power of the senses
anam	(untranslated)
pratyahara (for pratyaharah)	withdrawal

Result Of Sense Withdrawal

2.55   Extending that to the highest degree brings fitness for subjection of the power of the senses.

tataH   paramA   vaSyatA   IndriyANAm
*extended   in the   highest degree   fitness for subjection
the power of the senses*

Again pointing to the progressive nature of Yoga and personal evolution, the *Sutra* tells us that if we keep extending sense withdrawal we will come to fitness for conquering the hold the senses have upon us. It does not say that we have conquered or mastered them: it says that we have established a foundation for doing so. Learning to withdraw the senses from the external world gives us momentum toward eventual complete control over them.

Just as the mind does, the senses drive our life. Controlling our responses to them and telling them not to bother us at inappropriate times, by making them subject to our will, is a high state of accomplishment. An ongoing and constantly underlying theme of Yoga is the internal war between living in the world of the senses and living in the world of spirituality. The material/ sensory world and the senses, our only contact with that world, constantly draw us to them, making sensory fulfillment a continual drive. Our challenge is to escape their allure, and move toward a more spiritual life. There is a price for that. To get the more valuable benefits, we need to learn the price of relinquishing less valuable things and be willing to pay it.

Withdrawing the senses is critically necessary to growth of meditative skill and effectiveness. It is not in the realm of the novice, but it is not exclusively in the realm of the highly advanced yogi. The natural ability for it develops early in our practice toward meditative evolution and continually grows.

tataH paramA vaSyatA IndriyANAm

tata (for tatah)	extended
parama	the highest degree
vazyata (for vasyata)	fitness for subjection
indriyanam	

| indriya | power of the senses |
| anam | (untranslated) |

The Highest Three Limbs

Emphasizing their importance as the target zone of Yoga practice, Patanjali presents the remaining three limbs of Yoga within a separate part (*pada*), 'Superhuman',' which is next. 'Superhuman' refers to attaining consciousness experiences that are beyond the normal human reach.

VIBHUTI PADA

THE PART ON SUPERHUMAN

(Sutras 3.1 – 3.56)

Patanjali handled the transition from Part Two, 'Practice,' to Part Three 'Superhuman,' in a surprising way, but students of the *Sutras* learn to trust that there is always a reason. The *Sutras* contain no sloppiness or carelessness. Every word, progressive flow, and structure is meaningful. Most readers will not notice it, see it as a curiosity, or pause before moving on. Yet, what he has done is so striking that it will hook the seeker with curiosity until the questions resolve: the clarity of understanding that accompanies their resolution of the puzzle can bring breathlessness, waves of gratitude and thanks, or drifting into a wonderful wave of contemplation in which integration occurs.

The surprising element is his removal of the three highest 'practice' limbs of Yoga from his part (*pada*) on 'Practice' (*sadhana*), and placing them in his next part, 'Superhuman,' thereby drawing a firm and unbroken dividing line between them and the five lowest limbs. It is easy to see that the three highest limbs are meditative limbs, while the five others provide preparation for meditation, and are of a different character. Yet, that is not sufficient reason for splitting the eight limbs in this way.

As we come to understand the *Sutras* better, though, we see that the entire third part *is* about evolution into experiences of higher consciousness, experiences of consciousness not available in everyday human living, and the three highest limbs of Yoga are the means of attaining that evolution. The five lower limbs cannot bring us that high consciousness and that evolution. Patanjali will show us, even beyond that, that the evolution is not attainable except by *integrated practice* of the three high limbs.

The other books on the *Yoga Sutras* contribute much confusion through misrepresentation of the translation of this third part (*pada*), named *vibhuti*. The best translation is 'superhuman,' honoring the intent to move beyond the normal material/sensory human experience. Most of the *pada* titles of the others reference the Hindu concept of superhuman <u>powers</u>, not Yoga, and none is a valid translation of *vibhuti*:

Psychic powers
Accomplishments
Mystic powers
Extraordinary powers
Superhuman powers
Exceptional faculties
Supernormal powers
Supernatural abilities and gifts
Divine Powers of Perfection

Six of the nine *pada* titles tell us that it is about gaining 'powers,' which neither the *pada* nor the *Yoga Sutras* address. Only one of those *pada* titles, 'superhuman powers,' has dictionary support, but the inclusion of 'powers' makes it invalid. The Great Mystical Powers are a subject Patanjali does not cover. The dictionaries do discuss eight powers in detail, but as background, not as a translation. The term 'powers' has no broader meaning or usefulness than that. The idea of the Eight Powers developed much later in a religious context as eight powers of the god Siva. In the Faith system of some believers, sufficiently devout Siva devotees and accomplished gurus can attain those god powers. Among the few accounts of observation of the feats, though, most accounts are clearly mythical. Although the count and identification of the powers varies across texts, with some saying there are 11 and others claiming as many as 21, a typical authoritative set is:

Making the body minute
Achieving extreme lightness
Attaining or reaching anything
Irresistible will
Illimitable bulk
Supreme dominion
Subjugating by magic
Suppressing of all desires

In any case, whether factually true or not true, 'powers' are not part of core Yoga philosophy. Masters who promote these Hindu beliefs usually warn students of the dangers from ego-entrapment that await those who attain any of the powers, pointing out that attachment to them will arrest evolution.

Since the *Sutras* do not ever use the word *vibhuti*, other than for the *pada* title, no direct explanation or clarification of meaning is available within them. Nine meanings of *vibhuti* exist in texts earlier than or contemporary with Patanjali's life. From among them, 'abundant,' 'plentiful,' 'fortune,' 'welfare, ' and 'prosperity' could not be Patanjali's intent, since they are materialistic goals not consistent with the aspirations of Yoga. Similarly, the quest for power over others implied in the meanings of 'mighty,' 'powerful,' and 'presiding over' is not the trajectory of *Yoga* or the *Yoga Sutras*. The ninth definition 'superhuman' expresses exactly what this third *pada* is about, evolving to experiencing consciousness beyond the everyday level of human existence. Further, it is closely contemporary with the *Yoga Sutras*.

THE THREE HIGHEST LIMBS

In today's world, we use the word 'meditation' loosely. Its meaning and use have become greatly inconsistent, and many of the uses have little or nothing to do with the meditative aims and purposes of Yoga. Surprisingly, the *Yoga Sutras* also describe fifteen targets for meditation aimed at results separate from the core thrust of Yoga practice. In core Yoga aimed at Absolute Unity, it always refers to some technique of raising the level of consciousness experience, deriving from among the highest three limbs of Yoga, the second of which (limb 7) is formally named '*meditation*.' Many meditative techniques have developed for all three limbs. Those vary greatly from tradition to tradition, but a few practices cross many traditions. Put in the most basic terms, we 'meditate' (the term '*unified-restraint*' will replace '*meditation*' later) to put the mind on hold, to interrupt thought generation. That is what all Yoga meditative techniques do. They do it for many different reasons, to produce many different results. That is why there are hundreds of meditation techniques. We need to choose a technique that works for us in the singularly unique life that we each have, moving toward the individual eventualities that each of us moves toward.

In *meditation*, we stop thought generation for a reason so obvious and close to us that we do not notice it. Our conscious mind generates thoughts and other activities at a wild and crazy rate. It never stops. While we are awake, it never lets us rest. Each of us lives in a mental environment that contains some degree of chaos. Some of us are near the orderly end of the order-to-chaos scale. Others of us are near the chaotic end of the scale. Most of us are nearer the middle. None of us is at exactly the same point that others are. We are where we are partly because of our birth situation and partly because of the training imposed from outside ourselves. 'Fate,' our *karma*, has imposed those birth and training situations on us. We have no choice or control over them. We do have a choice in what we do with our situation. From any minute forward, we can begin to place our existence under our control. Through *meditation*, we can place our mind under our control. We can discipline the way it responds to internal and external stimuli that past training has conditioned.

Meditation is a training exercise. Through it, we discipline that scooting around mind. We discipline it, the way we discipline a puppy or a child, so that we are in charge. We do this through teaching it single-pointed attention. Disciplining it to single-pointed attention, we slow it down. We create gaps of time, at first tiny, during which it is doing nothing, generating no thoughts, analyzing nothing. If we aspire to harmonizing with the consciousness that exists beyond our daily thought-generating sensory awareness, we can use those gaps to open our mind to its presence.

Stress reduction, equanimity, inner quietness, and spirituality evolve from that, with the ultimate result of full spirituality (becoming more Spirit-like). All lives exist somewhere on the spirituality scale. Small percentages of us are toward the minimum and maximum extremes. Most of us are somewhere between the extremes. *Meditation* is a vital tool for increasing spirituality, for those who aspire to do that.

The list of practical applications of *meditation*, beyond the root purposes leading to spirituality and Absolute Unity, is too long to attempt here, but Patanjali will show you many such applications before his book ends. *Meditation* exercises exist to help with hundreds of common human situations. Among the most prevalent and most important to our health, meditation can help us to understand our individual psychology, to learn what our humanity truly is, and to discover our personal true nature. If we have discovered that we are indeed on a uniquely divined path, meditative practice can be a vital tool in following that path. Whatever our need for special application of meditation, a regular practice of a baseline meditative technique can open us to using appropriate specialized techniques.

Since this *pada* brings us toward the pinnacle of Yoga teaching and experience, the introduction above and the commentary on 3.1, 3.2, and 3.3 below receive extra attention here. You will see that in *concentration* we direct sensory flow with single-pointed awareness. During *meditation*, we allow flow of awareness, instead of directing the flow. Both are different yet from *intense absorption,* in which we become an open receptacle for whatever comes our way, leaving awareness behind. *Concentration* is an activity centered in the physical realm. *Meditation* is mind awareness centered. *Intense absorption* centers in consciousness, leading to experiencing the true self (soul), and absolute primal consciousness (oversoul).

The Sixth Limb - Concentration

3.1   Concentration of your mind is binding your mind to a place.

deSa   bandhaS   cittasya   dhAraNA
place   binding your mind   concentration of your mind

Patanjali tells us to bind our mind to one place. Being contemporary with Patanjali, 'binding' is a stronger statement of the intent than the modern translation as 'fixing.' Binding implies a state of intended union, while 'fixing' does not. He seems to leave the idea of place open for interpretation. However, he has said in 2.27 that the first stages of meditation, *savitarka samadhi* and *nirvitarka samadhi*, involve physical objects. Those stages of higher consciousness arte brought about by Limb 6 *concentration*. 'Place' is clearly a physical object.

When we choose a physical object as the target for *concentration* and enter into our practice, we examine it with any or all of the senses. We still the mind as well as we can at that point, and become deeply involved in sensually observing the object, putting aside all non-sensual influences. This is not an intellectual examination. Thoughts and analysis are not part of the game. Thoughts will present themselves during meditative sessions, but we let them drift away without becoming involved with them. Here, we invoke the senses as an agent of meditative work, not yet the mind. With practice and depth of concentration, knowingly experiencing the senses will drop away and we will experience the nonmaterial root nature of the object through a higher level of consciousness.

The practice of *concentration* develops willpower. It is an aggressive activity, a 'go for it' activity. One purpose of training ourselves through *concentration* is to eliminate obstacles to our ability to meditate and absorb. Another is to stabilize the mind by developing single-pointed concentration so that thoughts cannot interfere. The mind always wants to seize the knowledge and insights available to it and work further with them. That is its nature. If we put thoughts and activity on hold, we make space for insights to enter from the consciousness beyond materiality.

We can choose anything physical as a target for a *concentration* session, but it is best to choose something from nature at first and avoid emotionally loaded targets such as religious symbols or icons. If we choose to concentrate on a flower, that flower is the only thing that exists. We aspire to pierce its nature with our sensory awareness. That is all that exists for the time of our *concentration*. Some call this focus 'one-pointed.' In this one-pointed total attention, we do not allow extraneous thoughts, interpretations, or explorations. It is simply a game of staying focused on it with our senses. Consciousness will integrate all the sensory perceptions into a single holistic view of the object while adding insight. At the higher levels of one-pointed ability that come with practice, near the transition to *meditation*, we will have moved into progressive degrees of sensory withdrawal. Even during sensory merging with the target, we will not be aware of the senses. There will be no pain, sound, sight, or any other perception. When we can do this and keep the thoughts away, we are then fully prepared for *meditation*, the next limb.

Defined practices exist in greater number for *concentration* than for *meditation* and *intense absorption*, the next two limbs. That is how it should be. Defined *concentration* practice is easier for the beginner, and is strong training for the higher levels. With advanced techniques of *concentration*, the degree of challenge increases and the nature of the *concentration* changes, automatically shifting to using targets that phase into *meditation*. The practices exist on a continuous scale, with smooth, not jumpy transitions. *Concentration* practice will strengthen the will and personality, enhance health, and brighten awareness, while providing the foundation for the other two practices.

Remember, in all meditative techniques, the object is to keep the mind from thinking. We do not suppress thoughts; we simply refuse to become involved with them or the emotions that they generate, watching them pass. Thought generation will eventually slow. When we advance to *meditation*, we will give the mind specific things to work with, to the exclusion of all others. In *intense absorption*, we will step above the mind entirely. Leaving all senses and mind activity behind; we will approach the all-potent unknown. However, we need to maintain awareness that this is a barely noticeable smooth overlapping transition, not a leap from one limb to another.

deSa bandhaS cittasya dhAraNA

deza (for desa)	place
bandha (for bandhas)	binding
cittasya	
citta	mind
sya	(3rd person voice) your
dharana	concentration of the mind (joined with the retention of breath)

The Seventh Limb - Meditation

3.2 *Thither, when the mind is inviolably fixed on one object only, a notion, it is meditation.*

tatra   pratyaya   ekatAnatA   dhyAnam
thither   notion   attention fixed on one object only   inviolability   meditation

Under the conditions of sensuous comprehension created by Limb 6 *concentration* on physical objects, a strongly fixed mind eventually phases from the state of *concentration* to the state of *meditation*. 'Meditation' is the second of the three highest limbs, Limb 7' described in *Sutra 2.27* as *savitarka samadhi* and *nirvitarka samadhi*. At the *meditation* level of practice, the mind level of consciousness becomes the media for meditative effort. During *concentration*, meditative practice began in material/sensory consciousness. To describe this in terms of realms, *meditation* has left the physical realm behind. While meditating in the mind realm, we choose targets that are as surely parts of the material cosmos as physical objects are, but they are subtle objects, such as mental conceptions and notions. Objects in the subtle realm are not detectable by senses, but by the mind.

Use of the mind for *meditation* is not intellectual, nor is it analytical left-brain thinking. The meditative technique and accumulated experience free it to do its own intuitive exploration of the subtle-object target. A mind experiencing the world beyond physical/sensory consciousness follows a path initiated by a chosen target, using one of many specific *meditation* techniques to explore it. As always while meditating, the meditator allows the extraneous thoughts to drift by without becoming involved with them. At this level of evolution of the practice, the frequency of their arrival has diminished, causing larger gaps between the thoughts. Having thought-free gaps of longer duration allows the continuous flow of attention to the target and is characteristic of having developed meditative skill.

This is involvement with abstracts. The abstract meditative mind exploration can target any of many things. The targets might be emotions, intellect, language, a concept or idea, a spiritual goal, a virtue, a theme, a word, aspects of nature, the nature of Nature, the self, our lives, or just about anything nonphysical. The targets might be physical things, as well, but the mind exploration would address their subtle nature, not their sensory or physical characteristics.

When we meditate, we are disconnecting from the senses, detaching from the world, and blocking thoughts by focusing on a target just as we did during *concentration*. The difference is in the target. In the subtle realm, notions and mind activities of many kinds are 'objects.' We can make them targets for *meditation* as surely as we made flowers and other physical objects our targets. Just as with *concentration*, when our mind wanders from the directed path we will bring it back to the target. To achieve this, we will need the same stillness that we needed for *concentration*. It is often helpful to begin a *meditation* session by using one of the *concentration* techniques for a short while to achieve the proper preparatory state.

In doing the *meditation* practices, it will help to remember that these are not passive processes. There is active involvement, in which the mind engages fully, but is constrained to a zone of action. Opened within that zone, the mind plays freely with the selected theme, to examine that ground until it is content. We allow it to flow unrestricted, exploring all aspects of the theme, as long as it maintains loyalty to that theme. There is no willful escape from the other thoughts and feelings. There is just total attention to the theme, with dynamic intense focus on it. We treat extraneous thoughts, feelings, or emotions as uninvited guests to a party, politely turning them away, so that we can return to where we were. When we have become experienced meditators, our mind will be concerned only with the Truth. Sophisticated intellectualization will disappear, as we become the recipient for the Truth, not its creator. This requires total freedom of the mind, freedom to communicate with its roots, freedom from direction by our will. We are attempting to allow the mind to penetrate the heart of Reality.

Seekers do not actively and aggressively approach *isvara* during *meditation*, as they will do during *intense absorption* practices. They are just being there, doing what they are doing. *Isvara* may declare its presence or it may not. They do not care. It is not an issue. Mostly, they are deeply exploring the essence of things through a freed mind. There is no willfulness of thought, action, or emotion. They are just there at their center, doing their thing, and receiving what comes about as the mind processes things.

Meditation is mental perception and evaluation, without attempting control of its direction. Time and space will often disappear and many things may happen that do not directly relate to the target of the meditation. They might include light shows or patterns, visions, sounds, being spoken to, awareness of energy flow, feelings, movements, or unlimited and unpredictable other events.

tatra pratyaya ekatAnatA dhyAnam

tatra	thither
pratyaya	notion
ekatanata	
ekatana	attention fixed on one object only
ta	inviolability
dhyana (for dhyanam)	meditation

The Eighth Limb - Intense Absorption

3.3   *Intense absorption (samadhi) is in consequence of that way of acting, when there is only the matter itself without brightness, as if void of its own nature.*

tad eva artha mAtra nirbhAsaM sva rUpa sunya iva samAdhiH
consequently   way of acting   being only the matter itself   without   brightness its own   nature   void   as if   intense absorption

Intense absorption (*samadhi*) is the third and final limb of the meditative process. The *Sutra* tells us that it is a natural consequence of *dhyana* (meditation), which the preceding *Sutra* presented. In this stage of evolution, the seeker is aware of nothing but matter in its most primitive form, from which all things derive, without 'brightness' (no distinction, identification, or visibility) of any object. Among the experiences that may come about is *asmita samadhi* as described in *Sutra* 1.17 and elsewhere, telling us that it is an experience of matter in the form of *mula prakrti* and of the ego state of the universe before individuation.

To reach this level, the yogin has continued meditative practice through all three limbs. When mastered, *concentration* (*dharana*) phases into and becomes *meditation* (*dhyana*). As the seeker masters *meditation*, it phases into and becomes *intense absorption* (*samadhi*). Each phase, though, results in shifting to new types of targets and using new techniques. The transition may be invisible, happening naturally, but the new needs become clear and leave opportunities for modification of practice. The opportunities are obvious and easy when the meditator is ready for them. Defined practice techniques exist for each of the three meditative limbs, and the meditator always makes decisions that will affect progress.

As the meditator evolves through the progressive levels of consciousness experience, the single-pointed focus shifts to targets at higher levels of abstraction. We choose targets, but our choices increasingly move away from sense-detectable objects and subtle objects: new targets eventually come up without conscious selection. Higher *absorption* requires targets appropriate to higher consciousness, such as divinity, the qualities of a revered saint, the nature of Nature, abstract spirituality, *om, isvara,* or *brahman.*

During *meditation,* many seekers achieve insights about their life, seeing their history and developmental situations. During later stages of *intense absorption,* deeper self-insight may occur, seeing karmic flow and coming ever closer to knowing the inner self (soul). Over time, the yogin begins to intuitively understand the internal identity, moving toward the integrative depths of individual essence, the self as god-essence. Eventually breaking through the surface of soul consciousness, the seeker can leave even the awareness of *mula prakrti* and the universe behind and plummet deep into his or her nature. The duality of primal and individual existence disappears: knower and known, subject and object, meditation and meditator, seer and seen, self and Absolute, all become one thing. All individualities dissolve. At the higher reaches of it, nearly total physical, mental, and inner stillness begins, completely absorbed in a peaceful state. The yogin has transcended mind knowing into a new way of knowing, into Truth-knowing.

Further evolution occurs: with continued evolution, there is eventual seedless (*nirbija*) *samadhi.* With it, the *intense absorption* is on the threshold of experiencing the primal consciousness of the soul, *isvara,* and *brahman,* accomplishing the true union. That achieving of the ultimate consciousness experience through *intense absorption* is the highest of several levels of 'samadhi' in Yoga.

tad eva artha mAtra nirbhAsaM sva rUpa sunya iva samAdhiH

tad   consequently

eva	way of acting
arthamatra	being only the matter itself
nirbhasam	
nir	without
bhasa	brightness
sva	its own
rupa	nature
zunya (for sunya)	void
iva	as if
samadhi (for samadhih)	intense absorption

INTEGRATION OF THE HIGHEST LIMBS

Unified-restraint

3.4   Unified-restraint consists of three kinds in one.

trayam   ekatra   saMyamaH
of three kinds   in one   unified-restraint

Note: '*Unified-restraint*' is a term used only in this book. It represents the true definition of *samyama* as 'concentration of mind (comprising the performance of dharana, dhyana, and samadhi, or the last three stages in Yoga).'

Although Patanjali carefully led us along the path to believing that these are three independent and progressive practices, he how tells us that they are not. Mastering each of these three limbs does not complete the development of meditative skill. Effectively using them requires that the meditator carry all three forward as a single integrated skill, a skill that comes about automatically without deliberate practice. That integrated practice is *samyama* ('*unified-restraint*'). *Unified-restraint* is not a skill of doing three things at one time: it is doing one thing by integrating three previously developed and matured skills. Applying the skills of *concentration* enables single-pointed fixation. Skill at *meditation* enables freeing the mind for independent exploration and receptivity while experiencing higher consciousness. Skill at *intense absorption* enables progressively higher levels of consciousness experience. While in that higher consciousness experience, the meditator must have total single-pointed concentration, mind freedom, and deep absorption.

This integration is among the most important lessons the *Sutras* teach: yet, this prime key to Yoga and its meditative practice, this integration of skills, has been lost to modern teaching.

trayam ekatra saMyamaH

traya (for trayam)	of three kinds
ekatra	in one
samyama (for samyamah)	unified-restraint - paraphrase for 'concentration of mind (comprising the performance of dharana, dhyana, and samadhi, or the last three stages in Yoga)'

Insight Results From Victory Over The Senses

3.5   *In this manner, being constant in victory over the senses, there is the light of knowledge.*

taj   jayAt   prajNA   AlokaH
in this manner   to go constantly   victory over the senses   knowledge   light

When a yogin has become victorious over the senses and mastered the three-fold skill of *unified-restraint,* a new phase begins. Intuitive insight begins to deliver knowledge not accessible when blocked by sensuality, materialism, and the mind. That knowledge may come during experiences of higher consciousness, or may arrive separately from such experiences, but enabled by them. With the evolutionary progression that results from time and practice, the degree of intuitive knowledge will grow and come from increasingly higher consciousness levels.

Patanjali has slowly built to this point of experiencing insight, in a way that is important to see. In Part Two, before he introduced the meditative limbs, he provided some targets for meditative work, even telling us that we can choose any target we like. In this Part Three, he has so far provided three stages of training for that meditative work. With no prior hint of the trend, the *Sutras* have now said that they will integrate into a single meditative force. One of the results of that is the delivery of otherwise unavailable knowledge, the Truth (light of knowledge) that yogins aspire to.

The *Sutras* that follow this one will provide additional meditative targets, while unceasingly guiding us to use this fully integrated '*unified-restraint*' as our approach to our meditative practice.

taj jayAt prajNA AlokaH

tad (for taj)	in this manner
jayat	
jaya	victory over or restraint of the senses
at	to go constantly
prajja (for prajna)	knowledge
aloka (for alokah)	light

The Progression Of Insight Comes In Stages

3.6   Its use is brought about in stages.

tasya bhUmiSu viniyogaH
its brought about stages use

In telling us that higher levels of consciousness come about in stages, the term 'brought about' indicates that they come to us when we are ready, again emphasizing that the soul and we are partners. We will not acquire a stage until the soul sees us as fit for it, but we also will not acquire it without working to win it.

As acquired insights and ability accumulate, the material being, including the nervous system and the mind, transform and evolve. Meditative focus on a target provides new targets, just as studying something important continually leads to study of new aspects. The targets become ever more subtle as insights accumulate and evolution progresses. Starting at the gross level with physical objects as targets the seeker moves toward the subtlest of all things, such as the nature of Nature.

The natural progression of targets through those stages, the meditative techniques, and the levels of consciousness experience will coevolve in symbiotic mutual enablement. Over time, higher consciousness develops as a series of states. Patanjali has given us subtle guidance that we should let the stages develop, not trying to jump into the end game at the start.

tasya bhUmiSu viniyogaH

tasya
  ta   (pronoun indicator) it
  sya   (3rd person indicator)
bhumisu
  bhumi   stage
  su   brought about
viniyoga (for viniyogah)   use

These Three Are Internal Limbs

3.7 In the aforesaid effort of the mind to remain in its unmodified condition of purity, these threefold limbs are internal.

trayam antar aNgaM pUrvebhyaH
threefold internal limbs the aforesaid effort of the mind to remain in its unmodified condition of purity

These three aspects of Yoga (*concentration of the mind, religious meditation*, and *intense absorption*) are internal. The *Sutra* implies the obvious, that the first five aspects (*self-restraint, mind restraint, sitting, restraint of breath*, and *withdrawal*) have to do with our relationship with the external material/sensory world. Of different nature than the first five limbs, these three meditative practices change our relationship with our inner being through experiencing the nonmaterial consciousness. Patanjali confirms the progressive nature of Yoga here, showing the thrust to move from external consciousness to internal consciousness, with the level of internal consciousness continually advancing. The eight limbs continually draw us farther from materiality and closer to spirituality.

trayam antar aNgaM pUrvebhyaH

traya (for trayam)   threefold
antar   internal
anga (for aNgaM)   a limb
purvebhyah
  purva   aforesaid
  abhyasa (for abhyah)   the effort of the mind to remain in its unmodified condition of purity

Seedless Intense Absorption

3.8   Assuredly, going forth in this manner, a devoted man goes to his seedless state.

tad   api   bahir   arigaM   nirbIjasya
in this manner   assuredly   forth   devoted man   to go to a state   seedless his

A higher level of consciousness exists, which is not accessible through meditative practices alone, the highest reach of personal evolution. All the levels before that, the *Sutras* say, are 'seeded.' Led by some authors and our cultural leanings, many equate 'seed' (*bija*) with 'target' or meditative 'starting point.' That is an erroneous view that the *Sutras* will later clarify. 'Seeds' are the karmic 'impressions' (dubbed as 'karmic memories,' 'subliminal impressions' or 'subliminal activators' by some). At the preceding 'with seed' (*sabija*) levels, full deactivation of those impressions (seeds) had not yet happened.

Our beingness is not pure (fully quiet) while any seeds are still active. This seedless state comes about when the last seed has become inactive through all the purifications and other accumulated results of practicing the eight limbs and prolonged *unified-restraint*. Seedless (*nirbija*) *samadhi* occurs only when that committed practice has enabled it. In this state, the seeker experiences pure primal consciousness. In his marvelous flow of thought, Patanjali told us of that earlier in the *Sutras*, when he first introduced the eight limbs.

At this highest level of development of consciousness experience, something seemingly magical happens, an entirely new spiritual experience, but it is within the Laws, a result of 'how things work.' The preceding levels yield wonderful insights, mystical experiences, truth-bearing knowledge, psychic events, and many other wonders. Those who reach the seedless state are free from the entrapping allure and desire for repetition of those events. The karmic memories are no longer in a position to ripple the still mind and interfere with the experience of the pure consciousness. The *Sutras* will continue to make this clear, carefully laying out the progressive steps.

tad api bahir arigaM nirbIjasya

tad   in this manner

api	assuredly
bahis (for bahir)	forth
arigam	
ari	devoted man
gam	to go to any state
nirbijasya	
nirbija	seedless
sya	(3rd person indicator) his

EVOLUTIONARY PROGRESS TOWARD THE END

The *Sutras* will now expand on the idea of slow growth, describing the sequential process.

Blocking New Karmic Impressions

3.9   Awakening through suppression impressions that overpower and destroy manifestations at any instantaneous point in time following mind restraint.

vyutthAna nirodha saMskArayor abhibhava prAdur bhAvau
nirodha kSaNa citta anvayo nirodha pariNAmaH
*awakening   suppression   impressions   overpowering   manifestation
destruction   at any instantaneous point in time   mind
following   restraint   development*

Here, Patanjali introduces a vital piece of the puzzle of how meditation creates karmic change. He has previously led us through aspects of 'impressions' (subliminal activators, karmic memories, *samskaras*) that influence our life, and has told us that our Yoga life can lead to making them inactive. He introduced the concept of blocking future karmic memories in *Sutra* 1.50, where he discussed the dramatic effects of completing the fourth stage of meditative evolution in *nirvicara samadhi*.

The wording now shows us how that deactivation occurs, by telling us that a development comes about in which 'suppression impressions' emerge to destroy any future impressions that may come about. He will build on this through the next three *Sutras*, but here brings in the idea of continued evolution through 'suppression impressions' that actively prevent activation of any new impressions that might arise.

The *Sutras* have been slowly outlining the progressive development of a seeker's meditative life. Thoughts and other mind activity, more generally called 'notions' in the *Yoga Sutras*, leave behind new karmic memories (impressions). We begin gaining control over our mind through developing the skill of thought suppression during our sixth limb practice of *concentration*. The ability to do that strengthens as we evolve to experience progressively higher levels of consciousness. When we eventually reach a point in our evolution at which these suppression impressions automatically develop, we stop building an inventory of impressions. The properly practiced Yoga life will continue deactivating existing impressions, slowly reducing the inventory. Remaining *Sutras*, though, will add more to that progression.

vyutthAna nirodha saMskArayor abhibhava prAdur bhA-
vau nirodha kSaNa citta anvayo nirodha pariNAmaH

vyutthana	awakening
nirodha	suppression
samskarayor	
samskara	impressions
yor	(untranslated)
abhibhava	overpowering
pradurbhava (for pradurbhavau)	manifestation
nirodha	destruction
ksana	any instantaneous point of time
citta	mind
anvaya (for anvayo)	following
nirodha	restraint
parinama (for parinamah)	development

Purification Becomes Constant

3.10   With that, there is tranquility of mind with a constant flow of purification.

tasya praSAnta vAhitA saMskArAt
that   tranquility of mind   flow   purification to go constantly

With the prevention of new impressions (karmic memories), the inventory of active impressions cannot increase. The processes that deactivate impressions due to Yoga practices continue, and new processes will come into place as the yogin's evolution continues. With the constant flow of deactivation, the tranquility of mind that is the goal and result of Yoga practice grows. The eventual deactivation of the last active impression will initiate *nirbija samadhi*, the seedless state.

tasya praSAnta vAhitA saMskArAt

tasya
ta	(pronoun indicator) that
sya	(3rd person indicator)
prazanta (for prasanta)	tranquility of mind
vahita	flow
samskarat	
samskara	purification
at	to go constantly

All Physical Objects Become A Single Point

3.11   Evolution in intense absorption comes forth when all objects inviolably wane in the mind as it becomes one-pointed.

sarva   arthatA   ekAgratayoh   kSaya   udaya   cit-
tasya   samAdhi   pariNAmaH
all objects   inviolability   one pointed it   wane   coming forth   your mind
intense absorption   evolution

Patanjali has been laying out stages of evolution that come about as the yogin's evolution advances. Each of those stages has dramatic physiological, mental, and spiritual effects. The seeker actually becomes a different person in many ways, justifying the translation of *parinama* to 'evolution' rather than other worthy and valid meanings such as 'transformation into,' 'change,' and 'development.'

In this stage the long practice of meditation and a Yoga life, which partly includes single-pointed absorption in an individual physical object, yields an amazing result. All physical objects merge into oneness, in which physicality itself becomes a single thing with no distinctions between objects. This is a step in the direction of the ultimate in which everything physical, subtle, and spiritual becomes a unity.

sarva arthatA ekAgratayoh kSaya udaya cittasya samAdhi pariNAmaH

sarva + arthata		
	sarvartha	all objects
	ta	inviolability
ekagratayoh		
	ekagra	one pointed
	ta	it
	yoh	(untranslated)
ksaya		wane
udaya		coming forth
cittasya		
	citta	mind
	sya	(third party voice)
samadhi		intense absorption
parinama (for parinamah)		evolution

All Subtle Objects Become A Single Point

3.12   Extended further, evolution comes about with risen tranquility, when notions in your mind in like manner become inviolably one-pointed.

tataH   punaH   SAnta   uditau   tulya   pratyayau   cittasya
ekAgratA   pariNAmaH
*extended further   tranquility   risen   in like manner   notion   your mind
one point inviolability   evolution*

Experiencing the common oneness of all things in the physical world establishes a base for this new stage. Now, the yogin progresses to experience one-pointed oneness of the entire subtle realm, the realm of subtle objects such as mental notions. The higher experience of merger of physical and subtle worlds into oneness has not yet come about. Patanjali is showing us how the pattern of personal evolution is the reverse of cosmic evolution. When the cosmos evolved, the subtle world developed before the physical world. When we evolve, we experience the root physical world before we experience the root subtle world.

tataH punaH SAnta uditau tulya pratyayau cittasya ekAgratA pariNAmaH

tata (for tatah)	extended

punar (for punah)	further
zanta (for santa)	tranquil
udita (for uditau)	risen
tulya	in like manner
pratyaya (for pratyayau)	notion
cittasya	
citta	mind
sya	(3rd party voice)
ekagrata	
ekagra	one pointed
ta	inviolability
parinama (for parinamah)	evolution

All Things Are Told In Full

3.13   At this time the inaccessible evolution of the world, creation of the faculty of senses, the law, and array of forms are told in full.

etena bhUta indriyeSu dharma lakSaNa avasthA
pariNAmA vyAkhyAtAh
*at this time   the world   faculty of senses create   law   forms   array
evolution   tell in full   inaccessibility*

At the apex of the experience brought about by these three stages of evolution the blessing of the grand experience written about in so many texts comes to the yogin: all knowledge of the Universe is suddenly there. The yogin can see the entirety of evolution and existence. The birth and evolution of the world is there in full detail, all knowledge existing at the same time, not as sequential unfolding. The mystery of living beings with their powers of sensing and other wonders is no longer a mystery: the full knowledge of it is there. The underlying Law of everything, by which the Universe functions, is clear. The explanation includes everything about the seemingly unending variety of physical forms, both living and nonliving.

etena bhUta indriyeSu dharma lakSaNa avasthA pariNAmA vyAkhyAtAh

etad (for etena)	at this time
bhuta	the world
indriyesu	
indriya	faculty of sense

su	create
dharma	law
laksana	form
avastha	array
parinama (for parinamah)	evolution
vyakhyatah	
vyakhya	tell in full
ta (for tah)	inaccessibility

The Law Is Communicated

*3.14   Tranquil, following as a result of communication from the not to be defined
nature, the yogin knows the law.*

SAnta udita avyapadeSya dharma anupAtI dharmI
*tranquil   communication   not to be defined   nature   following as a result
knowing the law*

Continuing the lessons from the previous aphorisms, this now tells us
that with that nearly complete knowledge communicated by the consciousness of *brahman*, its very nature, the tranquil yogin knows the now exposed
Law. The Law that it speaks of is the infinite eternal Law that is intrinsic
within *brahman* and governs even how *brahman* does things. It is the Law of
spirituality and the Law of materiality. Nothing can exist or happen except
through precise following of that Law. Patanjali will later say, as a last step
in the evolution near the end of the book, that the Yogin will enter the Law
Cloud of consciousness experience.

There is a subtle point here, a point that all religions, traditions, and
philosophies might do well to absorb. Though we speak of the conscious existence behind everything, name some of its characteristics, describe some of its
involvement with things, and identify it as *brahman*, it is truly undefinable.
When we attempt to define it, we limit our ability to ultimately understand it.

SAnta udita avyapadeSya dharma anupAtI dharmI

zanta (for santa)	tranquil
udita	communicated
avyapadezya (for avyapadesya)	not to be defined
dharma	nature

| anupatin (for anupati) | following as a consequence or result |
| dharmin (for dharmi) | knowing the law |

We Evolve Differently Through The Stages

3.15   Evolution differences interweaving are the cause of succession differences.

krama anyatvaM pariNAma anyatve hetuH
succession difference evolution difference interweave cause of

This *Sutra* continues the series about high-level evolution with a simple and obvious truth. The transformational changes that occur in each of the meditative stages are not the same for all individuals. Each of us will experience them differently and evolve in ways different from each other. Those changes weave together to produce patterns of evolutionary succession that will be different in detail from individual to individual, but will trend in the same direction toward the same result.

krama anyatvaM pariNAma anyatve hetuH

krama	succession
anyatavam	
anyata	difference
vam	(untranslated)
parinama	evolution
anyatve	
anyata	difference
ve	interweave
hetu (for hetuh)	cause of

TWO UNIFIED-RESTRAINTS

The *Sutras* now begin to show other knowledge that will come about through meditation.

Knowing The Past And The Future

3.16   Consumed in threefold unified-restraint on evolution, the yogin will gain knowledge of the past and future.

pariNAma traya saMyamAd atIta anAgata jNAnam
evolution   threefold   unified-restraint consume   past   future   knowledge

As this series of *Sutras* closes, this one tells us of an additional knowledge that comes about from the evolutionary transformations. When a yogin reaches the heights of consciousness achieved through all consuming *unified-restraint* (*samyama*), the threefold integration of limbs 6,7, and 8, and meditates on evolution itself the window will open to full knowledge of the karmic path. The past that brought the yogin to this current situation, including all past lives, will be clear. The future path toward Absolute Unity, which is relatively short for such a high consciousness, will also be clear. That knowledge has always been present, but the opaque window has hidden it until this point. As the window opens, this highly evolved yogin enters the timeless zone of the soul. Since past, present, and future reside there without distinction between them, the seeker instantly sees their thrust through history, their interrelationships, direction of flow, and the trajectory to and through the future. To fully understand this, though, we must understand that Patanjali's words do not limit the knowledge to cover only personal evolution. The past and future of the universe, life, our species, a guru, a divine person, the planet, or anything else, depending on many factors, will be there, variably seen according to the karmic needs and evolution of the seeker.

pariNAma traya saMyamAd atIta anAgata jNAnam

parinama	evolution
traya	threefold
samyamad	
samyama	unified-restraint
ad	consume
atita	past
anagata	future
jjana (for jnanam)	knowledge

Knowledge Of The Divisions Of The World

3.17 A thing, its right word, and notions, constantly erroneously transferring from one to the other, bring intermixture confusion, therefore constant unified-restraint on the parts brings knowledge of how all the world is divided.

Sabda   artha   pratyayAnAm   itara itara   adhyAsAt   SaMkaras
tat   pravibhAga   saMyamAt   sarva   bhUta   rUta   jNAnam
right word   thing   notion   the one-the other
to go constantly erroneously transferring   intermixture confusion
therefore   part   to go constantly unified-restraint
the world   all   understanding   divided

When our senses observe a thing in everyday life, the word representing the thing (its name), the thing itself, and our historical and current mental understanding and beliefs about the thing intermix and merge in our consciousness as a single unified perception. We do not perceive them separately. By *unified-restraint* separately on the division of these three aspects - the word, the thing itself, and our mental notions about the thing, a highly accomplished yogin can come into such closeness to elementary nature that communication occurs at a different level, including understanding of communication itself at a non-intellectual, level. The concept of 'God' is an excellent example. The indescribable, eternal absolute becomes confused in our mind when we give it names, and develop ideas and beliefs about it. The ever-present intermixture in our mind makes true understanding difficult.

Patanjali has given us little insight about the true effects of meditating on the word representing an object. It is clear, though, that by meditating on that alone the seeker of Truth will develop some special intuitive insight. Perhaps knowledge will develop about the human trait to identify all things with names. Perhaps the insight will be about the relationship of the named thing to all other things, to how and where it fits in the overall organization of things. Perhaps understanding will come that names are an aspect of the subtle world completely different from such things as ideas, and beliefs. Perhaps the insight will be about the intellect (*buddhi*).

We have already seen that meditating on a physical object, a thing, brings us into oneness with it, attaining a deep understanding of the physical world. We have seen that different effects come about when we meditate on elements of the subtle world, which is the realm of the notions within the mind. Through meditation, the yogin can come to a deep understanding of the natural parts of the whole world, which would include the elementary structure of the physical and subtle worlds.

Sabda artha pratyayAnAm itara itara adhyAsAt saMkaras tat
pravibhAga saMyamAt sarva bhUta rUta jNAnam

zabda (for sabda)	the right word
artha	thing
pratyayanam	
pratyaya	notion
anam	(untranslated)
itara itara	the one - the other
adhyasat	
adhyaropa (for adhyasa)	erroneous transferring
at	to go constantly
samkara (for samkaras)	intermixture confusion
tad (for tat)	therefore
pravibhaga	part
samyamat	
samyama	unified-restraint
at	to go constantly
sarva	all
bhuta	the world
ruta	divisions
jjana (for jnana)	knowledge

HIGH KNOWLEDGE

Knowledge Of Prior Forms Of Existence

*3.18 Constantly producing the impressions before one's eyes, there is knowledge
of prior forms of existence (as man, animal, etc.) produced by birth.*

samskAra sAkSAt karaNAt pUrva jAti jNAnam
*impressions before one's eyes producing to go constantly prior
the form of existence (as man, animal, etc.) fixed by birth knowledge*

This *Sutra* nakedly exposes a powerful result of Yoga practice, without
speaking of the route to that result. It does not, for example, say that *unified-restraint* on the impressions produces a result. In the ongoing unfolding
of the steps and nature of evolving into higher consciousness experiences, it
simply tells of a condition that comes about, a state of non-sensory perception of the impressions. That intuitive insight reveals much about what lives

the yogin previously lived. More than memory of specific events or situations, personal cross-lifetime history will appear in integrated ways not readily imaginable. The long-term pattern of the events and their meaning in the *karma* of current life can become obvious, with cause and effect as well as the flow of issues of destiny falling into place.

The definition 'prior forms of existence produced by birth' includes the parenthetical phrase (as man, animal, etc.). It is natural for us to interpret revelation of previous lives as being about previous lives within our species. That is not what the definition says. Taking it as it is, it means that the experience reveals the entire chain of evolutionary history from the first bacteria up to animals, primates, predecessors of humans, through our species, and on through our individual multiple human experiences.

samskAra sAkSAt karaNAt pUrva jAti jNAnam

samskara	impressions
saksat	before one's eyes
karanat	
karana	producing
at	to go constantly
purva	prior
jati	the form of existence (as man, animal, etc.) fixed by birth
jjana (for jnanam)	knowledge

Knowledge Of The Past-life Notions

3.19   There is knowledge of their past mind notions.

pratyayasya   para   citta   jNAnam
their   notions   past   mind   knowledge

Having evolved to gain knowledge of previous birth forms and circumstances, the seeker also gains knowledge of what the mind was like during those previous times and of the notions that accompanied that current way of living.

pratyayasya para citta jNAnam

pratyayasya	
pratyaya	understanding
sya	their
para	past
citta	mind
jjana (for jnanam)	knowledge

Knowledge Of The World Without Objects

3.20   And at that time, there is no procuring of the foundation, that constant state of being of the past is out of reach.

na   ca   tat   sa   AlambanaM   tasya   aviSayaI   bhUtatvAt
no   and   at that time   procuring   foundation
that   anything out of reach   the past   the state of being   to go constantly

Following the teaching that in that high state of consciousness there is knowledge of the mental contents of the previous life, this *Sutra* clarifies a limitation on that. The Yogin knows what notion was in the mind, but has no access to the derivation of that notion. In other words, the yogin knows the content, but cannot know why or where it came from.

na ca tat sa AlambanaM tasya aviSayaI bhUtatvAt

na	no
ca	and
tad (for tat)	at that time
sa	procuring
alambana (for alambanam)	foundation
tasya	that
avisaya (for avisayai)	anything out of reach
bhutatvat	
bhuta	past
tva	state of being
at	to go constantly

UNIFIED-RESTRAINTS ON THE BODY AND ON FATE

From what the *Sutras* have said to this point it is easy to believe that meditative practice has the sole goal of advancing our consciousness experience to higher levels, perhaps all the way to enlightenment and on to the unification with the primal consciousness. They now correct that idea, by showing other benefits that derive from a variety of meditative targets. There is justifiable temptation to describe most of these as 'Applied Meditation,' while describing unification practices as 'Pure Meditation,' but Patanjali makes no such distinction. Perhaps he does not do that because all meditative experience conditions us for higher experience and the knowledge, practice, and even 'powers' attained are stepping stones toward the higher consciousness states. Although those powers are a reality that can come about through dedicated practice of Yoga, Masters warn that they have huge potential for entrapping us and arresting our evolution.

It is good to remember that in all the cases Patanjali describes in this part, the word *'meditation'* is sometimes a loose term, not referring specifically to the seventh limb. It usually refers to the integrated *unified-restraint* of mind *(samyama)*. The use of the word *samyama* to indicate the integrated *unified-restraint* signals that these are high-level practices, effective for those who have mastered and holistically merged *concentration*, *meditation*, and *intense absorption*.

Although the discussion here may sometimes seem esoteric and beyond reach, it is helpful to keep faith that the described yields from the *unified-restraint* are not fabrications. They are the results experienced and reported by mystics, Masters, and evolved seekers.

The Nature Of The Body As A Target

3.21   *Constant unified-restraint on the nature of the body, and suppression of occupation with the objects of sensual perception, brings disappearance through the absence of connection between appearance and the faculty of seeing.*

kAya   rUpa   saMyamAt   tad   grAhya   Sakti   stambha   cakSuH
prakAsa   asaMyoge   'ntardhAnam
the body   nature   to go constantly unified-restraint   and
the objects of sensual perception   occupation with   suppression
faculty of seeing   appearance   absence of connection   disappearance

Following the lead in *Sutra 2.54*, This *Sutra* further discusses withdrawal of the senses. In clear and simple terms, it tells us that the yogin who has become heavily committed will naturally evolve toward disconnection of the visual sense when deeply meditating. Deep and continual meditation on the nature of the body will bring intuitive insights about the physical world and greater harmony with the core nature and creative forces of the universe. The yogin who at the same time has strongly separated from involvement with physical things will be more free to experience the automatic disconnect of the visual sense. It is not a willful act: it just happens, because there is harmony with the aspects of the universe where senses do not exist.

Because Patanjali has included this in the stream of discussion about experiences in those who are highly evolved, we must take it as a description of an additional experience during evolution. However, moderately experienced yogins also experience spontaneous withdrawal from sensual experience. As they progress, the incidents are more frequent, deeper, and longer.

This aphorism applies specifically to the sense of sight. The following aphorism clarifies that all of the senses can spontaneously withdraw.

kAya rUpa saMyamAt tad grAhya Sakti stambha cak-
SuH prakAsa asaMyoge 'ntardhAnam

kaya	the body
rupa	nature
samyamat	
samyama	unified-restraint
at	to go constantly
tad	and
grahya	the objects of sensual perception
sakti	occupation with
stambha	suppression
caksus (for caksuh)	faculty of seeing
prakaza (for prakasa)	light
asamyoga (for asamyoge)	no connection
antardhana (for 'ntardhanam)	disappearance

Deactivation Of The Other Senses

3.22   In the manner said, sound and so on will disappear.

etena Sabdady antardhAnaM uktam
in that manner   sound and so on   disappearance   said
(Note: This *Sutra* is not in four of the other texts)

As with eyesight, under the conditions of deep meditation, the linkage between the faculty of sense and the stimulus will disappear. A high yogin can interrupt smelling, feeling, hearing, or tasting through disruption of the connection between emanations from outside and sensory organs so that they do not register and process in a normal way. It is a product of interaction with the elements of Nature, under aspects of the universal Laws.

etena Sabdady antardhAnaM uktam

tena (for etena)	in this manner
zabdadi (for sabdady)	
zabda	sound
adi	and so on
antardhana (for antardhanam)	disappearance
ukta (for uktam)	said

Fate As A Target

3.23   Being consumed in unified-restraint on fate with commencement and without commencement, then a natural phenomenon boding approaching death or knowledge of future end of life will come.

sa upakramaM   nir upakramaM   ca karma tat saMyamAd apara
anta jNAnam ariSTebhyo vA
*with commencement   without commencement   and   fate   then
consume unified-restraint   the future   end of life   knowledge
a natural phenomenon boding approaching death   come to   or*
(Note: This is 3.22 in some texts)

In this fascinating and different scenario, the *Sutras* give us two possible outcomes from a specific meditation on the nature of karmic results currently occurring (commenced) and karmic results that lay in wait (not commenced) for future action. One of the results could be the experiencing of some natural phenomenon that awakens a mystical boding of approaching death. In the other, the seeker would gain intuitive knowledge of when life will end in the future. This is clearly a high-level meditation that will only yield results for those who are harmonious with the processes of the universe. It is likely that the first of the two results will come about when life will still be long; the second would be likely to come about when death is near.

> sa upakramaM nir upakramaM ca karma tat saMya-
> mAd apara anta jNAnam ariSTebhyo vA

sa	with
upakrama (for upakramam)	commencement
nir	without
upakrama (for upakramam)	commencement
ca	and
karman (for karma)	fate (as the certain consequence of acts in a previous life)
tad (for tat)	then
samyamad	
samyama	unified-restraint
ad	consume
apara	the future
anta	end of life
jjana (for jnanam)	knowledge
aristebhyo	
arista	a natural phenomenon boding approaching death
abhye	come to
va	or

BENEVOLENCE, VIGOR, AND VISIONS

Benevolence

3.24 Benevolence sets in motion the first fruits of vigor.

> maitry AdiSu balAni
> *benevolence   first fruits set in motion   vigor*
> (Note: This is 3.23 in some texts)

Practicing benevolence will move the yogin toward greater vigor. The wording carefully tells us that it will yield the 'first fruits' of that trait. It does not tell us there will be an instant and magical total conversion. Continued practice and incorporating ongoing benevolent actions in everyday life will cause it to grow further.

maitry AdiSu balAni

maitri (for maitry)	benevolence
adisu	
adi	first fruits
su	set in motion
balani	
bala	vigor
ani	(untranslated)

Vigor Brings Character Strength

3.25   Vigor brings forth the noble-minded strength of an elephant.

baleSu   hasti   balAdIni
vigor set in motion   elephant   strength   noble-minded
(Note: This is 3.24 in some texts)

Following through on the previous aphorism, this one tells us that the vigor attained by the practice of benevolence develops our strength of character, described as the noble-minded strength of an elephant.

baleSu   hasti balAdIni

balesu	
bala	vigor
su	bring forth
hastin (for hasti)	elephant
baladini	
bala	strength
adina	noble-minded

Visions May Manifest

3.26   Manifesting vision may deliver knowledge of minute, concealed, and distant things.

pravRtty Aloka nyAsat sUkSmah vyavahita viprakRSTa jNAnam
manifestation vision delivering minute concealed distant knowledge
(Note: This is 3.25 in some texts)

As the last item in this series, the *Sutras* tell us that visions may manifest while in a high level of consciousness experience. Through them, the yogin may obtain intuitive insight about many wonders of the universe. While that tuned to nature, it is possible to gain knowledge of extremely small physical things that we cannot normally see, things that are far distant, and things obstructed from normal view. It is about information and knowledge, about knowing their existence and nature, not about magical eyesight.

This is not a low level practice where someone performs a 'parlor trick' to find a set of lost car keys. It occurs at high levels of experience, while in deep meditation by accomplished yogins. At those levels, meditators are so harmonious with the forces of nature that they can naturally experience them in supranormal ways. The physical senses and the mind do not provide the knowledge spoken of here: it comes from intuitive insight available in higher consciousness. This phenomenon of seeing 'beyond' occurs to diverse degrees at varying levels of personal evolution. The effects become ever stronger and more evident with continued higher-level practice.

pravRtty Aloka nyAsat sUkSmah vyavahita viprakRSTa jNAnam

pravrtti (for pravrtty)	manifestation
aloka	vision
nyasat	
nyasa	delivering
suksmah	minute
vyavahita	concealed
viprakrsta	distant
jjana (for jnanam)	knowledge

COMPONENTS OF THE NATURAL WORLD AS TARGETS

Although this text did not treat the preceding aphorisms as representing targets for *unified-restraint*, as other authors did, it is clear that Patanjali intended the upcoming series to be such meditative targets. A series of *unified-restraints* having to do with gaining insights to the natural world comes first. We of course, never will know what insights will arise until we experience them, but a larger message is obvious. We can make anything we want a target of our *unified-restraint* and receive insight about it. Meditating on anything in the cosmos, not just on the specifics identified here, will help us to better understand the nature of material existence.

The Sun As A Target

3.27   In constant unified-restraint on the sun, one gains knowledge of living beings.

bhuvana   jNAnam   sUrye   saMyamAt
living beings   knowledge sun   to go constantly unified-restraint
(Note: This is 3.26 in some texts)

No definitive description of the results of using the conceptual (not physical) sun as a meditative target is possible, because experiences may vary greatly from one meditator to another. It is clear, though, that meditating on such large physical objects will bring greater understanding of the universe. Arriving at a deep understanding of Nature and how it functions is a part of reaching the highest levels of consciousness, by whatever means that comes about.

In this case it will be likely to bring an understanding of the relationship of the sun to life on the planet. The world of Patanjali's time was unscientific, having no concept of the beginnings or nature of life.

As examples, the meditator might gain some insight to the sun's nature, the use and conversion of energies, or the seeming miracle of life. Over time, additional insights might cascade to other relationships throughout the universe. They would be very high insights, bringing the seeker ever closer to the endpoint of Absolute Unity (union). A true understanding of the primal energy of *prakrti*, the *gunas, causal body, subtle body, physical body,* and the universe's *soul* may even emerge.

This is not technical knowledge in a scientific sense, such as that of chemical and physical reactions. Whether through this *unified-restraint* or other yogic practices, the high yogin comes to conceptually know the deeper processes underlying those scientifically studied technical processes of life, the planet, or the universe. Such intuitive insights could lead people of the time to new paths of scientific exploration.

bhuvana jNAnam sUrye saMyamAt

bhuvana	living beings
jjana (for jnanam)	knowledge
surya (for surye)	the sun
samyamat	
samyama	unified-restraint
at	to go constantly

The Moon As A Target

3.28   (Unified-restraint) on the moon brings knowledge of the form of a fixed star.

candre tArA vyUha jNAnam
moon   fixed star   form   knowledge
(Note: This is 3.27 in some texts)

It seems that targeting the moon could bring a variety of intuitive results related to the nature of a fixed star. It is not clear what heavenly objects were 'a fixed star' in the perception of people at 250 BCE. It seems that, at a minimum, Patanjali meant to distinguish stars from moveable star-like things such as meteors or comets. Perhaps the moon was considered a fixed star in minds of that time.

candre tArA vyUha jNAnam

candra (for candre)	moon
tara	a fixed star
vyuha	form
jjana (for jnanam)	knowledge

The Eternal As A Target

3.29   (Unified-restraint) on the eternal brings knowledge of the meaning of its being.

dhruve   tad   gati   jNAnam
the eternal   it's   the being meant   knowledge
(Note: This is 3.28 in some texts)

Deep and long *unified-restraint* on the concept of being eternal will yield intuitive insight that could reveal its true meaning. Among other things, a yogi might learn much about how the eternal, beginningless, endless beingness relates to the material universe.

Such *unified-restraint* rewards are never as simple or shallow as they at first seem, nor possible to predict. Depending on personal nature and evolutionary progress, an early unscientific yogin may come to understand that the universe is not eternal and was created, and develop a foundation or spirituality.

dhruve tad gati jNAnam

dhruva (for dhruve)	the eternal
tad	its
gati	the being meant
jjana (for jnanam)	knowledge
(samyama)	(unified-restraint) assumed

PARTS OF THE BODY AS TARGETS

Navel As A Target

3.30   (Unified-restraint) on the circle at the navel brings knowledge of the orderly arrangement of the parts of the body.

nAbhi   cakre   kAya   vyUha   jNAna
the navel   circle a depression of the body   body
orderly arrangement of the parts of a whole   knowledge
(Note: This is 3.29 in some texts)

The aphorism presents no more information than to perform *unified-restraint* on the circle around the navel. Perhaps this is the source of the often heard, and often ridiculed, 'contemplate your navel.' It simply tells us that it will bring knowledge of the arrangement of the various parts of the body. It is difficult to come up with a reliable and accurate explanation of why that *unified-restraint* provides that added benefit, but one will come to know if they faithfully follow the guidance of the *Sutra*.

We again need to remind ourselves that this experience does not provide scientific knowledge. This knowledge is at a different level of consciousness. That higher consciousness can provide intuitive insight that helps in understanding the realities of how everything works together in the body. It may bring insight about the cells, organs, tissues, structures, what unifies it all, or to the harmony of the parts. It may lead to an understanding of the energy body, the *prana* zones, or other subtle (nonphysical) aspects of living beings, or about the symbiosis of causal, subtle, and physical aspects. No one can gain that knowledge from books or experiments. It comes only through the experience of high consciousness. Although there is much baseline commonality through the experiences of all who obtain the fruits of this *unified-restraint*, the experiences will be different for each, dependent on individual history, knowledge, and *karma* needs.

nAbhi cakre kAya vyUha jNAna

nabhi	the navel
cakra (for cakre)	circle
kaya	the body
vyuha	orderly arrangement of the parts (of a whole)
jjana (for jnana)	knowledge
(samyama)	(assumed) unified-restraint

The Throat Hollow As A Target

3.31 (Unified-restraint) on the hollow within the throat will bring cessation of hunger and thirst.

kaNTha kUpe kSut pipAsA nivRttiH

the throat   hollow   hunger   thirst   cessation
(Note: This is 3.30 in some texts)

This aphorism does not refer to a *cakra*, particularly not to the neighboring *Vishuddha cakra* in the throat, as some interpret. It refers simply to focusing on the hollow of the throat. As with many of these practices, this one will yield benefits of varying degree to those who have not yet developed the skill of *unified-restraint*. At high, but not highly advanced, levels of consciousness, this subduing of hunger and thirst can enable sitting for longer meditative sessions.

kaNTha kUpe kSut pipAsA nivRttiH

kantha	the throat
kupa (for kupe)	hollow
ksudh (for ksut)	hunger
pipasa	thirst
nivritti (for nivrttih)	cessation
(samyama)	(assumed) unified-restraint

The Tortoise Tube As A Target

3.32   (Unified-restraint) on the tortoise tube brings steadiness.

kUrma nADyaM sthairyam
tortoise   tube   steadiness
(Note: This is 3.31 in some texts)

The 'tortoise tube' is one specific *nadi* among the thousands, located near the bottom of the throat where the tipped chin touches in the V at the top of the sternum. Some say that the *nadi* has the shape of a tortoise, while others say that the name comes from the effect of this practice, to have a turtle-like ability to hold to a long stillness. The resulting physical and mental tranquility and steadiness are valuable to continued meditative practice for the accomplished yogin. Only yogins at high levels of consciousness can even begin to contemplate, recognize the importance of, accept the reality of, and focus on a single *nadi* to achieve the benefit. Those skilled at employing *unified-restraint* on this *nadi* achieve extreme states of stillness in which they can remain for unimaginably long periods.

kUrma nADyaM sthairyam

kurma	a tortoise
nadyam	
nadi	tube
yam	(untranslated)
sthairya (for sthairyam)	steadiness
(samyama)	(assumed) unified-restraint

The Head As A Target

3.33   (Unified-restraint) on the head brings perception of light as the unalterable divine principle of life.

mUrdha jyotiSi siddha darSanam
head   light as the divine principle of life   unalterable   perception
(Note: This is 3.32 in some texts)

The *Sutra* brings our awareness to a key issue about evolution of the universe and its beings: as an early materialization from *mula prakrti*, light is the progenitor of life and intelligence. Only the advanced yogin who achieves the intuitive insight brought about by this *samyama (unified-restraint)* on the head will truly know the meaning of light as the source. It is clear that the aphorism refers to light, as it existed at the earliest stages of universe evolution, when it first manifested. Patanjali was pointing to that physical process, not an esoteric light such as 'the light in the head' as represented by others. From the absolute beginning of physical manifestations from pranic energy, the divine forces were setting up the processes of intelligence and life.

mUrdha jyotiSi siddha darSanam

murdha	head
jyotis (for jyotisi)	light as the divine principle of life
siddha	unalterable
darzana (for darsanam)	perception

Perhaps Arising Of Intuition

3.34   Perhaps consuming manifold intuitions.

prAtibhAd   vA   sarvam
intuitive   consume   perhaps   various
(Note: This is 3.33 in some texts)

Practicing *samyama* (*unified-restraint*) on the head may bring additional intuitive knowledge, beyond the revelations about the role of light in evolution. That additional knowledge could be many things.

prAtibhAd vA sarvam

pratibhad	
pratibha	intuitive
ad	consume
va	perhaps
sarvam	manifold

The Heart As A Target

3.35   (Unified-restraint) on the heart, brings thorough knowledge of the mind.

hRdaye   citta   saMvid
heart   mind   know thoroughly
(Note: This is 3.34 in some texts)

The actual translation of *hrdaya* is 'the heart or interior of the body,' leading to a belief that the meditator could choose either and gain the same result of knowing the mind thoroughly. At the time, though,' heart' did not always mean the physical heart, but an area in the chest that was considered the seat of feelings and emotions. Perhaps it is best to separate the meditative focus from physical parts of the body that already have strong form in the mind.

If you pause to think about what the mind is, you will either fall into routine concepts related to the brain, or find yourself at a loss to clearly know. The mind is a mysterious element of human existence, existing in the subtle world and not easily definable. Its activities are broad, including thinking, reflecting, imagining, intention, aim, wishing, memory, intelligence, reason, understanding, perception, conscience, will, invention, opinion, affection, desire, mood, temper, and many other aspects. It is a vital element of existence, but full understanding of its nature can come about only through successful *unified-restraint*.

hRdaye citta saMvid

hrdaya (for hrdaye)	the heart
citta	mind
samvid	know thoroughly

SEPARATION FROM MATERIALITY

Three Core Ideas As A Target

3.36   Constant practice of unified-restraint on the ideas that existence and the Supreme Being are perpetually unmixed, that there is non-distinction during experience, and that self-interest is dependent on something else, brings knowledge of the Supreme Being.

sattva puruSayor atyanta asaMkIrNayoH pratyaya aviSeSo
bhogaH para arthatvAt sva artha saMyamAt puruSA jNAnam
*existence   the Supreme Being   perpetually   unmixed   idea
non-distinction   experiencing   dependent on something else   self-interest
to go constantly in unified-restraint   Supreme Being   knowledge*
(Note: This is 3.35 in some texts)

Intuitive understanding, fully different from intellectual/mental understanding, of three important points of Yoga philosophy will bring deep knowledge of the Supreme Being, *brahman*, the spiritual godness-essence underlying the universe. Deep and constant *samyama (unified-restraint)* on those three tenets will yield that understanding.

The first of the tenets is that the nature of the universe is two-fold, a material existence and a spiritual existence, which are perpetually present. Although the temporary material existence precipitated from the universally present eternal spiritual, they are separate forms of existence that maintain their purity. Although separate, both are inseparably necessary to material existence. Although spiritual existence can exist without material existence, it would be a pointless, empty, and inactive existence.

Second, the basic design of us aware beings enjoying Earth life is that it we are aware only of materiality, and unaware of the distinction between it and spirituality. Our sensual awareness is part of that manifested world, the material universe. Because it is, and by our nature, we relate to the world of experience, the short-term existence that our individual consciousness perceives. We think of it and our individual consciousness as reality and do not perceive it as temporary. Reality cannot be in the temporary: it exists only as the underlying, permanent, and eternal, soul/primal consciousness and existence that we have forgotten. In everyday life, we do not distinguish between the two cohabiting entities, recognizing only the material context. From a Yoga viewpoint, we have the potential to recognize both and make them active in our lives. From one perspective, that represents the essence of Yoga. A goal of Yoga practice is to escape that false understanding that traps us in material awareness where we cannot see the difference and find our spirituality.

Third, we do not act separately from the Supreme Being, but in concert with it. As the *Yoga Sutras* progress, they will bring us to see the interactive dance between our will and divine will. They will show us that, as an instrument of the Supreme Being, its awareness is present in all of our actions, not missing even the smallest thing, and it 'sees' the world though our own experience. Since it cannot experience anything except through materiality, it is dependent on us for that. We are dependent on it for our very existence and moving toward our self-interested aims. We cannot do it alone. When we take an action, follow a path, or make a decision we are selecting from among options provided by the Supreme Being.

sattva puruSayor atyanta asaMkIrNayoH pratyaya aviSeSo bhogaH
para arthatvAt sva artha saMyamAt puruSA jNAnam

sattva	existence
purusa (for pursayor)	the Supreme Being
atyanta	perpetually
asamkirnayoh	

asamkirna	unmixed
yoh	(untranslated)
pratyaya	idea
avizesa (for aviseso)	non-distinction
bhoga (for bhogah)	experiencing
pararthatva	dependent on something else
svartha	self-interest
samyamat	
samyama	unified- restraint
at	to go constantly
purusa	Supreme Being
jjana (for jnanam)	knowledge

Withdrawing From The Senses Brings Further Intuitive Knowledge

3.37   Expanded intuitive knowledge comes with victory over enjoying perception by the eyes, and perception by the ears.

tataH prAtibha SrAvaNa vedanA AdarSa AsvAda vArtA jAyante
expanded   intuitive   perceived by the ear   knowledge   the act of perceiving by the eyes   enjoying   victory
(Note: This is 3.36 in some texts)

The intuitive knowledge gained through that meditation will expand when the yogin is victorious in the effort to withdraw from sensory experience.

tataH prAtibha SrAvaNa vedanA AdarSa AsvAda vArtA jAyante

tatah	expanded
pratibha	intuitive
zravana (for sravana)	perceived by the ear
vedana	knowledge
adarza (for adarsa)	the act of perceiving by the eyes
asvada	enjoying
varta	(untranslated)
jaya and jayanta (for jayante)	victory

The State Of Awakening

3.38   Consumed by absorption in meditation together with letting go, one unalterably attains awakening.

te   sAmAdhav upasargA vyutthAne siddhayaH
consume   to be absorbed in meditation   together with   letting go   awakening
attaining unalterable
(Note: This is 3.37 in some texts)

The *Sutras* have been steadily advancing, showing the progression of a yogin's evolution. Having shown us the further blossoming of intuition to the nature of the Supreme Being and expanding into further intuition with withdrawal from physical sensing, they now bring our perspective to a new level. The yogin's experience of consciousness has advanced sufficiently that experiencing awakening to the reality behind the illusory daily experience can come about by fully 'letting go' of the material world and entering deep absorption in meditation.

The final words are far more potent than the casual reader will catch. When the evolution has reached the state of 'awakening,' permanent physical, psychological, metabolic, and spiritual changes occur. 'Awakening' is the actual term the Gautama Buddha used to describe his final stage of transformation. Although many moderns call his transformation 'enlightenment,' he never used that term, nor does Patanjali. It is more likely that the transformation described in *Sutras* 1.50 and 3.9 is equivalent to the modern concept of enlightenment, and that described here is a much higher level, but lower than that of the Buddha.

te sAmAdhav upasargA vyutthAne siddhayaH

te	(flag for verb action status)
samadhav	
samadha	to be absorbed in meditation
av	consume
upasarga	
upa	together with
sarga	letting go
vyutthana (for vyutthane)	awakening (a particular state in Yoga)

siddhayah
> siddha   unalterable
> ya   attaining

Effects Of Attachment To The World

3.39   Attachment to this world is a cause of depression, wandering perception of your mind, and being openly occupied with the body.

bandha kAraNa SaithilyAt pracAra saMvedanAc
ca cittasya para SarIra AveSaH
*attachment to this world   a cause   depression   wandering   perception
your mind   and   intent upon   the body   joining one's self*
(Note: This is 3.38 in some texts)

This simple statement of Yoga philosophy caps a series of *Sutras* that bring the yogin to progressively higher consciousness. It separates that series from a new series that presents the effects of *unified-restraint* on *prana*. The aphorism itemizes some effects of remaining attached to the material/sensory world and its pleasures. Mental depression is a condition experienced by far more materially oriented people than spiritually oriented people. Overcoming the wandering, unfocused, fast-moving nature of the mind is a prime goal of Yoga practice as it moves us toward greater stillness. As other *Sutras* emphasize, the opposite of spirituality is the belief that we are body alone and placing our attention on it.

bandha kAraNa SaithilyAt pracAra saMvedanAc ca cittasya para SarIra AveSaH

bandha   attachment to this world
karana   a cause
zaithilya (for saithilyat)   depression (of the mind)
pracara   wandering
samvedana (for samvedanac)   perception
ca   and
cittasya
> citta   mind
> sya   your (3rd person voice)
para   occupied with

zarira (for sarira)   the body
avis (for avesah)   openly

CONTROL OVER THE FLOW OF TWO PRANA FORMS

In this next *Sutra*, Patanjali introduces another nearly unnoticeable interruption of the flow, but noticeable enough to cause a feeling of discontinuity. He begins to discuss 'conquering' of a new class of targets having to do with *prana* and its zones in the body. Again, he does not tell us to use our *unified-restraint* practice or any other methodology, but clearly has waited to introduce this subject while discussing high-level practices that require much evolution and skill at *unified-restraint*. He tells us of the benefits derived from gaining control of that *prana* (which many in today's culture inaccurately know as 'life-force energy,' a modern characterization). For whatever reason was important to him, he has deliberately inserted his discussion of mastering pranic energy at this point in his exposition of the philosophy and practice. He will soon shift to a new class of targets: when he does, he will again not say that he is changing the subject. It is his way, and the reader has to be vigilant.

Omnipresent and existing in different forms within regions of the body, pranic energy is a part of the material world, one of its first creations. As pure creative energy, it is the source of physical objects, subtle objects, and altered forms of itself, five of which are within the body. As a field of undetectable energy, whose characteristics we do not know philosophically or scientifically, it is not clearly in either the physical or subtle realm. The *Sutras* do not tell us. Neither the original pure *prana* nor the forms of it that derived from the original seem to have separate parts that would be equivalent to physical particles or atoms, nor to subtle thoughts, or ideas, but the philosophy is also silent about that. However, it is possible to modify, manipulate, and move *prana* around, because it is real. It has 'substance,' even though it is not what we normally perceive as substance. It is not Spirit, because it is a part of the limited-life temporary world: consisting of a fixed, though very large, amount, it is finite; since it will pass away when the universe does, it is not eternal.

The *Sutras* and other texts repeatedly tell us to gain dominance over parts of our existence. That dominance could be over our body, our breath, our senses, or our mind. Leaving out detailed instruction, Patanjali is now telling us to gain dominance over the *prana* within us, so that we are its master, and not its slave. The wording will make it clear that this set of *Sutras* specifically refers to the flow of *prana*, or the *nadi* channels it flows through. There is no reference to the *cakras*, which Hinduism defined later.

Prana In The Head And Neck

3.40   And conquering the udana (upwards vital air), one is liable to begin try-
ing to move without the obstacles of water, mire, and thorns.

udAna jayAj jala paNka kaNTaka AdiSu asaNga utkrAntiS ca
upwards vital air   conquest   water   mire   thorn   lia-
ble to become beginning with
moving without obstacles   stepping up to   and
(Note: This is 3.39 in some texts)

The *Sutra* does not tell us <u>how to</u> move without obstacles, only that we will be able to try doing it. The ability is there, but not ready for instant and complete execution. Further, it does not tell us <u>how to</u> 'conquer' the '*udana* vital air,' the *prana* flow from the neck upwards into the cranium: it only tells us what happens when we do. Since this is a high level of advancement, the control of the vital air will come from accumulated yogic practices.

It seems fair to assume, and consistent with the evolutionary process, that 'conquer' means gaining control of the *prana* (vital air) flow. Some translators assume that *unified-restraint* (*samyama*) on that zone is the way to do it, but this is not a *Sutra* about *unified-restraint*. Again, this is not about moving *prana* through the seven *cakras* of Hindu philosophy (the number of *cakras* varies somewhat from sect to sect and tradition to tradition) in the way that such later traditions as Kundalini Yoga do.

On one level we could properly read the teaching of this aphorism as a metaphor for the general ability to deal with the difficulties and obstacles of life, while on another it is a description of physical realities. At that higher level, the power of the advanced yogin to control and to act upon the elements of nature comes into play, working with the forces and materials of Nature, possibly with little more effort than visualizing the intended result. The result may be a reconditioning of the skin and metabolism to withstand thorns without pain, akin to what happens within those who walk on hot coals. It could manifest as walking on water, in the manner depicted for the Christ, or resisting the downward pull of mire. The Yogin would have accumulated a broad range of abilities for separation from the effects of the physical world.

Here, Patanjali brings our awareness to the natural occurrence of abilities (not 'powers') that come about as we reach higher levels of consciousness experience. However, we should know that all such experiences have lower levels of manifestation, such as the ability of trained novices to walk on coals, lie on beds of nails and so on. These harmonizations with Nature are not sudden events, as if throwing a switch. They are products of gradual evolutionary transformation of the entire being.

udAna jayAj jala paNka kaNTaka AdiSu asaNga utkrAntiS ca

udana	upwards vital air - one of the five vital airs of the human body (that which is in the throat and rises upwards)
jaya (for jayaj)	conquest
jala	water
pagka (for panka)	mire
kantaka	a thorn
adiz (for adisu)	to undertake
adi	beginning with
su	liable to become
asagga (for asanga)	moving without obstacle
utkrantis	stepping up to
ca	and

Prana In The Torso

3.41   Conquering the samana (common vital air) brings fire.

samAna jayaj jvalana
common vital air conquering fire
(Note: This is 3.40 in some texts)

The abdominal region, ranging from the navel to the upper body, is another of the zones of circulation for a type of *prana*, this one called the *samana,* 'common vital air.' *Samana* is the *prana* that controls the metabolic effects of processing food into the energy units needed for survival and functioning of all of the cells within the body. Later forms of Yoga, Hinduism, and Buddhism refer to its movement as the *samana vayu* (*samana* wind or *samana* air) or 'middle breath,' and describe it as '*one of the five vital airs (that which circulates about the navel and is essential to digestion).*' This *Sutra* tells us that if we gain dominance over the workings of *samana*, we will experience fire. Whether or not this is an enhancement of the fire of metabolism, the oxidation of food, or some similar physical happening, the yogin feels a heat rising, with the strength depending on the yogin and circumstances: it is a delicious heat, not painful. Externally, those nearby may observe a radiance emitting from the body. Being a light of a single color and special character, it is more than just causing the normally present aura to be visible. The glowing radiance known to emit from some Great Masters attests to the truth of this. Yet, even lower yogins easily experience the heat. Colloquially, some call it 'the burn.' Their shine may sometimes be lightly visible to a sensitive few: high quality cameras have recorded it as a white glow.

samAna jayaj jvalana

samana	common vital air
jayaj	conquer
jvalana	fire

THE BODY AND THE SURROUNDING ETHER AS A TARGET

The Organs Of Hearing And The Ether

3.42   Consumed in unified-restraint on the organs of hearing and the connection with the ether, the yogin gains divine hearing.

Srotra   AkASayoH   saMbandha   saMyamAd   divyaM   Srotram
organ of hearing   ether   connection   unified-restraint consume   divine   hearing

(Note: This is 3.41 in some texts)

An accomplished meditator who consumedly practices *samyama* on the connection between the organs for hearing and the surrounding ether (a "*subtle and ethereal fluid*" that pervades the universe) will gain access to divine hearing: some refer to it as the 'divine ear.' Others erroneously refer to the 'divine voice,' a poor characterization that limits the range of hearing experience to that of voice.

Divine hearing is not sensory hearing. No sound waves travel through air to cause physical and nerve reactions. It is if stimulation of the part of the brain that processes sound had occurred, with a result not distinguishable from the vibratory hearing from the material world. The recipient may hear words, bell sounds, tones, a wind-like roar, the sound of wordless angel-like singing, or many other manifestations. The experience may produce a perception of guidance, leave an insight or symbolic lesson, seed a puzzle to be solved, or just leave a feeling state in its wake: afterglows of joy, peace, love, or extreme quietness may follow.

The mysterious and unfamiliar term 'ether' has not come up in any previous *Sutra*, and many authors and readers misconstrue it. Ether is not air, space, or atmosphere: it is more encompassing and closer to the divine source than all of those are. The early philosophical definition/description was "the subtle and ethereal fluid (supposed to fill and pervade the universe and to be the peculiar vehicle of life and of sound)." Air is limited to its range around the Earth, but ether is pervasive throughout the cosmos. It is present in all physical and subtle objects: it is a carrier for everything, including all physical objects, thoughts, ideas, abstracts, forms of energy and forces. Although the word *akaza* does not translate to 'space,' modern scientific thought considers space as a transparent substance made of the tiniest of particles: its description is close to that of the 'ether.' Both the scientific and philosophical entities are primitive substances that existed before all material things came about, and pervade all material things. Each is a carrier for everything. The temptation is great to say that ether is the active form of Nature as *prana* (*mula prakrti*), carrying all creative potentials, and that may be right, but Patanjali does not name it as that and it could be a byproduct of the earliest prana.

Yet, he is clearly pointing to something within the cosmic creation that is close to the root substance of all things, and is the medium for transmission of divine sound.

Again, please understand that the *Sutra* describes the extreme end of a scale of happenings. A high level yogin who effectively practices *samyama* on that connection between human hearing organs and the ether achieves the fullness of divine hearing: the results are beyond any expectation or description other than by those who experience it. The reports of those experiences are highly variable. Divine hearing, though, occurs at many levels and in many ways. You may have heard the angelic wordless singing, bells ringing, or 'the voice' speaking to you. People whose *karma*, life experiences, or other factors bring them to experiences of that type sometimes feel a magnetic draw toward Yoga or another spiritual pursuit. Depending on many factors it may begin to develop early on a yogin's path, and build as the path progresses and narrows: it becomes stronger, deeper, more long lasting, more varied, more intuitive and more revealing as personal evolution progresses.

Srotra AkASayoH saMbandha saMyamAd divyaM Srotram

zrotra (for srotra)	the organ of hearing
akasayoh	
akaza (for akasa)	ether
yoh	(untranslated)
sambandha	connection
samyamad	
samyama	unified-restraint
ad	consume
divya (for divyam)	divine
zrotra (for srotram)	the act of hearing

The Body And The Ether

3.43   *With unified-restraint on the connection between the body and the ether,*
the yogin can attain falling into a state of being as light as cotton and go
to the ether.

kAya   AkASayoH   saMbandha   saMyamAl   laghu   tUla
samApatteS   ca   AkASa   gamanam

*body ether connection unified-restraint light cotton
attain falling into a state of being and ether going to*
(Note: This is 3.42 in some texts)

The *Sutra* says that through proper practice of *unified-restraint* on the connection between the body and the ether, the meditator may feel that the body feels as light as cotton, and roam the ether. It does not define or suggest how that happens.

In perhaps the best and most likely of several scenarios from respected gurus, the subtle body separates while remaining an ongoing linkage, and travel while the physical body remaining stoically where it is. Some proponents of that say that if the linkage breaks, perhaps by fear triggered by the experience, the two bodies cannot reunite and the physical body will die. Whatever the mechanism and process, this is an out-of-body experience by evolved seekers, allowing them awareness of new places as a non-participating observer.

The next *Sutra*, 3.44 (3.43 in some texts), links to this one, in Patanjali's typical style of logic development: it tells us of happenings during out of the body experience, verifying that this current aphorism refers to an out-of-body experience, not to the body levitation experience portrayed by some authors.

kAya AkASayoH saMbandha saMyamAl laghu
tUla samApatteS ca AkASa gamanam

kaya	body
akasayoh	
akaza	ether
yoh	(untranslated)
sambandha	connection
samyamal	
samyama	unified-restraint
al	(untranslated)
laghu	light
tula	cotton
samapattes	
samapatti	falling into any state
es	attain
ca	and

akasa   ether
gamana (for gamanam)   going to

Destruction Of The Covering On The Light

3.44   *Extended, apart from your natural occupation with the intellectual prin-*
       ciple and being bodiless, there is destruction of the covering on the light.

bahir   akalpitA   vRttir   mahA   videha   tataH
prakASa   AvaraNa   kSayah
apart from   natural   occupation with your   intellectual principle
bodiless   extended   light   covering   destruction
(Note: This is 3.43 in some texts)

The term 'intellectual principle' refers to the attributes of self-consciousness (*ahamkara*) and of the mind. Evolution of that principle happened in
the early universe. In this species, the most advanced of all, self-consciousness
and mind activities keep us constantly busy. During the ultimate out-of-body
experience, the seeker passes fully beyond intellectual and mental activities, as
well as occupation with awareness of the self. During that journey, intellect,
intelligence, understanding, perception, sense cognition, conscience, will,
thought, imagination, invention, reflection, opinion, belief, intention, inclination, affection, disaffection, desire, mood, temper, and so on are beyond
the awareness. The yogin's usual involvement with them is not active. After
lifetimes and years of evolution, now experiencing pure consciousness near
the ultimate primal level, no obstacles remain to receiving the light (opening
to intuitive insights) of pure knowledge: in the metaphor of the aphorism,
there has been destruction of the covering on the light of knowledge pos-
sessed by the primal existence, *brahman/sat/isvara*.

As with other high level experiences, this is a progressive happening.
Yogins of low levels of evolution will have early and minimal out-of-body
experiences with excursions into higher consciousness experience, some
of which will yield insights (pieces of the total knowledge). As evolution
advances, these experiences advance, eventually reaching the ultimate level.

Since this translation differs strongly from all of the modern attempts at interpretation, it would be helpful to read the notes in Volume 2 for an understanding of why that is.

bahir akalpitA vRttir mahA videha tataH prakASa AvaraNa kSayah

bahis (for bahir)	apart from
akalpita	natural
vrttir	
vrtti	occupation with
ir	(indicator of second or third person) your
mahat (for maha)	the intellectual principle
videha	bodiless
tata (for tatah)	extended
prakaza (for prakasa)	light
avarana	covering
ksaya (for ksayah)	destruction

UNIFIED-RESTRAINT ON YOU, THE TANGIBLE, AND THE INTANGIBLE

Victory Over The World

3.45 Consumed in unified-restraint, according to your purpose, on the association of the tangible, one's own nature, and the intangible, brings victory over the world.

sthUla sva rUpa sUkSma anvaya arthavattva saMyamAd
bhUta jayaH
tangible one's own nature intangible association
according to a purpose your unified-restraint consume the world victory
(Note: This is 3.44 in some texts)

The material world of the universe consists of objects of the tangible physical world detectable by the senses and of the undetectable intangible subtle world that include such things as subtle bodies, thoughts, forces, mind, and abstracts. Material existence and its living beings would be impossible without the presence of both worlds. Our nature is as a union of both: they are present within each of us and in all things from the hugeness of the universe itself to the smallest of subatomic particles.

The guidance of this *Sutra* leads to *unified-restraint* on the interrelationships of both aspects of existence and our own nature. Patanjali put an additional thought before us, unrecognized by modern authors, that each person will approach the *samyama* according to their own *karma* and its life path, 'according to the purpose' of their life. Through that, we will come to intuitively understand the aspects of the cosmos and their mutual functioning. It advises us to use this particular *unified-restraint* to discover how everything works. Such *unified-restraint* will yield deep knowledge of how evolution of the world functions. It is victory over the hidden mysteries, not victory as in conquest. The yogin can then be victorious in the long war against the lure of the sensual/material world that so easily overpowers spirituality. Now being so close to the roots of Nature, the ability to use the divine Laws to manage Nature is present. The spirituality of the yogin, or other factors, may cause him or her not to use the ability, but the opportunity for use of the natural forces, elements, and objects of both the physical and subtle worlds is present when experiencing the highest levels of consciousness.

sthUla sva rUpa sUkSma anvaya arthavattva saMyamAd bhUta jayaH

sthula	tangible
sva	one's own
rupa	nature
suksma	intangible
anvaya	association
arthavattva	
arthavat	according to a purpose
tva	(2nd person indicator) your
samyamad	
samyama	unified-restraint
ad	consume
bhuta	the world
jaya (for jayah)	victory

Result Of Victory Over The World

3.46   In that place, consequently knowing the law, beginning with the smallest particle, manifestation of body excellence, they will cause no damage.

tato' aNima Adi prAdurbhAvaH kAya saMPat
tad dharma anabhighAtaS ca

in that place   the smallest particle   beginning with   manifestation   the body excellence   consequently   knowing the law   cause no damage   and

(Note: This is 3.45 in some texts)

Now in the rare state of opening to experience and conquering the basic aspects of nature, and continuation of the physiological alteration, the body reaches a peak of excellence: it proceeds from the smallest particle of the body to the overall mass. With that physical transformation and now knowing the ultimate Laws of everything, the *Sutra* tells us that this advanced individual will not be capable of causing damage. This writing assumes that it means 'damage to anything,' not just to the body or self.

Because there are many fables about and tales taking this body excellence to unthinkable extremes, take caution against literal interpretation. There is nothing in the *Yoga Sutras* that should lead to an expectation of the body of an athlete, movie star, the pretzel body of a modern posture-obsessed yogin, or strength to wrestle lions.

The reader should be aware that many other *Yoga Sutras* texts reverse this, saying that the yogin will be impervious to damage. They say that he or she will gain protection of the body from forces or objects that would harm it. They mistranslate to say that the body will not break or injure. It is hard to imagine, though, that walking away after a jump from a high cliff, deflection of bullets or explosions, or harmlessly ingesting cyanide are real possibilities. In "The Only Dance There Is," Ram Das tells of his newly found guru taking his bag full of drug pills and ingesting them all at one time, without any effect on him. Students of Ram Das say that he learned in later years that it was an illusion and no drugs were taken.

This is not a *Sutra* about mystical 'powers' (*siddhis*).

tato' aNima Adi prAdurbhAvaH kAya saMPat tad dharma anabhighAtaS ca

tatas (for tato')	in that place
animan (for anima)	the smallest particle
adi	beginning with
pradurbhava (for pradurbhavah)	manifestation
kaya	the body
sampad (for sampat)	excellence
tad	consequently
dharma	knowing the law
anabhighata (for anabhighatas)	
an	(negation) not
abhighata	damage
ca	and

Excellence Of The Body

3.47   In the robust state of body excellence, there is the splendor, loveliness, and strength of a diamond.

rUpa lAvaNya bala vajra saMhananatvAni kAya saMpat
splendor   loveliness   strength   diamond   robustness
state of being   the body   excellence
(Note: This is 3.46 in some texts)

It is easy to misinterpret this *Sutra* and miss its relationship to having experienced and integrated a very high experience of consciousness. Since its meaning is conditioned by the requirement of the previous *Sutra*, 3.46, it can only come about through that victory over the world, victory over sensuality and materiality.

You can find many modern translations or interpretations that tell you that you will gain 'beauty,' rather than the 'splendor' of this translation. Although this experience will bring another level of metabolic transformation to the body, beauty is not the intent. Those who conquer the forces, elements, and subtleties of Nature and themselves, and develop the natural abilities that accompany that level will not willfully transform themselves to that: they will not transform to a romantically handsome man or to the movie star or model image of a beautiful woman. They will not become Yoga athletes or posture models.

The body excellence, splendor, charm, and strength will come from the effects of *prana*, good nutrition, breathing, meditation, and yogic practices of all eight limbs. Greater physical, mental, and spiritual health will bring an inner glow of happiness, and compassion will radiate to those around them. A natural grace will emerge from their careful movements, slow pace, accumulated wisdom, and confidence. A few saints have gained extraordinary physical strength, because of their desire to move in that direction, but mainly the *Sutra* refers to the personal strength of full yogic being. The clarity, willpower, and strength of character will be indomitable. The patience, fortitude, devotion, health, character, and faith will provide the ability to endure anything and have great vitality on the path.

For all levels of yogins, physical excellence of the body is a worthy intent that will enhance progress - unless the intent is narcissistic. Splendor, of course, can mean many things. A healthy body has a different appearance than an unhealthy one, through its skin tone, hair quality, muscle tone, and other obvious characteristics. A happy or joyful person will be more likely to attract positive reaction than one who is the opposite. Beauty emanating from Spirit is appealing, perhaps as the inner beauty that radiates from a person who has achieved serenity. Improved health and strength and the confidence of knowledge could have the yogin flow through the world with graceful ease.

The 'strength' of this aphorism is not muscle strength. When introduced earlier in *unified-restraint* on friendliness and personal qualities, it referred to strength of personality or being. Knowledge of the nature of things at such a deep and intimate level would undoubtedly yield that form of personal strength. The continually practiced yogic way of living will harden the yogin against the will and intrusion of unwanted philosophies and teachings of others. The firm and solid stature will yield equanimity and communicate the strength of character to others. Together all these yield great health, perseverance and endurability. Remember that this root Yoga is a meditative pursuit. It is not a physical bodybuilding pursuit, as many of the Yoga practices of today would lead us to believe. We cannot forget that *asana* translates to 'sitting,' not to 'posture.' Yet, good health and modern posture practice will also make us physically stronger, tone and cleanse the muscle and nervous systems, stimulate the pranic system, and remove blockages in nerve, blood, and *prana* flow.

rUpa lAvaNya bala vajra saMhananatvAni kAya saMpat

rupa	splendor
lavanya	loveliness
bala	strength
vajra	diamond
samhananatvani	
samhanana	robustness
tva	state of being
ni	in
kaya	the body
sampad (for sampat)	excellence

HIGHER EXPERIENCE LEADING TO ABSOLUTE UNITY

Association Of Organs Of Sense, One's Nature, And Egoism

3.48   Consumed in unified-restraint, according to your purpose, on the association of an organ of sense, one's own nature, and egoism, one gains victory over the power of sense.

grahaNa sva rUpa asmitA anvaya arthavattva
samamyAd indriya jayah
organ of sense one's own nature egoism association
according to purpose your unified-restraint consumed power of sense victory
(Note: This is 3.47 in some texts)

Withdrawal from the senses is the fifth of the eight limbs of Yoga. Since it is instrumental to further quieting of the mind, it is critically necessary to progressive consciousness experience resulting from practice of the three higher limbs, the meditative limbs. Having taken other major steps in victory over material living, achieving high consciousness experience, the yogin is ready for victory over the power the senses.

Although Patanjali began by telling us that meditation is about restraining the activity of the mind, he has been unfolding a scenario of conquests, as if they were freestanding goals of Yoga, not telling us that they contribute to the quieting. Adding to the conquest of attachments, the body, the elements, and worldly living he now focuses on defeating the power that the senses have over our lives. These conquests are not goals in their own right but evolutionary victories necessary to the conquest over the activity of the mind, toward ever-greater quietness.

The aphorism begins by pointing us toward *unified-restraint* on any of our five sense organs. By itself, that meditative practice might lead to amazing discoveries. Perhaps even by doing the unified-restraint the meditator would recognize that those five simple things are the only ways we have of connecting to the material world: we could not experience the world in any way or function at all without at least one of them. He then leads us to considering the association between the sense organs and the egoism that separates us from our spirituality and makes us feel disconnected from others and all things in the universe. As a third association, he ties the senses, and the egoism to our physical/spiritual nature, in the context of the karmic purpose of our life.

The very existence of the samyama points to the Yoga view that we are in a war in which our senses team with our ego against our spirituality. Our senses want to keep us entrapped, tying us firmly to the material existence: our ego ties us firmly to our physical self and the beliefs within the mind of our subtle being. The spiritual drive wants to separate us from those material entanglements to rediscover the always-present divine side of our existence.

grahaNa sva rUpa asmitA anvaya arthavattva samamyAd indriya jayah

grahana	an organ of sense
sva	one's own
rupa	nature
asmita	egoism
anvaya	association
arthavattva	
arthavat	according to a purpose
tva	(2nd person indicator) your

samyamad
     samyama   unified-restraint
     ad   consume
indriya   power of the senses
jaya (for jayah)   victory

Result Of Mind Stilling And Surmounting The Senses

3.49   And consequently of being deprived of organs of sense and your quick mind, there is victory in being in the state of the original source of the material universe.

> tato   mano   javitvaM   vikaraNa   bhAvaH   pradhAna   jayaS   ca
> *consequently   mind   your quick   deprived of organs of sense*
> *state   original source of the material universe   victory   and*
> (Note: This is 3.48 in some texts)

In the flow of *Sutras* that reveal the evolution of the yogin, we have seen a progression through experiencing states of increasingly higher consciousness as we overcome the powerful attractions of materiality. This *Sutra* advances it another step, bringing consciousness experience closer to the root of all things, the earliest step of bringing the cosmos into existence. Having quieted the mind and surmounted the senses, the yogin is in a new level of interruption-free clarity. This experience of high consciousness exceeds any level yet encountered, the consciousness at the time of the evolutionary source substance that preceded creation of the subtle and the physical worlds, *maha prakrti*. In this aphorism, Patanjali uses the more specific word *pradhana*, not *prakrti*. The translation of *pradhana* as 'original source of the material universe' points to the source of the causal, subtle, and material existences, the three prime aspects of the material world, *maha prakrti*. To make it easier to relate to, the discussions in *Sutras* 1.40 and 2.19 dub *maha prakrti* as 'creative prana.'

> tato mano javitvaM vikaraNa bhAvaH pradhAna jayaS ca

tatas (for tato)   consequently
mano   mind
javitvam

javin (for javi)	quick
tvam	(2nd person indicator) your
vikarana	deprived of organs of sense
bhava (for bhavah)	state
pradhana	original source of the material universe
jaya (for jayas)	victory
ca	and

Attaining Discrimination Between The Soul And The Material World

3.50   And perception comes of the difference between the existence of the soul and its elementary matter in various states, and that the Supreme Ruler state of being knows all states of being.

sattva puruSa anyatA khyAti mAtrasya sarva bhAva
adhiSThAtRtvaM sarva jNAtRtvaM ca

*existence   soul   difference   perception   elementary matter   its   various   state
Supreme Ruler   state of being   all   one who knows   state of being   and*
(Note: This is 3.49 in some texts)

At this stage, the yogin clearly sees the difference between the pure spiritual purusa at its macro level as the soul of the universe, and the various pure elementary states of materiality that it caused to manifest. The other aspect of the *Sutra*, which is the important point here, is that the Supreme Ruler knows all states in the finest detail. The Supreme Ruler is omniscient. Every thought, motivation, action, cause, and result is in the awareness of the god-essence. There are no secrets.

sattva puruSa anyatA khyAti mAtrasya sarva bhAva
adhiSThAtRtvaM sarva jNAtRtvaM ca

sattva	existence
purusa	the soul (of the universe, not the individual soul))
anyata	difference
khyati	perception
matrasya	
matra	elementary matter
sya	(3rd person indicator) its

sarva	various
bhava	state
adhisthatrtvam	
adhisthatr	the Supreme Ruler
tva (for tvam)	the state of being
sarva	all
jnatrtvam	
jjatr (for jnatr)	one who knows
tva	state of being
ca	and

Final Detachment And Deactivation of Remaining Seeds Come About

3.51   At that time, with freedom from worldly desires and deficiencies, waning of the remaining seeds and detachment from all other connections come about.

tad   vairAgya   api   doSa   bIja   kSaye   kaivalya
at that time   freedom from worldly desires   and   deficiency   seed   waning detachment from all other connections
(Note: This is 3.50 in some texts)

After lifetimes of Yoga practice, purification, and elimination of human desires and imperfections, the yogin nears the goal of Absolute Unity of the individual and the one Source of all, in which there will be permanent experience of the consciousness of the Supreme Being (*brahman*). Some seeds (karmic memories) are still active, but their almost inevitable deactivation has begun. This *Sutra* is forward-looking, not a statement of accomplishment. Final Absolute Unity (*kaivalya*), and its providing freedom from future worldly living, has not yet come about.

In the following *Sutras*, Patanjali will describe a test and the final evolutionary steps necessary to completion of the journey.

tad vairAgya api doSa bIja kSaye kaivalya

tad	at that time
vairagya	freedom from all worldly desires
api	and

dosa	deficiency
bija	seed
ksaya (for ksaye)	wane
kaivalya	detachment from all other connections

Lures From The Path

3.52   In the event of pride in worldly attachment to offers from those being in
the right place, causing absence of action in the opposite direction will be
disadvantageous.

sthAny upanimantraNe saNga smaya akaraNaM
punar aniSTa prasaNgAt
being in the right place   to offer   worldly attachment   pride in
absence of action   in an opposite direction   disadvantageous   event
(Note: This is 3.51 in some texts)

The *Sutra* issues another strong warning to the seeker. Even at this high
level of attainment, at the doorstep of the ultimate consciousness and emancipation from materiality, even the highest, and most accomplished seeker
may succumb to a lure away from the path. From a practical standpoint in
the everyday world, the aphorism recognizes both the fact, and the dangers
that come from the fact: kings, military leaders, and other high persons of
the time often sought the advice and company of high yogins. Many yogins
depended on wealthy people for support, shelter, and protection. Without
taking actions to resist those tendencies, attachment to the people and the
benefits received, or pride, could lead the yogin off the path.

It would seem that people at this stage of evolution would be invulner-
able to pride or attachment, because there is little ego left. Yet, it does not
take royalty, rich people, or others of popular or political influence to lure
us away. The temptations are nearby, always awaiting their opportunity to
attract us. They exist in many forms, including things that we have successfully renounced in the past, which could still lure us into renewed desire and
attachment. Reports abound of highly developed spiritual seekers falling into
self-destruction or entrapment in this way. Slipping back is always a possibility, even for the advanced seeker.

sthAny upanimantraNe saNga smaya akaraNaM punar aniSTa prasaNgAt

sthanin (for sthany)	being in the right place
upanimantr (for upanimantrane)	to offer
sagga (for sanga)	worldly attachment
smaya	pride in
akarana (for akaranam)	absence of action
punar	in an opposite direction
anista	disadvantageous
prasagga (for prasangat)	event

The Instant Of Time And Its Course As A Target

3.53   Consumed in unified-restraint on the instant and its course, there is knowledge born from discrimination (i.e. the power of separating reality from mere semblance or illusion).

kSaNa tat kramayoH saMyamAd viveka jaM jNAnam
instant   its   course   consumed in unified-restraint   discrimination born from   knowledge
(Note: This is 3.52 in some texts)

Time passes as separate events in a series; each event is individually so small that we do not notice the separations. We normally experience time as if it were a continuous flow, never suspecting that it has pieces. *Unified-restraint* on the exact instant of time and the tiny sequential elements of time leading to and away from that moment enables final and meaningful discrimination between things at the root level of the cosmos. That discrimination yields intuitive insight and knowledge not previously available to the aspirant. It is accurate to describe it as the power of separating the invisible Spirit from the visible world, the Spirit from matter, truth from untruth, or reality from mere semblance or illusion. They are equally correct ways of expressing it. That discrimination will become important to emancipation from the necessity for material living.

kSaNa tat kramayoH saMyamAd viveka jaM jNAnam

ksana	instant
tad (for tat)	its

kramayoh	course
samyamad	
samyama	unified-restraint
ad	consume
viveka	discrimination (the power of separating reality from mere semblance or illusion)
ja (for jam)	born from
jjana (for jnanam)	knowledge

Fine Distinction Between Things

3.54   Extended, there is perception of the differences in those of comparable welfare where non-distinctions constantly go on in their forms of existence (as man, animal, etc.) fixed by birth, characteristics, and place.

jAti lakSaNa deSair anyatA anavacchedAt tulyayos tataH pratipattiH
*the form of existence (as man, animal, etc.) fixed by birth   characteristic
place   difference   non-distinction to go constantly   comparable   welfare
in that place   extended   perception*
(Note: This is 3.53 in some texts)

In that deep withdrawal into the high state of *samadhi* where the yogin perceives the underlying reality, new perceptions arise of the previously unseen differences in similar things. Throughout life, all states of existence have become steady in the everyday awareness. Tulips are tulips, wolves are wolves, stars are stars, and people are people. The new perception reveals much individuality, detail, and subtle characteristics between comparable healthy or undamaged things, beyond what is available to normal consciousness. The human ways of seeing and describing at a gross level through characteristics, location, and such birth situations as species, class, caste, race, or ethnicity describe things in dimensions that are inferior to the perceptions in higher-level understandings of the physical world and the subtle world. These new perceptions are from the roots of material existence.

jAti lakSaNa deSair anyatA anavacchedAt tulyayos tataH pratipattiH

jati	the form of existence (as man, animal, etc.) fixed by birth
laksana	characteristic
desair	
deza (for desa)	place
ir	(untranslated)
anyata	difference
anavacchedat	
an	(negation) non
avaccheda	distinction
at	to go constantly
tulyayos	
tulya	comparable
yos	welfare
tata (for tatah)	extended
pratipatti (for pratipattih)	perception

Discriminating The Invisible Spirit From The Visible World

3.55   Born from that knowledge, the yogin is enabled to pass over all sensuality in the highest degree, and happening at once, any special worldly objects, aims, or matters of business, thus gaining the power of separating the invisible Spirit (brahman, sat, isvara) from the visible world.

tArakaM sarva viSayaM sarvathA viSayam akra-
maM ca iti viveka jaM jNAnam
*enabling to pass over   all   sensuality   in the high-
est degree   any special worldly object
or aim or matter or business happening at
once   and   thus   the power of separating
the invisible Spirit from the visible world   born from   knowledge*
(Note: This is 3.54 in some texts)

Now deeply and intuitively able to discriminate between Reality and illusion, as well as fully seeing the hidden differences not available to the mind, the yogin is nearing emancipation from materiality, the final Absolute Unity with the spiritual essence, godness (*brahman*). Personal evolution has reached a level where there is full separation from sensuality and its awareness of material objects. The subtle world involvement with attachments, ego issues, needs, and human drives has succumbed to spirituality. It has all come to fruit simultaneously, yielding experience at nearly the highest consciousness level, that of the original bringing about of materiality from spirituality, things precipitated from god-essence. The seeker now intuitively knows the root difference between, and interdependence of, the spiritual real and the material realm, in a way that no intellect could comprehend. The only consciousness level higher than that is *brahman/isvara/sat* consciousness. The seeker will experience it, fully and permanently, at Absolute Unity.

tArakaM sarva viSayaM sarvathA viSayam akra-
maM ca iti viveka jaM jNAnam

taraka (for tarakam)	enabling to pass over
sarva	all
visaya (for visayam)	sensuality
sarvatha	in the highest degree
visaya (for visayam)	any special worldly object, aim, matter, or business
akrama (for akramam)	happening at once
ca	and
iti	thus
viveka	the power of separating the invisible Spirit from the visible world
ja (for jam)	born from
jjana (for jnanam)	knowledge

Absolute Unity

3.56 Thus, having equal purity, the mind and the Supreme Being are in absolute unity.

sattva puruSayoH Suddhi sAmye kaivalyam iti
mind Supreme Being purity equal absolute unity thus
(Note: This is 3.55 in some texts)

In the first of his four parts, 'Samadhi' (Intense Absorption), Patanjali showed the progress of individual evolution from everyday consciousness to the high consciousness state at which new karmic impressions will not occur, arriving at the threshold of Absolute Unity. The second part, 'Sadhana'

(Practice), again showed the process of evolution, this time toward laying the foundation for full withdrawal of the senses. Here, as he will do again in the fourth *pada* entitled 'Kaivalya (Absolute Unity),' he has shown the development of the evolution to its absolute endpoint.

The second *Sutra*, 1.2, spoke of bringing the mind to stillness through meditation, the true goal of Yoga. Throughout the *Sutras*, there have been reminders that the process is about purification. In Yoga terms, purification is the process of stilling the mind, purifying it of its activities. The final purification cannot come about until there is complete disassociation with the senses and the material world. With the individual mind being pure and still through yogic practices that cause that disassociation, and deactivate the last karmic memories, there is nothing to disturb the stillness. The mind of the individual soul becomes as still as the primary consciousness of *brahman*. This is the merging into union, the aspiration of the seeker. Reaching this stillness, the yogin achieves the state of *kaivalya*, Absolute Unity.

With that evolutionary development to an individual nature as pure and still as that of the primal beingness (*brahman*), the seeker has reached the point of full freedom from materiality, and from attachment to or involvement with the world or any other being. Knowing Truth, the yogin is in final release from the thoughts, understandings, and beliefs of all individuals. Having attained that, the freed one is in a state of oneness with all and everything. No sense of distinction between things remains, and there is no need for further births. When total purification has occurred, mind activity no longer blocks the full experience of absolute consciousness. In the satisfaction of the evolutionary purpose, the individual soul has no more need to purify the mind. It can rest in full oneness with the absolute consciousness.

In his final part to follow, Part Four, Patanjali goes on to bring us toward a more clear understanding of that Absolute Unity, starting from a different perspective and building again toward that endpoint in freedom from further material living.

sattva puruSayoH Suddhi sAmye kaivalyam iti

sattva   mind

purusa (for purusayoh)	Supreme Being
zuddhi (for suddhi)	purity
samya (for samye)	equality
kaivalya (for kaivalyam)	absolute unity
iti	thus

KAIVALYA PADA

THE PART ON ABSOLUTE UNITY

(Sutras 4.1 – 4.34)

Having brought us step by step to what the philosophy of Yoga is ultimately about, attaining Absolute Unity; this ending part continues to unfurl surprises as it explores issues related to that. It first reminds us that the game of Yoga is wide open. There are many paths to the completed union.

FACTORS LEADING TO SUCCESS

4.1   Attaining success is produced by birth, herbs, prayer or song of praise, religious austerity, and intense absorption.

janma   oSadhi   mantra   tapaH   samadhi   jAH   siddhayaH
*birth   herb   a prayer or song of praise   religious austerity   intense absorption
produced by   successful   attaining*

Patanjali starts this final *pada*, Absolute Unity, by pointing to multiple factors leading to higher consciousness. He is speaking of success, but not specifically of attainment of Yoga, which is the Absolute Unity of *kaivalya*. In one brief statement, he tells us that the laws of *karma*, chemicals, religion, personal discipline, and intense absorption can each contribute to our karmic evolution.

He begins by stating that some people are predisposed at birth. On the surface, this seems to make aspiration and a committed life irrelevant, but only because the surface view does not reflect the workings of *karma*. Under the Law of Karma (not a formal term in the philosophy), positive and negative influences carry from life to life - perhaps for many lifetimes, as long as at least one karmic impression remains active. Some highly evolved yogins who have come a long way, perhaps having attained very high consciousness experiences through their unified practices and intense absorption during their previous life, may have little karmic influence left to deactivate: they will be predisposed to becoming an illustrious yogin in their current life. Perhaps they even could be among the very few who have the potential for attaining ultimate union during that lifetime, entering this round of material living already approaching the endgame.

Surprisingly, he then says that herbs can be a factor in bringing us to experiencing high consciousness. Considering what we know about some modern plants and drugs, it would be foolish to argue that no drug could ever provide at least a temporary consciousness 'high.' Their influence can provide those experiences by restructuring the mind, body, and sense complex in some of the ways that Yoga practices do. However, herbs and drugs do not accomplish the purification, nonharming, reduction of karmic memories, and accumulation of effects that Yoga practice does. They can poison the body and bring a high level of attachment to using them, both of which can impede further evolution. If the effects are not cumulative or directional, such shortcuts to temporary experiencing of higher consciousness, even experiencing the divine, are not shortcuts to moving on to final union.

Patanjali so easily and naturally included herbs, though, that we know that some understanding of the culture, the availability of special herbs, or of his intent, may be missing. Rumors and speculations abound that nonharming consciousness-enhancing plants, possibly prepared through careful and complicated processes, were in use during his time. As one example, priests used the fermented juice of the soma plant as ritual offerings to gods and for self-intoxications, but it may have been no more magical than alcohol or marijuana of today. Many have aggressively searched for information about 'soma' and other 'magic pill' herbs and recipes without success. However, there is no choice but to accept, without passing judgment, that some chemical approach was and is a valid approach to aiding higher consciousness, even if it violates our belief against the 'end justifying the means.' We simply do not have enough good information.

Prayer or song of praise (*mantras*) takes many forms from a broad range of contexts. *Mantras* may be spiritual, religious, mystical, or otherwise. Typically, they involve repetitive chanting of sounds or ideas. They may be religious *mantras* from sacred texts, representative of spiritual goals or beliefs, pure sound patterns, or otherwise. Repetition of *mantras* is a prime meditative path toward the higher consciousness necessary for attaining *kaivalya*: it is an obvious path, since the design of *mantras* is usually spiritual, whether contained in religious terms or not. The constant repetition of one of the many names for gods, the symbol *om*, spiritual passages, or recognition of the infinite consciousness will bring the committed yogin ever further down the path, continually purifying the mind and focusing attention on the path. A *mantra* is among the most potent thought-blockers, a key to meditation of all forms.

Religious austerity is severe discipline in the way that those cloistered in religious orders practice it, living quiet lives dedicated to their pursuit. The word 'austerity' carries a lot of negative implication these days, but it is clearly consistent with the flow of Yoga practice, without the negative connotations. Whether considered in a religious context or not, the limbs of Yoga are about self-discipline. Limbs 1 and 2 are about disciplining our way of living. The next two discipline the body. The other four discipline the mind. When combined they are potent tools.

Ample discussion of <u>intense absorption</u> (samadhi) has preceded this and more will follow.

The itemized tools are neither mutually exclusive nor sequential. Many use multiple tools in the same timeframe.

janma oSadhi mantra tapaH samadhi jAH siddhayaH

janman (for janma)	birth
osadhi	herb
mantra	a prayer or song of praise
tapas (for tapah)	religious austerity
samadhi	intense absorption
ja (for jah)	produced by
siddha	successful
ya (for yah)	attaining

MAN, ANIMAL, ETC., ARE TRANSFORMATIONS OF THE PRIMAL SUBSTANCE

Everything Derived From The Primal Substance

4.2   The constantly abundant original passive power of creating the material world (consisting of 3 constituent essences or gunas) transforms into different forms of existence (as man, animal, etc.) fixed by birth.

jAty antara pariNAmaH prakRty ApUrAt
*forms of existence (as man, animal, etc.) fixed by
birth   different   transformation into
the original passive power of creating the material world (consisting of 3 constituent essences or gunas)   abundance to go constantly*

The wording here has broad implications, but specifically says that all life forms developed under the passive power of the creator (*brahman/isvara/ sat*). We and all other living beings are primal substance, shaped into different forms by that creativity, as fixed by birth. Beginning with a base of bacteria-like organisms, all the species of the world have slowly evolved to what they are today, all developing through transformation of the substance under the invisible force of the creative power.

Our lives evolve moment by moment from the time we are born. Even our thoughts evolve with every instant. The experience of consciousness by a practicing yogin evolves. Evolution of everything, whether of life forms, objects of subtle matter, or of physical matter, is simply transformation over time into new manifestations of the primal substance, responding to the continual creative power that brings about different forms of existence. On Earth, oceans, mountains, continents, volcanoes, and deserts slowly evolve. Galaxies evolve: the chemistry and nature of each star evolves. The universe and all its parts continually evolve to what they are at the moment.

'Seers' from before Patanjali's time said that our universe bubbled up from the great beingness beyond, under the force of 'intention.' What bubbled up was undifferentiated primal substance from which all physical things, subtle objects, and much more manifested. Today's scientists tell us that before our

universe a huge pool of undifferentiated energy manifested from the nothing-
ness void and subsequently precipitated into matter, forces, and various forms
of energy. The difference between scientists and mystics is mainly semantic.

jAty antara pariNAmaH prakRty ApUrAt

jati (for jaty)	forms of existence (as man, animal, etc.) fixed by birth
antara	different
parinamah	transformation into
prakrti	the original passive power of creating the material world (consisting of 3 constituent essences or gunas)
apurat	
apura	abundance
at	to go constantly

We Cannot Affect The Supreme Being

4.3   *Instrumental causes have no effect on the original producer of the material
world (consisting of 3 constituent essences or gunas) in its act of choosing
changes: it has extended authority, like the owner of a field.*

nimittam aprayojakam prakRtInAM varaNa bhedas tu tataH kSetrikavat
*Instrumental cause   not affecting   the original producer of material world
(consisting of 3 constituent essences or gunas)   the act of choosing
change   to have authority   extended   like the owner of a field*

Although the wording is not smooth and easy to immediately grasp, the
message is simple. As much as we may think we make things happen, the
human events, motives, efforts, desires, actions, and changes do not affect
the original producer of our material world (*brahman/isvara/sat*). Nothing
can affect Iт, change Iт, or cause Iт to do anything. Iтs complete authority
extends over everything: Iт is the originator and producer of all things from
the beginning of the universe on. That includes all events, occasions, and
happenings. Iт causes things, but no one can cause Iт to do things.

nimittam aprayojakam prakRtInAM varaNa bhedas tu tataH kSetrikavat

nimitta (for nimittam)	the instrumental cause
aprayojaka (for aprayojakam)	not effecting
prakrtinam	
prakrti	original producer of the material world (consisting of 3 constituent essences or gunas)
nam	(untranslated)
varana	the act of choosing
bheda	change
tu	to have authority
tata (for tatah)	extended
ksetrikavat	
ksetrika	the owner of a field
vat	like

EGOISM AND SEPARATION OF INDIVIDUAL MINDS

Origin Of Egoism

4.4   Forming within mind, egoism is of the material world.

nirmANa cittAni asmita mAtrAt
forming within mind egoism material world

There is strong insight here into the nature of evolution of mind in the universe. Since it speaks of mind in general, with no reference to individuation it is pointing to the common mind of the universe, the mind from which other minds individuate. It simply says that egoism is part of mind, and that mind and egoism are part of the manifested material world, not of the eternal spiritual world.

This is a logical and clear step in the evolution of the universe. The universe is material, (made of matter, both physical and subtle). It is materialized Spirit (*brahman, isvara, sat,* primal existence, Absolute). Everything created is matter, because everything created is temporary, mortal, and disposable, including the universe itself. Spirit is the creator, not the created: it is eternal, not disposable.

The first step of establishing the universe was the primal essence, the 'stuff' from which subtle world and physical world material derives. Early manifestations in the material world are the universal mind and its egoism, from which all individuation derives. Beings in the universe have individual soul and individual consciousness, individuated from common consciousness (*caitanya*) and common soul (*purusa, isvara, sat*). Since soul and consciousness are eternal and spiritual, the spiritual forces individualize them: it is not done by the universal ego, which is material. That ego can cause individualization only of material things, such as mind, body, and intellect, which are mortal and belong to the material existence.

nirmANa cittAni asmita mAtrAt

nirmana	forming
cittani	
citta	mind
ni	within
asmita	egoism
matra (for matrat)	material world

Many Minds From The Common Mind

4.5   *Progressing with that distinction leads to the mind that happened only once being separated.*

pravRtti bhede prayojakaM cittam ekam anekeSAm
manifestation alteration leading to mind, happening only once separated

With a singular happening ("happened only once") at the birth of the universe, the creative drive formed one soul of the universe with one consciousness manifested from the *brahman* oversoul and Its consciousness. Varied cultures know this universal consciousness as Common Consciousness, Cosmic Consciousness, Christ Consciousness, and Krishna Consciousness. That soul level eternal consciousness gave rise to a common mind of the universe, part of its materiality. The preceding *Sutra* spoke of that material mind being newly influenced by a sense of self-identification, egoism. The presence of that egoism in that common mind lead to creation of separated individual minds.

The universe would not be what it is without forming individuals from those common entities, souls individuating from the universe soul, individual consciousness from the common consciousness, individual bodies from the universe body, and individual minds with their own egoism from the common mind with its egoism.

pravRtti bhede prayojakaM cittam ekam anekeSAm

pravrtti	progress
bheda	distinction
prayojaka	leading to
citta	mind
eka (for ekam)	happening only once
anekesam	
aneka	separated
sam	not translatable

SOME ASPECTS OF KARMA

Karmic Influences Are Inactive During Meditation

4.6   There, while in continually consuming meditation there is no stock (i.e. karmic influences).

tatra   dhyAna   jam   anASayam
there   meditation   consuming continually   no stock

Actions we take within our normal consciousness level leave memories in the mind. Key memories become karmic 'impressions' (informally - subliminal activators, karmic seeds, karmic memories) in both the mind and the soul. The *Sutras* refer to them as the 'stock.' This stock of impressions will affect the future existence of the individual in the current life and following lives. The deactivation of existing impressions and discontinuation of accumulation of new ones are important steps to the goals of Yoga. The message here is simple and clear. A mind consumed with devoted continual meditation will not create new karmic impressions during the meditation. Activity from existing impressions, will not affect the meditation.

The *Sutras* have just begun an exploration: as the text further develops, and the marvelous flow of logic brings the pieces together, we will see how the deactivation and discontinuation processes work.

tatra dhyAna jam anASayam

tatra	there
dhyana	meditation
jam	consuming continually
anasyam	
an	no
azaya	stock (i.e. karmic influences)

For Yogins, Actions Are Neither Black Nor White

4.7   Actions of those regarded as devotees are not black and not white. Those different from them have three kinds.

karma   aSulka   akRSNaM   yoginah   trividham   itareSAm
action   not black   not white   devotee   regard as   three kinds   different from

The Sanskrit of this aphorism refers to 'yogin,' for which this text uses the definition of 'devotee.' There is no fine line dividing yogins from those who are not yogins. By definition, yogins are followers of the Yoga system of practice. It is clear, though, that the *Sutra* refers to those yogins who practice Yoga with devotion and dedication, aspire to its goals, and commit to the yogic life, not those who have just begun to experience the practices. The yogins that experience the effect described here are those that have evolved to experience higher consciousness well beyond material/sensory consciousness.

Patanjali tells us here that the acts by those who have evolved to sufficiently high attainment are on neither side of any coin: their acts are dispassionate. Their way of being has changed, so that the things they do are no longer at extremes or exclusively from one viewpoint or its opposite. Being in continuous equanimity, they have become neutral. However, viewing that evolutionary transformation as coming about through a one-time switch-closing event would be incorrect. As experience in higher levels of consciousness extends, things move proportionally toward that neutral situation. The acts of those 'not black or white' yogins will not affect *karma* by leaving new karmic seeds (impressions) to affect the future. Nor will those acts cause deactivation of old ones. Only already existing karmic memories will generate consequences.

Patanjali speaks of the effects of those karmic memories, their management, and deactivation in subsequent *Sutras*, particularly 4.8, 4.11, and 4.30.

On the other hand, those who have not progressed to that level of evolution will engage in three types of actions, black, white, and mixed. Some call the mixed actions 'grey,' but we should be clear that they occur at all points on the scale from nearly black to nearly white.

karma aSulka akRSNaM yoginah trividham itareSAm

karman (karma)	action
azukla (for asukla)	not white
akrsnam	not black
yoginah	
yogin	devotee
ah	regard as
trividha (for trividham)	three kinds
itaresam	
itara (for itare)	different from
sam	(indicates a grouping)

No New Impressions Form

4.8   *After that, consequently with maturing, manifestation is only according to the impressions of anything remaining unconsciously in the mind.*

tatas   tad vipAka anuguNAnAm eva abhivyaktir vAsanAm
*after that   consequently   maturing   according to   only   manifestation
the impression of anything remaining unconsciously in the mind*

This *Sutra* and the next one seamlessly continue from the previous one, which described the karmic step of a yogin reaching the evolutionary status at which actions are neutral. Being neutral, they do not bring about karmic cause and effect results at the time of the act or in the future, and they do not affect the seeds. All consequences experienced by the yogin now derive from still active karmic impressions. Since no new karmic influences will accumulate, the door is open for gradual decrease of remaining karmic influences through deactivation of seeds, leading toward the endgame.

Although Patanjali uses *samskara* throughout the book, to represent karmic memories, he does not use it here. The precise definition of samskara
is 'impression on the mind of acts done in a former state of existence.' He
instead uses the word *vasana* here, which has a translation of 'the impression
of anything remaining unconsciously in the mind.' Although they seem close
to being the same, *samskara* clearly refers to all storage of karmic memories: as
used here, *vasana* refers to remaining active karmic impressions. He is setting
the stage for deactivation of those remaining impressions.

Karma is a process in which we are continually building a storehouse of
event memories, reflecting our past actions. Each of them is an object in the
subtle realm of the universe, just as a flower is an object in the physical realm.
As you have seen, this book uses an informal term, 'karmic memories,' for the
stock of stored impressions, simply for easier recognition, but it is a characterization, not a translation. By whatever name, that stock of retained seeds
from past events affects future life. If we build a history by treating someone
with meanness or unfairness, for example, we will at some time experience
meanness and unfairness from others. We will experience it in such a way that
a wise person - a spiritually tuned person - can perceive the lesson and learn
from it. If we practice compassion or love, compassion or love will return to
us. Uncountable life factors affect our future life.

The karmic effect is not an automatic switch-throwing kind of thing, but
a potential that can lay dormant, awaiting the right mix of conditions and
factors. When the conditions are right ('mature'), the karmic response will
come about. Although the divine guidance through the response can often be
harsh and painful to our life, it is not retribution, nor punishment. It is the
teaching of lessons and provision of needed experience. We learn from experiencing both sides of the coin. Life, Yoga, and evolution are largely about experiencing. We need to learn in order to evolve, but that cannot happen without
experience. It is almost impossible to properly understand and hold in mind,
though, that the divine is truly the experiencer. We play roles through which
the divine experiences. It can only experience through its creations.

tatas tad vipAka anuguNAnAm eva abhivyaktir vAsanAm

tatas   after that

tad	consequently
vipaka	maturing
anugunanam	
anuguna	according to
anam	(untranslated)
eva	only
abhivyakti	manifestation
vasanam	the impression of anything remaining unconsciously in the mind

Mind Memories And Soul Memories

*4.9   Moreover, since birth, place, and time incline toward separation of imme-
diate sequence, your forms of memory and impressions are identical.*

jAti   deSa   kAla   VyavahitAnam   apy   AnantaryaM
smRti   saMskArayor   eka   rUpatvat
*birth   place   time   separation incline   moreover   immedi-
ate sequence   memory   impressions   identical   form your*

The karmic cycle of effects from actions may take a long time to come
about, or may happen in the short term. Death may interrupt those effects
until the next rebirth, when the soul's copy of the impressions enables the
karmic cycle to refresh. Because the mind passes away at the body's death, its
intimate connection with the soul to share its karmic impressions has enabled
them to be the foundation for the continuing cycle. If the impressions were
not shared by the soul, they could not convey the influences from one life to
the next.

The impressions will be present in those future times no matter how
much time separates lives, and in all future places, no matter where we go,
what mental health conditions come about, or what conditions we live under.
They will travel into future existences, where they will again be in intimate
contact with newly formed individual mental memory, providing the karmic
seeds that condition that life. As the new life accumulates new karmic seeds,
those seeds will condition the situation and actions in yet another future
existence that will, in its turn, leave additional karmic memories. This is the
'chain of cause and effect,' customarily known as the *Law of Karma.*

jAti deSa kAla VyavahitAnam apy AnantaryaM
smRti saMskArayor eka rUpatvat

jati	birth
desa (deza)	place
kala	time
vyavahitanam	
vyavahita	separation
anam	incline
api (for apy)	moreover
anantarya (for anantaryam)	immediate sequence
smrti	memory
samskarayor	
samskara	impression
yor	(untranslated)
eka	identical
rupatvat	
rupa	form
tvat	(2nd person indicator) your

Eternity Of Karmic Memories

4.10   They are in a state of having no beginning, and zealousness to overcome
them is a constant innate state of being.

tasam   anAditvaM   ca   Asiso   nityatvAt
they   state of having no beginning   and   to make zealous to overcome
innate the state of being to go constantly

The *Sutra* teaches that impressions ('karmic memories,' 'subliminal activators,' etc.) are an eternal feature of the primal existence. They never began:
they have always been there: the oversoul carries them: the universe soul carries them, and all individual souls carry them. They were present before there
was any universe, for use in evolution in material beings. The zealous human
drive to overcome the active karmic memories is innate, but not eternal. In
a more general way, this *Sutra* tells us that the process of evolution through
cause and effect, using stored impressions is eternal, without beginning or
end, part of the equipment for building a universe.

Patanjali is saying here that it is not correct to think of karmic memories as beginning with the first human or the first being. The subliminal impressions are an innate and eternal part of the universe system, within the beginningless soul that preceded the universe, awaiting the inevitable appearance of living beings. This teaching does not speak of it, but even inanimate entities have souls, leaving a question as to whether they have karmic impressions. The strongest example of an inanimate soul is the soul of the universe. At a detailed level, a new embryo has a carried forward karmic memory, whether an elephant, ant, or human. The sperm and egg that produced the embryo also each had one. All cells have one. All life of any form anywhere has karmic impressions. There would be no evolution without them. Associated with all souls are the potentials for modifying *karma* and for overcoming karmic influences by deactivating them. Those potentials become realities at appropriate times in evolution.

tasam anAditvaM ca Asiso nityatvAt

tasam	they
anaditva (for anaditvam)	state of having no beginning
ca	and
asiso	
azi (for asi)	to make zealous
sah	to overcome
nityatvat	
nitya	innate
tva	the state of being
at	to go constantly

Reducing Karmic Memories

4.11 *Seeking nullity and consequently non-existence is the foundation on which the state of being collected from cause and effect depends.*

hetu phala ASraya AlambanaiH saMgrhI-
tatva eSAm abhAve tad abhAvah
*cause effect on which anything depends foundation col-
lected state of being seeking nullity consequently non-existence*

The previous aphorism told us, "Zealousness to overcome them (the impressions) is a constant innate state of being." This one follows that lead by pointing to 'seeking' as the final zealousness factor that holds us to the cycle of evolutionary rebirth through the cause and effect cycle. In each of our sequential lives we, largely unknowingly, have an internal drive to overcome our karmic residue. As we become more conscious of cause and effect and begin looking for new ways of being in the world, that drive comes closer to awareness. The further a yogin progresses the more conscious, purposeful, automatic and fixed the seeking to overcome becomes, the more fixed the drive becomes. That seeking ends with the final nullification of the impressions. Freedom from seeking enables us to escape the tyranny of the ego over our lives and the karmic rule of cause and effect over our future, approaching the Absolute Unity of *kaivalya*, the nonexistence the *Sutra* points to. The *Sutras* will point to other factors necessary to attaining the final freedom, but this one points to that seeking as a necessary step.

Patanjali has earlier described causes of karmic accumulation, such as materiality and ignorance, which have the effect of having us take actions of one sort or another. The actions we choose result in effects that lead to karmic memories, the seed deposits for future steering of our living. In addition, they continually point to the problems created by the ugly twins of attachment and desire, which add many seeds. Stimuli such as sensory awareness, actions of others, and perceptions (correct and incorrect) play into all of those, causing new actions, effects, and thoughts that help generate seeds.

Continuing the teaching about impressions (karmic memories), while leading us toward understanding the endgame of Yoga, this *Sutra* gives us a vital insight. The key to understanding that insight is in 'nullity.' The final step on the path to full union is nullification (deactivation) of the final remaining impressions. When we have abandoned all seeking for something, in an environment where no new impressions form, Yoga practices will continually nullify (deactivate) remaining impressions to decrease the collected stock while not adding new ones.

hetu phala ASraya AlambanaiH saMgrhItatva eSAm abhAve tad abhAvah

hetu	cause
phala	effect
asraya (for azraya)	on which anything depends

alambana	foundation
samgrhitatva	
samgrhita	collected
tva	state of being
esa (for esam)	seeking
abhave (for abhava)	nullity
tad	consequently
abhava (for abhavah)	non-existence

Past And Future Are In All Things

4.12   Past and future exist in one's own form; the journey changes, holding to the law.

atIta anAgataM sva rUpato 'sty adhva bhedAt dharmANAm
*past   future   one's own   form   exist   journey   change
holding to the law*

For humans, past and future are always present within the human com-position of physical world body, subtle world mind, and eternal soul. They determine the nature we are born to, the complex of mind, karmic memories, physical body, subtle body, causal body, genes, and everything else that makes us who we are. Although our view of what is the past continually changes in our perception, the true past has shaped our journey and created the changes that brought us to where we are, always under the eternal Laws. The future exists as possibilities for choice. The karmic memories, and the way we choose to act under those influences, continually change the journey. The journey brings us through our evolution, to become the person of the moment. The differences may be minor for some and major for others. During a lifetime, we have added to our past and have prepared ourselves to select a new future.

Past, present, and future are simply elements of path selection. Past never goes away. Our path through it does not change. Future is waiting for us to choose it. The present, which is unmeasurably small, exists for all manifested things, inanimate, animate, physical, or subtle. Past and the future equally exist for those things. As a star evolves, due to an array of past path events and circumstances, it may become a supernova, pulsar, white dwarf or something else. The universe itself would be a fully different universe if different events had happened in the past, setting up different futures.

To understand this from a different perspective, put your imagination in the situation of the seeker who has gained the nearly highest sought for consciousness experience, just short of the state of *kaivalya*, Absolute Unity. That is the consciousness of The All through the omniscient eye of godliness, from a perspective where time and sequence do not exist. From that high yoga philosophy view, beyond the time-oriented universe, all moments of all things are simultaneously there, with no distinction between past, present, and future. To us, past has passed and future has not arrived, but in that extremely high experience of consciousness all past, present and future events are infinite concurrent collections of objects.

In the reality of this world, time moves. We ride time and see the changing forms of existing things as we pass by them. We can see an egg and then a chick's beak making a hole. If we could make time go backward we could see all past states again, as momentary objects in reverse flow, because they are material-world real and there. We would see the beak retract and the egg close. Yet, time moves only forward and we encounter the future states on whatever path we have chosen in order to meet the needs of our karmic influences, responding to ever-changing circumstances. The future state of a nail encased in plastic will be different than the future state of an identical nail soaked in brine.

The gene pool of a living thing provides a useful analogy to this. It contains every gene of every past being that led to the current being through evolution. It carries billions of unused genes which, in part, may define the options for what it will be in the future, depending on the changing circumstances. Yet, it is more than simply responding to conditions: each individual, species, even inanimate forms, and the entire universe respond to the pressure of an unfulfilled karmic destiny. For genetically based beings, neither the full set of genes defining past forms nor the genes possibly defining future forms are currently active.

atIta anAgataM sva rUpato 'sty adhva bhedAt dharmANAm

atita	past
anagata (for anagatam)	future
sva	one's own
rupa (for rupato)	form
asti (for 'sty)	exist
adhvan (for adhva)	journey
bheda (for bhedat)	change
dharmanam	
dharma	holding to the law
anam	(untranslated)

THE BODY CONSISTS OF THE PHYSICAL, THE SUBTLE, AND GUNAS

4.13 Regard the whole body (i.e. 'the person or whole body considered as one and opposed to the separate members of the body.') as perceptible by the senses, subtle objects, and the constituents of prakrti.

te vyakta sUkSmA guna AtmAnah
*perceptible by the senses   subtle   constituent of prakrti   the whole body
(i.e. 'the person or whole body considered as one and opposed to
the separate members of the body.') regard as*

Whether the body is the individual person, the universe, or any other body, Yoga philosophy tells us that its composition is of physical sense perceptible things, non-detectable things of the subtle realm, and the basic constituents of *prakrti*, the *gunas*. The *gunas* pervade everything physical and everything subtle. The physical objects and subtle objects could not exist without them. Whether we think of them as properties, forces, qualities, or characteristics, nothing material can exist without their creative and balancing presence. Those three counterbalancing constituents are continually active present within everything of our universe. The relative power or control of each of the three within an entity shifts over time. *Rajas* (activity) may be predominant at one time, *tamas* (lethargy or resistance) may be predominant at another, and *sattva* (balance and stillness) at another. At the end of evolution, *sattva* predominates.

te vyakta sUkSmA gunaAtmAnah

te	denotes verb action status
vyakta	perceptible by the senses
suksma	subtle
guna	constituent of *prakrti*
atmanah	
atman	the whole body ('the person or whole body considered as one and opposed to the separate members of the body.')
ah	regard as

TRANSFORMATION TO INDIVIDUAL THINGS FROM PRIMAL ONENESS

4.14   *The tattvas (the 24 true principles of Nature) cause transformation of the oneness (of the primary essence) to the real.*

pariNAma ekatvAd vastu tattvam
transformation   oneness   the real   tattvas (the 24 true principles of Nature)

This *Sutra* brings our awareness to something new, the 24 *tattvas* at the base of evolution of the universe, which act in harmony within everything that exists, varying their influences and nature as needed. These 24 foundational 'principles of Nature' anticipate and lay the foundation for 'the real,' all the forms of physical world and subtle world evolution, including all life forms. Working with the *gunas*, which the *tattvas* also modify, each comes into play in the flow of universe evolution as conditions ripen.

1 *prakrti* - the substance of Nature

2 *buddhi* - intelligence or higher mind

3 *ahamkara* - the ego maker, or principle of individuation

4 *manas* - mind, or lower mind

5-9 *jjnanendriyas* - five instruments of sensing

10-14 *karmendriyas* - five instruments of action

15-19 *tanmatras* - five subtle elements

20-24 *mahabhuttas* - the five physical elements

Everything there is, physical or subtle, is the current form of the original singular undifferentiated oneness, the primal essence of *mula prakrti* (the first *tattva*) that has undergone transformation. No matter how many times it transforms in new ways, it is the primal substance in a different form. Physical and subtle things are not static. They continually break apart and then regenerate at invisible and undetectable speed, under control of the *tattvas* and the *gunas*, which introduce modifications, causing change and evolution to occur. Yet, the essence of the object remains the same. A rock remains a rock and a nail remains a nail, even though increasingly weathered. They do not become a stick or a sail, but they may eventually disappear or merge with something else.

Nothing would exist, subtle (non-detectable) or physical (sense detectable), if the principles of Nature (*tattvas*) did not work in integrated harmony to create it and continually modify it. Their continuous presence in everything is necessary to the functioning of our universe. Yet, they do not work alone. They interact harmoniously with the forces of the three *gunas*, existence (*sattva*), activity (*rajas*), and resistance to activity (*tamas*). No subtle or physical thing can exist without the *guna* quality of beingness (existence), because nothing can exist without being there. Being there is nothing by itself. Being there will not mean anything unless there is activity: activity provides the drive that changes things. In a universe of opposites, activity must have its counterpart, inertia - resistance to activity, to keep things in balance.

pariNAma ekatvAd vastu tattvam

parinama	transformation
ekatva (for ekatvad)	oneness
vastu	the real
tattva (for tattvam)	tattvas (the 24 true principles of Nature)

MORE ABOUT MIND

Individual Minds Perceive Differently

4.15   Constant differences in minds on the sameness of the real move variously.

> vastu sAmye citta bhedAt tayoh vibhaktah panthAh
> *the real   sameness   mind   differences constant   various   move*

Having earlier showed the existence of common and individual minds, Patanjali is now beginning further discussion of the individual minds. Here he is simply telling us that two minds observing the same 'real' (things, objects, words, sounds, anything) will always understand it differently. Although the 'real' things have their own existential reality, their own intrinsic nature, each individual mind perceives them differently and interprets the perception differently. The same mind will see the real variously over time. We each see characteristics that we relate to, while not seeing others, and then color them in with our history of associations, subconscious impressions, and emotions.

> vastu sAmye citta bhedAt tayoh vibhaktah panthAh

vastu	the real
samya (for samye)	sameness
citta	mind
bhedat	
bheda	difference
at	to go constantly
tayoh	(untranslated)
vibhakta (for vibhaktah)	various
panthah	
path (for panth)	move
ah	(untranslated)

Existence Is Independent Of Perception

4.16 And moreover, therefore, the real is not dependent on a single mind. How could that be, even in the case of small incorrect knowledge.

na ca eka citta tantraM ced vastu tad apramANakaM tadA kiM syAt

*not moreover single mind depending on and the real there-
fore incorrect knowledge small in that case how it may be*

Some other philosophies espouse an idea that things do not exist, but are completely fabrications of our mind, that they do not come into existence until the mind constructs them. The *Sutra* tells us that our minds do not create physical things. Things exist due to their own nature. If multiple minds incorrectly created things, the banana on the breakfast table would be a physically different thing for each person. That cannot be. Regardless of how individual minds perceive a thing, it continues to exist as it is.

The aphorism tells us that the material world actually exists. In other places the philosophy tells how it came into being, what its nature is, and it is a transient product of an eternal nonmaterial existence. Being transient, it is an ever-changing false world of illusions compared to the unchanging eternal reality, but it exists.

na ca eka citta tantraM ced vastu tad apramANakaM tadA kiM syAt

na	not
ca	moreover
eka	single
citta	mind
tantra (for tantram)	depending on
ced (cet)	and
vastu	the real
tad	therefore
apramanaka (for apramanakam)	
aprama	incorrect knowledge
anaka	small
tada	in that case
kim	how
syat	it may be

The Object Is Not Known Until It Affects The Mind

*4.17   And, it is required that one's mind be affected for the dawning of that
which is known from that which is the unknown.*

ad   uparAga   apekSitvAt   cittasya   vastu   jNAta   ajNAtam
*and   affecting   required   one's mind   dawning   that which is known
that which is not known*

Many objects exist, whether known or unknown at any given time.
Having stated in the preceding aphorism that the objects exist independent
of the mind, this one says that the object will not exist for an individual, and
will remain unknown, until it affects the mind. The only way that that will
happen for physical objects is through the senses. Non-physical objects can
affect the mind without using the senses. Subtle objects such as an insight, a
thought, an emotion, or a dream image can affect the mind spontaneously
without sensory initiation. All things, millions upon millions of things, exist
independently of our minds. We come to know only a small number of them.

tad uparAga apekSitvAt cittasya vastu jNAta ajNAtam

tad	and
uparaga	affecting
apeksitvat	
apeksita (for apeksitvat)	required
vat	(untranslated)
cittasya	
citta	mind
sya	(3rd person indicator) one's
vastu	dawning
jnatam (for jnata)	that which is known
ajnatam (for ajnata)	that which is not known

THE SUPREME BEING AND INDIVIDUAL MINDS

The *Sutras* now begin to close in on an understanding of the eternal invisible existence underlying everything, and clarify the meaning of the 'divinity
within.' The relationship between the mind, individual consciousness, and
the primal consciousness will clarify and become the key to understanding

many things. The fact that it has not surfaced until this point shows Patanjali's mastery of writing. The story has slowly unfolded before us, with each added piece augmenting previous pieces: the unfolding has often caused us to go back and refresh our understanding.

Primal Consciousness Is Aware Of The Mind

4.18   So also, the Supreme Being master, which is a state of being of constant unchangeableness, continually cognizes the mind behavior as it froths up.

sadA jNAtAs citta vRttayas tat prabhoH puruSasya apariNAmitvAt
continually   cognizance   mind   behavior   to froth up   so also
master   Supreme Being   unchangeableness   state of being to go constantly

The *Sutra* makes the vital point that things continually bubble through the mind, whether they are thoughts, memories, observations, insights, or many other things, and that the consciousness of the Supreme Being, the soul and master of the universe, is continually aware of the mind, experiencing every nuance. Yet, being unchangeable, what it observes does not affect it.

It is important to note that Patanjali is referring to the soul of the universe (isvara/sat), not the *brahman* oversoul of all universes, or the soul of the individual. That is shocking at first, because it seems to downplay the role of the individual soul and wall us off from the *brahman* soul. Yet, because the primal consciousness of the universal soul is the creator of the individual souls and minds, it remains connected to all of them, as does the *Supreme Being's* originator, *brahman* - through the *Supreme Being*. In the highest view of things, *brahman* is the originator of the universe's soul and any other soul that the power of *isvara* may have created for other universes, and continuously aware of them. Although we think of the *brahman* soul, universal soul, and individual souls as types or levels of soul, only one soul exists, acting in different roles. That is highest of the meanings of 'we are all one.' We have a natural tendency to think of only our individual soul.

Since souls have no thought-waves or activity to filter or alter perception, and are completely unaffected by what they observe, nothing in them blocks or warps the accurate perception of the happenings in individual minds. The

Supreme Being is aware of every perception, thought, mental action, nuance, and emotion of our personal individual being: nothing can, fool, delude, or deceive it.

As the line of thought initiated here unfolds in remaining *Sutras*, the importance of this piece of knowledge will become more obvious.

sadA jNAtAs citta vRttayas tat prabhoH puruSasya apariNAmitvAt

sada	continually
jjnatas (for jnatas)	cognizance
citta	mind
vrttayas	
vrtta	behavior
yas	to froth up
tad (for tat)	so also
prabhu (for prabhoh)	master
purusasya	
purusa	Supreme Being
sya	(3rd person indicator)
aparinamitvat	
aparinama	unchangeableness
tva	state of being
at	to go constantly

We Do Not Perceive On Our Own

4.19   It is not so that its (the mind's) own light produces the visibility state of being.

na   tat   sva   AbhAsaM   dRSyatvA
it is not so   that   its own   light   visible   state of being

When we look at a candle, a tree outside the window, or the window itself, we experience visibility. The mind has become aware of something our vision has absorbed. Yet, as obvious as the situation seems, the mind cannot accomplish that by itself. Visibility is a joint venture of the mind and primal consciousness of the universe, a partnership. Although the *Sutra* does not say so, that is equally true of awareness brought to the mind by touch, smell, hearing, and taste. We could not be aware of things without primal consciousness energizing the mind to its awareness.

The individual mind is always an object to the primal consciousness of *purusa* (isvara, sat), just as a stone or a flower is an object to the human individual mind. They are partners in perception. While the mind could not perceive unless lighted (activated) by the primal consciousness, the primal consciousness uses a mind as a tool in order to experience our perception. The individual mind interacts with the world as a surrogate for the primal consciousness: it mentally manipulates its observations, produces thoughts, and takes actions: the primal consciousness has no thoughts and takes no responsive actions.

To look at it from a slightly different perspective, when humans perceive, the primal consciousness is doing the perceiving, through and with the individual. From another view, individual mind is the primal consciousness taking the form of an individual mind, so they are the same thing, a duality of action and observation. Even while perceiving the vibrational material world through the vibrational individual mind, primal consciousness maintains its absolute stillness.

Although it sometimes becomes confusing, Patanjali primarily uses *purusa* or Supreme Being to represent the soul of the universe (*isvara/sat*), but *purusa* also sometimes represents the individual soul, depending on the context. However, the two souls are aspects of one soul, the Absolute primal consciousness of *brahman.* Some other texts sometimes use the capitalization, *Purusa*, to represent *brahman* (Sanskrit does not use capitalization). The absolute stillness of all three never fluctuates. Souls are 'self-illumined,' active and aware in their own right. That self-illumination allows that consciousness to observe the mind as an object and perceive everything that happens with that mind. On the other hand, even through the highest forms of individual consciousness, the meditative seeker can never directly perceive the changeless soul or its primal consciousness as an object, in the way it perceives a flower. Yet, a high-level seeker that has gained the ability to move the mind out of the way can perceive *as* the soul consciousness perceives.

na tat sva AbhAsaM dRSyatvA

na   it is not so

tat	that
sva	its own
abhasa (for abhasam)	light
drsyatva	
drzya (for drsya)	visible
tva	state of being

No Simultaneous Mind And Consciousness Experience

4.20   Yet, you cannot newly have both kinds at the same time.

eka   samaye   ca   ubhaya   anavadhAraNam
the same   time   yet   both kinds   not newly having

It is possible to experience the primal consciousness of the oversoul that is illuminating our power to sense. However, it is not possible to experience the transient, material world mind, and the eternal spiritual world consciousness at the same time. If we are experiencing one and move to experiencing the other, we give up the current experience for the alternative one. While we are in perception of a rock, attractive person, windstorm, the smell of an orange, or anything else, it is impossible to simultaneously experience the root consciousness. This is core Yoga philosophy: the degree to which we disengage the mind is the degree to which we enter higher consciousness. It is not possible to experience higher consciousness and mind activity without switching from one to the other. In meditative practice, we will increasingly withdraw our individual mind from objects, not to perceive the primal consciousness, but to experience higher consciousness. It is impossible to perceive that higher consciousness as if it were an object: we can only experience it, and can only do that when our mind and lower forms of consciousness are not in the way.

eka samaye ca ubhaya anavadhAraNam

eka	the same
samaya (for samaye)	time
ca	yet
ubhaya	of both kinds
anavadharana (for anavadharanam)	
a	(negation)
nava	newly

dharana   having

Minds Cannot Be Visible To Each Other

*4.21   And if a mind were visible to another, an intellect would procure intellects
for itself: excessive attachment would yield memory confusion.*

citta antara dRSye buddhi buddher atiprasaNga smRti saMkaraS ca
*mind   another   visible   intellect   procure for itself   intel-
lect   excessive attachment   memory   confusion   and*

Although it is not immediately obvious, this *Sutra* tells us that good reason exists for individual minds to be individual, and not interconnected. If
interconnected, each mind, particularly the intellectual faculty of mental perception, would have access to all the intellects of other minds, including their
memories, resulting in great confusion. That everyday confusion of dealing
with the different memories in the minds of others (even of the same event)
as well as our own, is just one level of the problem. Since the lengths of our
individual lives define the life span of memories associated with our material
world mind and intellect, the system of *karma* requires copying them to the
soul so that they can affect our next life. Placing multiple memories of multiple individuals in one individual soul would destroy the process of *karma*,
which aims at the evolution of an individual.

The problem is even bigger than it at first appears. If your mind could
perceive another mind, perhaps of someone named John, it could store memories of that mind. John's mind, and others that it could perceive, could in
turn perceive Wendy's mind and store memories of it. Through John, you
could then receive memories of Wendy's mind. This would cause infinite levels and cross webbing of memories.

citta antara dRSye buddhi buddher atiprasaNga smRti saMkaraS ca

citta	mind
antara	another
drsye (drzya)	visible
buddhi	intellect

buddher
    buddhi   intellect
    er   procure for oneself
atiprasagga (for atiprasanga)   excessive attachment
smrti   memory
samkara   confusion
ca   and

The Individual Mind Has The Power To Form Conceptions

4.22   Causing perception that has no intermixture, that form enters a state that has its own power to form conceptions from perceptions.

citer   apratisaMkramAyAs   tad   AkAra
Apattau   sva   buddhi   saMvedanam
perceive   cause   having no intermixture   that   form   entering into a state its own   the power of forming conceptions   perception

    This *Sutra* continues discussing the nature of the mind, linking it to the background theme of evolution of the universe and its beings. It tells us that when the individual mind with its single intellect, not intermixed with others, rose from the common mind of the universe it had the power and ability to form conceptions from what it perceived.

citer   apratisaMkramAyAs   tad   AkAra   Apattau   sva   buddhi   saMvedanam

citer
    cit   perceive
    er   cause
apratisamkramayas
apratisamkrama   having no intermixture
    yas   (untranslated)
tad   that
akara   form
apatti (for apattau)   enters into a state
sva   its own
buddhi   the power of forming conceptions
samvedana   perception

The Individual Corrupts The Perceptions

4.23   For all objects of the senses, the mind influences the one who sees the visible.

draSTR dRSya uparaktaM cittam sarva artham
one who sees visible influenced by mind all objects of the senses

Perception by the senses is never pure. The individual perceiver ('the one who sees') warps everything the senses deliver, based on experience, expectations, psychological processes, errors made by faulty sensory organs, or many other things. The registered perception does not accurately map the reality of the observed object.

draSTR dRSya uparaktaM cittam sarva artham

drastr	one who sees
drzya (for drsya)	visible
uparakta	influenced by
citta (for cittam)	mind
sarva	all
artha	object of the senses

It All Serves Primal Consciousness

4.24   And, the innumerable different impressions of anything remaining unconsciously in the mind, and your acts work together for another.

tad asaMkhyeya vAsanAbhih citra api parArtham saMhatya kAritvAt
*and innumerable the impression of anything remaining unconsciously
in the mind different and for another working together act your*

In *Sutras* 4.18 and 4.19, the *Sutras* addressed ways in which the Supreme Being, *purusa*, interacts in our lives. This takes that theme a step further. Everything about us, whether it is subtle or physical, our memories, our currently active *karma*, and our acts work for the sake of that primal being. Those things do not work for the sake of improving It: It cannot improve. They work for the sake of providing that primal being with experience and fulfilling its directional intentions.

Patanjali drives home the nature of our relationship to that existence by constructing an aphorism that shows us as Its agents. The mind, physical objects, the subtle entities, and karmic impressions exist for no reason but to join with and serve the interests of that primal existence. They do not exist for their own sake: they exist solely to support, and act on behalf of, that primal existence, which depends on them to fulfill Its purpose. Without them, there could be no evolution. The spiritual entity not only needs an agent in the material world, It also needs a mechanism for evolution.

Of course, that leaves the question of 'Why?' What does the primal consciousness get from this? Surprisingly, it seems that the primal consciousness needs to experience through its creations. That is why It creates things. If It did not create things, It would have nothing to experience. If things were static, without evolution, it would not be different from having no things at all. An eternally still observer, with nothing to observe, nothing to remember, and nothing to create, would have no function. An observer over a static creation would have nothing to experience.

tad asaMkhyeya vAsanAbhih citra api parArtham saMhatya kAritvAt

tad	and
asamkhyeya	innumerable
vasanabhih	
vasana	the impression of anything remaining unconsciously in the mind
bhih	(untranslated)
citra	different
api	and
parartha (for parartham)	for another
samhatya	working together
karitvat	
kari	act
tvat	(2nd person indicator) your

CLOSING IN ON ABSOLUTE UNITY

Distinction Between Reality And Not-Reality Ends

4.25   Understanding the individual soul, the distinction between reality and not-reality comes to an end.

viSeSa   darSina   Atma   bhAva   bhAvanA   vinivRtti
distinction   understanding   individual soul   reality   not-reality comes to an end

The preceding *Sutras* referred to the interlocking relationship between the individual mind, physical world things, subtle world things, and the primal existence (*brahman, isvara, sat,* soul). This one points to the truth that as we develop as yogins and reach higher consciousness, that knowledge allows us to see the spiritual entity (reality) and the material entities (not reality) as a singularity, not as separate interlocked entities. It is all simply the oversoul Supreme Being, with its individual souls, using us to play roles to fulfill its purpose.

That achieved understanding is not an intellectual understanding derived from thought, but a deep intuitive understanding of the relationship between individual existence and primal existence: having that intuitive deep understanding, the incorrect ideas of separation of the material and spiritual existences and of separate and independent selves dissolves. When we have reached that high level of consciousness experience, we are coming close to the understanding of the oneness, in which all beings and things are one being. It is not just that our minds and impressions are one with Spirit; everything *is* Spirit, non-materialized Spirit and materialized Spirit.

Evolving to that point, we are nearing 'home.' This is high 'Wisdom,' the opposite of 'Ignorance.' In Yoga terms, Wisdom is spiritual understanding, while Ignorance is lack of spiritual understanding. However, this is not a black and white situation or a sudden switch throwing. Every one of us exists somewhere on the scale from Ignorance to Wisdom. As the Yogin evolves, he or she advances along the scale through an ever-greater component of

Wisdom and lesser component of Ignorance. The degree of a seeker's progress is the degree of spiritual understanding.

viSeSa darSina Atma bhAva bhAvanA vinivRtti

vizesa (for visesa)	distinction
darzin (for darsina)	understanding
atman (for atma)	the individual soul
bhava	reality
bhavana	
bhava	reality
na	(negation) not
vinivrtti (also nivrtti)	coming to an end

Prepared For Absolute Unity

4.26   At that time, in the depth of discrimination, the yogin is not far from meditation into absolute unity of the mind.

tadA viveka nimnam prAgbhAraM kaivalya cittam
at that time discrimination depth the being
not far from yogas (i.e. meditation
absolute unity mind

As we near the final *Sutras* in his well-woven book, the word Yogas appearing for the second time, this time within a definition, brings us back to the purpose established in *Sutra* 1.2. The seeker is nearing the end of personal evolution by arriving at intuitive understanding of the distinction between the non-material Spirit and the material world, truth and untruth, as well as reality and illusion: the yogin deeply experiences the depth of the primal existence. According to the philosophical evolutionary process, a yogin's evolution of consciousness experience maps to the evolution of the universe in reverse. Here the yogin's consciousness experience now nears that cosmic evolutionary point where the force of illusion (*maya*) was about to bring about the material world. In Yoga philosophy, the material world is an illusion, not reality, and the primal existence is reality. That state of material manifestation from primal spiritual energy is not yet the state of Absolute Unity, where unequivocal freedom (often called Emancipation) from the material/sensory world comes about, but it is coming close.

tadA viveka nimnam prAgbhAraM kaivalya cittam

tada	at that time
viveka	discrimination
nimna (for nimnam)	depth
pragbhara (for pragbharam)	the being not far from Yogas (i.e. meditation)
kaivalya	absolute unity
citta (for cittam)	mind

Arising Notions

When we at first meditate, our undisciplined minds do what they want, firing many types of thoughts and notions at a fast pace. Those things capture our attention, trapping us into following their lead. It is difficult to settle into stillness. The periods of full stillness are brief. Most notions are memories of the past and fantasies or plans for the future. They cause us to live there, not seeing the present moment. When we become involved in those memories or anticipations, they generate emotions, regrets, anxieties, and desires.

As time and practice go by, the activity arrival rate declines and the periods of stillness increase. We become gradually less attached to and involved with the activities, though, and we learn to let them drift by to dissolve like puffs of smoke. At high levels of evolution, the activity-free times become long.

4.27   *At that time, during openings of the practice, notions arise from the impressions.*

tac chidreSu pratyaya antarANi saMskArebhyaH
at that time opening imperfections notions during impressions practice

At first, the periods of achieving that fine discrimination will be brief and the time between the periods of discrimination will be long, but that ratio will reverse with continued evolution. Even at the stage of evolution where the seeker holds to the discrimination for long periods, openings between those periods will occur during which notions (memories, ideas, and related emotions) will still arise from the karmic memories (impressions) that still remain. However short the remaining mountain path may be, the need for evolution is still present, and the openings are necessary for it to happen. The arising notions may relate to memories, desires, anxieties, regrets, love, or many other human things. Even at this stage, the seeker is not perfect and faith is not perfect.

tac chidreSu pratyaya antarANi saMskArebhyaH

tac (tad)	at that time
chidra (for chidresu)	opening
pratyaya	notion
antarani	
antar	within
ani	limit
samskarebhyah	
samskara (for samskare)	impressions
abhyas (for abhyah)	practice

Stopping Thoughts

4.28   Seeking getting rid of them, affirm that said about the afflictions.

hAnam   eSAM   kleSavad   uktam
getting rid of   seeking   affirm   afflictions   said

In *Sutra* 2.1, Patanjali began detailing Kriya Yoga practices and their relationship to overcoming the afflictions. To decrease the need for openings it is necessary to deactivate the remaining karmic impressions and the mind-noise that draw attention away from the discrimination. This teaching advises to reaffirm the commitment to practice the methods of Kriya Yoga that reduce the afflictions. When the mind disturbances decrease due to deactivation of karmic impressions and the mind activity declines, the discrimination periods free of interruptions will become more frequent and longer. The same advice would apply to a yogin at any level of evolutionary advancement who becomes susceptible to slipping back or moving away from the path into more materialistic territory. Although the likelihood decreases as we evolve, we are never free from those possibilities.

hAnam eSAM kleSavad uktam

hana (for hanam)	getting rid of
esa (for esam)	seeking
klesavad	
kleza	affliction
vad	affirm
ukta (for uktam)	said

ENDING IN CONSCIOUSNESS STATE OF THE LAW CLOUD

As all good stories do, the story of the philosophy and practice of Yoga reaches its climax with final resolution of the struggle. After living through lifetimes of experiencing states of high consciousness, the seeker reaches the highest consciousness possible for an Earth dweller, the Dharma Cloud state. In rough interpretation, although there are many meanings to 'dharma,' the best of them for this *Sutra* is 'Law Cloud.' While experiencing that consciousness, the seeker comes to know the Laws as the primal existence knows them.

The Law Cloud Consciousness Experience

4.29   One uniting to meditation without gain, procuring the highest degree of discriminative knowledge, attains intense absorption in the Law Cloud.

prasaMkhyAnE'py akusIdasya sarvathA viveka khyAter
dharma meghaH samadhih
*meditation uniting to   without gain   one   in the highest degree
discrimination   knowledge procure   law   cloud   intense absorption*

The Sanskrit word 'dharma' translates to many meanings, some similar to each other and some dissimilar: many non-dictionary meanings are also in popular usage. From among the valid dictionary uses, this interpretation uses 'law,' referring to the basic Laws of everything, the Laws that *brahman* and all creation must follow. Law Cloud (Dharma Cloud) consciousness is seedless (*nirbija*) *samadhi*, the highest consciousness.

The *Sutra* tells us that the doorway to the ultimate intense absorption leading to Absolute Unity (*kaivalya*) is near to opening. It will open only when the seeker no longer has an interest in gain, and is in a continuous, unbroken state of meditative discrimination as discussed in previous aphorisms, without error or interruption or opening. It is important to remember that it is necessary to master all other elements of practice to reach that point of discrimination, and that it cannot happen while carrying a karmic load. The seeker has truly reached the peak of the mountain that has been such a long climb.

During this *Dharmamegha samadhi* (Law Cloud intense absorption) consciousness state, stillness of the mind becomes a continuous state, with no intervening moments for mental activity generation, whether from thoughts, karmic seeds, or anything else. To attain it, continuous detachment from the ego must have already taken place. That ego detachment would be complete, with unequivocal faith in and profound experience of the primal existence, relinquishing all elements of personal will. With that and all Yoga practices fulfilled, the yogin is ready to give up all expectations or wishes, including one that expects to gain the sought union.

Now the knowledge of Truths and Laws at the foundation of all existence becomes available.

prasaMkhyAnE'py akusIdasya sarvathA viveka khy-
Ater dharma meghaH samadhih

prasamkhyana	meditation
api (for 'py)	uniting to
akusidasya	
akusida	without gain
sya	(3rd person voice) one
sarvatha	in the highest degree
viveka	discrimination
khyater	
khyati	knowledge
er	procure
dharma	law
megha (for meghah)	cloud

Afflictions And The Cycle Of Karma Cease

4.30   Extended from that, afflictions and effects cease.

tataH kleSa karman nivRtti
extended   affliction   effects   ceasing

When the seeker has reached and sustained this state of evolution, the afflictions will cease and the lures of materiality will never bother her or him again: since no active impressions (karmic seeds) remain, no karmic effects will ever generate. With the long voyage near completion, the yogin is no longer subject to the *Law of Karma*. The cause and effect cycle no longer exists. The Dharma Cloud experience does not bring the end of life: the purified individual continues to live out a physical life, but in a new condition not subject to afflictions or karmic cycles.

tataH kleSa karman nivRtti

tata (for tatah)	extended
kleza (for klesa)	affliction
karman	effect
nivrtti	ceasing

Infinite Knowledge

4.31   *At that time, you are free from obstruction and impurity, and your higher knowledge drives toward immortality with trifling little to be known.*

tadA sarva AvaraNa mala apetasya jNAnasya AnantyAj jNeyam alpam
*at that time   all   an obstruction   impu-
rity   free from you   higher knowledge your
drive   immortality   to be known   trifling   little*

The yogin is now free of all impurities that would ripple the mind: the cause and effect karmic influence is no longer active, and no other obstructions to the final step remain. The infinite higher knowledge, with little left to learn, opens to the vast nonsequential storehouse of experiences of all time in all places, driving the yogin toward immortality.

tadA sarva AvaraNa mala apetasya jNAnasya AnantyAj jNeyam alpam

tada	at that time

sarva	all
avarana	an obstruction
mala	impurity (physical, moral, and of the mind)
apetasya	
apeta	free from
sya	(3rd person indicator) your
jnanasya	
jjana (for jnanam)	higher knowledge
sya	(3rd person indicator)
anantyaj	
anantya	immortality
aj	to drive towards
jjeya (for jneyam)	to be known
alpa (for alpam)	little

Purpose Fulfilled

4.32   *Extended from that, purpose thus accomplished, indeed the constituents of prakrti complete their succession of evolution.*

tataH   kRta   arthAnAm   pariNAma   krama   samAptir   guNAnAm
extended   accomplished   purpose thus   evolution   succession   completion   constituents of prakrti indeed

The purpose of the seeker's life has been to have experiences that lead toward evolution into full spirituality: there is no further need for material existence to accomplish that. The material being has fulfilled its purpose here as agent for the primal existence: the role of giving It the opportunity to vicariously observe this individual experience has finished. The *gunas* and the primal consciousness have fully evolved this unique individual, reaching absolute equilibrium: *sattva* (being) has prevailed, *while rajas* (activity) and *tamas* (resistance) have become dormant. When death comes about at the right future time, the *prakrti* for the individual being, with its three gunas, dissolves back into the undifferentiated oneness that began the universe. Yoga philosophy does not cover the status of the three bodies, but it is reasonable to assume that, since they will never be needed to support a new life, the subtle and causal bodies, also made from *prakrti*, dissolve along with the gunas, while the soul remains intact. Now omnisciently knowing and joining the experience of seeing everything, the individual being no longer exists for rebirth. Its soul will become one with *brahman*. Now omniscient, the quest is over. The seeker has found the object of the search, permanently experiencing the Great Oneness.

tataH kRta arthAnAm pariNAma krama samAptir guNAnAm

tata (for tatah)	extended
krta	accomplished
arthanam	
artha	purpose
ana (for anam)	thus
parinama	evolution
krama	succession
samaptir	completion
gunanam	
guna	the constituents of *prakrti*
ana (for anam)	indeed

Perceiving The Progression Of All Previous Lives

4.33   At this point of extreme end to a yogin's evolution, it is a suitable moment for perceivable succession.

kSaNa pratiyogI pariNAma apara anta nirgrAhyaH kramaH
a suitable moment at this point the yogin evolution extreme end perceivable succession

There is a popular thought that when we die our lifetime passes before our eyes. The *Sutras* now teach us that at the final death, when personal evolution ends, the seeker sees the entire progression through all lifetimes. This is consistent with the understanding that at this point the yogin has all knowledge of all things.

Perspective

From the moment of the initial birth in the karmic cycle, the *gunas* of our body are changing their relationship and us, leading us toward the end of this lifetime in physical death. Life does not end then, since evolution along our path takes many lifetimes. Although between deaths we exist as subtle bodies and are aware beings, no evolution occurs during that experience. We are eventually reborn to the material world for our next karmic evolutionary stage. Once we are reborn, and our soul associates with our new physical-world body/mind, a new process starts, for the mind, body, subtle body, and causal body. The soul does not evolve: It is an observer of our life and evolution, experiencing it voyeuristically, without the experience affecting It.

In this way, the *gunas* continually evolve us through life after life, moving us toward *kaivalya* and Emancipation, the freedom from rebirth. At completion, the individual soul and its memories will exist, but will never occupy another body for a new Earth-plane experience. In that spiritual existence the experience of Time ceases: past, present, and future no longer exist. The individual consciousness merges with the primal consciousness, which in itself is void of Time. In the state of primal consciousness, there are no fluctuations for the emancipated soul to experience. The individual soul has completed its part in the universe's purpose of evolving souls toward pure spiritual existence.

kSaNa pratiyogI pariNAma apara anta nirgrAhyaH kramaH

ksana	a suitable moment
pratiyogi	
prati	at this point
yogin (for yogi)	the yogin
parinama	evolution
aparanta	the extreme end
nirgrahya (for nirgrahyah)	perceivable
krama (for kramah)	succession

The End

4.34   *The soul thus void of purpose, indeed the constituents of prakrti return to their original state, with one's own nature standing very still, the layers of attachment end. Absolute Unity.*

puruSa artha sUnyAnAM guNAnAM pratiprasavaH kaivalyaM sva rUpa
pratiSThA vA citi Saktir iti

soul   purpose void thus   constituents of prakrti indeed   return
to the original state   absolute unity   one's own nature   stand-
ing still   very   layer   attachment   end

Now that the yogin has achieved the final state of evolution, experiencing the most primal universe state, the sought after stillness (purity) is now complete throughout the individuals nature, its mind, physical body, subtle body, and causal body. The individual loses all attachment to the things of material living.

The individual has merged with the Absolute, but has retained its individual identity, with all its memories. The soul keeps those memories, as part of the vast unending knowledge of the primal existence. Our individual soul will retain its identity, but not be an active participant. It has all the characteristics of the Absolute. It does not experience Time, since there is no Time beyond the material world, and past present and future are not sequential for it, causing the concept of being there through eternity to be meaningless. Patanjali leaves us there, with no further comment. Yet, the philosophy leaves us with many things to reflect on, things we may never know answers to until we pass through the Law Cloud.

puruSa artha sUnyAnAM guNAnAM pratiprasavaH kaivalyaM sva rUpa
pratiSThA vA citi Saktir iti

purusa	soul
artha	purpose
sunyanam	
zunya (for sunya)	void
ana (for anam)	thus
gunanam	
guna	constituents of *prakrti*
ana (for anam)	indeed
pratiprasavah	return to the original state
kaivalyam = kaivalliyam	absolute unity
sva	one's own
rupa	nature
pratistha	standing still
va	very (stressing the preceding word)
citi	layer
sakti (for saktir)	attachment

iti   end

BIBLIOGRAPHY

Aranya, Swami Hariharananda. *Yoga Philosophy of Patanjali.* State University of New York Press, Albany, 1983.

Bouanchaud, Bernard. *The Essence of Yoga, Reflections on the Yoga Sutras of Patanjali.* Rudra Press, Portland, 1995

Bryant, Edwin. *The Yoga Sutras of Patanjali, A New Edition. Translation, and Commentary.* North Point Press, New York, 2009

Carrera, Reverend Jaganath. *Inside the Yoga Sutras, A Comprehensive Sourcebook.* Integral Yoga Publications, Buckingham, 2006

Dvivdedi, Manilal Nabhubhai. *The Yoga-Sutra Of Patanjali.* Rajaram/ Tuckaram, Bombay, 1914

Feuerstein, Georg. *The Yoga Sutras of Patanjali, A New Translation and Commentary.* Inner Traditions International, Rochester (VT), 1979

Hartranft, Chip. *The Yoga-Sutra of Patanjali.* Shambhala, Boston, 2003

Govindan, Marshall. *Kriya Yoga Sutras of Patanjali and the Siddhas, Translation, Commentary and Practice.* Kriya Yoga Publications, Quebec, 2000

Iyengar, B. K. S. *Light on the Yoga Sutras of Patanjali.* Thorsons, London, 1993.

Miller, Barbara Stoler. *Yoga, Discipline of Freedom.* University of California Press, Berkeley, City, 1996

Prabhavananda, Swami, and Isherwood, Christopher. *How to Know God.* New American Library, New York, 1953.

Saraswati, Swami Satyananda. *Four Chapters on Freedom, Commentary on the Yoga Sutras of Patanjali.* Yoga Publications Trust, Bihar (India), 1976

Satchidananda, Sri Swami. *The Yoga Sutras of Patanjali, Translation and Commentary.* Integral Yoga Publications, Yogaville, 1978.

Savitripriya, Swami. *Psychology of Mystical Awakening, Patanjali Yoga Sutras.* A New World Translation, New Life Books, Sunnyvale, 1993

Shearer, Alistair. *The Yoga Sutras of Patanjali.* Random House, New York, 2002

Stiles, Mukunda. *Yoga Sutras of Patanjali.* Red Wheel/Weiser, Boston, 2002

Vivekananda, Swami. *Raja Yoga.* Ramakrishna-Vivekananda Center, New York, 1956

APPENDICES

APPENDIX 1

WORDS AND PHRASES

Absolute Unity *kaivalya* (2.25) (3.56) (4.26) (4.34)

Absolute Unity (often loosely called Emancipation) is the end of the yogic journey. It occurs when the yogin has reached total and permanent purity (stillness of the mind), completing the purpose of life. There is then freedom from the material/sensory world, with no requirement to return for another lifetime of experiences. The word *kaivalya* has several context sensitive meanings also, for stages leading to Absolute Unity.

Activity of mind *vrtti* (1.2) (1.41) (2.15)

The vibratory movement of the otherwise stilled mind, in which mind activities are observations, thoughts, emotions, and other mental flows in the nonphysical, subtle, realm of material existence.

Afflictions *avidya* (2.3 - 2.10) (2.24)

The *Sutras* tell us of five afflictions that interfere with stilling the mind and experiencing levels of higher consciousness: they are spiritual ignorance, egoism, vehement desire, repugnance, and affection. All are subtle world mental/attitudinal factors that counter our spirituality.

Aim of Yoga (1.2) (1.3) (1.4) (4.34)

The Yoga taught by the *Yoga Sutras* is about purifying (stilling) the mind to achieve Absolute Unity.

Approaching Absolute Unity *kaivalya* (2.25) (2.26) (2.27) (3.49 - 3.56) (4.27 - 4.34)

We reach the ultimate results of Yoga through developmental steps.

Attachment *sakti* (2.23) (4.34) *bandha* (3.39) *sangha* (3.52) (4.21)

A core problem of human existence is that we possessively attach to things — want to hold onto them no matter what, and then come to fear their loss and to desire more things. We attach to physical things, physical 'objects' in Yoga terminology, such as cars, homes, jewels, money, land, or people. We equally attach to subtle realm 'objects,' such as beliefs, thoughts, ideas, or emotions. Whether physical or subtle, either side of the eternal dichotomies of love or hate, valor or fear, sweet or sour, presence or absence, and so on may become the glue that binds us to the object of attachment.

Concentration *dharana* (2.29) (2.53) (3.1) (3.4) (3.7)

This is the Yoga meditative practice of single-pointed focusing of the mind. It is also a specific limb of Yoga, Limb 6, *dharana*.

Consciousness (see also *samadhi*) (There are many references)

That part of our existence that is continuously aware. Consciousness is a flow, not made of discrete time-limited individual parts, as all material things are, both physical and subtle. Being beyond the constraints of time, it travels from point to point, no matter the distance, with no intervening delay.

Consciousness - seven stages (2.27)

The evolutionary path of the yogin leads through seven progress levels of consciousness experience, beyond normal material/sensory consciousness. Concentration on a physical object provides the first and experience of the godhead is the last.

Destiny

See 'Karma.'

Dharma Cloud (4.29)

This is a very high consciousness state, the last stage of evolutionary experience before *kaivalya*, Absolute Unity (informally called Emancipation, a modern characterization).

Effects   (results) *vipaka* (1.24) (2.13) *phala* (2.14) (2.34) (2.36) (4.11) *karman* (4.31)

Effects are the results of causes. Causes produce effects in the physical and subtle realms and leave karmic influences (impressions) to be resolved. Some call it the Law of Karma, and others the 'karmic cycle.'

Ego *sva* (2.23)

The ego, a role of mind, binds us to the material world and causes spiritual ignorance.

Egoism *asmita* (1.17) (2.3) (2.6) (3.48) (4.4)

Egoism is continually being unaware of the soul's existence and role, thinking that personal perception is all there is.

Eight Limbs (2.28 - 2.55) (3.1 - 3.3)

There are eight limbs of Yoga practice. Devoted practice of all leads to the ultimate result.

Enlightenment (a speculation) (1.47 - 1.50)

Enlightenment is not a topic of the *Yoga Sutras* and there is no Sanskrit word for it. However, there is a specific point of personal evolution (Stage 4) where the experience matches many accounts of the enlightenment experience.

Eternal *nitya* (2.5) *ananta* (2.34)

Eternal means to have no beginning point or ending point. At the root of everything, there has to be an Absolute that exists without beginning or end, never created and never subject to ending.

Ether (3.42) (3.43)

The element *ether* is both a primary substance used to make other substances and a background omnipresent substance of particles so tiny that they fill everything in the universe, even the space within atoms and subatomic particles. It is everywhere that space is. Some say it is the medium that carries the sound of *Om*, but the concept is not Yoga philosophy and may have originated in Hinduism or Vedanta.

<u>Evolution of the yogin</u> (1.14) (1.15) (1.16) (3.9 - 3.20) (3.38) (3.42-3.56)

From the start of the journey, the yogin slowly evolves to experience progressive levels of consciousness and learn continually more about how everything works.

<u>Five states of mind</u> (Active consciousness) (1.5 - 1.11)

This is the everyday level of mind characterizing human life in the physical world. Yoga opens us to higher levels of consciousness beyond the mind. The five states of mind are,

> Means of acquiring certain knowledge
> Misapprehension
> Imagination
> Sleep
> Attaining remembrance

<u>Godhead</u>

> See 'Primal Existence'

<u>Gunas</u> (See' Nature' for Sutra references)

The three gunas are basic qualities or essences of *prakrti* (Nature). They are part of the material world, ubiquitous in all things, but are not subtle matter or physical matter. Force-like they are vital to forming things from *prakrti*, as they act against each other for dominance. *Rajas* is the quality of motion. *Tamas* is resistance to motion. The neutral *sattva* is quietness.

<u>Higher consciousness</u>

This is a loose term, generally meaning any consciousness beyond sensory consciousness and mental consciousness. The term covers a wide range, from experiencing the nature of physical objects at the first stage to experiencing the consciousness of the oversoul at the highest stage.

<u>Impressions</u>   *samskara* (1.18) (1.50) (2.15) (3.9) (3.18) (4.9) (4.27) *azaya*
(1.24) (2.12) (4.6) *vasana* (4.8) (4.24)

Actions and mental activities leave their karmic records within us.
Individual mind memory and soul consciousness equally record (remember,
store) them. Authors use a variety of non-translation substitutes to represent
them, 'subliminal traits,' 'subliminal activators,' 'depth memory,' 'subconscious memories,' 'subliminal impressions,' and karmic memories.' They carry
the karmic cycle from lifetime to lifetime.

<u>Individual consciousness</u>

This is the consciousness of the individual soul, as compare to the consciousness of the oversoul, which could be seen as *brahman, izvara,* or *sat.*

<u>Inner self</u>

See 'soul.'

<u>Insight or intuition</u>

A state of inner perception, received from the soul's omniscience.

<u>Intense absorption</u>   *samadhi* (1.17) (1.18) (1.20) (1.21) (1.40 - 1.44) (1.46)
(1.47) (1.50) (1.51) (2.2) (2.19) (2.27) (2.29) (2.33) (2.45) (3.3) (3.4)
(3.11) (4.1) (4.29)

We think of *samadhi* as one thing, perhaps the highest consciousness,
enlightenment, the equivalent of *nirvana,* or some mystical experience.
However, there are seven well-defined and documented stages of *samadhi,*
each of which has its individual name. (See also 'Samadhi - forms.')

<u>Isvara</u> (1.23 - 1.27) (2.1) (2.32) (2.45)

The primal existence (*brahman*) performs in the role of *isvara* to establish
an immanent Presence in the universe. For all practical purposes it is equivalent to God-immanent, *brahman,* or *sat.*

<u>Karma</u> (2.12) (3.18) (3.23) (4.6 - 4.11) (4.30)

Under the Law of Karma, the soul-packet keeps track of positive and negative actions and their effects. Those effects influence future life. 'Impressions'
are the vehicle for communicating karmic effects across lifetimes. (See
'Impressions')

Kriya Yoga (1.1) (2.1) (2.2) (2.28)

The *Yoga Sutras* combined Samkhya philosophy and Kriya Yoga, as it existed at the time. Samkhya provided the philosophy and spirituality and Kriya (action) provided the ways to practice.

Manifest

When the spiritual primal existence (*brahman*) transitions to material forms through a creation process, it has manifested. Essentially this means, 'something comes into place from something else.'

Material/sensory consciousness

This is our normal mode or level of consciousness, part of the material world existence - our everyday sensory awareness. In a strong way it is 'mind consciousness' as compared to the spiritual consciousness of the souls and oversoul.

Matter *matra* (2.19) (2.20) (3.3) (3.50)

Matter is anything that has form, anything that is material. This may be either subtle matter (invisible and undetectable) or physical matter (detectable by the senses and scientific equipment).

Mental pain, troubles, difficulty, and sorrow   *abhyam* (1.12) *klista* (1.5) *duhkha* (1.31) (1.33) (2.5) (2.8) (2.15) (2.16) (2.34) *soka* (1.36) *tapa* (2.15)

Indian and Buddhist philosophies often use the word 'suffering,' stating that our goal is to relieve our suffering. In today's world wording indicating pain, sorrow, difficulty, or great discomfort often replaces 'suffering.' It is easy to misunderstand the intent if one thinks of the physical and psychological results from disease or accident. The words, however, are intended to bring our attention to the mental pain that we experience, often bringing it on ourselves, in response to both the severe and more ordinary situations of life. Mostly, it means the pain of internal chaos.

Mind   *citta* (1.2) (1.30) (1.33) (1.37) (2.54) (3.1) (3.9) (3.11) (3.12) (3.19) (3.35) (3.39) (4.4) (4.5) (4.15 - 4.24) (4.26)

Mind is of the subtle realm, not the physical realm. It begins with a common mind for the entire cosmos and then individualizes for separate beings.

Nature   *prakrti* (1.19) (3.49) *dharma* (3.14) *pradhana* (3.49) *tattvas* (4.14) *gunas* (1.16) (2.15) (2.19) (4.2) (4.3) (4.13) (4.14) (4.32) (4.33) (4.34)

Nature is everything created to form our universe, whether subtle, material, or otherwise. The words 'the Creation' would mean the same thing.

Object *grahya* (1.41) (3.21) *artha* (1.42) (1.43) (2.22) (3.11) (4.23) *visaya* (1.11) (1.37) (2.54) (3.55) *vairagya* (1.12) (1.15) *ekatana* (3.2)

Everything that manifests with form from primal essence is an object. The object can be a physical thing such as an atom of hydrogen or flower, or it can be a nonphysical subtle object such as a thought or emotion. Objects are targets for all forms of *concentration, meditation, intense absorption*, and *unified-restraint*.

Obstacles *antaraya* (1.29) (1.30)

Sickness, apathy, doubt, carelessness, sloth, intemperance, erroneous understanding, not obtaining your next degree, and instability, are nine defined obstacles to Yoga practice and evolution.

Om *pranavah* (1.27) (1.28)

Om is the *pranavah*, the mystical and sacred (to some) syllable symbolizing the unnamable god-essence. Sects of Yoga philosophy say many varying things about Om. What some say is outlined here.

It is the intelligent cosmic energy manifesting as vibration in the universe. In the presence of the cosmic laws of karma and the divine intelligence of Kutastha chaitanya (Cosmic consciousness, Krishna consciousness or Christ Consciousness) it causes the creation of matter. It is, therefore, the link between the material and spiritual realms.

Our universe began with a single sound that continues as its background sound. Humans emulate its sound by combining the sounds of oooooooo, ahhhhhh and mmmm, but the real vibration is not audible to human physical hearing and is nothing like the emulation. In the ancient literature the sound is described as many things, including the root sound of everything in the universe and the name of everything.

Patanjali points to its original importance as the symbol of the immanent-primal existence, *isvara*, without any other such characterization.

One's own nature *sva rupa* (1.3) 2.54) (3.45) (3.48) (4.34)

The term 'our own nature' points to the reality that our basic nature is as a physical and spiritual entity, not just a body. That basic nature is universal, the same for each of us. Our personal nature is determined by our karma and our stock of karmic impressions.

Success - factors leading to it (4.1)

Birth, herbs, prayer or song of praise, religious austerity, or intense absorption can influence success at Yoga intention.

Philosophy of Union (Yoga) (1.1)

The philosophy of Union (Yoga), which began to accumulate more than 5000 years ago, is the subject of this book. A culture that existed in prehistory (before written words) near the location of the first known civilization at Harappa originally developed it. Harrapa, now on the maps of southwestern Pakistan, was home to a mixture of Aryan (probably Persian immigrants) and Ancient Indian peoples.

Prakrti – types *mula, mahat, para, and apara prakrti* (2.19)

The *prakrti* (primal essence or primal substance) passed through four stages driven by the gunas to create the universe.

Prana - cosmic types *avisesa, visesa, alinga, linga* (2.19)

Along with *prakrti*, the *prana* of the universe passed through four stages of evolution.

Primal consciousness

Not a phrase used in the *Yoga Sutras*, it is the consciousness that underlies everything in our universe and beyond. It is all pervading, completely still, beginningless, and endless. It is the consciousness of the divinity, *brahman*, or god-essence by whatever name. See also 'Primal Existence.'

Primal essence (primal substance)   *mula prakrti* (2.12) (2.13) (2.19) (3.3) (3.33) (4.14)

The primal unmanifested undifferentiated 'stuff' (*mula prakrti*) that arose from the eternal pool of potentials, is in every creation that manifests in both material and not material forms. 'Primal energy' and 'root energy' are close to being alternate names, but the word energy is not technically correct. Primal essence is more like potential energy. To exist as matter, it would first manifest as energy and then transition to matter.

Primal Existence

'Primal existence' is a word-symbol used here to represent the being existence transcendent of the universe that is the Source of everything, variously named as the infinite, All, Absolute, Spirit, isvara, or *brahman*. It is the root of all things, which has no beginning or end, no forebearer. It is the source of all things, the ultimate consciousness, the provider of creative drive and destructive drive. It is unmoving (totally still) intelligent awareness.

See also 'Primal consciousness,' and 'Supreme Being.'

Purity *abhyasa* (1.12) (1.13) (1.18) (1.32) (3.4) *jyotismat* (1.36) *punya* (2.14) *suddhi* (2.28) (2.41) (2.43) (3.56) *sauca* (2.32) (2.40) *mala* (4.31)

In the *Yoga Sutras*, purity is stillness of the mind. The ultimate effect of Yoga is total mind stillness. All other purifications are for the purpose of mind purification.

Purpose of materiality (2.18) (2.21)

The universe exists to support life, experience, and beatitude.

Samadhi

See 'intense absorption.'

Samadhi - forms of (1.40)

The discussion included under 1.40 details the seven forms of samadhi.

Samyama

See '*unified-restraint.*'

Soul - individual *atman* (2.5) (2.6) (2.41) (4.25) *purusa* (4.34)

Often called 'the self' in Indian philosophy, it is the soul of an individual being. As such, it is one step away from the common soul of all beings, that of primal consciousness. Although language will never describe it accurately, one description has the soul as an aspect of the common soul, or a zone within it. Since the individual soul and the common soul of all are not physical, however, the idea of location and zone can be greatly misleading. The soul is not locatable by place or time.

Seed *bija, sabija, and nirbija* (1.40) (1.46) (1.50) (1.51) (3.8) (3.51)

In this context, a seed is a karmic 'impression.' Authors give it several names, such as 'subliminal activator,' 'subliminal impression,' karmic memory,' 'subconscious memories,' which are not translations. It is an effect, left in mind and soul memory by an action or event. In the cause and effect scheme, it is the effect of a cause and a seed for another cause. It is an important subject to *karma, unified-restraint*, and Union.

Sorrow

See 'Mental pain.'

Soul memories

See 'Impressions.'

Stillness

Stillness is a state of mental inactivity where the mind is devoid of vibrations produced by thoughts, emotions, or other stimuli. See 'Purity.'

Subtle forms *suksma* (1.44) (1.45) (2.10) (2.19) (2.50) (3.45) (4.13)

These are abstract nonphysical material creations, such as thoughts.

Suffering

See 'Mental pain.'

Supreme Being   (universal soul) *purusa/isvara* (1.16) (1.23 - 1.27) (2.1) (2.32) (2.45) (3.36) (3.50) (3.56) (4.3) (4.18) *adhyatma* (1.47) *viveka* (3.55) *adhisthatr* (3.50)

The Supreme Being is the primary existence and soul within the universe, often called the oversoul. *Yoga Sutras* do not mention the oversoul, but it is included in the discussions of *Sutras*. It is the common soul of all souls. All souls are one soul, differentiated by the god-essence into individuals. The word *purusa* can also refer to the individual soul. See also 'primal existence.' In the modern set of colloquialisms the capitalization of Purusa refers to that oversoul without distinguishing between *brahman* and the Supreme Being, and it truly is both. That capitalization convention is not followed here.

Transformation/evolution *parinama* (3.11 - 3.16) (4.2) (4.14) (4.32) (4.33)

As things evolve, they change from one form to another.

Unified-restraint (of mind) samyama (3.4 - 3.6) (3.16 - 3.37) (3.42 - 3.49) (3.53)

When the seeker of transformation has mastered the progressive practices of *concentration*, *meditation*, and *intense absorption*, the integration of those three practices can occur. This integration yields a meditative force treated here as '*unified-restraint*,' which means *unified-restraint of mind*.

Unified-restraint (of mind) samyama (3.4 - 3.6) (3.16 - 3.37) (3.42 - 3.49) (3.53)

When the seeker of transformation has mastered the progressive practices of *concentration*, *meditation*, and *intense absorption*, the integration of those three practices can occur. This integration yields a meditative force treated here as '*unified-restraint*,' which means *unified-restraint of mind*.

Unified-restraint targets (3.16 - 3.48)

The *Yoga Sutras* contain many targets for meditative practice. Some are purely in line with aspiration to *kaivalya*, while others have limited intent. This text refers to those with limited intent as 'applied meditation.'

Vital airs (*prana*) *udana* (3.40) *samana* (3.41)

Everything derives from a singular primal energy, *prana*, which spawns other pranic energy types. Those energy types mix and interact to create all things, maintain them, and annihilate them, riding the creative drive from the primal consciousness. The forms of *prana* (such as *udana* and *samana*) concentrate in different zones of the body where they perform specific functions. We live in a sea of this energy, *prana*, and continually absorb it, without realizing that it is there.